Twenty-First Century Arab and African Diasporas in Spain, Portugal and Latin America

This volume considers the Arabic and African diasporas through the underexplored Afro-Hispanic, Luso-Africans, and *Mahjari* (South American and Mexican authors of Arab descent) experiences in Spain, Portugal, and Latin America. Utilizing both established and emerging approaches, the authors explore the ways in which individual writers and artists negotiate the geographical, cultural, and historical parameters of their own diasporic trajectories influenced by their particular locations at home and elsewhere. At the same time, this volume sheds light on issues related to Spain, Portugal, and Latin American racial, ethnic, and sexual boundaries; the appeal of images of the Middle East and Africa in the contemporary marketplace; and the role of Spanish, Portuguese, and Latin American economic crunches in shaping attitudes towards immigration. This collection of thought-provoking chapters extends the concepts of diaspora and transnationalism, forcing the reader to reassess their present limitations as interpretive tools. In the process, Afro-Hispanic, Afro-Portuguese, and *Mahjaris* are rendered visible as national actors and transnational citizens.

Cristián H. Ricci is a professor of Iberian studies and North African studies at the University of California, Merced. His literary research interests and experience include the narrative of Spain, the literature of Morocco written in Western European languages (Castilian, Catalan, French, Dutch, English), and the literatures of Equatorial Guinea and Latin America from 1800 through the present. He is the author of *El espacio urbano en la narrativa del Madrid de la Edad de Plata, 1900–1938* (2009), *Literatura periférica en castellano y catalán: el caso marroquí* (2010), *¡Hay moros en la costa! Literatura marroquí fronteriza en castellano y catalán* (2014), and *New Voices of Muslim North African Migrants in Europe* (2019). He is the codirector of *Transmodernity. Journal of Peripheral Cultural Production of the Luso-Hispanic World*.

Routledge Studies in Latin American and Iberian Literature

This series is our home for cutting-edge, upper-level scholarly monographs and edited collections, focusing on literatures from Central America, South America and the Iberian Peninsula. Books in the series are characterized by dynamic interventions and innovative approaches to established subjects and ground-breaking criticism on emerging topics in literary studies.

Female Criminality and "Fake News" in Early Modern Spanish
P liegos Sueltos
Stacey L. Parker Aronson

Medicine, Power, and the Authoritarian Regime in Hispanic Literature
Oscar A. Pérez

Queer Rebels
Rewriting Literary Traditions in Contemporary Spanish Novels
Łukasz Smuga
Translated by Patrycja Poniatowska

Human Rights in Colombian Literature and Cultural Production
Embodied Enactments
Edited by Carlos Gardeazábal Bravo and Kevin G. Guerrieri

A Posthumous History of José Martí
The Apostle and His Afterlife
Alfred J. López

The Intellectual and Cultural Worlds of Rubén Darío
Kathleen T. O'Connor-Bater

Twenty-First Century Arab and African Diasporas in Spain, Portugal and Latin America
Edited by Cristián H. Ricci

For more information about this series, please visit: www.routledge.com/ Routledge-Studies-in-Latin-American-and-Iberian-Literature/book-series/ RSLAIL

Twenty-First Century Arab and African Diasporas in Spain, Portugal and Latin America

Edited by Cristián H. Ricci

NEW YORK AND LONDON

First published 2023
by Routledge
605 Third Avenue, New York, NY 10158

and by Routledge
4 Park Square, Milton Park, Abingdon, Oxon, OX14 4RN

Routledge is an imprint of the Taylor & Francis Group, an informa business

© 2023 selection and editorial matter, Cristián H. Ricci; individual
chapters, the contributors

The right of Cristián H. Ricci to be identified as the author of the editorial
material, and of the authors for their individual chapters, has been
asserted in accordance with sections 77 and 78 of the Copyright, Designs
and Patents Act 1988.

All rights reserved. No part of this book may be reprinted or reproduced
or utilised in any form or by any electronic, mechanical, or other means,
now known or hereafter invented, including photocopying and recording,
or in any information storage or retrieval system, without permission in
writing from the publishers.

Trademark notice: Product or corporate names may be trademarks or
registered trademarks, and are used only for identification and explanation
without intent to infringe.

Library of Congress Cataloging-in-Publication Data
Names: Ricci, Cristián, editor.
Title: 21st century Arab and African diasporas in Spain, Portugal and
   Latin America / Cristián H. Ricci.
Description: New York : Routledge, 2023. | Includes bibliographical
   references and index.
Identifiers: LCCN 2022036756 (print) | LCCN 2022036757 (ebook) |
   ISBN 9781032156446 (hardback) | ISBN 9781032424293 (paperback) |
   ISBN 9781003245117 (ebook)
Subjects: LCSH: Immigrants in literature. | Immigrants—Spain. |
   Immigrants—Portugal. | Immigrants—Latin America. | Arabs—Spain. |
   Arabs—Portugal. | Arabs—Latin America. | Africans—Spain. |
   Africans—Portugal. | Africans—Latin America.
Classification: LCC PN56.5.I55 A14 2023 (print) | LCC PN56.5.I55
   (ebook) | DDC 809.89206912—dc23/eng/20220803
LC record available at https://lccn.loc.gov/2022036756
LC ebook record available at https://lccn.loc.gov/2022036757

ISBN: 978-1-032-15644-6 (hbk)
ISBN: 978-1-032-42429-3 (pbk)
ISBN: 978-1-003-24511-7 (ebk)

DOI: 10.4324/9781003245117

Contents

List of Contributors		viii
Introduction		1
CRISTIÁN H. RICCI		

PART I
Spain 21

1 Integration, School, and the Children of North African
Immigrants in Spain 23
DANIELA FLESLER

2 Finding and Recording the Invisible: The *Porteadoras* of
the Spanish-Moroccan Border in Documentary Film 36
RAQUEL VEGA-DURÁN

3 Saharaui Women Writers in Spain: Voices of Resistance
in *Mil y un poemas saharauis II [One Thousand and
One Saharaui Poems II]* 50
DEBRA FASZER-MCMAHON

4 Sex, Identity, and Narration in the Equatoguinean
Diaspora 67
MAHAN L. ELLISON

5 Mothering, *Mestizaje* and the Future of Spain 81
ANNA TYBINKO

vi *Contents*

PART II
Portugal 95

6 Black Migration, Citizenship, and Racial Capital in
Post-Imperial Portugal 97
DANIEL F. SILVA

7 We Are Not Your Negroes: Analyzing Mural Representations
of Blackness in Lisbon Metropolitan Area 113
MARGARIDA RENDEIRO

8 Reclaiming an Individual Space: The Angolan Diaspora
in Portugal 135
SANDRA SOUSA

9 Luso-Arabic Poetry: Reviewing the Concept 150
CATARINA NUNES DE ALMEIDA

10 Portugal Against the Moors in the 21st Century:
Invisible Diasporas and the "Mediatic Romanticism"
of a Contemporary Opera 163
EVERTON V. MACHADO

PART III
Latin America 179

11 Chilestinians and Journalism 181
HEBA EL ATTAR

12 Writing South, Facing East: Arab Argentine Narratives 194
MARCUS PALMER

13 Chronicling "the Death of the Arab" in Colombian
Literature 207
ANGELA HADDAD

14 The Otherness That Remains. The Past From The Future:
Cuaderno de Chihuahua [*Chihuahua Notebook*] by
Jeannette Lozano Clariond 223
ROSE MARY SALUM

Contents vii

15 The Idea of Translation in *Ancient Tillage*, by Raduan
Nassar   237
NAZIR AHMED CAN

Index   251

Contributors

Introduction

Cristián H. Ricci is a Professor of Iberian Studies and North African Studies at the University of California, Merced. His literary research interests and experience include the narrative of Spain, the literature of Morocco written in Western European languages (Castilian, Catalan, French, Dutch, English), and the literatures of Equatorial Guinea and Latin America from 1800 through the present. He is the author of *El espacio urbano en la narrativa del Madrid de la Edad de Plata, 1900–1938* (CSIC, 2009), *Literatura periférica en castellano y catalán: el caso marroquí* (Biblioteca Clásica–U of Minnesota, 2010), *¡Hay moros en la costa! Literatura marroquí fronteriza en castellano y catalán* (Iberoamericana, 2014), and *New Voices of Muslim North African Migrants in Europe* (Brill, 2019). He is the codirector of *Transmodernity. Journal of Peripheral Cultural Production of the Luso-Hispanic World*.

Spain

Daniela Flesler is Associate Professor and Chair of the Department of Hispanic Languages and Literature at Stony Brook University in NY, U.S.A. She is the author of *The Return of the Moor: Spanish Responses to Contemporary Moroccan Immigration* (Purdue UP, 2008) and co-editor of *Revisiting Jewish Spain in the Modern Era* (Routledge, 2013) and *Genealogies of Sepharad* (Quest. Issues in Contemporary Jewish History 18, 2020). She has been the recipient of ACLS and NEH fellowships. Her most recent book is *The Memory Work of Jewish Spain* (Indiana University Press, 2020), co-authored with Adrián Pérez Melgosa and winner of the 2021 National Jewish Book award in the Sephardic culture category.

Raquel Vega-Durán is Senior Lecturer in Peninsular and Transatlantic Film and Literature and Chair of the program Ethnicity, Migration, Rights at Harvard University. Her research focuses on Spanish Peninsular Studies; Migration and Borders; Gender and Identity Studies; Social Activism; and Transatlantic and Mediterranean literature, film, and photography.

She is the author of *Emigrant Dreams, Immigrant Borders: Migrants, Transnational Encounters, and Identity in Spain* (Bucknell UP, 2016). She is currently working on a new book-length project entitled *Vanishing Europe: Abandoned Villages and the Repopulation of Europe in the Twenty-First Century*. Until 2017, Raquel Vega-Durán was Associate Professor at Claremont McKenna College.

Debra Faszer-McMahon is Professor of Spanish and Dean of the School of Humanities at Seton Hill University. Her research interests include transnational poetics, immigration, cultural studies, and women writers. She has published *Cultural Encounters in Contemporary Spain: The Poetry of Clara Janés* (Bucknell UP 2010), *African Immigrants in Contemporary Spanish Texts: Crossing the Strait* (Routledge/Ashgate Press 2015 – co-edited with Victoria L. Ketz), and *A Laboratory of Her Own: Women and Science in Spanish Culture* (Vanderbilt UP 2021 – co-edited with Victoria L. Ketz and Dawn Smith-Sherwood), as well as articles in *Hispania*, *Afro-Hispanic Review*, *Letras Femeninas*, *Transmodernity*, and other journals. She is currently working on a book-length project about La Generación de la Amistad and Saharawi poetics in Spain.

Mahan L. Ellison is Associate Professor of Spanish at Furman University. His research focuses on the literary and historical connections between Spain and Africa. He is the author of the book *Africa in the Contemporary Spanish Novel, 1990–2010* (Lexington Books 2021), and he has published articles in *Research in African Literatures*, *CELAAN* (Review of the Center for the Study of Literatures and Arts of North Africa), the *Vanderbilt e-Journal of Luso-Hispanic Studies*, *Confluencia*, and other journals. He was a 2020–2021 Fulbright Scholar to Morocco and Spain, and his research has been supported by grants from the National Endowment for the Humanities and the Virginia Foundation for Independent Colleges Mednick Memorial Fellowship. More information can be found at www.mahanellison.com.

Anna Tybinko is a NEH Collaborative Humanities Postdoctoral Fellow at Vanderbilt University in the Department of Spanish & Portuguese. Previously, she was the John Hope Franklin Postdoctoral Research Associate in the Franklin Humanities Institute's From Slavery to Freedom Lab at Duke University where she also received her doctorate in Romance Studies. She specializes in Migration and Border Studies in the Iberian world. She has been the recipient of fellowships from the Council for European Studies, the Mellon Foundation and the American Council of Learned Societies for her research on questions of race, racialization, and urban borderlands in contemporary Spain.

Portugal

Daniel F. Silva is Associate Professor of Luso-Hispanic Studies at Middlebury College, where he is also Director of the Black Studies Program. He

x *Contributors*

is the author of *Embodying Modernity: Race, Gender, and Fitness Culture in Brazil* (University of Pittsburgh Press, forthcoming); *Anti-Empire: Decolonial Interventions in Lusophone Literatures* (Liverpool University Press, 2018); and *Subjectivity and the Reproduction of Imperial Power: Empire's Individuals* (Routledge, 2015). He is also the co-editor of *Decolonial Destinies: The Post-Independence Literatures of Lusophone Africa* (Anthem Press, 2021), *Emerging Dialogues on Machado de Assis* (Palgrave, 2016), and *Lima Barreto: New Critical Perspectives* (Lexington Books, 2013). He is co-editor of the book series Anthem Studies in Race, Power, and Society with Anthem Press and has published scholarship in *Hispania, Chasqui, Portuguese Cultural Studies,* and *Transmodernity*.

Margarida Rendeiro holds a PhD in Portuguese studies from Kings College, London. She is an integrated researcher in the Centre for the Humanities (CHAM) at NOVA University of Lisbon and an Assistant Professor at Lusíada University of Lisbon. She has co-edited *Challenging Memories and Rebuilding Identities: Literary and Artistic Voices that undo the Lusophone Atlantic* (Routledge, 2019) with Federica Lupati and authored *The Literary Institution in Portugal since the Thirties: An Analysis under Special Consideration of the Publishing Market* (Peter Lang, 2010). Her research interests broach questions of contemporary Portuguese literature and cultures, identities, resistance, and utopias.

Sandra Sousa holds a PhD in Portuguese and Brazilian studies from Brown University. Currently, she is Assistant Professor in the Modern Languages and Literatures Department at the University of Central Florida. Her research interests include colonialism and post-colonialism; Portuguese colonial literature; race relations in Mozambique; war, dictatorship, and violence in contemporary Portuguese and Luso-African literature; and feminine writing in Portuguese, Brazilian, and African literature. She has articles published in the United States, Brazil, and Portugal. She is the author of *Ficções do Outro: Império, Raça e Subjectividade no Moçambique Colonial* (Esfera do Caos, 2015) and has co-edited *Visitas a João Paulo Borges Coelho. Leituras, Diálogos e Futuros* (Colibri, 2017).

Catarina Nunes de Almeida (PhD, NOVA University of Lisbon, 2012) is an Assistant Researcher at the School of Arts and Humanities, University of Lisbon. Full Member of the Centre for Comparative Studies (CEC), she is the PI of the collective research project ORION. Portuguese Orientalism since 2019. At CEC she has also developed an individual research project on *The Journey to the Orient in Portuguese Contemporary Literature* (1990–2020). Before starting her PhD in Portugal, she had a contract as a Portuguese language lecturer at the University of Pisa (Italy) for two academic years (2007–2009). Her work is mainly focused on Portuguese Orientalism and Portuguese contemporary literature. She has published several articles on these subjects in anthologies and journals, and she is also the author of six poetry books.

Everton V. Machado received a PhD in comparative literature from the University of Paris-Sorbonne/Paris IV in 2008. He is currently Principal Researcher (equivalent to Associate Professor) at the Centre for Comparative Studies (CEC) of the School of Arts and Humanities of the University of Lisbon (FLUL). He co-directed the CEC (2016–2019), where he also developed the exploratory research project "The Portuguese Representations of India: Power and Knowledge in a Peripheral Orientalism (19th and 20th centuries)," funded by the Foundation for Science and Technology of Portugal (IF/01452/2013). Among his publications is *O Orientalismo Português e as Jornadas de Tomás Ribeiro: caracterização de um problema* (Lisbon, National Library of Portugal, 2018), as well as a scientific edition of India's first Portuguese-language novel, *Os Brahamanes* (1866) by Francisco Luís Gomes (1829–1869) (*Les Brahmanes*, translated from Portuguese to French by L. de Claranges-Lucotte, Paris, Classiques Garnier, 2012). He is now co-editing a volume of essays entitled *Colonial Periodical Press in the Portuguese Empire: Theorising Approaches* that will be published in the series Routledge Studies in Cultural History.

Latin America

Heba El Attar is Professor of Spanish at Cleveland State University. Her traditional scholarship includes articles and book chapters on novels, poetry, presses, and films by Chileans of Palestinian descent. Among her published translations and co-translations are novels and books by Carlos Fuentes and Gabriel García Márquez, both into Arabic. Her nontraditional/creative scholarship includes two documentaries on Chileans of Palestinian descent.

Marcus Palmer is an Assistant Professor at Texas A&M University-San Antonio, where has been a faculty member since 2016. He is the coordinator for the Spanish program and directs the Language Learning Center. Dr. Palmer completed his PhD at the University of Iowa and his undergraduate studies at the University of Nevada-Reno and Weber State University. His research interests include Latin American literature, Arab diaspora, and Orientalist writing practices, specializing in the Southern *Mahjar* writing. He has performed translations of research projects published in peer-reviewed journals or edited books and has published in the areas of the *Mahjar* and writers of Arab heritage in Argentina.

Angela Haddad is a doctoral candidate in the Department of Comparative Literature at New York University and works between Arabic, Spanish, and French. Her research focuses on the literary and cultural entanglements of the Arab world with areas outside of Western Europe and the United States from the late 19th century onward, and her current project treats the connections between the Eastern Mediterranean and the Caribbean basin through themes of migration and travel.

xii *Contributors*

Rose Mary Salum is Founding Editor of the bilingual literary magazine *Literal: Latin American Voices and Literal Publishing*. She has authored *El agua que mece el silencio*, winner of the International Latino Book Award and the prestigious Panamerican Award Carlos Montemayor (Vaso Roto, 2015); *Tres semillas de granada. Ensayos desde el inframundo* (Vaso Roto, 2020); *Una de ellas* (Dislocados, 2020); *Delta de las arenas, cuentos árabes, cuentos judíos*, winner of the International Latino Book Award (Literal Publishing, 2013); and *Spaces in Between* (Tierra firme, 2002). She was the guest editor for *Hostos Review* with the issue titled *Almalafa y Caligrafía, Literatura de origen árabe en América Latina*. Her awards and recognitions include Author of the Year 2008 for the Hispanic Book Festival, four Lone Star Awards, two Council of Editors of Learned Journals Awards, St. Thomas University's Classical Award, a recognition from the U.S. Congress, and a nomination for PEN America's Nora Magid Award. She is a member of the Academia Norteamericana de la Lengua.

Nazir Ahmed Can is the Serra Húnter Lecturer in Portuguese Language and Translation at the Department of Translation, Interpreting and East Asian Studies—Autonomous University of Barcelona, and also the vice dean of the Faculty of Translation and Interpretation and coordinator of the area of Portuguese. Can has a PhD in theory of literature and comparative literature from Autonomous University of Barcelona. He was an associate professor of African literatures at the Federal University of Rio de Janeiro, a visiting professor at the University of Salamanca, a postdoctoral researcher at the University of São Paulo, and a visiting predoctoral researcher at University of Liverpool. He is the author of the books *João Paulo Borges Coelho: ficção, memória, cesura* (Rio de Janeiro: Folha Seca, 2021), *O campo literário moçambicano. Tradução do espaço e formas de insílio* (São Paulo: Kapulana, 2020), *Discurso e poder nos romances de João Paulo Borges Coelho* (Maputo: Alcance, 2014), and co-editor, among others, of *Racism and Racial Surveillance. Modernity Matters* (London/New York: Routledge, 2022), *The Africas in the World and the World in the Africas: African Literatures and Comparativism* (Holden, MA: Quod Manet, 2022), *Geografias literárias de língua portuguesa no século XXI* (Roma: Tab Edizioni, 2021) and *Visitas a João Paulo Borges Coelho. Leituras, diálogos e futuros* (Lisboa: Colibri, 2017).

Introduction

Cristián H. Ricci

In their seminal works, William Safran and Ted Lewellen determine that definitions of diaspora commonly refer to displacement, generally through coercion, from one's homeland and settlement in foreign places while maintaining a deep, often mythical, attachment to the homeland. However, in recent years this definition has been widely discussed and reevaluated. Diaspora studies have, over time, embraced varying degrees of flexibility regarding what constitutes the diasporic condition. Consequently, diasporas may not always develop through a long passage of time and may or may not be the result of forced migration (Moser and Racy 281). This volume considers the Arabic and African diasporas through the underexplored Afro-Hispanic, Luso-Africans, and *Mahjari* (South and North American authors of Arab descent)[1] experiences in Spain, Portugal, and Latin America. Utilizing both established and emerging approaches, the authors explore the ways in which individual writers and artists negotiate the geographical, cultural, and historical parameters of their own diasporic trajectories, influenced by their particular locations at home and elsewhere. At the same time, this volume sheds light on issues related to Spain's, Portugal's, and Latin American's racial, ethnic, and sexual boundaries; the appeal of images of the Middle East and Africa in the contemporary marketplace; and the role of Spanish, Portuguese, and Latin American economic crunches in shaping attitudes towards immigration. This collection of thought-provoking chapters extends the concepts of diaspora and transnationalism, forcing the reader to reassess the limitations of current interpretive tools. In the process, Afro-Hispanic, Afro-Portuguese, and *Mahjaris* are rendered visible as national actors and transnational citizens.

With Edwige Tamalet Talbayeb and Daniela Merolla, I believe that Arab and African diasporas to France and England have garnered significant critical attention. Its corollary in other European countries remains conspicuously absent from the discipline's discourse on migration. Because *Francophonie* and Anglophone studies have "failed" to provide a successful model to critically engage with other European languages, texts hailing from the postcolonialities, such as those reflected in this volume,

DOI: 10.4324/9781003245117-1

2 Cristián H. Ricci

develop critical connections along lateral axes with other Arab and African literatures written in Spanish, Catalan, and Portuguese. Colonial and postcolonial "poetics of transition" (Merolla), a feature of English and French writings since the beginning of the nineteenth century, has progressively characterized Spanish, Portuguese, and other European literatures thanks to new writers who have attracted public and critical attention. A growing number of migrants and children of immigrants have become artistically active over the last few decades. As a result, some of the new writers and artists have managed to establish a reputation in the literary field and theatre, cinema, and music. This artistic renewal has prompted discussion on matters pertaining to creation and language, cultural essentialism, social identity, and political choices.

The narrative and artistic representations addressed by Arab and African diasporic subjects in Europe and Latin America occupy a contingent "in-between" space that innovates and interrupts the discourse of the past. These are texts sentenced to live interstitially in the frontier, in ambiguous indolence in the storm of exile, a liminal space, in between designations of identity (Homi Bhabha). The liminal space in postcolonial writing and artistic performance permits Arab and African writers to approach their tradition from a transcultural perspective. This "third space"/"the interstice," the borderline between East and West, grants them the agency of speaking/writing about their experience as "alien," "clandestine" women and LGBTQ people, as well as about general grievances.

While this volume is interdisciplinary in nature and takes into consideration political and statistical analysis, it mainly concentrates on the field of cultural production coming from Arab and African authors living their diasporic experiences in the Iberian Peninsula (Spain and Portugal) and Latin America (Chile, Argentina, Colombia, Mexico, and Brazil). This volume aims to show alternative views on Orientalism (including counter-Orientalism), along with new studies dealing with the Islamic world, the Maghreb, and sub-Saharan Africa. While still dealing with interpretations of the East and South by Western outsiders, the fact that this cultural production comes from the two European countries that not too long ago were considered parts of Africa (perhaps most eloquently summed up in the well-known expression that "Africa begins at the Pyrenees") and Latin America, which also suffered European and U.S. imperialism and colonialism for centuries, this volume brings a corrective to Edward Said's conceptual framework by excavating readings of "oriental" cultures from a position of familiarity and entanglement. As will be demonstrated, even though prejudice and racism, as could be expected, are still prevalent in many Orientalist aesthetic practices coming from the Iberian Peninsula and Latin America, the perspective is radically different, as Catalan-Moroccan writer Juan Goytisolo astutely points out in his prologue to the Spanish version of Said's *Orientalism* (Kushigian 109). According to the latter, we infer that Islam is not foreign or an enemy to

Introduction 3

the Iberian Peninsula's cultural identity, particularly Spain; it is part of it. The stereotypical ideas of Oriental exoticism, corruption, and despotism; the notions of cultural inferiority, endemic passivity, and stagnancy; a libidinized Orient of sensual odalisques and harems; a homogenized Islamic world; and multiple types of Africanness and *Negritude*, among many other topics, are thus explored from a very different perspective. Now the Orient has become the "Other" of countries with a colonial past that are also trying to define themselves as culturally independent nations.

According to the Instituto Nacional de Estadística-INE (National Statistics Institute), Spain has over 7 million immigrants from a population of 47 million (close to 1 million from Morocco). The Serviço de Estrangeiros e Fronteiras-IFE (Immigration and Borders Service) reports that Portugal has 1 million immigrants from a population of 11 million (30 percent from Angola, Mozambique, and Cape Verde). The Comisión Económica Para América Latina-CEPAL (Economic Commission for Latin America) estimates that today in Latin America, there are over 133 million Afro-descendants (Afro-Latinxs) and the largest number of Arab descendants outside the Middle East, with anywhere between 17 to 20 million people. While most of the Afro-Latinxs' ancestors were forced into slavery, the Arabs were obligated to escape their native countries due to poverty, violence, and insecurity, creating one of the largest exoduses in Latin America and one of the world's largest displacements since 1860.

Thus, the chapters in this volume study the concept of modern diasporic subjects and diaspora in general, as well as historical forced displacements, trying to provide potential lasting analyses of the many cultural paradigms associated with this situation. This volume is not only timely but expansive, as it moves from the pressing immigration and refugee crisis to examine the limits and possibilities of "shared experiences" and how they can become the basis for socio-historical linkages, identity formation, cultural participation, and solidarity work. The chapters address cross-disciplinary boundaries, including literary and film studies, urban and cultural studies, popular and mass culture, subcultures, performing and visual arts, and Luso-Hispanic thought.

Rather than a celebration of ethnic or cultural identity, this volume is more concerned with processes of racialization, hybridization, transculturation, liminality, creolization, syncretism, and mestizaje. The chapters equally deal with exile, migration, transnationalism, citizenship, social and cultural memory, glocalization, assimilation, and strategic (self) orientalization and the orientalization of both Eastern and non-Eastern cultures and peoples in the Luso-Hispanic world. Therefore, this volume focuses on new intercultural and inter-(semi)peripheral paradigms that claim their own place beyond the traditional Western modernity that had previously excluded them. It addresses decentering interplays among "peripheral" areas of the Third World, "semiperipheral" areas (Spain and Portugal since the second part of the seventeenth century), and

4   *Cristián H. Ricci*

marginalized social groups of the globe (Maghrebis, Saharauis, and sub-Saharans). This approach responds to the objective of "provincializing" the metropolis and disrupting the traditional center-periphery dichotomy, thus bringing about multiple and interchangeable centers and peripheries whose cultures interact with one another without the mediation of the European metropolitan centers.

Several books and scholarly essays address sub-Saharan African diasporas to Latin America. Still, few studies concentrate on the cultural production of Arab/North African vis-à-vis sub-Saharan African diasporic subjects in the Iberian Peninsula and Latin America. While this volume leans firmly towards the study of Arabic/North African diasporas in the Iberian Peninsula and Latin America, the inclusion of chapters focusing on sub-Saharan African diasporas in Portugal and Spain aims at situating them in a broader Black diasporic epistemology and world-making. Throughout the twenty-first century, the competing claims that "Africa begins at the Pyrenees" and "Europe ends at the Atlas" give a measure of the paradoxical status of Spain and Portugal as at once orientalized and orientalizing. At the same time, this volume highlights the historical, political, and cultural contexts in which Latin American identities have engaged in the debate about the precise nature of their Arab and African legacies.

Before giving an overview of the different chapters that constitute the three parts of this volume, I want to acknowledge the invaluable contribution of scholars and critical works that separately addressed sub-Saharan African, North African, and Arab migrations and diasporas into Spain, Portugal, and Latin America and their cultural representations. Many of them have served as a starting point of analysis or theoretical reference for many of the chapters in this volume. For the Spanish field, I would like to highlight Susan Martin-Márquez's *Disorientations: Spanish Colonialism in Africa and the Performance of Identity* (2008); Daniela Flesler's *The Return of the Moor: Spanish Responses to Contemporary Moroccan Immigration* (2008); Adolfo Campoy-Cubillo's *Memories of the Maghreb: Transnational Identities in Spanish Cultural Production* (2012); Raquel Vega-Durán's *Emigrant Dreams, Immigrant Borders: Migrants, Transnational Encounters, and Identity in Spain* (2016); and my own *New Voices of Muslim North African Migrants in Europe* (2019). These books offer rich and exciting readings of Spanish national identity about colonialist and post-colonialist endeavors in Morocco, Western Sahara, and Equatorial Guinea, as well as critical analyses of literature, film, music, art, websites, and blogs produced by African authors in Spanish and Catalan.

Regarding Portugal, Kesha Fikes's *Managing African Portugal. The Citizen-Migrant Distinction* (2009) deals with Cape Verdean women. This is a study of migrant phenomena that considers not only how the enactment of citizenship by the citizen manages the migrant but also how citizens are simultaneously governed through their uptake and assumption of new European Union citizen roles. In turn, Michelle Johnson's

Remaking Islam in African Portugal: Lisbon–Mecca–Bissau (Framing the Global) (2020) explores the religious lives of migrants in the context of diaspora, highlighting what being Muslim means in urban Europe and how Guinean migrants' relationships to their ritual practices must change as they remake themselves and their religion.

Concerning the field of Arab diasporas in Latin America, there are some important titles, such as Christina Civantos's *Between Argentines and Arabs. Argentine Orientalism, Arab Immigrants, and the Writing of Identity* (2005) and Camila Pastor's *The Mexican Mahjar: Transnational Maronites, Jews, and Arabs under the French Mandate* (2017). Both authors use established and emerging approaches such as literary analysis and cultural studies (class, race, and gender) to explore the production of historical and contemporary identities and cultural practices within and beyond the boundaries of the nation-state. There is also a journal devoted to this type of cultural production and their corresponding diasporic communities: *Mashriq & Mahjar: Journal of Middle East and North African Migration Studies*.

Twenty-First Century Arab and African diasporas in Spain, Portugal, and Latin America's innovative 15 chapters, covering the cultural production of authors and works from or that refer to 18 different countries and four continents (Spain, Portugal, Argentina, Brazil, Chile, Colombia, Mexico, Equatorial Guinea, Morocco, The Sahrawi Arab Democratic Republic [Western Sahara], Benin, Cape Verde, Mozambique, Guinea-Bissau, São Tomé and Príncipe, Palestine, Lebanon, and Syria), were written by a host of scholars who have left their mark on this academic subfield. The volume is divided into three geographical sections: Part 1. Spain, Part 2. Portugal, and Part 3. Latin America. While the initial two chapters of Part 1 pay particular attention to Morocco's film and literature, the third chapter includes female Saharawi writers. The other two chapters of Part 1 focus on sub-Saharan diasporas to Spain (Equatorial Guinea and Benin). Part 2 includes sub-Saharan African diasporas and the neo-Orientalist revival of the North African/Muslim presence through literature and the arts in Portugal. The first three chapters of Part 2 cover Black cultural production, racism, identity, and different forms of coloniality. For their part, the other two chapters of Part 2 analyze Luso-Arabic poetry and drama through counter-orientalist approaches and national identity. The third and final part covers the *mahjar* cultural production in Chile, Argentina, Colombia, Mexico, and Brazil. Its five chapters cover ethnocultural writing, literary journalism, Hispanic-American orientalism, literary works by women, literary criticism, and translation.

Part 1. Spain

Over 8,000 migrants, including some 2,000 minors, from North Africa (mostly Moroccans) arrived in the Spanish North African enclave of Ceuta

6 *Cristián H. Ricci*

between May 17 and 18, 2021. This latest crisis of May 2021 came after 20,000 migrants tried to enter the Canary Islands in 2020, boosting the anti-immigrant propaganda of the nationalist, far-right Vox Party, which showcases, in its political campaign meetings, re-enactments of the Reconquista, the medieval battles waged by Spain's Roman Catholic Kings to end eight centuries of Muslim occupation. The Spanish Government, led by a coalition of the Socialist Party (PSOE) and the anti-austerity Unidas Podemos, prides itself on its forward-thinking progressiveness regarding immigrant communities' integration and promoting an amnesty for undocumented immigrants in the country to regularize their situation. However, on the shores of Ceuta – and in the rest of the Iberian Peninsula – the tide is turning. A common discussion topic among staff members at diverse Spanish NGOs is the lack of preparation for the influx of African immigrants and the deficient role of communities, institutions, and the state in accepting and integrating those Afro-Spanish children born on Spanish soil. Indeed, modern Afro-Spanish minors often face discrimination in school settings and on the streets and are disproportionately targeted by the Spanish police. Though this type of behavior is often brushed off as isolated incidents of xenophobia, in reality, this discrimination rarely considers whether the individuals targeted are recent immigrants or Spanish-born citizens.

In this context, Daniela Flesler's chapter, "Integration, School, and the Children of North African Immigrants in Spain," focuses on educational discourses and classroom interactions in Spanish schools in relation to Moroccan immigrant children's membership and identity. Flesler also includes, in her chapter, two fictional texts centered on young women negotiating their cultural identity: Xavi Sala's short film *Hijab* (2005) and Najat El Hachmi's novel *La hija extranjera* (The Foreign Daughter, 2015). The chapter shows how teachers and governmental institutions buy into essentialist notions of children's ethnolinguistic identities, upholding, as a result, discriminatory practices, deteriorating inter-ethnic relations, and weakening social cohesion in communities, cities, and Spain's autonomous regions. It also examines how Moroccan immigrant children contest Spanish institutions' essentialist formulations of citizenship by asserting multiple, hybrid forms of membership and belonging.

The second chapter of the volume takes us back to the Spanish enclaves in North Africa, Ceuta and Melilla, which were originally two among several presidios (military penal settlements) established by the Spanish along the North African coast following the end of the Reconquista (1492). Initially, these military garrisons functioned as penal settlements for noblemen and political deportees; over time, they grew into regional trading hubs and became the military headquarters whence the Spanish colonial project in northern Morocco was launched (Soto Bermant). After Morocco's independence in 1956, Ceuta and Melilla remained under Spanish sovereignty, and today, the two enclaves are part of the European

Introduction 7

Union. As reported by Phillipa Payne, every day on the border between Morocco and Spain's North African enclaves, thousands of women act as porters – known in Spanish as *porteadoras*, in French as *femme mulets* (mule women), and in Moroccan Arabic/Darija *hamalas* (mule women) – to transport huge packages to trading points in Morocco. A tax loophole means that anything carried by hand is exempt from tax and can be transported into Morocco duty free. Often involved in the organized smuggling of goods such as clothes, fabrics, and toiletries, many of these women suffer from the aggression and corruption of officials and other porters at the border point. These porters have historically been female and are frequently single mothers who may be divorced, widowed, or victims of abuse. Such women have no choice but to work as porters since they must feed their families, and there is no other work available in Morocco.

A job as a porter translates into obtaining minimum resources for survival. However, the border or customs is what ends up gradually structuring these *porteadoras*' lives in every way. In other words, what began with the idea of a temporary job that allowed them to continue taking care of their families ends up becoming a way of life that derives from that traditional figure of the absent provider. Eventually, the border plays a key role in all areas of their lives, including daily conversations between them; their entire lives revolve around the border. While the *porteadoras* have been described in newspaper articles and news reports as a shapeless mass of individuals carrying large bundles on their backs, Raquel Vega-Durán's chapter, "Finding and Recording the Invisible: The *Porteadoras* of the Spanish-Moroccan Border in Documentary Film," concentrates on a series of Spanish documentaries that create a more complex framework, thus enabling the viewer to see the social and moral significance of different forms of exchange across the Spanish–Moroccan border through the voice of the *porteadoras* themselves. This essay depicts them in the private sphere, collectively (re)defining their experiences and elaborating strategies to make inroads on both sides of the border and on the unexplored space of the border itself, which is revealed through highly intentional camerawork as a space of connection.

In an unprecedented volume about Western Sahara, published in the flagship academic journal *Transmodernity*, the guest editors, Jill Robbins and Adolfo Campoy-Cubillo, indicate that Moroccan King Hassan II's Green March marked the *de facto* occupation of Western Sahara by Morocco in 1975. As the Spanish dictator Francisco Franco lay dying in Madrid, 350,000 Moroccan citizens arrived in Daoura, Hausa, Mahbes, and Laayoune. Although Hassan II presented the march as an effort to free the Saharaui from Spanish colonization, it resulted in a takeover of the territory by Morocco that did not account for Saharaui demands, as expressed by the Polisario Front, which had begun the Saharaui insurgency against Spanish colonialism in 1973. The United Nations issued a verdict through the International Court of Justice in 1975 in favor of the

8   Cristián H. Ricci

right of self-determination for Western Sahara. In 1976, Spain withdrew from Western Sahara, and over 40,000 Saharauis began to abandon their homes and move eastward. When the Polisario Front declared war on Morocco and Mauritania, Algeria was quick to provide them with weapons and logistical support. The ensuing war lasted for more than 15 years until the United Nations negotiated a ceasefire in 1991 on the condition that a referendum be held to decide on the territory's sovereignty. In 2015, the European Court of Justice nullified a previous trade agreement between the European Union and Morocco for the liberalization of the agricultural exploitation of Western Sahara. The court's decision was significant in that it recognized Polisario Front's right to defend its interests in the territory. Despite the favorable ruling of the European Court of Justice, the celebration of the long-promised referendum over the self-determination of Western Sahara remained a remote possibility (Robbins and Campoy-Cubillo 1–4).

In 2021, diplomatic tensions resurfaced when the Spanish government allowed Brahim Ghali, leader of the Polisario Front, to be treated for COVID-19 in a Spanish hospital. After Ghali's hospitalization, the aforementioned 8,000 migrants arrived in Ceuta as Moroccan border forces failed to act in what was seen as a retaliatory move against Spain. On March 18, 2022, the government of Spain announced a "new stage" in relations and said it now backed the kingdom's plan of limited autonomy under Moroccan sovereignty for Western Sahara. In this context, Debra Faszer-McMahon's chapter, "Saharaui Women Writers in Spain: Voices of Resistance in *Mil y un poemas saharauis II [One Thousand and One Saharaui Poems II]*," analyzes the contributions of three Saharaui women poets, demonstrating how digital media has effectively contributed to popularizing feminist, historical, literary, and cultural perspectives on the gendered and paternalistic colonial history of Spanish, Moroccan, and European interventions in Western Sahara. The three women writers analyzed by Faszer-McMahon resist and recast old patriarchal traditions to find a new women-centered way of writing, which in turn facilitates the insertion of feminist goals into the Sahraoui nation-building project.

Equatorial Guinea was a colony of Spain until 1968. As with the case of Morocco and Western Sahara, Equatorial Guinea provides ambivalent literary responses toward autonomous, indigenous, and national identities. The different ethnic groups who make up the state are Fang (85 percent of the population), Ámbö, Bubi, and Ndowè, each with its own ethnocultural and historical diversity. Despite a veneer of Spanish culture and Roman Catholic religion that is thicker on the island of Bioko than on the mainland, many Equatorial Guineans live according to ancient customs, which have undergone a revival since independence. Religious beliefs, often derogatively described as witchcraft; traditional music; and storytelling survive among the Fang of the mainland. After the country's independence, two consecutive dictatorships propitiated a mass exodus of

Introduction 9

writers, intellectuals, and artists. The works of exiles explore the results of colonialism and dictatorship as manifested through identity, poverty, and violence in its multiple dimensions in national and international contexts. At the same time, the fact that Spain had been in this country for over 200 years and that nowadays, the presence of the Spanish government has been replaced by private corporations, Spanish satellite TV, Spanish NGOs, and official institutions forces readers to deconstruct the inevitable processes of hybridization of identity markers between the autochthonous and the Spanish/European in the Central African country's cultural production. Equatorial Guinean writers combine their national and exile experiences with a variety of theories and techniques like the fantastic, interior monologue, and stream of consciousness to communicate postcolonial themes prevalent in the African, European, and American contexts to render unique literary perspectives.

Mahan L. Ellison's chapter, "Sex, Identity, and Narration in the Equatoguinean Diaspora," focuses on a new generation of female Equatoguinean authors who are directly engaging with the themes of sex and identity in the diaspora. Ellison's chapter analyzes how the subaltern voices of women disrupt and antagonize the modern canon of the literatures of the Peninsula, all the while establishing how hybrid discourses can dismantle power structures. The chapter further explores the cultural attitudes towards African women through their own voices as well as those of the male characters. More interestingly, it addresses new questions arising from the growing conflict between the patriarchal Fang tradition and the realization of a changing modern present.

Postcolonial Spain is a critical term that reassesses Spain in its past imperial pluralities and current divergent multicultural scenarios, articulating its present-day racist and xenophobic situation as an integral part of its territorial indeterminacy. The history of slavery, colonialism, and imperialism, which many nations and individuals in Europe would willingly forget and erase, resurfaces in the narratives produced by Afro-Spanish writers. This is the case of Agnès Agboton, a storyteller and poet from Benin who has lived in Barcelona since 1978. Her position may differ from most sub-Saharan African writers living in Spain, mainly from Equatorial Guinea. As such, she is among the writers coming from countries whose historical relation with Spain is not strictly "postcolonial." However, as Anna Tybinko rightly points out in her chapter, "Mothering, *Mestizaje* and the Future of Spain," Agboton "pushes the 'migrant narrative' label," thus making other Afro-Spanish authors carve out a space for Blackness and Black identity in the Spanish imaginary. Agboton is not unaware of the racism and general ignorance about Africa in the West. In her self-portrait, she is honest about her experiences as an African woman living in Spain. Her poetry and narrative are a point of departure from African women writers in Spain and other Afro-Spanish/Afropean woman writers. To this end, the numerous histories and herstories contained in

10 *Cristián H. Ricci*

Afropean narratives also have another valuable effect: they can teach us to devalue the pompous oratory of Western nations on egalitarianism, human rights, democracy, freedom, and so many other tall words that are so often employed with an unjustifiable degree of self-complacency to celebrate our purported unique social, economic and political achievements. Tybinko's chapter, which examines Agboton and the other Afro-Spanish writers' narratives, provides a new viewpoint of the different methodological schools and theories undertaken by the foremost scholars in the field of Black, women, migration, and borderland studies and validates modern research orientations to the intercultural relationships between Africa and Europe.

Within the context of cultural nationalism, identity politics, and the politics of cultural belonging, Tybinko's representative chapter portrays a Black-female-second-generation consciousness in the context of making and unmaking contemporary racial identities in Spain. The determination of who belongs and who gets to decide the boundaries of belonging is being called into question in increasingly vocal ways by activists attentive to the singular dynamics of race as a political concept. By focusing on populations of African descent, Tybinko's chapter is at the forefront of cutting-edge research on diaspora and postcolonial studies.

Part 2. Portugal

Portugal's colonial history begins in the fifteenth century when finding new lands for agriculture, riches, and ambition was the main motivation to build an empire. Soon after, ships started transporting Africans for use as enslaved workers on sugar plantations in the Cape Verde and Madeira islands in the eastern Atlantic. Angola and Mozambique were colonized in southern Africa at the end of the sixteenth century, thus becoming the first European territorial colonies in Africa. The Atlantic slave trade ended in the mid-nineteenth century, but enslaved people continued to be imported into São Tomé and Príncipe until prohibition in 1908. Enslaved people were then replaced by African workers who had to be repatriated after a certain number of years. By the twentieth century, many of the Portuguese colonies were lost to either rival powers or internal warfare. Of those that remained, Madeira and the Azores became autonomous regions of Portugal, Goa became a part of India in 1962, and Macau returned to Chinese rule in 1999. The Portuguese government, then a military dictatorship under António de Oliveira Salazar (ruled 1932–1968), refused to see the futility of fighting African independence movements, and bloody wars followed in both Angola and Mozambique. The Cape Verde islands, São Tomé and Príncipe, East Timor, Angola, and Mozambique all gained independence from Portugal in 1975 (Cartwright).

Portugal's mid-1990s economic and social integration into the European Union fundamentally changed everyday encounters between

Introduction 11

Portuguese citizens and African immigrants. The enactments of European Union modernity gave birth to a new practice of engaging difference in Portugal, which privileged European "multicultural" or "integrationalist" approaches as well as the Portuguese *Lusotropicalism* of the middle twentieth century, a representation that emphasizes the uniqueness of the Portuguese colonial relations based on Portuguese empathy and capacity to deal with people from different cultures. Therefore, according to Warwick Anderson, Ricardo Roque, and Ricardo Ventura Santos, Lusotropicalism became an attempt to spin a unitary narrative out of a series of unequal encounters, forced migrations, and living patterns ordered by the priorities of Portuguese settler colonialism – a story that would be elevated to the level of national (and civilizational) identity. In this sense, Lusotropicalism reminds us that attempts to reckon with racial mixing in the context of national identity have a long and perhaps underexplored history while also underlining the need to scrutinize accounts that celebrate and romanticize "mixedness" as something inherently progressive (Anderson et al. 12–14). Daniel F. Silva's chapter, "Black Migration, Citizenship, and Racial Capital in Post-Imperial Portugal," based on an analysis of fiction and music, examines the relationship between the Lusotropicalist representation of the history of Portuguese colonization and overt (as well as latent) expressions of anti-immigrant prejudice. The findings presented in this chapter suggest that this Lusotropicalist representation may explain the salience of the norm against prejudice in Portugal and may contribute to weakening the traditional association between national identity and overt discrimination.

In 2014, Lisbon officials decided to improve the district's image. They invited Portuguese and foreign artists to paint murals for what they now call "the biggest open-air art gallery in Europe." At street level, artists have transformed entire neighborhoods with giant murals and colorful graffiti. In this sense, Lisbon has become a canvas in constant transition. However, as Margarida Rendeiro argues in her chapter, "We Are Not Your Negroes: Analyzing Mural Representations of Blackness in Lisbon Metropolitan Area," when street artists choose to depict international Black icons, such as Nelson Mandela or Tupac Shakur, as the few Black figures represented in the city center's street art murals, they are not actively engaged with a discussion about Portuguese postcolonial race relations. The Portuguese government, particularly the Lisbon City Council, chose to continue with a Lusotropicalist narrative in the city center, marginalizing representations of Portuguese Black figures and problems associated with the Black community to the periphery. Rather than operating primarily as a political and cultural identity, non-Portuguese blackness is used to draw in tourists, customers, and capital to the city center's spaces. Rendeiro's chapter encompasses the need to manage the existing tensions between the process of institutionalizing graffiti and street art on the one hand and the several layers of impact that this action may have on urban

12 Cristián H. Ricci

life and on the structuring of this art world on the other. It also reflects on the urban image and on the symbolic management of the territories involved; on the creation of mechanisms of economic value, including real-estate valorization and gentrification processes, on the social value enhancement; on the promotion of inclusion, participation, and citizenship mechanisms, and on the governance of the city's known use conflicts (Costa and Lopes). Blackness itself is a space of practice and productivity, where a different kind of politics is possible – and where blackness is not mimicry, desire, or loathing. Therefore, it is essential in this cultural moment that scholars continue some of the work that is being done in art, culture, and politics by recognizing the aesthetics of Portuguese blackness as deeply interwoven into politics and visual culture.

In his celebrated book, *Afropean*, Johny Pitts claims that there is a space where blackness is taking part in shaping European identity at large. Pitts suggests the possibility of living in and with more than one idea: Africa and Europe, or, by extension, the Global South and the West. Pitts is driven by the possibility that Afropean is a unifying concept, a riposte to the nativism of Marine Le Pen and Nigel Farage. If Afropean is a concept whose time might have come, there have been numerous rehearsals since the early 1900s, at least in terms of recasting Black identity, including Pan-Africanism, the New Negro Movement, the Harlem Renaissance, Marcus Garvey's Back-to-Africa project (including Rastafarianism), Black Power, *Negritude*, and many others. Pitts pauses on many of these stepping stones as he journeys to Paris, Lisbon, Moscow, Berlin, and Stockholm, as he walks by homeless and comatose drunks lying under a sign that reads, "Lisboa, City of Tolerance." For all the talk about mixing and miscegenation, Portuguese culture had long had a way of keeping a White elite in luxury and shunting the poor to the sidelines in powerful ways. These impoverished areas on the edge of Lisbon became places that cultivated the kind of safety, community, and social capital Cape Verdeans, Mozambicans, and Angolans had at home, things that could be leveraged against their situation as impoverished outsiders in a European society. Sandra Sousa's chapter, "Reclaiming an Individual Space: The Angolan Diaspora in Portugal," is written on the premises of Johny Pitts's *Afropean*. The chapter correlates new Angolan diasporic voices in a broader European context by showing epistemological and corporal aesthetic forms of resistance to ongoing forms of coloniality through social, historiographic, and anthropologic studies with literary works of fiction. Focusing on the city as a narrative of modernity, coloniality, and decoloniality, the chapter examines how Angolan authors question these notions. Assuming that today the modern/colonial boundaries are being recast into the city as an extension of power relations between dominant and dominated subjects, the chapter unveils the voices of those who have been relegated to the city margins through the standpoint of the cultural production that is being produced in the city center.

Introduction 13

In 711, Arab and Amazigh-speaking Muslims from North Africa invaded the Iberian Peninsula. They quickly conquered what is now southern Portugal and ruled it for centuries. However, they were unable to subdue northern Portugal permanently. Compared to Spain, the presence of an Arabic-Islamic culture and language suffered from a lack of visibility in Portuguese history due to the ideological discourse of colonialism, only partially corrected after the Carnation Revolution of April 25, 1974. The five centuries of Muslim rule are only briefly studied in Portuguese schools. Textbooks place more emphasis on a triumphant Reconquista of the territory by Christian rulers, aided by crusaders, that ended in the thirteenth century. Even though a significant part of the population converted to Islam – by the tenth century, half of the population was Muslim – Portuguese identity has been constructed in opposition to the Moors, historically depicted as enemies. Today, less than 0.5 percent of the population of 11 million is Muslim. However, in 2019 a newly formed far-right party, *Chega* (Enough), won a seat in Portugal's parliament for the first time since the end of Salazar's rule. The party has proposed excluding "the teaching of Islam" from public schools and emphasizes the need to combat "Islamic fundamentalism" and to defend Europe's borders from an "invasion" from the south of the Mediterranean. At the same time, as Marta Vidal noticed, Portugal's Islamic past is slowly clearing the way for a kind of historical reparation. To correct this historical erasure, Portuguese writer Adalberto Alves has spent the last 38 years documenting the influences of al-Andalus in Portugal – from poetry and language to music, carpet-weaving, and pastries, to minaret-shaped chimneys. But it was perhaps through the study of Arabic poetry that Alves most contributed to changing the way Islamic heritage is perceived in Portugal. With his collection and translation of Arabic poetry from the al-Andalus period into Portuguese, poets such as al-Mu'tamid, the last Muslim ruler of Seville and one of the most celebrated Andalusian poets, are coming to be known as "local" poets.

In her chapter "Luso-Arabic Poetry: Reviewing the Concept," Catarina Nunes de Almeida discusses the current use of the concept of *Luso-Arabic poetry*, presenting it as an example of Counter-Orientalism. She analyzes how the concept of *Luso-Arabic poetry* introduced a selective discourse about the *Gharb al-Andalus* through the exaltation of its poets and significant aspects of its culture. Based on Adalberto Alves's *Meu Coração é Árabe: a Poesia Luso-Árabe* [My Heart Is Arab: Luso-Arabic Poetry] and Portuguese poets inspired by Islamic poetry and philosophy, Nunes de Almeida shows how *Gharb al-Andalus* paved the way for a historical narrative to build a more "authentic" Portuguese identity. The outcome of the study results in a confluence of languages, styles, ideas, and points of view displayed by contemporary "Luso-Arabic" Portuguese poets who do not follow the normative orientation of a school but instead reflect a choice, a reading, a personal inquiry and, even more, an art of living that

14 *Cristián H. Ricci*

is far removed from the identity standards deemed as "Portuguese." The specific poetic phenomena discussed in this chapter show that contemporary Portuguese literature is now a space of hospitality, where new forms, themes, and genres from the Arab tradition have begun to be accepted, blended, and reconfigured.

Much aligned with the previous chapter, Everton V. Machado's "Portugal Against the Moors in the 21st Century: Invisible Diasporas and the 'Mediatic Romanticism' of a Contemporary Opera" analyzes the possible connections between a persistent "mediatic romanticism" (riddled with Orientalism) and the cultural and political "invisibility" of those who are today the "Moors" of Portugal: the Muslim diaspora communities from former Portuguese colonies (especially Mozambique and Guinea Bissau), as well as those from other former European colonies (Pakistan, Bangladesh, and Senegal). In order to analyze the modern revival of Luso-Arabism, Machado goes back to *The Lusiads*, an epic sixteenth-century poem by Portuguese poet Luís de Camões that celebrates the glory of Portuguese kings and explorers at a time of imperial expansion at the expense of the "vile and treacherous Muslims," together with the influence of Islam in the southern cities of Beja and Mertola, where the pioneering efforts of archeologist Claudio Torres have been aimed at debunking the stereotype of an Arab-Muslim invader and at recovering the Islamic past as a foundational element of Portuguese identity and heritage (Vidal). Regardless of Portugal's relationship with Islam, which dates back to the founding of the nation, the romanticization of history is not without consequence, as there are still instances of verbal abuse on the streets towards people who appear to be Muslims (intersection of race, gender, Islamophobia), vandal attacks on places of worship, and dissident voices from within society claiming that Muslims pose a threat to society's secular base.

Part 3. Latin America

Waïl S. Hassan observes that due to British and U.S. political influence in the Middle East, many Arabs already knew some English before immigrating to the United States in the late nineteenth and early twentieth century. By contrast, their compatriots who settled in Latin America did not begin to acquire Portuguese or Spanish until they arrived there. Thus, while Anglophone Arab immigrant literature began at the beginning of the twentieth century, most Arab immigrants in Latin America wrote only in Arabic. They are known collectively as the "southern *mahjar*" (or immigrant) group to distinguish them from, while also denoting their affinity to, the North American *mahjar* writers. Likewise, the North American Al-Rābiṭa al-Qalamiyya (the Pen League), founded by Kahlil Gibran in 1920 in New York, had its counterpart in the Brazilian Al-'Uṣba al-Andalusiyya (the Andalusian League), founded in São Paulo in 1933, and Al-Rabiṭa al-Adabiyya (The Literary League), established in Argentina in 1949. In

Latin America, Arab immigrant writers remained even closer to both the political concerns of the Arab homelands and the Arabic poetic tradition, which they venerated, than the North Americans, who rebelled against the conventions of Arabic poetry and exhibited great interest in mysticism and universal themes. Both groups, however, have played an important role in the history of modern Arabic literature, and much scholarship has been devoted to their work. In the second half of the twentieth century, a few immigrants and dozens of second- and third-generation writers have written in Portuguese and Spanish, including some of the most prominent poets, novelists, journalists, and scholars (Hassan 168–169).

Arab migrations to Chile occurred in great waves. The first one was very large and took place from the end of the nineteenth century through the beginning of World War I. The second Arab wave was smaller and took place between the two world wars. The third migratory flow occurred after World War II: more Palestinians than Syrians and Lebanese entered the country due to the fall of the Ottoman Empire and the establishment of the mandates of France and England. Initially, this migratory flow was called Turkish or Ottoman migration due to the Turkish passport carried by young Palestinians, Syrians, and Lebanese, as subjects of the Ottoman Empire. For this reason, Latin Americans associate Arabs with the term *turco* (Turk). It is the literature of the *neomahyar* (Arab Chileans) that, from their particular perspectives, poetically reproduced this displacement to observe how the problems of identity and alterity manifest themselves and how a portion of their ancestral identity traits had been lost. It is a narrative full of dynamism, playfulness, questioning, and rebellious creativity in which one can see an integrated journey of uprooting, longing, intolerance, and integration into mainstream Chilean society. These characteristics have been illustrated mainly through novels published by descendants of Palestinians (*Chilestinians*) and Syrians. At the same time, sentiments of anti-Turkism or Turkophobia also developed among parts of the Chilean population who considered the arrival of Arabs in the country an unsustainable situation. To dispel the feelings of rejection from Chilean society that afflicted the Levantine community, Christian editors created The Arab Press, a space to encourage the revival of the community's identitarian traits, provide cohesion, and denounce suffering in response to Turkophobia.

The Arab Press reported not only on literary and economic activities but also on the sustained sociocultural integration of Arab migrants in Chile and the rest of Latin America. In this context, Heba El Attar's chapter, "Chilestinians and Journalism," analyzes Chilestinians' contributions to Chilean print media and underscores how their immersion in mainstream press builds upon early Palestinian-Chilean immigrants' engagement with journalism through their communal press.

Arab immigration to Argentina began massively around 1890. Most of the migrants, mainly from Lebanon and Syria, settled in Buenos Aires,

16   *Cristián H. Ricci*

Cordoba, and in some towns in the northern regions of the country, quickly becoming a real force in many fields, including politics, journalism, and literature. Gladys Jozami indicates that most of these immigrants – of which some 70 percent were originally Christians – became part of the Argentine population between 1890 and 1950 and today have second-, third-, fourth-, and even fifth-generation descendants. Before the 1980s, they were, for the most part, absorbed in a process of acculturation that was, by 1980, almost complete (Jozami 41–42). However, for many of the children, grandchildren, and great-grandchildren of Middle Eastern immigrants, their ethnicity survives in their home environment, cuisine, preservation of the extended family, survival of specific values and customs, and an intangible sort of feeling as displayed fictional and non-fictional representations focalized through different narrative voices. Marcus Palmer's chapter, "Writing South, Facing East: Arab Argentine Narratives," examines the recovery of the homeland and the recording of family histories in relation to diaspora studies, with special attention given to lesser studied genres in the Argentine *mahjar*: Spanish-language short stories.

Several gaps in the study of the Arab diaspora in Colombia are yet to be filled. Odette Yidi David argues that existing research on the Arab diaspora in Colombia generally focuses on the migratory restrictions and discrimination faced by early migrants, explored through local newspapers and legislative decrees; on their economic networks reconstructed from public records; and on their active participation in regional and national politics (Yidi David 208). On the other hand, with very few exceptions (Odette Yidi David), studies on identity and cultural politics of this diaspora are yet to be thoroughly undertaken, in contrast with, for example, the well-known works regarding literature and identity negotiation among Arabs in Argentina (Christina Civantos), Chile (Heba El Attar), or Mexico (Camila Pastor). By exploring case studies from the late literature of the Colombian *mahjar*, Angela Haddad's chapter, "Chronicling 'the Death of the Arab' in Colombian Literature," sheds new perspectives on the Arab diaspora in Colombia, revealing how canonical and non-canonical novelists served as cultural mediators and how they related to the image of the Arab migrant or traveler. More importantly, the chapter explores the narratological structure of novels dealing with Arab protagonists as a constitutive component of Hispanic-American Orientalism that is concerned with authorship and knowledge production.

With 400,000 Arabs in Mexico – including recent migrants and the descendants of historical migrations – the ethnic group would seem too small to matter, were it not for the common ancestry between Arabs and Mexicans derived from the times of al-Andalus and the amazing social mobility of some Arab immigrants and their children in the country, such as telecommunications mogul Carlos Slim Helu, ranked number 9 (2022) in Forbes World's Billionaires list. Yvonne Yazbeck Haddad observes that during the last decade of the nineteenth century and the beginning of the twentieth century, many immigrants from Lebanon settled in the northern states of Mexico – Chihuahua, Sonora, Nuevo Leon, Coahuila, and Durango – as these states have been traditionally more isolated and, therefore, more open to foreign migration since Spanish colonization. Recent scholarship on Mexican identity and culture rarely mentions the immigrant tradition to Mexico. The discourse tends to focus on the mestizo paradigm, on persons of indigenous and/or Spanish descent to the exclusion of "Others." It is within this mestizo construct that the *turco* (Turk) stereotype is perpetuated (Yazbeck Haddad 279). Rose Mary Salum's chapter "The Otherness That Remains. The Past from The Future: *Cuaderno de Chihuahua* by Jeannette Lozano Clariond" acquaints the reader with the nature of the Levantine migration to Mexico by using the voices of its descendants as its basis, even though this chapter of Mexico's migration was officially considered over by 1930.

Today, Brazil is home to the largest community of Arab descent in the Americas, with an estimated population of seven to twelve million (some other estimates range from twelve to fifteen million) or 3.5–6 percent of the population. Sixty percent of Arab Brazilians are of Lebanese ancestry. The most significant influx of Arab immigration to Brazil occurred beginning in 1904, with the large majority settling in the city of São Paulo. However, as studied by Jeffrey Lesser, significant contingents eventually settled in the states of Pará, Rio de Janeiro, and Rio Grande do Sul (48). Most Syrians and Lebanese who immigrated to Brazil were Christian, from various denominations, including Eastern Orthodox, Melkite, Maronite, and Protestant (Moser and Racy 283). Over a century of Levantine migration to Brazil has produced unique literary genres in both Arabic and Portuguese languages. Many migrants were also journalists and dabbled in prose genres like essays, travelogues, autobiographies, short stories, plays, and novels. While writing exclusively in Portuguese, authors such as Raduan Nassar, Alberto Mussa, Milton Hatoum, Carlos Nejar, William Argel de Mello, and Salim Miguel bring themes related to their identities as descendants of Levantine migrants to the forefront in their novels. Nazir Ahmed Can's chapter, "The Idea of Translation in *Ancient Tillage*, by Raduan Nassar," analyzes the fluidity of the homeland as a concept. It considers relevant translation theories in the study of diaspora and seeks to understand the intricacies of migrant experiences that occur when communities leave one geographical space and contend with issues of home, space, and belonging, to coalesce around different markers of identity in a new geographical space (Dueck and Jacoby 50).

Overall, the chapters that make up *Twenty-First Century Arab and African Diasporas in Spain, Portugal, and Latin America* explore the peculiarities of Arab, sub-Saharan, and North African diasporic literatures and artistic representations, as well as their synergies with the European and Latin American fields of cultural production. Within the context of social,

18 Cristián H. Ricci

political, historical, and cultural events, the 15 chapters trace the transcultural and heterogenous genealogies of diasporic literary and artistic representations, their development in the first quarter of the twenty-first century, efforts to consolidate transnational literature and art, and the eventual attainment of a place in the global literary and artistic map. From multiple thematic and theoretical perspectives, this book thus provides a comprehensive and inclusive view of little-known and non-canonical works and authors, which have traditionally marginalized and silenced. In short, it hopes to encourage new research on more inclusive Luso-Hispanic literary and artistic productions.

Note

1. In Arabic, *muhājirīn*, or those who have left for or have been living in the *mahjar* – literally, the place of immigration.

Works Cited

Anderson, Warwick, Ricardo Roque, and Ricardo Ventura Santos, eds. *Luso-Tropicalism and Its Discontents: The Making and Unmaking of Racial Exceptionalism*. Berghahn Books, 2019.

Bhabha, Homi. *The Location of Culture*, 1994. Routledge 1998.

Cartwright, Mark. "Portuguese Empire." *World History Encyclopedia*, 19 Jul. 2021. Web. 03 May 2022, n.p.

Costa, Pedro, and Ricardo Lopes. "Is Street Art Institutionalizable? Challenges to an Alternative Urban Policy in Lisbon." *Métropoles*, vol. 17, 2015, n.p.

Dueck, Jennifer, and Tami Amanda Jacoby. "Sites of Identity Among Middle Eastern Diasporas in North America." *Mashriq & Mahjar: Journal of Middle East and North African Migration Studies*, vol. 4, no. 1, 2017, pp. 50–58.

Goytisolo, Juan. "Presentación." *Orientalismo*, edited by Edward W. Said, Debolsillo, 2003.

Haddad, Yvonne Yazbeck, ed. *Muslims in the West: From Sojourners to Citizens*. Oxford UP, 2002.

Hassan, Weil S. "Arabs and the Americas: A Multilingual and Multigenerational Legacy." *Review: Literature and Arts of the Americas*, Issue 99, vol. 52, no. 2, 2019, pp. 166–169.

Jozami, Gladys. "The Return of the 'Turks' in 1990s Argentina." *Patterns of Prejudice*, vol. 30, no. 4, 1996, pp. 27–42.

Kushigian, Julia Alexis. *Orientalism in the Hispanic Literary Tradition: In Dialogue with Borges, Paz, and Sarduy*. 1st ed., U of New Mexico P, 1991.

Lesser, Jeffrey. *Negotiating National Identity: Immigrants, Minorities and the Struggle for Ethnicity in Brazil*. Duke UP, 1999.

Lewellen, Ted C. *The Anthropology of Globalization: Cultural Anthropology Enters the 21st Century*. Bergin & Garvey, 2002.

Merolla, Daniela. "Poetics of Transition: Africa and Dutch Literary Space." *Migrant Cartographies. New Cultural and Literary Spaces in Postcolonial Europe*, edited by Elisabeth Bakers et al., Rodopi, 2009, pp. 35–55.

Moser, Robert H., and A.J. Racy. "The Homeland in the Literature and Music of Syrian-Lebanese Immigrants and Their Descendants in Brazil." *Diaspora*, vol. 19, no. 2–3, 2017, pp. 280–311.

Payne, Phillipa. "'Porteadoras' Suffer Exploitation and Violence on the Border Between Morocco and Spain's North African Enclaves." *The Organization for World Peace*, 26 May 2019, https://theowp.org/reports/porteadoras-suffer-exploitation-and-violence-on-the-border-between-morocco-and-spains-north-african-enclaves/

Pitts, Johny. *Afropean: Notes from Black Europe*. Penguin, 2019.

Robbins, Jill, and Adolfo Campoy-Cubillo. "Considering the Western Sahara: Multi-Disciplinary Approaches to Post-Colonialism. Special Issue on Western Sahara." *Transmodernity: Journal of Peripheral Cultural Production of the Luso-Hispanic World*, vol. 5, no. 3, 2015, pp. 1–4.

Safran, William. 1991. "Diasporas in Modern Societies: Myths of Homeland and Return." *Diaspora*, vol. 1, no. 1, pp. 83–99.

Said, Edward W. *Orientalism*. Vintage Books, 1979.

Soto Bermant, Laia. "The Myth of Resistance: Rethinking the 'Informal' Economy in a Mediterranean Border Enclave." *Journal of Borderlands Studies*, vol. 30, no. 2, 2015, pp. 263–278.

Tamalet Talbayeb, Edwige. "The Languages of Translocality: What Plurilingualism Means in a Maghrebi Context." *Expressions Maghrébines: Revue De La Coordination Internationale Des Chercheurs Sur Les Littératures Maghrébines*, vol. 11, no. 2, 2013, pp. 9–25.

Vidal, Marta. "The Portuguese Rediscovering Their Country's Muslim Past." *Al Jazeera*, 10 Jun. 2020, Web 03 May 2022, n.p.

Yidi David, Odette. "From Khalil Gibran to Meira Delmar: Reflections on the Literature of the Colombian Mahjar." *Los rostros del otro: colonialismo y construcción social en Medio Oriente y norte de África*, 2019, pp. 206–233.

Part I
Spain

1 Integration, School, and the Children of North African Immigrants in Spain

Daniela Flesler

On July 13, 2015, the Spanish parliament passed Law 19/2015, which contained a revision of the procedure for naturalization through residence for all immigrants living in Spain. What was added to the requirements was a method to establish "la acreditación del suficiente grado de integración en la sociedad española" [the accreditation of a sufficient degree of integration into Spanish society]. This accreditation took the form of two exams: one on Spanish language and the second on knowledge of the Spanish Constitution and the "realidad social y cultural españolas" [Spanish social and cultural reality] ("Ley 19/2015"). This revision followed the French model, heavily influenced by discourses of Islamophobia weaponizing fears of Muslim immigrants' supposed lack of integration into European societies. Not coincidentally, it was added to the naturalization requirements in the context following the attacks on *Charlie Hebdo* and customers in the Hypercacher kosher supermarket in Paris in January of that same year, 2015.

A 2008 PEW survey showing an increase of unfavorable views of Muslims in Europe showed that Spain was the country with the most negative view of them: 52% admitted to negative views. A 2018 PEW survey that included strongly worded negative statements about Muslims found greater ambivalence: asked whether "Muslims want to impose their religious law on everyone else," Spain's percentage of people agreeing was the highest after Belgium, 40%. But when asked whether Islam was incompatible with their country's values and culture, 37% answered yes in Spain, on the lower side compared with other European countries. At the same time, Spain and Portugal had the highest percentage of people saying that they knew not much or nothing at all about Islam (PEW, "Nationalism" n.p.). These statistics show us that the situation of Muslim immigrants in Spain partakes of a European context of great suspicion about their integration, with the additional charge and ambivalence that these discussions carry in Spain due to the centuries-long presence of Muslims in Iberian territory. This presence not only marked Spain's own cultural identity but also determined a European view of Spain as

DOI: 10.4324/9781003245117-3

24 *Daniela Flesler*

Oriental and Semitic, a racial and religious Other of Europe (Fuchs 6–9, Hillgarth 160).

In Spain, North African Muslim immigrants have focalized most of the debates over immigrants' integration and assimilation, and they have become the most ill-regarded immigrant group (Martín Muñoz 32–33). North African immigrants are identified, through their characterization as "Moors," with the Arab and Berber Muslims who conquered the Iberian Peninsula in 711 and with their subsequent reincarnations as threatening "Moorish invaders" throughout Spanish history, including, in the twentieth century, Moroccan mercenaries that fought in the Nationalist side of the Spanish Civil War (Flesler 3–4). As Gema Martín Muñoz has explained, this characterization has persisted until today, notwithstanding the visible gap that exists between this perception of "invasion" and their actual numbers (Martín Muñoz 15–17).

This latent Islamophobia has been weaponized by the new extreme right political party Vox.[1] As Sebastiaan Faber and Bécquer Seguín explain, together with an extreme centralism and Spanish nationalism incensed by the push for Catalan independence, anti-immigration animates Vox's voters, for whom immigrants are "a threat to 'Spanishness itself'" (Faber and Seguín n.p.). It is not surprising, then, that its leader, Santiago Abascal, has embraced "Reconquista" symbols, such as the launching of his political campaign in April of 2019 in Covadonga, in the northern region of Asturias, where the Christian King Don Pelayo supposedly defeated the conquering North African troops in the year 722. However, This perception of threat, especially focalized on Muslim immigrants and their children, precedes Vox's recent popularity and has purchase beyond Vox's base.[2]

Following Vatican II, the Francoist law of religious freedom of 1967 had recognized non-Catholic religious minorities, although with limitations. The Constitution of 1978 guaranteed freedom of religion, prohibited discrimination based on religion, and established that no religion would have a state character, although it explicitly mentioned the Catholic Church, which was able to secure a privileged status. As Aitana Guía explains, "[w]hile the Spanish Constitution guarantees equal treatment of minority confessions by the state – including access to public funds on par with that enjoyed by the Catholic Church – the imbalance remains egregious" (102). A new Law of religious freedom in 1980 and recognition of their "deeply rooted" (notorio arraigo) character in 1985 paved the way for Cooperation Agreements with Muslim, Jewish, and Evangelical religious representatives in 1992. However, these agreements have yet to be truly fulfilled in matters of consideration of religious holidays, access to prayer sites and public funds, religious teaching in schools, and actual state neutrality and equality in religion (Guía 96–105).[3]

The European Commission Against Racism and Intolerance (ECRI) Report analyzes every five years the situation in each of the member states of the Council of Europe, covering legislative issues, hate speech, violence,

Integration, School, and the Children of Immigrants in Spain   25

and integration policies. It follows up on recommendations made in the prior report and requests their implementation by the corresponding authorities of each country. In the 2018 report about Spain, ECRI regrets that its prior recommendation concerning the right to equality to be granted to all individuals by the Constitution, not just Spanish citizens, was not implemented. It also notes that the Migrant Integration Policy Index identifies the field of education as "the greatest weakness in Spain's integration policies," with averages of school enrollment and completion much lower than the EU average and with only limited support for children of immigrant families in learning Spanish and other official languages and catching up academically. "Decisive action and investment in the education of children with migration backgrounds is needed in order to provide them with equal opportunities," states the report (ECRI 28).

School has become a rich site of exploration among the growing literature on the experiences of children from immigrant families. In *Constructing Inequality in Multilingual Classrooms*, Luisa Martín Rojo analyzes the results of a team ethnography of four multilingual and multicultural schools in Madrid. In the last 30 years, these schools have incorporated growing numbers of children whose parents emigrated from, mostly, Ecuador, Colombia, Romania, Peru, Morocco, Bolivia, China, and the Dominican Republic. In Madrid's city center, they make up around 34% of students (Martín Rojo 5), although in some schools, the percentages are 50 or even 90%. These percentages do not reflect residential segregation but differential school choice (as in Spanish-born parents sending their children to state-subsidized private schools to avoid sending them to schools perceived as "sub-standard") (Martín Rojo 262; see also Colectivo Ioé 43–44, 57; El Hachmi, *Jo també* 78). Martín Rojo and her team wished to discover whether these demographic changes had resulted in changes in the schools' understanding of community, the role of education, and what is considered "normal" in school. However, they found that cultural and linguistic differences had virtually no visibility in the schools: "students' voices, languages and experiences are rarely included by the teacher . . . inequality and social exclusion . . . is exercised and constructed within everyday classroom interactions" (Martín Rojo 10). Moroccan students, in particular, are tokenized, controlled, sidelined, silenced, stereotyped, and constructed as "other" of a white, European "us" composed of the teacher and the local students (Martín Rojo 263–89; see also García-Sánchez 485–88).

These experiences, specifically those of North African Muslim girls, are critically explored in the short film *Hiyab*, by Xavi Sala, and in several texts by Najat El Hachmi. *Hiyab* consists of the dialogue between a teacher and a girl, Fatima, who is attending high school for the first time. In a school hallway, peering through a classroom door, they discuss the headscarf Fatima is wearing. The teacher tries to convince her to remove it before entering the classroom. Fatima does not want to. The teacher

26 Daniela Flesler

uses several arguments, speaking for most of the time of the short, pushing for the desired result. Her tone is condescending and paternalistic. Fatima is embarrassed, nervous, and mostly silent. "¿No ves cómo van las otras?" [Can't you see how the other (female) ones dress?] begins the teacher, playing, almost cruelly, to the common desire to conform and not be overly conspicuous of many young people. Moments later, as if there was any doubt to how far she will press this point, she insists, "Tú has visto alguien aquí que lo lleve? No querrás ser la rara de la case, no?" [Have you seen anybody here wearing it? You don't want to be the weird one in class, right?]. "Pero soy musulmana" [but I am Muslim], replies Fatima. "That has nothing to do with it," sentences the teacher, with all the authority conferred by her position of power over the new student. "Lo que intento explicarte es que esta es una escuela laica y todos somos iguales. No queremos diferencias entre los alumnos. Tú te imaginas qué pasaría si a cada uno se le ocurriera venir vestido de su religión? Pues que la libertad de culto, de pensamiento, y todo eso se nos iría directamente a la basura" [What I am trying to explain to you is that this is a lay school and we are all the same. We don't want any differences among the students. Do you imagine what would happen if each person came dressed in their religion? Well, religious freedom, freedom of thought, and all that would go down the drain].

The teacher keeps pressing her faulty logic, knowing very well that being "dressed in their religion" only constitutes a problem when that religion is not Catholicism. Nobody would ever ask a girl not to wear a necklace with a cross to school. As Sander Gilman argues, "[s]cratch secular Europe today, and you find all the presuppositions and attitudes of Christianity concerning Jews and Muslims present in subliminal or overt forms. Secular society in Europe has absorbed Christianity into its very definition of the secular" (145). As Colectivo Ioé also explains, the public schools that define themselves as not religious follow a Catholic calendar as part of a hidden curriculum never questioned (64). The teacher then voices the widespread, common prejudice, "¿Tus padres te pegan si no lo llevas? [Do your parents hit you if you don't wear it?] to which Fatima responds, increasingly upset, "no, ellos también quieren que me lo quite" [no, they also want me to take it off].[4]

After several minutes of relentless arguments, and when it becomes obvious that her own reasons will not be heard, Fatima very slowly takes the headscarf off. It is evident she does not want to, and the moment captures the symbolic violence of the pressure exerted upon her. Without the headscarf, Fatima enters the classroom. The last scene of the short film is shot from Fatima's point of view. The camera shows us what she sees when entering the classroom. In contrast to what the teacher said, the students staring at her are not "all the same." We see one by one staring back at Fatima. Their gaze, captured from her point of view, seems almost taunting. Several are wearing different styles of scarves on their

Integration, School, and the Children of Immigrants in Spain   27

heads, another one a wool hat, another one several piercings. Each of them looks at Fatima from a highly individualized personal choice of hairstyle, clothing, and style that nobody in the school has questioned. The message of the short film is clear: some differences are seen as more different than others, or certain bodies have a right to wear and style their differences and individuality, and other bodies do not. In terms of how this relates to the process of social and cultural integration, which the teacher in the film is supposedly pursuing, it exemplifies Martín Rojo's observation of school officials' interactions with children of immigrant backgrounds: "A process of essentialization is revealed, by means of which cultural non-adaptability resides in the inferior, essentialist features of the other's culture" (301).

When the Partido Popular (governing right-wing party) presented the draft of what ended up passing as Law 19/2015, the PSOE (Socialist Party), PNV (Basque Nationalist Party), and EPC (group of left Catalonian parties) objected, among other items, to the language and culture exams. The PSOE and EPC explained their opposition using the same argument:

> el nuevo modelo mediante el que, para la concesión de la nacionalidad por residencia, se pretende acreditar el suficiente grado de integración en la sociedad española. . . . supone dar un salto hacia un modelo aislacionista, abandonando un itinerario de integración bidireccional y una adaptación mutua que aproxime a los inmigrantes y a la sociedad de acogida con la máxima del respeto mutuo
> [The new model by which nationality through residency is granted expects [that immigrants] prove a sufficient degree of integration into Spanish society. . . . It endorses an isolationist model, abandoning a bidirectional program of integration and of mutual adaptation, which brings immigrants and the receiving society closer through the maxim of mutual respect.]
>
> ("Proposiciones de Ley")

The violence depicted in *Hiyab* is, precisely, the assimilationist, isolationist model referenced by PSOE and EPC and explained by Martín Rojo: the violence of interpreting integration as a one-way process. In their study of the children of Moroccan immigrants in Spanish schools, Colectivo Ioé reached the same conclusion: the criteria by which teachers evaluated the integration of these children was their degree of assimilation of preexisting rules in Spanish schools. From this perspective, their difference was perceived as a lack and a problem (88–90): "Al identificar 'lo de aquí' con modernidad y 'lo de allí' con retraso cultural y social, se justifica la necesidad de integrar a los niños marroquíes en lo de aquí" [by identifying 'what is from here' with modernity and 'what is from there' with cultural and social backwardness, we justify the need to integrate Moroccan children in what is from here] (Colectivo Ioé 98).[5]

28   Daniela Flesler

Najat El Hachmi describes this understanding of integration when, in her autobiographical essay, *Jo també sóc catalana*, she explains, "Quan algú et diu que t'integris, el que en realitat t'està demanant és que et desintegris, que esborris qualsevol raster de temps anteriors, de vestigis culturals o religiosos, que ho oblidis tot i només recordis els seus records, el seu passat" [when somebody tells you to become integrated, what they are really asking you is to disintegrate, that you erase any trace of times before, of cultural or religious vestiges, that you forget everything and only remember their memories, their past] (90).

The experiences of physical and cultural migration and dislocation are a central focus of El Hachmi's written work. So is her experience as an intercultural translator or mediator and the psychological toll these positions take. El Hachmi has literally worked as an intercultural mediator for the education office of Vic's Town Hall. Especially after the success of her novel *L'últim patriarca* (2008), which received the prestigious Ramon Llull Catalan Letters Award, she became a public figure who often finds herself positioned as transcultural mediator in her columns, interventions, and interviews in Catalan and Spanish newspapers, radio and television. As Cristián H. Ricci has observed, "the written, plural and transgressing insubordination of El Hachmi becomes a fight, a negotiation of the difference, an encounter-(dis)encounter between the obsession of North African markers and 'the anxiety of influence' of the European" (Ricci, "Postcolonial" 34). As other critics have explained, she articulates "a fluid Catalan-Amazigh identity" (Campoy-Cubillo 142), inhabiting "a hybrid space" (Joan Rodríguez 64).[6]

Her novel *La hija extranjera* [The Foreign Daughter] describes the internal conflict of the young, nameless protagonist and narrator in her relationship with her mother and her desire for independence. The narrative shows the process by which she slowly begins carving a separate space from that of her mother and her mother's expectations. The protagonist speaks Catalan perfectly, having grown up in Catalonia, and knows very well what the rules to follow are to become "la perfectamente integrada" [the perfectly integrated one] (El Hachmi, *La hija* 66). However, once and again, she ironically incorporates into the narrative and comments on the often-hypocritical discourses of integration and on the limits of her "almost" acceptance into Catalan society. Speaking to herself in second person, the protagonist reminds herself: "No tienes ningún motivo para quejarte, como hablas su lengua igual o mejor que ellos casi ni recuerdan de dónde eres o quién eres. Casi" [You do not have any reason to complain, since you speak their language as well or better than them, they almost do not remember where you are from or who you are. Almost] (El Hachmi, *La hija* 23). The word "almost" marks the limits: she might know Catalan perfectly well, but other identity markers "betray" her as not Catalan enough.

This "almost" exists in correlation to the concept of "sufficient" of Law 9/2015, when its text speaks of immigrants having to prove "sufficient

Integration, School, and the Children of Immigrants in Spain 29

degree of integration into Spanish society." But what happens when that "sufficient" is impossible to reach because no matter how well someone knows the language and the "social and cultural reality" evaluated in the residency exams, they are still perceived as "Other," racialized, and discriminated against? This "almost" becomes evident when the protagonist and her mother look for a new apartment and their applications are rejected time and again (El Hachmi, *La hija* 94–95). If mother and daughter go in person, her mother's headscarf results in the apartment that was available not being available anymore. On other occasions, the narrator is able to go much further in the process and almost close the deal: if she goes by herself, and they do not "detect" her as Moroccan. Or on the phone, where there are initially no problems since the protagonist "sounds" Catalan. But in these cases, explains the narrator, the disappointment is worse. The illusion of belonging and integration sooner or later is crushed:

> los que me generan más frustración son los que al principio no se dan cuenta de que soy marroquí . . . pero, mira tú por donde, cuando envío la fotocopia de mi permiso de residencia va y aparece, como por arte de magia, un sobrino de la propietaria que necesita el piso. . . . Podría incluso llegar a creerme la historia si no fuera porque en todos los casos se trata de un sobrino
>
> [the ones who produce the most frustration for me are those who, in the beginning, do not realize that I am Moroccan . . . but, well, what do you know, when I send them the copy of my residency permit, suddenly, as by a magic trick, appears the owner's nephew needing the apartment. . . . I could even begin to believe the story if it wasn't because, in every case, it is a nephew.]
>
> (El Hachmi, *La hija* 95)

The narrator's experiences at school occupy a central place in her psychological development and in the widening of a horizon of expectations for herself, but they also reveal to her the limits of her acceptance and integration into Catalan society. She returns several times, in her narration, to a key episode in the construction of her self-image. Her grades for the Spanish University Admission Test (EvAU), the "sele," produce a great commotion in the city. The grades were not the best from her high school, but a journalist noticed her foreign last names in the list of grades. Because of this, the grades become news, and she is interviewed in several newspapers and on TV. The protagonist immediately resents the excess entailed in the attention, which would not occur if the same grades had been earned by someone not labeled as a Moroccan immigrant. "Fairground monkey! Fairground monkey!" she repeats to herself, given the exhibition that she has become an object of (El Hachmi, *La hija* 67).

30   *Daniela Flesler*

When attending a sewing workshop for "women at risk of social exclusion" with her mother, the mayor's daughter recognizes her from TV as "la chica que sacaste un nueve en la 'sele'" [the girl that got a nine in the Cert] and congratulates her for such a high score, the narrator feels the mayor's daughter's condescendence and paternalism. She notes how she feels flattered and immediately chastises herself for feeling that, translating the context and connotation of the mayor's daughter congratulations, explaining to the reader what the young woman is probably thinking:

> Y a ti te encanta que te digan estas cosas, aunque sepas de sobra que es denigrante, que lo que piensa esta chica es que, de entrada, solo por ser lo que eres, solo por haber nacido donde has nacido, estás destinada a no ser nada, a no hacer nada, que en tu ADN están inscritos el atraso y la inferioridad. Por eso, superar estos condicionantes es ya de por sí un mérito extraordinario, casi un milagro
>
> [And you like people saying these things to you, even though you know it's insulting, since what this girl is really thinking – since the start, given only that you are who you are, given only that you were born where you were, you are destined to be a *nobody*, to achieve nothing, inferiority and backwardness are inscribed in your DNA. That's why it's such an extraordinary merit, practically a miracle, you overcame these conditioning factors.]
>
> (El Hachmi, *La hija* 88)[7]

While in the short film *Hiyab*, the "price of admission" to the Spanish classroom was the violence of the pressure of abandoning an important element of Fatima's own sense of self, in El Hachmi's *La hija extranjera*, we see the violence of the prejudice of low expectations. Martín Rojo documents this widespread and openly expressed opinion among high school teachers about Moroccan female students, which has extremely negative consequences for the students:

> they explain their low level of expectations by the supposition that the girls, especially those from Morocco, will not continue with their studies because, like their mothers, they will remain at home and give priority to motherhood over studying for a career.
>
> (284)

The danger of these low expectations is that they can often end up becoming self-fulfilling prophecies (Colectivo Ioé 71). *La hija* explores these expectations, positing that this path of domesticity and motherhood as opposed to studying for a career is precisely what the protagonist's mother expects of her. The novel describes the process by which she will reject this paradigm and abandon her mother and her mother's world.[8]

Integration, School, and the Children of Immigrants in Spain 31

In this novel, we also see a reflection on the mediating role that school-age children and young people often occupy between their immigrant parents and local authority figures. This mediating role that the protagonist assumed since childhood becomes more complex and formalized as she grows up and is hired as mediator by Vic's Town Hall. Although we can think that this kind of work is essential and not many people are qualified to do it well, she receives minimal compensation for it. The salary is less than what she earns in her cleaning job, which reveals the real social value assigned to it. Having "sufficient" knowledge to mediate between the two (to use the language of Law 19/2015) will not be enough for the protagonist to be able to afford leaving the marginalization of her immigrant neighborhood (181). Her first experience as mediator is her participation in an "intercultural forum." Soon, however, she realizes that the forum is neither a forum nor intercultural. It is not a space of exchange where the Town Hall might be interested in listening to the factors that make Moroccan immigrants' integration more difficult and how to help them overcome these obstacles but a platform for public figures to air their complaints about Moroccan immigrants (El Hachmi, *La hija* 124). At the end of the day, the narrator realizes her innocence: "no me habían invitado para hablar de los problemas de los marroquíes sino de los problemas que provocan los marroquíes" [they had not invited me to talk about Moroccans' problems but of the problems caused by Moroccans] (127).

Her second experience as mediator is equally painful and revelatory. Her task is to go early in the morning to the house of a Moroccan woman and to make sure that her two daughters, including the three-year-old one, get on the bus to go to school. The issue, she soon realizes, is that the girls are supposed to go to a school that is significantly far away from where they live, and thus they will be all day away. This is not "por su bien" [for their own good], because the mother "debe entender que es lo mejor para todos" [should understand that this is the best for everybody] (187), as the authorities want the protagonist to tell the mother (here, again, we see the novel's incorporation of the condescending discourse of one-way integration). The reason is that they want to "repartir" [share] Moroccan children in different schools to avoid their "concentration" in the same school (as we saw is the case in the Madrid schools where Martín Rojo and her team conducted their ethnographic research). The narrator repeats what she was told, knowing it is a lie: that in the school nearby there are no vacancies and that "here" children begin school when they are three (188). The narrator does as she was told and yanks the screaming little girl from her mother's arms to put her on the bus. She gets home "con la sensación de haber hecho algo sucio o, como mínimo, injusto. . . . me utilizan para convencer a las familias de que acepten lo que las familias 'de aquí de toda la vida' no aceptarían nunca" [with the feeling of having done something dirty or, at least, unfair. . . . They use

32 *Daniela Flesler*

me to convince families to accept something that the families 'who have always been here' would never accept] (190).

While the Town Hall authorities evaluate this mother's situation as one of a Moroccan woman not wanting her daughters to go to school, the protagonist sees and understands more. Her understanding is possible because she, like the children featured in Inmaculada M. García-Sánchez's study, "take an active part in asserting multiple forms of belonging" (482). As García-Sánchez explains, even as teachers, often inadvertently, participate in the exclusion of children from immigrant families, these children are also capable of contesting the limitations imposed upon them (482). This contestation implies, for teachers and authorities, a confrontation with more complex forms of cultural, ethnic and national identity. This complexity is certainly not encompassed in Law 19/2015's assimilationist, differentialist exhortation to demonstrate "a sufficient degree of integration into Spanish society." But the presence and voices of an increasing number of children of immigrant families embodying more complex forms of belonging to their communities and nations bring with them an unavoidable reckoning with the fact that they, themselves, are already part of that Spanish society invoked in the law.

Notes

1. Together with Islamophobia, Vox espouses features also found in other European far right parties: heightened nationalism, hard-line anti-immigration positions, and traffic in antisemitic conspiracy theories (as in "George Soros finances the Islamization of Europe") at the same time as support for Israel (see Baer, "The Rise"). The Asociación Musulmanes contra la Islamofobia [Muslims against Islamophobia Association] denounced Vox's secretary general, Javier Ortega Smith, for incitement to hatred against the Muslim population after he declared, in a political rally in September 2018, that European civilization was threatened by a common enemy, "the Islamic invasion" (Marraco). See Soyer for an analysis of this type of current "demographic panic" in relation to the development, throughout the sixteenth century, of a perception of Spain's Moriscos as a demographic and security threat to the state.
2. An infamous, notorious example was the incendiary speech pronounced by former president José María Aznar in Georgetown in 2004 characterizing Spanish identity as forged against Islam. For an overview of Muslims in Spain and Spanish Islamophobia, see Planet Contreras and Aguilera-Carnerero.
3. See Guía for a discussion of religious teaching in schools and Astor for an analysis of the opposition to the building of new mosques throughout Spain, especially in Catalonia.
4. For a discussion of the politics and controversies over the use of the headscarf in Spain, see Flesler, 156–60, Nair, Mijares and Ramírez. In her 2019 essay *Siempre han hablado por nosotras* [They have always spoken for us], El Hachmi controversially defends the prohibition of the use of headscarves in schools (67–68).
5. See Balibar for a theorization of how these assumptions underline differentialist or culturalist racism. In *The Return* (131–62), I analyze this dynamic in relation to a series of Spanish films on immigration.

Integration, School, and the Children of Immigrants in Spain   33

6. See Ricci's article for a thorough contextualization of El Hachmi's work as part of a group of Moroccan-Amazigh writers who have lived in Catalonia since childhood and write in Catalan and, more widely, of a new type of postcolonial praxis by Moroccan and Amazigh writers in Spain. For more on El Hachmi's writing, see also Ricci's "L'últim," Campoy-Cubillo, Martin-Márquez, Murray, Joan Rodríguez.
7. A similar situation is described by the protagonist of El Hachmi's 2021 novel, *El lunes nos querrán.* Like the protagonist of *La hija extranjera*, she is an excellent student, and she wins a short story contest at her school. Her achievement causes a commotion both in her neighborhood and in the school: "Algunos interpretaron que mi logro era una prueba de mi integración en la sociedad; otros me dieron palmaditas en la espalda y se asombraron de que alguien como yo hubiera podido escribir un relato como ese. Ya lo sabes, creían que no podíamos ni hablar, ¿cómo íbamos a escribir?" [Some people interpreted that my achievement was proof of my integration in society; others patted me on the back and were surprised that somebody like me could have written a short story like that. You know, they think we cannot even talk, how were we going to write?] (El Hachmi, *El lunes* 149).
8. The mother-daughter relationship in this novel and the daughter's search for agency and independence is analyzed in Bourland Ross's excellent article. As she explains, "[i]n order for the narrator to establish her own identity, the author portrays a struggle in which the narrator must ultimately reject her mother and her cultural heritage" (358).

Works Cited

Aguilera-Carnerero, Carmen. "Islamophobia in Spain: National Report 2018." *European Islamophobia Report 2018*, edited by Enes Bayraklı and Farid Hafez, SETA, 2019, pp. 775–794.

Astor, Avi. *Rebuilding Islam in Contemporary Spain: The Politics of Mosque Establishment, 1976–2013.* Sussex Academic Press, 2017.

Balibar, Etienne. "Is There a "Neo-Racism?" *Etienne Balibar and Immanuel Wallerstein Race, Nation, Class: Ambiguous Identities.* Verso, 1991, pp. 17–28.

Bourland Ross, Catherine. "Left Behind: Cultural Assimilation and the Mother/ Daughter Relationship in Najat El Hachmi's *La hija extranjera* (2015)." *Hispanófila*, vol. 183, 2018, pp. 351–365.

Campoy-Cubillo, Adolfo. *Memories of the Maghreb: Transnational Identities in Spanish Cultural Production.* Palgrave Macmillan, 2016.

Cesari, Jocelyne. "Is There a European Islam?" *The Oxford Handbook of European Islam.* Oxford UP, 2014, p. 802.

Colectivo Ioé (Miguel Angel de Prada, Walter Actis, Carlos Pereda). *La educación intercultural a prueba. Hijos de inmigrantes marroquíes en la escuela.* Universidad de Granada: Madrid, 1994, www.colectivoioe.org/uploads/14506ad4d90 195fd39ae34d3115735b5d372e61a.pdf. Accessed 22 Mar. 2022.

ECRI (European Commission Against Racism and Intolerance) Report on Spain 2018, https://rm.coe.int/fifth-report-on-spain/16808b56c9. Accessed 20 Mar. 2022.

El Hachmi, Najat. *Jo també sóc catalana.* Columna, 2004.

———. *La hija extranjera.* Destino, 2015.

———. *Siempre han hablado por nosotras.* Destino, 2019.

34 *Daniela Flesler*

Faber, Sebastiaan, and Béquer Seguín. "Spain's Radical Right Is Here to Stay – But Did It Ever Leave?" *The Nation*, 10 Jan. 2019. www.thenation.com/article/archive/spain-vox-radical-right-populism-catalonia/. Accessed 20 Dec. 2020.

Flesler, Daniela. *The Return of the Moor: Spanish Responses to Contemporary Moroccan Immigration*. Purdue UP, 2008.

Fuchs, Barbara. *Exotic Nation: Maurophilia and the Construction of Early Modern Spain*. U of Pennsylvania P, 2008.

García-Sánchez, Inmaculada M. "The Everyday Politics of 'Cultural Citizenship' among North African Immigrant School Children in Spain." *Language & Communication*, vol. 33, 2013, pp. 481–499.

Gilman, Sander L. "The Case of Circumcision: Diaspora Judaism as a Model for Islam?" *Antisemitism and Islamophobia in Europe. A Shared Story?*, edited by James Renton and Ben Gidley, Palgrave, 2017, pp. 143–164.

Guía, Aitana. "Completing the Religious Transition? Catholics and Muslims Navigate Secularism in Democratic Spain." *New Diversities*, vol. 17, no. 1, 2015, pp. 95–110.

Hiyab. Dir. Xavi Sala. Spain, 2005.

Hillgarth, J. N. *The Mirror of Spain, 1500–1700: The Formation of a Myth*. U of Michigan P, 2000.

Joan Rodríguez, Meritxell. "Transitando el Mediterráneo: etiquetas literarias y subjetividades híbridas en la tríada migratoria de Najat El Hachmi." *Transmodernity: Journal of Peripheral Cultural Production of the Luso-Hispanic World*, vol. 9, no. 4, 2020, pp. 45–67.

"Ley 19/2015, de 13 de julio, de medidas de reforma administrativa en el ámbito de la Administración de Justicia y del Registro Civil." *BOE* (Boletín Oficial del Estado) 167–7851, 14 Jul. 2015, 58125.

Marraco, Manuel. "La Fiscalía no ve delito de odio en las 'abominables' palabras de Javier Ortega Smith sobre el islamismo." *El Mundo*, 3 Jul. 2019, www.elmundo.es/espana/2019/07/03/5d1c7f80fdddffec758b45e7.html. Accessed 20 Mar. 2022.

Martin-Márquez, Susan. *Disorientations. Spanish Colonialism in Africa and the Performance of Identity*. Yale UP, 2008.

Martín Muñoz, Gema. *Marroquíes en España: estudio sobre su integración*. Fundación Repsol YPF, 2003.

Martín Rojo, Luisa. *Constructing Inequality in Multilingual classrooms*. De Gruyter, 2010.

Mijares, Laura, and Ángeles Ramírez. "Mujeres, pañuelo, e Islamofobia en España: un estado de la cuestión." *Anales de Historia Contemporánea*, vol. 24, 2008, pp. 121–135.

Murray, Michelle. "Migration and Genealogies of Rupture in the Work of Najat El Hachmi." *Research in African Literatures*, vol. 48, no. 3, 2017, pp. 18–32.

Nair, Parvati. "Moor-Veiled-Matters: The Hijab as Troubling Interrogative of the Relation between the West and Islam." *New Formations*, vol. 51, 2003–04, pp. 39–49.

Pew Research Center. "Unfavorable Views of Jews and Muslims on the Increase in Europe." *The Pew Global Attitudes Project*. Pew Research Center Study, Released 17 Sep. 2008, http://pewglobal.org/reports/display.php?ReportID=262-. Accessed 28 Dec. 2021.

Integration, School, and the Children of Immigrants in Spain   35

———. "Nationalism, Immigration and Minorities." *Being Christian in Western Europe Survey*, 29 May 2018, www.pewresearch.org/religion/2018/05/29/nationalism-immigration-and-minorities. Accessed 28 Dec. 2021.

Planet Contreras Ana I. "Islam in Spain." *Handbook on European Islam*, edited by Jocelyne Cesari, Oxford UP, 2014, pp. 311–349.

"Proposiciones de Ley. Enmiendas." *Boletín Oficial de las Cortes Generales*. Senado. X Legislatura. Núm. 509, 24 de abril de 2015.

Ricci, Cristián H. "*L'últim patriarca* de Najat El Hachmi y el forjamiento de una identidad amazigh-catalana." *Journal of Spanish Cultural Studies*, vol. 11, no. 1, 2010, pp. 71–91.

———. "The Reshaping of *Postcolonial Iberia*: Moroccan and Amazigh Literatures in the Peninsula." *Hispanófila*, vol. 180, no. 1, 2017, pp. 21–40.

Soyer, François. "Faith, Culture and Fear: Comparing Islamophobia in Early Modern Spain and Twenty-first-century Europe." *Ethnic and Racial Studies*, vol. 36, no. 3, 2013, pp. 399–416.

2 Finding and Recording the Invisible

The *Porteadoras* of the Spanish-Moroccan Border in Documentary Film

Raquel Vega-Durán

The Spanish cities of Ceuta and Melilla in North Africa are surrounded by high triple fences topped with barbed wire, control towers, and other surveillance systems, rendering the notion of the border omnipresent and overwhelming. With the signing of the Schengen Agreement in 1985, these fences became a visual symbol of the impenetrability of Europe's southern border. A closer look, however, reveals what Xavier Ferrer-Gallardo calls its "selective impermeabilization" (131) with various gates that open and close at different times of the day. Every day, thousands of Moroccan women cross this border on foot. They are the so-called *porteadoras*, women who travel from the border towns of Morocco to Ceuta and Melilla to pick up goods in Spanish industrial warehouses, carry them on their own backs as they walk back to Morocco, and receive a small amount for their labor. Every day presents many unknowns for them. They never know in advance if the border gates will even open that day or whether they will have time to cross and return before it closes for the day. They also enter the border without knowing if there will be enough bales to transport for everyone on the Spanish side or if the goods on their backs will be confiscated by border agents (the *porteadoras* do not know what is inside their cargo).

Although these women are key players in the Europe-Africa transborder economy, they are almost completely invisible beyond the space of the border. This claim may seem paradoxical since the *porteadoras* have been the focus of numerous photojournalism series, reports from human rights associations, official conversations between Morocco and Spain, and documentary films.[1] They are the "mule women," "carrier women," "cargo women," "mule ladies," "porteadoras," and "hamalas" (in Darija).[2] In numerous newspaper articles and news reports, they have been depicted as a shapeless mass of individuals carrying large bundles on their backs. Nevertheless, although these images make visible the reality of this border exchange at the Spanish periphery, the *porteadoras* themselves appear as an indistinguishable mass rather than as individuals.

DOI: 10.4324/9781003245117-4

Finding and Recording the Invisible 37

A series of Spanish documentaries have proposed a different narrative. Although they share, along with articles and news reports, the narrative of the *porteadora* as part of a social and economic fabric, they also create a more complex framework, enabling the viewer to see this invisible figure through three main perspectives: the voice of the *porteadoras* themselves (making visible their existence as individuals); the diversity of voices and contexts that they present (fracturing the sense of homogeneity); and the hitherto unexplored space of the border itself, which is revealed through highly intentional camerawork as a space of connection. Even though documentary films are produced independently, their common approach allows us to perceive an organic dialogue among the stories they tell. This chapter explores how the resulting dialogue manages to make the invisible visible by weaving a narrative that makes *porteadoras* an integral part of the border.

The figure of the *porteadoras* exists because, although there is no commercial customs with Morocco in Ceuta and Melilla, a Moroccan citizen can introduce goods from Spain into Moroccan territory as long as they carry them on top of their bodies, with no limit in weight or quantity. In other words, everything that a person carries on their body (whether wrapped around them, carried on their back, or held in their arms) is considered carry-on baggage and is therefore not subject to customs duties. This fact allows thousands of women to carry bales of 120 to 200 pounds on their backs through the border without being penalized. Nevertheless, this transport is not legitimized either. It is not an illegal crossing for Spain, but "alegal" – neither prohibited nor regulated – and thus, it "does not exist." For Morocco, it is, in effect, smuggling. This activity receives various names, such as illicit trafficking, illegal trade, or underground economy; whatever it is called, the *porteadoras*' labor is not recognized as "work," so they do not have the right to social, labor, or health benefits. Since this exchange is essential to the functioning of the economy in the border cities,[3] the Spanish and Moroccan governments agree to perceive these women as a minor nuisance for the security forces. Meanwhile, the exchange of goods they carry out every week has become the livelihood for thousands of Moroccan families and a profitable business for just a few. The bales bend the backs of the women, but they allow the border economy to grow exponentially.

Until March 2020, the daily crossing of these women made numerous headlines of newspaper articles, perhaps the main and most frequent source of information for the general public.[4] The proliferation of images that illustrate the news reports, which often show large numbers of women huddled together along the border, carrying large bundles of shoes, clothes, blankets, hardware tools, tech accessories, and cleaning products on their backs, makes the *porteadoras* highly visible. But can we really *see* them? Invisibility is usually equated with the lack of an

38 *Raquel Vega-Durán*

image. The invisibility of the *porteadora*, however, originates paradoxically in their hypervisibility. Their hypervisibility and over-exposure end up stereotyping them, causing a visual information overload. They are presented as an immense group of individual bodies that seem to merge into a shapeless mass, a spectacularization that deprives them of their individuality.[5] This condition, in turn, becomes exacerbated by the collectivization resulting from the use of the plural form to refer to them. Thus, if on the one hand, the news photographs make their existence visible, on the other hand, they end up functioning as vectors of opacity. If we add the fact that they only seem to exist outside the peninsular territory (and at the border of the peripheral cities of Ceuta and Melilla), their "ec-centric" condition undoubtedly places them outside the hegemonic Spanish narrative. As Georges Didi-Huberman explains in *Peuples exposés, peuples figurants*, "Les peuples exposés au ressassement stéréotypé des images sont, eux aussi, des peuples exposés à disparaître" [peoples exposed to the stereotyped repetition of images are also peoples exposed to disappearance] (15).

If we turn from the news media to documentary film, we find a somewhat different situation. Since 2008, a number of documentary filmmakers have attempted to convey the experience of the *porteadoras*, whether in short (2–3-minute) clips or in longer films. In this chapter, I will consider four of these films: *Barrio Chino: porteadoras y porteadores* [Chinese Quarter: Mule Women and Men] (Ana Vílchez, 2015, 6.5 minutes), *Con el mundo a cuestas* [With the World on Their Back] (Fernando Santiago, 2019, 34 minutes), *Porteadoras, las esclavas del sur* [Mule Women, the Slaves of the South] (Amparo Climent, 2017, 10 minutes), and the longest of all the documentaries, *Cien metros más allá* [A Hundred Meters Away] (Juan Luis de No, 2008, 67 minutes). All four documentaries are a combination of public and private productions. They are all Spanish and have a Spanish viewer as their primary audience; thus, it may not be surprising that all of them focus on the *porteadora* from and for a Spanish gaze, approaching the Moroccan-Spanish border as the "southern" border. Nevertheless, they all focus on the roundtrip of the *porteadoras* – from Morocco to Spain and back – and they all share a desire to *see* the *porteadora*'s experience from many points of view. *Porteadoras, las esclavas del Sur* opens with this voice-over narration: "La historia que os voy a contar sucede en España y sus protagonistas son cientos de mujeres marroquíes conocidas como las porteadoras de la frontera sur" [The story that I am going to tell you happens in Spain, and the protagonists are hundreds of Moroccan women known as the *porteadoras* of the southern border]."[6] Immediately a Spanish space is opened up to Moroccan protagonists. Among the voices represented in these documentaries are border security forces, merchants, intermediaries, porters, and their families in Morocco. The *porteadoras* are at the center of their narratives, but they appear from different perspectives. *Barrio Chino: porteadoras y porteadores* chooses to focus on the story of a single *porteadora*, Hachi Mimond (83 years old); *Con el mundo a cuestas* includes the point of view of several figures; *Porteadoras, las esclavas del sur* moves away from an informative tone, presenting us with aesthetically rich storytelling; and *Cien metros más allá* offers the voices of three men and one woman. By putting in conversation the different voices and perspectives they offer, we can understand how these documentaries denounce the social invisibility of these women, portraying instead the history of the space they inhabit (both the Rif and the border itself) and the border space where we get to meet them. Through the cinematographic language of the camera, they manage to record the invisible.

Spain's relation to the geographical and cultural region of the Rif in northern Morocco is one of the most overlooked historical episodes among Spaniards. The women who work as *porteadoras* inhabit this border space, so we need to take a brief look at its past to understand their present existence. Ceuta and Melilla are two Spanish cities located in North Africa. The west side of Ceuta borders with Fnideq (Morocco), and today that border is controlled by a 16-mile triple fence. It is a polysemic border since it separates Ceuta from Fnideq, but also Spain from Morocco and Europe from Africa. Portugal occupied this territory in 1415, and with the annexation of Portugal in 1580, it thus passed to the Spanish Crown. The city of Melilla was conquered by Pedro de Estopiñán y Virués in 1497, and in 1510 it became part of the Spanish Crown. Thus began the history of the Spanish presence in North Africa, which is full of paradoxes, conflicts, and friendships. In her book, *España en el Rif: crónica de una historia casi olvidada* [Spain in The Rif: Chronicle of an Almost Forgotten History], María Rosa de Madariaga traces the history of encounters between Spain and Morocco starting in the fifteenth century, showing how periods of war and siege alternated with periods of greater acceptance. In 1904 France and England signed the Entente Cordiale, which allowed Spain to maintain some interests in Morocco. Spain, at the time weak and hurt due to its colonial defeat in 1898, nevertheless decided to seize this opportunity in the hopes of re-establishing its reputation and exploiting the iron mines of the eastern part of the Rif. In 1912 Spain officially declared its territories in Morocco a protectorate. After this, Spain would have many bloody encounters with The Republic of the Rif, including the Rif War (1921–1926), the occupation of Tangiers (1940–1945), and the Ifni War (1957–1958).

This long history of Spain's intense and often hostile presence in North Africa does not usually have a significant space in history books, and in most Spanish textbooks, the so-called "Moroccan Wars" are not studied until the tenth grade (and even then in a very sketchy way). The prolonged presence of Spain in Africa is thus reduced to a mere anecdote that is difficult to incorporate into the general historical narrative of Spain. In addition to the long history of domination and lack of independence the

40   *Raquel Vega-Durán*

Rif has suffered as a result of the European presence in Northern Africa, this area has also been subject to abuse by the Moroccan government. On November 11, 1958, two years after the independence of Morocco, Amghar Mohammed Ameziane, leader of the Moroccan Rifian resistance, presented a program to King Mohammed VI, demanding job creation and representation in the government for Rifians. But Rifians had already risen up to protest against the neglect of their territory by the Moroccan crown (by both Hassam II and Mohammed VI). The Rif Revolt started, but the Rifians were defeated. As a result, the Rif suffered a brutal military rule during the subsequent years, and it was condemned to complete indifference and discrimination by the Moroccan government for decades.

This history of colonization, marginalization, and lack of resources and agency that the Rif has experienced for centuries (both from Spain and Morocco) is key to understanding the invisibility assigned to the figure of the *porteadora*. For decades, the Rif has been one of the most impoverished areas of Morocco, a difficult position exacerbated by its lack of political representation. Its inhabitants have been neglected and oppressed by both Spain and Morocco, and they have been deprived of nearly any voice. The lack of job opportunities in Morocco led many people to rely on the borderland trade to make ends meet. And in this borderland, thousands of women have found their space. They are one of the most, if not the most, marginalized constituencies of the borderland, and the invisibility of their existence coincides with the lack of historical visibility of the area they inhabit. Thus, like the history of Ceuta and Melilla themselves, the *porteadoras* tend to appear as anecdotal and peripheral episodes, rarely relevant to the larger Spanish narrative.

Where textbooks and media fail to provide the necessary context to understand why the *porteadoras* are so marginalized, documentary films have attempted to provide some answers. If we analyze the documentaries individually, we might conclude that their narrative runs parallel to the hegemonic narratives, given their lack of historical depth. However, if we look at our four chosen documentaries together, a different story emerges. All of them include brief mentions of historical facts that, complemented by each other, arouse our curiosity and allow us to gain a more encompassing understanding of the space the *porteadora* inhabits. For example, all documentaries mention the Schengen Agreement as a key moment for the current transborder trade relations. In all of them, a voice-over narrator explains that when Spain signed the Schengen Agreement in 1991, it managed to include a specific visa exception regime between the Spanish cities of Ceuta and Melilla and the Moroccan provinces of Tetouan and Nador. This is important for the viewer to understand why it is so easy for the residents of Tetouan and Nador to cross the border and the reason the *porteadoras* do not need a visa to do so. As the narrator of *Con el mundo a cuestas* explains, this exceptional regime "se fundamenta en los vínculos culturales entre la región

Finding and Recording the Invisible 41

fronteriza, una schegenización selectiva que se realizó en gran parte para no dañar las relaciones diplomáticas con Marruecos, que reclama como propias las ciudades de Ceuta y Melilla" [is based on the cultural ties between the border region, a selective schengenization that was carried out largely in order not to damage diplomatic relations with Morocco, which claims Ceuta and Melilla as its own]. The documentaries thus succeed in providing a historical context that, in the form of bullet points, helps us to understand the nature of the transborder flows and relations. Documentaries do not provide long explanations about why Ceuta and Melilla are free ports, the reasons Morocco does not recognize Ceuta and Melilla as Spanish cities, or what the "cultural ties" in the borderlands are so that one could interpret this schematic historical context as a failure. Most of them are fairly short (around 6–34 minutes), so a longer explanation of these historical facts would have diverted the narrative from their main focus. These brief contextual mentions are more like a set of brushstrokes; if up close they seem confusing, sketchy, and out of context, from a distance, when we put the four narratives in dialogue and consider them jointly, they provide an impressionist reading. This approach invites us to move away from considering documentaries individually and to look at them instead as pieces of a larger narrative. All the historical mentions point at the *porteadora*, who thus become the focal point of the border stories. The prominence that the *porteadoras* gain with their images and their voices allows them to challenge the idea of their condition as peripheral since all the information tells us they are central to the survival of the transborder economy.

Moreover, their constant movement between Spain and Morocco makes us question the idea of the border as a separating line since their work presents it as a communicating membrane. The transborder movement appears as essential to the survival of the Spanish and Moroccan economies, and the *porteadora* makes it possible. But this movement is also essential for the porteadora, since, as Fatima clearly explains in *Cien metros más allá*: "Si trabajas, comes. Si no trabajas no comes. Es lo que hay" [If you work, you eat. If you don't work, you don't eat. That is the way things are]. This idea of bare survival is echoed by a nameless *porteadora* in *Con el mundo a cuestas*: "Con esto la gente sobrevive" [With this (work), people just survive]. As we will see, the documentaries look for these women because they want to "see" them, but they do not find them as *porteadoras* solely in Spain or in Morocco. It is thanks to the border, a place neither in Spain nor in Morocco, that the documentaries complete their transborder stories. History books and newspaper articles tend to focus either on the Moroccan or the Spanish side, presenting the border as a line splitting the space in two. By contrast, the documentary camera decides to penetrate the line, finding a third space that connects and disconnects both countries simultaneously.

42 *Raquel Vega-Durán*

The first thing that stands out is that, counter to the homogeneity conveyed by articles and photographs, the documentaries invite us to meet women who have their own names, voices, experiences, and motivations. Most of them are widows, single, or separated; many of them are in their 40s (although they range from adolescents to over 80 years of age), and the majority are illiterate or have a very low educational level. Through interviews, we hear them describe themselves in their own voices: they all are mothers with young children or other people who depend on them; they all come from the *wilayah* (administrative division) of Tetouan or Nador, since only those registered in these *wilayat* can enter Spain without a visa; none of them can legally spend the night in Spain, since the agreement between the two countries only applies to working hours – when the border closes, they need to return to Morocco; almost all of them are the sole breadwinners for their family; none of them enjoy their work; and most of them plan to leave portage once their children become independent.

In order to go beyond anecdote, the documentaries delve into the routine of these *porteadoras*. Since the women share many similar experiences, we might identify this narrative with the homogenizing approach of other media reports. However, the Spanish documentaries offer a novel approach, deciding to explore their lives in Morocco (the "other" side of the border) – a perspective that tends to be invisible in Spanish narratives since it falls beyond the limits of Spain. Through their polyphonic narrative, we become familiar with the *porteadoras'* daily practices: they wake at dawn, prepare food, get a taxi (often in the company of other transborder workers), and arrive at the border when it is still dark. They will then have to wait several hours lying on a piece of cardboard until the border gates open (usually between 7:00 and 9:00 in the morning in Ceuta, and a little later in Melilla). Once the border opens, time is of the essence: they must cross the border and run to the Spanish warehouses (Ceuta) or to the esplanade next to the border fence (Melilla) to pick up bundles that sellers in Spain have been preparing. Luck and experience will determine the fortune of each *porteadora*.

After picking up a bundle, the women immediately return to the border, hoping not to find it closed. At this point, the documentaries we are examining all abandon a fixed camera position, turning to the handheld camera as a tool for empathy, facilitating an emotional connection with the women's feelings of anguish, instability, and confusion. As we follow the women running towards the gate, the camera shakes from the movement of the operator, transmitting a sense of urgency. Upon reaching the border, the women form a line along the fence, waiting to enter the metal tunnels connecting Spain and Morocco, known as *la jaula* (the cage) in Ceuta or the *pasadizo* (passage) in Melilla. This is one of the most dangerous parts of the trip.

In his newspaper article "La jaula" (2009), the writer Eduardo Jordá described this space from a Spanish perspective:

> A finales del año pasado, . . ., crucé a pie el paso fronterizo de El Tarajal, en Ceuta. . . . A un lado, el izquierdo, había un pasillo rodeado de vallas metálicas, lleno de mujeres marroquíes cargadas con grandes fardos que forcejeaban y gritaban. Cuando íbamos a meternos por allí, un policía corrió a advertirnos: "No, no, por la jaula no. Vayan por el otro lado, el de los españoles". En el otro pasillo no había vallas metálicas ni mujeres gritando y empujando. En realidad no había nadie. Cruzamos tan tranquilos, mientras las mujeres de la "jaula", con sus grandes fardos a cuestas, intentaban abrirse paso como si fueran una manada de vacas obligada a meterse a fustazos en la pequeña abertura de un corral. Y por el ruido que venía de la "jaula", estaba claro que en cualquier momento podría producirse una estampida.
>
> At the end of last year, I crossed El Tarajal border (Ceuta) on foot. . . . There was a corridor surrounded by metal fences on the left side, full of Moroccan women carrying large bundles, struggling, and screaming. When we were preparing to go through there, a policeman ran to warn us: "No, no, not by the cage. Go to the other side, the side for Spanish people." There were no chain-link fences or women yelling and pushing in the other corridor. Actually, there was no one. We crossed so calmly while the women of the "cage," with their large bundles on their backs, tried to make their way as if they were a herd of cows forced to squeeze into the small opening of a corral. And from the noise coming from the "cage," it was clear that a stampede could break out at any moment.

This account of the space of the cage, although visually powerful, is typical in portraying it as foreign to a Spanish audience, even though it is partly regulated by Spain. Unlike Jordá, the Spanish documentaries' cameras attempt to infiltrate this space from Ceuta and Melilla. In most cases, the camera remains physically outside the *jaula* or *pasadizo*, even as it shows the viewer what is happening through the bars that line the tunnel. In all four documentaries, these bars work in many ways: as a reminder that this is a foreign space the viewer can never be part of, as the bars of a jail where the *porteadoras* seem to be trapped, and as an invitation to look through them to enter into an unknown world.

In several instances, however, the lens of the camera manages to poke through the bars of the tunnel, providing a more "open" view of what is happening inside. And in *Cien metros más allá*, the camera actually infiltrates the *pasadizo*, functioning as a spy to record what happens there. In this documentary, we do not see the camera operator, but we understand they have somehow managed to get inside the tunnel while carrying a

44 Raquel Vega-Durán

concealed camera that none of the *porteadoras* seem to notice. The resulting shots are an unedited series of low-resolution black and white images, showing people moving urgently through the passage and attempting to cross as quickly as possible. The sense of authenticity is powerful. The shots are subjective and taken from a low angle; in most situations, this height would be unusual, but this camera choice situates us at eye level with the *porteadoras*, whose heads are low because the weight has forced their bodies to bend down. Continuing with the aesthetic choice of the handheld shot, the camera follows the *porteadoras* as they squeeze their large bundles through the long narrow tunnel. The shaky cam and the canted angles heighten the intensity of the moment, conveying a feeling of duress, of being trapped and in constant danger – a fall would inevitably lead to being crushed and suffocated, which has in fact been the cause of several deaths in these tunnels in recent years. The handheld camera enhances an unsettling moment, providing a sense of instability to make us feel we are moving along with the *porteadoras* into an otherwise inaccessible and unknown world.

Due to the narrowness of the tunnel, the *porteadoras* seem to fill the entire available space of the *pasadizo*, almost as if they were blending into the bars of the tunnel. Bundles and women seem to blend into one as well, and they become part of a strong current that moves through the tunnel. This homogenization is exacerbated in turn by the dehumanizing nature of the space since the tunnels are intended for "merchandise traffic" while, as Jordá explained, the gate next to it (inaccessible to the *porteadoras*, but open to Spaniards in both Ceuta and Melilla), is reserved for "people." The *porteadoras* become invisible as they are inexorably reduced to the bundles they carry. Thus their existence and very humanity are made invisible, turning them into animal-like figures that go through a narrow corridor that guides them to a revolving barred door, through which, one by one, they will end up on the other side. Moreover, their bales are marked, so the buyers on the Moroccan side can recognize their goods.[7] In his article, Jordá pejoratively referred to the *porteadoras* as a "herd of cows," and in the documentaries we see policemen using their clubs to keep the women in one organized line before entering the tunnel. The sense of animalization is strikingly evident through long shots in the documentaries, providing location and context to this dehumanizing treatment. Throughout the documentaries, however, the audience has also been listening to the *porteadoras*, whose voices were intended to encourage identification with their stories; moreover, in the dehumanizing context of the crossing of the border, the documentaries also organically incorporate close-ups (which in themselves lack context), which only make sense in juxtaposition to the collective shots, reminding the audience that, even though they are shown as a collective, they are also individuals and may have different experiences.

Finding and Recording the Invisible   45

Exiting this dehumanizing tunnel is seen as a victory, as their smiles show, but it is a bittersweet triumph. Although it is true that they will take home the payment for their bundle (barely 5–15 Euros per trip), they will not return home with their heads held high as breadwinners. As they themselves explain to the camera, their job carries a social stigma, and many try to disguise the origin of the money, pretending to their families that they are domestic workers on the other side of the border. Moreover, not only is their work as *porteadoras* not recognized, but neither is their status as *porteadoras*, because as Cristina Fuentes Lara explains,

> la sociedad marroquí relaciona el trabajo como porteadora con la prostitución. Los argumentos del símil se basan en la baja reputación social de sus profesionales laborales, en el uso del cuerpo como principal herramienta de trabajo, [y] en el modo de vida alternativo a roles tradicionales de la mujer marroquí.
>
> [Moroccan society associates work as a *porteadora* with prostitution. The rationale for this simile is based on the low social reputation of their job, the use of the body as their main work tool, [and] the alternative way of life to traditional roles of Moroccan women.]

(253)

Thus, although many of them talk to the camera, only a few of them agree to show their faces. Many of the voices we hear are those of women who are trying to hide their identities, either talking with their back to the camera or covering half of their faces with a kerchief so they won't be recognized (thus perpetuating their social invisibility through camouflage). We hear that their work is hard, uncertain, poorly paid, and subject to multiple humiliations and risks. We learn from their testimonies that their passports are usually not stamped, so their crossing stays unrecorded. Nor does their activity exist as a job officially, since, while Morocco considers it smuggling (allowed, but not authorized), for Spain it is "alegal." The labor of these women is what Arlene Kaplan Daniels calls the "invisible work" of people who are systematically excluded from society (405). The invisibility of their work is part of their larger effacement; philosopher Axel Honneth explains that social invisibility produces feelings of social exclusion and disaffiliation. The lack of affiliation that comes with their invisibility makes them impossible to be part of a narrative since they are not recognized. In *Porteadoras: las esclavas del Sur*, Fátima tells us heartbreakingly that "En mi país las mujeres como yo no servimos para nada" (In my country, women like me are not useful for anything). They do not exist in the narrative, an invisibility that translates into the spaces they inhabit during their workday where, as unrecognized individuals, they do not have access to basic needs such as water, bathrooms, or shade. The *porteadoras* thus seem to become a mere means of transportation, so

46 Raquel Vega-Durán

the load on their backs, their reduction to objects, and their invisibility in Morocco dehumanize their existence (a violent act that translates into a sense of exclusion from society).[8] Even though the *porteadoras* would like their labor to be recognized so their lives could improve, their motivation goes beyond themselves. In *Con el mundo a cuestas*, a *porteadora* who wants to remain anonymous speaks with her back to the camera, explaining that "los jóvenes son quienes nos dan mucha pena. Donde vayan siempre encuentran las puertas cerradas. . . . ¿A dónde va esta pobre gente?" [We feel sorry for the young people. Everywhere they go they find doors closed. . . . Where can this poor people go?] Her question remains unanswered but provides a dimension until now absent from narratives about the border, which tend to focus on the present. Perhaps the *porteadoras* cannot alter what happens to them now, but their voices and experiences can become vectors of change for future generations.

By entering the *passages* that connect Spain and Morocco – the very space of the border itself – these documentaries open our eyes to a new way of looking at the border. The subjective camera shows us how this apparently two-dimensional separating line acquires volume and depth, becoming a zone that widens to make room for the figure of the *porteadora*. The border is not part of the hegemonic narratives that focus either on the Spanish or the Moroccan side. It is, instead, a space that belongs to two spaces, and to neither of them, connecting both sides. In the documentaries, the border space becomes the key link that helps us understand the *porteadora* as a complex figure. Taking into consideration that their crossing goes unrecorded and that their job is "alegal," they are not recognized on the Spanish side either. They are neither from here nor there. The documentaries connect the two sides by entering the border itself, thus completing their transborder reality. While they are *in* the border, the transborder economy depends on them, and the weakest link in the chain becomes essential, and thus the portage becomes an action that deserves to be recognized as work. The border thus helps documentaries contextualize the activity of the *porteadoras*. As borders cannot be one sided (for example, we cannot talk about the "Spanish" border, but the "Spanish-Moroccan" border), the transborder figure of the *porteadora* does not exist only in Spain or in Morocco. The documentaries were interested in finding the *porteadoras*, and thanks to the border and their presence and voices on both sides, they succeed. By focusing on the figure of the *porteadora* as a continuum, documentaries move beyond the one-sided hegemonic narratives of the countries that the border both unites and separates. They use a subjective camera in the border, provide a context to the existence of the *porteadoras*, and use straight-to-camera testimonies on both sides of the border (thus fracturing with their voices the invisibility they have in hegemonic narratives, where their presence goes unrecorded in Spain and their labor is a source of shame in Morocco). These three perspectives (which cover the Moroccan and the Spanish side of the border and the space that connects these two spaces) manage to provide the viewer with an encompassing narrative where we finally *see* these women. It is through this encompassing narrative that the invisible and the unrecorded become visible. These documentaries open the viewers' eyes to an until now inaccessible and unknown narrative connected not by a line but by a *practice* with real consequences. And it is with this connecting space, this line with depth, that documentaries are able to present the multidimensional and complex identity of the *porteadora*.

This diversity of voices, articulated in different ways by the *porteadoras* in the documentaries, creates a strong intimacy between the *porteadora* and the viewer, evoking strong emotion in the latter. Their words create the type of ethical dilemma that Carl Plantinga discusses in his *Screen Stories: Emotions and the Ethics of Engagement:* How should we respond to that emotion? The films close with an open call: the struggle against the invisibility of the *porteadoras* cannot fall on them alone. Their voices are directed to the viewer, and the end of the documentaries is thus not the end of their stories but an invitation to continue them. The voices of the *porteadoras* tell us about their labor, the constant obstacles, and their lives beyond the border. They reveal their stories until then hidden by the culture of spectacle and hypervisibility in dialogue with their social inexistence on both sides of the border. They make us think about their present and future, and they want their stories to be known. We get to meet them in the three spaces they inhabit: Morocco, Spain, and the border, and it is in the convergence of these three spaces that we can see them as complete identities. Now it is the viewer's turn to decide what to do with their stories. The directors choose the documentary form to recount the experiences of the *porteadoras* and call into question the audience's own civic engagement. The documentaries do not address the viewer as a private individual (something fiction does), but as "a citizen, member of civil society, putative participant in the public sphere" (Chanan, vi). The achieved intimacy between the viewer and the *porteadora* in these documentaries extends the story beyond these women to include the viewers themselves. Like the concept of border, which cannot be understood from just one side, the *porteadoras* come into contact with the Spaniards through the documentary, inviting the audience both to consider the *porteadoras'* relevance in the Spanish narrative and to enter the space where they live to make their existence visible. Now we know, and it is our turn to decide what to do with that knowledge.

Notes

1. Since 2012, human rights groups have written lengthy reports and declarations, such as the *Declaración de Tetuán* [Declaration of Tetouan] (2012), *Respeto y dignidad para las mujeres marroquíes que portan mercancías en la frontera de Marruecos y Ceuta* [Respect and Dignity for Moroccan Women Who Carry Bales at the Morocco-Ceuta Border] (2016), the manifest *Restablezcamos la*

48 *Raquel Vega-Durán*

legalidad en la Frontera Sur [Let's Reestablish Legality at the Southern Border] (2017), and *Porteadoras: la feminización de la pobreza en la Frontera Sur* [Mule Women: The Feminization of Poverty in the Southern Border] (2021), among others.

2. Examples of this are "Morocco's long-burdened 'mule women' face new struggle," "'Carrier' Women: a Grounded Theory Approach," "Morocco's 'cargo women' carry goods worth millions of euros on their backs," "Morocco's Mule Ladies," and "La batalla de la hormiga: la azarosa vida de las porteadoras en la frontera sur de Europa" [The Battle of the Ant: the Hazardous Life of Mule Women at the Southern Border of Europe]," among many others.

3. The Human Rights Association of Andalusia (ADPHA) estimates that this atypical transborder trade generates 1,400 million Euros for Ceuta and Melilla each year (in Tohaira, Mar. "Las mujeres porteadoras.")

4. Since March 14, 2020, the Spanish-Moroccan land border has been closed due to the Covid-19 pandemic, and the *porteadoras* have disappeared from the media.

5. This idea aligns with Guy Debord's idea of spectacle: "reality rises up within the spectacle, and the spectacle is real" (8).

6. All translations from Spanish to English included in this chapter are my own, unless noted otherwise.

7. In addition to marking their cargo, the numbers seem to mark them in the manner of cattle passing through the corridor to the slaughterhouse (reminiscent of a branding iron).

8. They are socially stigmatized, economically impoverished, and deprived of agency as political subjects. Even though they are not slaves per se, documentaries like *Porteadoras, las esclavas del sur* use the term "slave" to bring to mind a condition similar to "social death" (coined by Orlando Patterson to refer to disposable people not accepted as fully human).

Works Cited

Asociación Pro Derechos Humanos de Andalucía. *Respeto y dignidad para las mujeres marroquíes que portan mercancías en la frontera de Marruecos y Ceuta.* Sevilla: APDHA, 2016, www.apdha.org/media/informe-mujeres-porteadoras-2016.pdf. Accessed 22 Feb. 2022.

———. *Porteadoras: la feminización de la pobreza en la Frontera Sur.* Sevilla: APDHA, 2021, www.apdha.org/wp-content/uploads/2021/03/Porteadoras-feminizacion-pobreza-2021.pdf, Accessed 22 Feb. 2022.

Asociación Pro Derechos Humanos de Andalucía, Asociación Pro Derechos Humanos de Melilla, et al. *Declaración de Tetuán,* 22 Apr. 2012, www.apdha.org/media/declaracion_tetuan_porteadoras2012.pdf. Accessed 22 Feb. 2022.

Barrio Chino: porteadoras y porteadores. Dir. Ana Vílchez, Coleccionista de Momentos, 2015.

Castilla, Amelia. "La batalla de la hormiga: la azarosa vida de las porteadoras en la frontera sur de Europa." *El País,* 17 Jan. 2020, https://elpais.com/elpais/2020/01/13/eps/1578930916_678797.html. Accessed 22 Feb. 2022.

Chanan, Michael. *The Politics of Documentary.* British Film Institute, 2007.

Cien metros más allá. Dir. Juan Luis de No. Chello Multicanal, 2008.

Con el mundo a cuestas. Dir. Fernando Santiago. Diputación de Cádiz, 2019.

Debord, Guy. *Society of Spectacle.* Black & Red, 1983.

Del Berro, Fernando. "Morocco's 'Cargo Women' Carry Goods Worth Millions of Euros on Their Backs." *Middle East Monitor*, 2 Oct. 2017, www.middleeastmonitor.com/20171002-moroccos-cargo-women-carry-goods-worth-millions-of-euros-on-their-backs/. Accessed 22 Feb. 2022.

Didi-Huberman, Georges. *Peuples exposés, peoples figurants*. Éditions de Minuit, 2012.

Ferrer-Gallardo, Xavier. "Acrobacias fronterizas en Ceuta y Melilla: explorando los perímetros terrestres de la Unión Europea en el continente africano." *Documents d'Anàlisi Geogràfica*, vol. 51, 2008, pp. 129–149.

Fuentes Lara, Cristina. "'Carrier' Women: A Grounded Theory Approach." *Revista Internacional de Estudios Migratorios*, vol. 7, no. 3, 2017, pp. 153–175.

———. *La situación de las porteadoras en la frontera sudeuropea: el caso de Ceuta*. Centro de Investigaciones Sociológicas, 2019.

Honneth, Axel. "Visibilité et invisibilité. Sur l'épistémologie de la 'reconnaissance'." *Revue du MAUSS*, vol. 23, no. 1, 2004, pp. 137–151.

Jordá, Eduardo. "La jaula." *Diario de Sevilla*, 27 May 2009, www.diariodesevilla.es/opinion/articulos/jaula_0_263074104.html. Accessed 22 Feb. 2022.

Kaplan Daniels, Arleene. "Invisible Work." *Social Problem*, vol. 34, no. 5, 1987, pp. 403–415.

Legalidad Frontera Sur. "Restablezcamos la legalidad en la Frontera Sur: Medidas políticas urgentes." *Legalidad Frontera Sur*, 2017, http://legalidadfronterasur2017.org.

Madariaga, Maria Rosa de. *España y el Rif: Crónica de una historia casi olvidada*. UNED, 1999.

Mekouar, Hamza. "Morocco's Long-Burdened 'Mule Women' Face New Struggle." *France 24*, 2 Feb. 2020, www.france24.com/en/20200202-morocco-s-long-burdened-mule-women-face-new-struggle. Accessed 22 Feb. 2022.

Patterson, Orlando. *Slavery and Social Death: A Comparative Study*. Harvard UP, 2018.

Plantinga, Carl. *Screen Stories: Emotion and the Ethics of Engagement*. Oxford UP, 2018.

Porteadoras, las esclavas del sur. Amparo Climent. Melgares Producciones, 2017.

Toharia, Mar. "Las mujeres porteadoras en la ciudad de Melilla." *El País*, 5 Feb. 2018, https://elpais.com/elpais/2018/02/02/seres_urbanos/1517564563_111545.html. Accessed 22 Feb. 2022.

Toral, Almudena. "Morocco's Mule Ladies." *New York Times*, 30 Mar. 2014, www.nytimes.com/video/world/africa/100000002787986/trapped-and-burdened.html. Accessed 22 Feb. 2022.

3 Saharaui Women Writers in Spain

Voices of Resistance in *Mil y un poemas saharauis II [One Thousand and One Saharaui Poems II]*

Debra Faszer-McMahon

Immigrant literature and culture in Spain have received much-warranted attention over the past two decades, and in the context of immigrant poets, some of the most active authors have been Saharaui writers living in Spain and publishing in Spanish – those belonging to the Generación de la Amistad Saharaui. Spain's Saharaui immigrant community has received increasing attention and media exposure as evidenced by documentary films such as Javier Bardem's *Sons of the Clouds: The Last Colony* and in-depth news articles like that published in *El País Semanal*.[1] Within the group of six authors highlighted in the *El País* article, two are women, Zahra Hasnaui and Sukeina Aali-Taleb. Their presence in the news story and the poetic group highlights an important issue, namely the active voices of women in Saharaui immigrant and poetic culture in Spain, as well as their absence from most existing analyses of Saharaui poetry.

It is perhaps not surprising that women poets have been overlooked, since theoretical approaches to Saharaui literature, in general, are still relatively rare. In addition, Saharaui women writers have not published many individual works, and they have only recently begun contributing in larger numbers to poetic anthologies. Yet, despite these obstacles, it is important to consider how immigrant women are representing themselves and likewise being represented in Spanish literature. Postcolonial feminist criticism highlights the potential pitfalls of reading global women writers through the lens of western feminisms.[2] However, poetry focused on markers of gender and sexuality appears with frequency in collections by and about Saharauis, and thus the approach to female immigrant experience represented in these texts warrants consideration, albeit with an openness to new ways of hearing women's voices that are not circumscribed by western feminist norms. The aim of this chapter is to theorize how the representation of Saharaui women relates to broader questions of African immigration, gender studies, and contemporary poetry in Spain. This analysis explores such questions through the writing of three female

DOI: 10.4324/9781003245117-5

Saharaui poets whose works appear in the digital anthology *Mil y un poemas saharauis II* (2013), particularly the poetry of Zahra Hasnaui, Fátima Galia, and Darak Mohamed. I argue that poetry currently produced by Saharaui women offers an alternative to the male-dominated and Franco-era inspired concept of a Spanish-Saharaui fraternity, instead focusing on transnational feminist concerns in an effort to critique not only the plight of the contemporary Saharaui community but also the gendered and paternalistic colonial history of Spanish interventions in Western Sahara.

The anthology *Mil y un poemas saharauis II* is part of a larger digital poetic project composed of eight volumes, all titled *Mil y un poemas saharauis*.[3] The series was published online between February 2013 and July 2015, and each volume contains exactly 101 poetic texts by a range of Saharaui and Spanish contributors. The second volume does not depart from this norm, offering 101 poems by 24 authors, as well as an introduction by the editor, Xabier Susperregi, and brief biographies of contributors. This analysis is focused on volume II of the series because that work contains a particularly large percentage of female authors. Thirteen women writers are highlighted in volume II, outnumbering the male contributors and demonstrating the presence of Saharaui women writers in the global Hispanophone community.[4]

The format of *Mil y un poemas saharauis* is unusual and highlights the strategic use of digital forms within Saharaui immigrant culture in Spain. The multi-volume anthology has been published entirely online via free digital book publishers like ISSUU.com, making the texts themselves accessible to anyone in the world with internet access free of charge. They thus provide both poets and readers with a digital and globally accessible format in which to interact with Saharaui work. While the Saharaui immigrant community in Spain has long employed websites, blogs, and other forms of digital media to share poetry and voice political dissent, *Mil y un poemas saharauis* marks the first fully digital multi-volume publication, and it is thus significant that it is also the first anthology, via volume II, in which large numbers of female Saharaui immigrants have been included. Isabelle Rigoni notes in her article "Intersectionality and Mediated Cultural Production in a Globalized Post-Colonial World" that contemporary research into digital media must address the "ways in which race and gender operate in tandem to produce and maintain the unequal distribution of power in the mediascape of countries of post-colonial immigration" (834).[5] In the case of Saharaui immigrants in general, and particularly Saharaui women writers, limited access to Spanish mainstream media and publishing houses has meant limited publications and difficulty accessing works that are published, despite prolific poetic production within the Generación de la Amistad. Yet through the medium of a free digital anthology, Saharaui women have been able to move away from the mainstream mediascape and resist the "unequal

52 Debra Faszer-McMahon

distribution of power" noted by Rigoni previously. Their work is thus becoming available to a larger public (the whole world) at an attractive price (free), shifting the power dynamic and allowing a more direct exchange of ideas across a global framework and outside the traditional power structures of dissemination and reception, marked as they are by ideologically charged political aims and mixed colonial histories in relation to Western Sahara.

Susan Martin-Márquez's *Disorientations* was one of the first studies to analyze in depth the way contemporary cultural production about the Western Sahara is implicated in a history of colonial intervention and Orientalizing gazes. She charts the way a Franco-era discourse of "brotherhood" or fraternity has been employed to connect Saharaui and Spanish culture. According to Martin-Márquez, this concept of brotherhood has been deployed by Spanish nationals to ventriloquize Saharauis, representing them as friends in need of Spanish assistance in order to regain their rightful freedoms, as if Spain had not been a primary cause of the loss of independence in the first place (329–30).

The issue of troubling colonial histories is an important one to address in an anthology whose title self-consciously references the *1001 Arabian Nights*. As Edward Said's foundational study *Orientalism* highlights, western cultural production has a long history of creating and disseminating distorted notions about nonwestern cultures and using those representations to justify and support imperialist aims. One thus might justifiably question what an anthology titled *Mil y un poemas saharauis* signifies in the context of Spain's own history of imperialist efforts in Western Sahara. While the title should give readers pause, it is helpful to contextualize the complexities of Orientalism within the Spanish context. As Said himself notes in the introduction to the 2nd Spanish edition (2002) of his ground-breaking work, Orientalism in Spain offers some notable exceptions to the broader European Orientalist discourse. The power dynamic between European, North African, and Islamic cultures on the peninsula was complex, with the forces of empire shifting in the region between east and west, other Europeans often Orientalizing Spain, and Spanish cultural producers at times acknowledging and at others eschewing the deep impact of diverse African and Islamic influences on Spanish identity (*Orientalismo* 9).[6] As Anna McSweeney and Claudia Hopkins note in their analysis of Spain and Orientalism,

> Spanish artists, architects, writers, and patrons were aware of the orientalizing gaze of foreign artists who regarded all Spaniards, whether in the past or present, as "exotic," but at the same time Spanish artists and architects were also capable of orientalizing parts of their own culture and other cultures.
>
> ("Editorial: Spain and Orientalism" 3)

The question of Orientalism in *Mil y un poemas saharauis* is similarly complex, particularly since the work, while focused on Saharaui culture and incorporating many Saharaui voices, is edited by non-Saharaui Spanish authors. Nevertheless, the work officially lists "Various Authors" as the copyright authorship on the title page, and the way the work has been organized, into eight separate publications, each with 101 poems focused on the Saharaui cause, recalls connections between the literary impetus for the *1001 Nights* and the motivations of the Saharaui poetic community.

The allusion to the *Arabian Nights* in the title invites readers to consider parallels between Scheherazade's strategic use of art in a struggle for survival and the similarly urgent (and seemingly interminable) struggle for justice and survival within the Saharaui poetic community. What could be more appropriate than an anthology where Saharaui authors use their literary talents, like Scheherazade, to connect with powerful audiences in order to try to gain control of their own narrative? As Martin-Márquez notes in *Disorientations*, the Saharaui community has a successful history of employing powerful tropes, like the Spanish-Saharaui brotherhood, or in this case, the *1001 Arabian Nights*, for their own political and literary ends. Martin-Márquez terms this "ventriloquizing Spaniards," noting how Saharauis "have learned to co-opt Spaniards' identitarian strategies in order to advance their own struggle" (*Disorientations* 339).

Adolfo Campoy-Cubillo's *Memories of the Maghreb* also analyzes the implications of colonial interventions and orientalizing gazes on Saharaui cultural production, particularly the notion of a "Hispano-Maghrebi brotherhood" or the "Hispano-Saharawi" fraternity. Campoy-Cubillo highlights the gendered aspect of this rhetoric, focused as it is on male actors and relationships, noting that while the idea of brotherhood initially stemmed from Franco-era colonialism, "the notion of a Hispano-Saharawi brotherhood has gradually ceased to be associated with the Francoist colonial discourse and been presented as a progressive concept that is deemed to exemplify an anticolonial stance" (153). One of Campoy-Cubillo's principal critiques is that in contemporary Spanish cultural production, this notion of fraternity is invoked, rather than human rights, to argue for the Saharaui cause, despite the fact that, as Martin-Márquez points out, the basis of such fraternity is questionable at best since Saharaui culture has far less claim to Spanish connection and influence than Moroccan culture, which is rejected in this same discourse. As Campoy-Cubillo notes, tracing Martin-Marquez's argument, "Saharawis cannot claim an Andalusi heritage in common with Spaniards, their cultural traditions draw from sub-Saharan cultures much more than they do from North Africa, and their intermarriage with black Africans makes it difficult to associate them with Ibero-Berbers" (154). He then continues with his critique of the human rights stance: "Yet, it is the concept of fraternity that is invoked much more than human rights in Spanish cultural production" (154).

54   *Debra Faszer-McMahon*

The issue of human rights versus brotherhood is important in the context of poetry produced by female Saharaui immigrants writing in Spanish. This chapter argues that in the case of female Saharaui poets in *Mil y un poemas saharauis II*, it is in fact human rights that are evoked, rather than a male-centered concept of brotherhood or fraternity, in order to represent the plight of Saharaui people and to negotiate the discourses of postcolonial agency.

This emphasis on human rights rather than a Spanish Saharaui fraternity is evident, for example, in the second poem in the anthology *Mil y un poemas Saharauis II*, in a contribution by Zahra Hasnaui, the only female founding member of the Generación de la Amistad.[7] Her poem also demonstrates how work by Saharaui women subverts the nostalgia or forgetfulness that is often present in Spanish-Saharaui fraternal discourse. The poem, titled "Se me olvidó," offers an intriguing transnational feminist reflection on the process of forgetting and the creation of artificial borders:

"Se me olvidó"

Se me olvidó
dedicar un poema
a la fuerza invisible
de la mujer afgana.

A la niña Malala
que con letra carmesí
pinta caminos prohibidos.
A la espiga que se dobla
en un monte andino.

Al poeta,
al músico,
al cooperante
que se sacude la mano
y limpia de espinas la tiende,
al amigo sin fronteras.

A la caricia del viento
en un lunar de Tiris,
a las sonrisas del sol
en mis ondas marinas.

Al enigma de tus ojos
cómplice de mi insomnio.

Al silencio de tu boca,
a veces, afluente

y otras, espada.
Se me olvidó tanto . . .
(*Mil y un poemas saharauis* II 13)

[*"I forgot"*

I forgot
to dedicate a poem
to the invisible strength
of the Afghan woman

To the child Malala
who with crimson letter
paints prohibited paths.
To the grain that bends
on an Andean hill.

To the poet,
to the musician,
to the aid worker
who shakes hands
and removes the barbs outstretched,
to the friend without borders.

To the wind's caress
under a Tiris moon,
to the smiles of the sun
in my marine waves.

To the enigma of your eyes
accomplice to my insomnia.

To the silence of your mouth
at times, a tributary
and others, a sword.
I forgot so much . . .
(*One Thousand and One
Saharaui Poems* II 13)

The poem begins with an acknowledgment of forgetting, "se me olvidó," that is repeated in the title as well as the first and final lines. What is forgotten is the task of dedicating a poem, thus highlighting the importance of poetry for marking and remembering. In this case, what is marked and remembered begins with a reference to women's human rights movements on the border between Afghanistan and Pakistan. The poet references "la niña Malala/que

56 Debra Faszer-McMahon

con letra carmesí/pinta caminos prohibidos" [the child Malala/who with crimson letter/paints prohibited paths], highlighting the experience of the young Pakistani educational activist Malala Yousafzai, who was accosted and shot in the head by Taliban forces on her way home from school in 2012. The poetic voice transforms Malala's contribution into something more than a political act – it becomes textual and creative, a painting in the red letters of her body's life-blood leading through forbidden trajectories. But this transnational call for women's dignity is not limited to the Swat Valley, as the following stanza implies, referencing the Andes in South America; Tiris in Western Sahara; and a range of cultural producers and forms including musicians, poets, volunteers, activists and friends without borders ("al amigo sin fronteras"). Hasnaui's poem works against the strictures of borders, calling instead for a remembering of the transnational points of commonality across divides. Martin-Márquez notes in her critique of contemporary cultural production that "Saharawi women are described by most contemporary Spanish sources as radically distinct from their counterparts in the rest of the Muslim world, a characterization that facilitates their ventriloquization as 'daughters' and 'sisters'" (331).[8] However, in this poem by Hasnaui, the opposite seems to be the case. Here, a Saharaui woman emphasizes the connection between Saharaui culture, human rights, and the rest of the world – noting a shared hope that touches Afghani, Pakistani, South American, and Western Saharan women. The poem emphasizes connections across the globe, as well as the importance of not forgetting. As Said, Martin-Márquez, and Campoy-Cubillo point out, the tendency to forget colonial histories leads to ventriloquization and orientalism, forms of control within cultural production, such that Saharaui women are represented as daughters or sisters without a sense of the colonial past. In this poem, by contrast, the poet insists that through poetry such forgetfulness can be resisted, and that it is precisely the "amigo sin fronteras" or the borderless friends across national divides that will offer a gaze less "complice de mi insomnia" but rather one that reaches out to shake hands – entering into Saharaui cultural space via a shared welcome: "que se sacude la mano/y limpia de espinas la tiende,/al amigo sin fronteras" [who shakes hands/and removes the barbs outstretched,/to the friend without borders] ("Se me olvidó" 13).

Hasnaui's poem is not the only one by a Saharaui female author to challenge the notion of brotherhood and address transnational divides from a human rights perspective. While Hasnaui is arguably the most well-known female Saharaui poet, Fátima Galia, whose work also appears in *Mil y un poemas*, is certainly the most prolific, having published several poetic and prose texts as well as poems in various anthologies.[9] She has lived in the Basque Country for more than 20 years, and her work represents another aspect of Saharaui resistance to Spanish ventriloquization. Susan Martin-Márquez notes that

> Saharawis have become equally practiced at fomenting alternative notions of brotherhood and sisterhood with Spaniards that do not

Saharaui Women Writers in Spain 57

imply acceptance of presumably Western feminist values, or of the language of colonization. These forms of alliance . . . seek to underline commonalities between myriad nationalist struggles in Spain and the POLISARIO's fight for political independence.

(335)

One clear example of such nationalist resistance appears in Galia's contribution to *Mil y un poemas saharauis II* in the form of the poem "Luali." At first glance, Galia's poem comes across as a strident call to arms, a war poem lacking subtlety and glorifying violent martyrdom. However, deeper analysis reveals how the poem subverts efforts to downplay the urgent resistance of Saharaui nationalism, and the poem focuses on a shared battle as the defining feature of brotherhood:

"Luali"

Levántate, ya todos sabemos cómo
te llamas y quién eres.

Las palomas repartieron tu nombre
en el combate y en los campamentos.
Eres la gloria, eres el valor, eres la fuerza.

Levántate, para que todos los guerrilleros, niños,
ancianos y mujeres, digan ansiosamente
allí viene el Líder de nuestro pueblo.

La sangre que corre en nuestras venas,
el oxígeno que respiramos y el fusil
de nuestra batalla.

Nunca olvidamos que estés y estarás presente
en nuestros hogares, en nuestras trincheras,
en nuestros pensamientos y en nuestros corazones,
siempre eres el héroe inmortal queridísimo

Luali. (26)

[*"Luali"*

Stand up, now we all know your
name and who you are.

The doves shared your name
in combat and in the camps.
You are glory, you are valor, you are strength.

58 *Debra Faszer-McMahon*

Stand up, so that all the fighters, children,
elders and women, will say anxiously
here comes the Leader of our people.

The blood that runs in our veins,
the oxygen that we breath and the rifle
of our battle.

We will never forget that you are and will be present
in our homes, in our trenches,
in our thoughts and in our hearts,
you will always be the immortal beloved hero
                                    Luali.] (26)

The name "Luali," the titular hero of the poem, refers to the revered
nationalist leader and founder of the Polisario Front, El-Ouali Mustapha
Sayed, who was also the first president of the Sahrawi Arab Democratic
Republic.[10] After studying constitutional law as a young university student, Luali became concerned about political abuse in Western Sahara
by Spanish colonial forces and began peaceful demonstrations, which
soon led to his torture at the hands of Moroccan military forces and
subsequently to his founding of the Polisario. His leadership helped
force the withdrawal of Spanish troops from the region, and he died in
an armed battle against Moroccan military forces while attempting to
sabotage water supplies in the disputed territory.[11] Galia's poem thus
glorifies and honors a forceful political dissident who worked tirelessly
to overthrow not just Moroccan control but also Spanish colonial forces.
While the poem is not aesthetically innovative, it demonstrates something important: Saharaui women poets like Galia are not as concerned
as their Spanish counterparts with couching Saharaui brotherhood in
inoffensive or westernized feminist guises. The emphasis here is on battle
and fighting, with references to "rifle," "battle," and "trenches," all in
the context of "glory."

The stanza in "Luali" about "sangre" or blood is particularly important for a discussion of the Spanish-Saharaui fraternity and Saharaui
women's poetic resistance to the gendered, patriarchal, and colonial sense
of brotherhood. The fifth stanza begins with a metaphor that links Luali's
revolutionary struggle with the blood of all living Saharauis: Luali, "the
Leader of our people" is equated with "The blood that runs in our veins,/
the oxygen that we breath and the rifle/of our battle." The brotherhood
described here is a communion among all Saharauis that links them to
"our battle" through the memory of Luali. This is not a fraternity between
Spaniards and Saharauis but rather a link between the armed martyrs
of the Saharaui cause who fought against both Spain and Morocco and
the current generation of Saharauis still suffering "in combat and in the

Saharaui Women Writers in Spain 59

camps." The poem redeploys Franco-like war discourse to highlight and trump a revolutionary leader fighting for freedom against colonialism and against Francoist and Spanish forces: "We will never forget that you are and will be present/in our homes, in our trenches,/in our thoughts and in our hearts,/you will always be the immortal beloved hero/Luali." The poem ends "we will never forget," referring to the work of Luali, but also implying a rejection of Franco-era colonial discourse, eschewing the Spanish "immortal beloved hero" and instead supporting the Saharaui's own home-grown savior, who is being called to rise again, "levántate," via those warriors, "the fighters, children, elders and women" who will resurrect Luali's work in the future. The poem thus directly subverts Spanish fraternal discourse, linked as it is to Franco-era colonial roots, while at the same time employing that same genre and language to praise a martyr who died fighting to protect Saharauis against Spain and other colonial aggressors.

In an article about celebrity and representation of Saharaui culture, Jill Robbins notes that the directors of Javier Bardem's *Sons of the Clouds: The Last Colony* took tremendous care to make certain that Saharauis were not presented as Islamic radicals and that the Polisario was represented as a non-threatening organization. The goal was clearly to disconnect Saharauis from any sense of militant Islam (124). However, the poetry included in *Mil y un poemas II* by female Saharaui authors themselves seems to be far less concerned with representing Saharaui culture in such a brotherly way. "Luali" is a battle hymn, almost mimicking the style of Franco-era civil war propaganda, but here the leader being praised is one who fought directly (and successfully) against Spain and against Franco's government.

The repetition of the word "Levántate" two times in the poem recalls the desire to reawaken this kind of resistance – it is not just Luali who is being called back for resurrection from the dead, but indeed Saharauis themselves who, having the "sangre," the blood and weapons, are called to resistance, called to take on the role of this revolutionary leader "en nuestros hogares, en nuestras trincheras, en nuestros pensamientos y en nuestros corazones." The leader of the Saharaui cause is not a Spanish poet or Spanish government protector or Spanish filmmaker (or any other foreigner who can take on a paternalistic or colonialist stance) but rather a leader from Saharaui history who symbolizes resistance and battle on all fronts.

While the issue of brotherhood, sisterhood, and fraternity is only dealt with implicitly in the poetry discussed thus far by Hasnaui and Galia, in the work of Darak Mohamed, another female Saharaui contributor to the collection, the language of fraternity is explicitly addressed. In the case of Mohamed, the framework for that discussion involves the complexity of Saharaui subject positions in relation to global conflicts. One can see this tension in Darak Mohamed's poem "Gritos por el Sahara":

60 *Debra Faszer-McMahon*

"Gritos por el Sahara"

¡Libertad!, ¡paz!, ¡esperanza!
Entre la vida y la muerte,
entre el paraíso y el infierno,
¡allí estoy!
Entre el mar y el enemigo,
entre montañas de arena,
¡allí estoy!
Encarcelada en mis sueños
escapada del destino
y grito por el Sahara:
¡Libertad!, ¡paz!, ¡esperanza!

Grito al mundo a ver si me escuchan,
grito a la humanidad a ver si me ven,
grito a la hermandad a ver si me hablan,
grito a la Amistad a ver si me salvan.
Lucho contra el tiempo y grito:
¡Libertad!, ¡paz!, ¡esperanza!
. . . .

(102)

[*"Cries for Sahara"*

Freedom! Peace! Hope!
Between life and death,
between paradise and hell,
there am I!
Between the sea and the enemy,
between mountains of sand,
there am I!
Imprisoned in my dreams
an escapee of destiny
and I cry for the Sahara:
Freedom! Peace! Hope!
I cry to the world to see if they hear me,
I cry to humanity to see if they see me,
I cry to the brotherhood to see if they speak to me
I cry to Friendship to see if they save me.
I fight against time and I cry:
Freedom! Peace! Hope!
. . . .

(102)

The poem offers a sense of being present in a liminal, placeless kind of
zone. The speaker begins by crying for freedom, peace, and hope, and the

Saharaui Women Writers in Spain   61

second stanza clarifies the location of the poetic speaker: an in-between state between life and death, paradise and hell, the sea and the enemy: "Between life and death,/between paradise and hell,/there am I!/Between the sea and the enemy,/between mountains of sand" ("Gritos" 102). This sense of being in-between is critical for interpreting the poet speaker's rejection of a simple discourse of "fraternity" with Spain. While post-structural theorists have long critiqued western cultural forms for their reliance on binary opposition, here the poetic speaker places herself somewhere within those differences. The polarization does not lead to freedom, but rather as the poet notes, to being "encarcelada" and "escapada." It is useful to note that this sort of in-between stance is not merely theoretical for the poet. Darak Mohamed has experienced precisely this kind of displacement, having been born in Auserd, a small commune on the border of the disputed territory between Western Sahara and Morocco surrounded by a giant Moroccan berm constructed in 1987, six years before her birth. While Morocco technically controls the village of Auserd, it has always been contested and has proven a difficult space to occupy. Darak Mohamed thus understands quite clearly what it means to live in-between polarized forces.

The poem includes the refrain "¡Libertad!, ¡paz!, ¡esperanza!" [Freedom! Peace! Hope!], and it is interesting that each cry that the poet chooses to emphasize and repeat is also a feminine noun in Spanish. All three exclamations take feminine linguistic form, and while that might be accidental, the emphasis is suggestive since Mohamed, in other poems in the anthology, makes very explicit gendered calls. Consider for example her poem "Amor mío no me dejes" [My Love Do Not Leave Me," which begins with a similar list of three repeated anaphoric items: "Madre mía . . . hermana mía . . . amiga mía" [My mother, my sister, my friend] (130–31). This latter poem is focused on a kind of gender-bending feminism, particularly evident in the powerful closing line: "Eres el hombre y la mujer de mi vida./Te amo mama" [You are the man and the woman of my life./I love you mom]. In the previous "Gritos" poem, the feminist call is less obvious, but it is still important to note. The speaker employs feminine adjectives, describing herself as "encarcelada" [a female prisoner] and "escapada" [a female escapee] and uses feminine nouns to announce the call to action.

The third stanza is the most significant in the context of the concept of "brotherhood," sisterhood," or "fraternity" between Spain and Western Sahara because it explicitly references the notion of "hermandad." That term in Spanish is gender neutral, as in "siblinghood," although it is linguistically feminine. The stanza begins with the poetic speaker crying out to various groups in an effort to seek freedom, peace, and hope: "I cry to the world to see if they hear me,/I cry to humanity to see if they see me,/I cry to the brotherhood to see if they speak to me/I cry to Friendship to see if they save me" ("Grito" 102). The cry begins on the broadest level, a call to the whole world ("al mundo") to see if they will listen. The use of the

62 Debra Faszer-McMahon

term "grito" is important to consider, since it refers not just to the poetic speaker's cry for attention, but also has strong political implications in Spanish, particularly for a group of poets primarily trained in Cuba and with close ties to Mexico and Venezuela. That "grito" is followed by a cry to humanity in general, in an attempt to be seen, to no longer be invisible but to establish a human connection across cultures and other barriers. The poem continues with a cry to sister and brotherhood using the term "hermandad" and thus explicitly signaling the key language that we have seen so prevalent in the representation of Saharaui immigrant culture. The question raised by the speaker here is "a ver si me hablan" – to see if they will speak to me, implying a request for dialogue. The reference to speaking may imply a nod to a shared language, with its ensuing connection with Spanish brothers and sisters, but seeking linguistic connections to bridge divides could just as easily signal a call to Latin American ties, particularly in a poem where the term "grito" is repeated. In addition, one might also read the stanza from the context of the *1001 Arabian Nights*, as the call of a desperate storyteller trying every kind of linguistic and literary strategy in order to stay alive. The poem continues with a cry for friendship, which likely alludes to the Generación de la Amistad, or the group of Saharaui poets. "Amistad" is the only term capitalized in the poem, signifying its function as a proper noun. The poetic speaker describes the call to this Saharaui poetic community as the group from whom she seeks salvation ("to see if they save me"). The earlier reference by the poetic speaker to "siblinghood" or "hermandad" is in fact just one of several strategies used by the poet in order to garner attention for this battle that the speaker fights against time ("I fight against time"). As Martin-Márquez notes, Saharaui women have become adept at using the notion of sisterhood, brotherhood, or fraternity to meet their own ends, a reverse ventriloquization, and here readers can see this explicit acknowledgment: this "hermandad" is one of many efforts to make the cry and plight of the Saharauis heard.[12]

This chapter has analyzed the way Saharaui women writers are challenging colonial tropes and redeploying powerful discourse such as the notion of a Spanish-Saharaui brotherhood, offering new transnational feminist lenses for understanding Saharaui identities and their relationships with former colonial powers. Zahra Hasnaui's contribution to *Mil y un poemas saharauis II* highlights the importance of transnational human rights movements in Afghanistan, Western Sahara, and Latin America and the way the notion of sisterhood can be understood in broader social justice terms. Fatima Galia's poetry recalls a militant and defiant posture towards Spanish colonial ambitions, one that requires a recollection of historical and contemporary conflict rather than any mollified Spanish notion of peaceful brotherhood. Darak Mohamed's work engages explicitly with gendered critique, offering a non-gendered approach to "hermandad" that places linguistic ties to Spain as one strategy within a

Saharaui Women Writers in Spain 63

broader attempt to communicate across intractable spatial, political, and gendered divides. While this chapter has only been able to address a few key poems from one volume of the much more extensive eight-volume work *Mil y un poemas saharauis*, it is helpful to recall that the voices of Saharaui women have more to offer, not only in the eight volumes of this collection but also in the two volumes of the "1001 poemas" as yet unpublished, as well as in the many other writings by Saharaui women authors, published and unpublished, to date. Perhaps the unfinished nature of this anthology signifies the unfinished business of Saharaui political aims. In that sense, the female poets of this collection, like Scheherazade, are weaving their narratives in order to stay alive. *Mil y un poemas saharauis* continues an ongoing effort to ensure the survival of the community and Saharaui political aims amid a challenging power dynamic and short global attention spans. If volume II is any indication, Saharaui women writers represent female immigrant experience in ways distinct from the discourse of Saharaui fraternity so familiar when they are represented by others. Their works offer a transnational, feminist, and literary battle cry for self-determination and freedom over and against European and Spanish colonial hegemony.

Notes

1. See Lola Huete Machado's thoughtful article on the Generación de la Amistad in "Poetas castellanos del Sáhara." *El País Semanal*. Ediciones El País SL. 27 March, 2013.
2. See, for example, the foundational work by Reina Lewis and Sara Mills, eds., *Feminist Postcolonial Theory: A Reader* (2003), and the article by Sandoval, Chela. "US Third-World Feminism: The Theory and Method of Oppositional Consciousness in the Postmodern World" in that same volume. See also the more recent studies on diasporic feminisms by Boulila, *Race in Post-Racial Europe: An Intersectional Analysis* (2019), Hartman's "The Anarchy of Colored Girls Assembled in a Riotous Manner," (2018), and Small's "Theorizing Visibility and Vulnerability in Black Europe and the African Diaspora" (2018).
3. The first volume in the five-part series was published in February, 2013 and edited by Xabier Susperregi. The following volumes were published in June 2013 (vol. II), December 2013 (vol. III), December 2014 (vol. IV), March 2015 (vol. V), March 2015 (vol. VI), April 2015 (vol. VII), and July 2015 (vol. VIII). The first three volumes were edited by Susperregi, with volume IV edited by Fátima Nascimento and volumes V–VIII by Susperregi and Nascimento together.
4. In volume I, only 16 total authors appear as contributors, 8 of them women. In volume II, 24 authors appear, and more than half are women, including 5 Saharaui. In volume III, which includes many Latin American poets, 21 women authors appear, but only 2 are Saharaui. In volumes IV–VIII, focused more on Spanish-Portuguese bilingual translation, fewer women appear, and they are mostly Spanish and Portuguese, with almost none Saharaui. Volume 8 references a future volume, including a cover image, in a section titled "próximamente" (285); however, no additional volumes have been published

64   *Debra Faszer-McMahon*

since 2015. Thus, the current multi-volume work stands at 808 poems, two volumes short of the titular number.

5. For more theoretical background on the intersectional issues facing female immigrant writers in Spain, see Small, "Theorizing Visibility and Vulnerability in Black Europe and the African Diaspora," as well as Ahmed, "A Phenomenology of Whiteness," and Boulila's *Race in Post-Racial Europe: An Intersectional Analysis.*

6. See McSweeney and Hopkins, "Editorial: Spain and Orientalism," (2017) for a brief and thoughtful analysis of this complex history.

7. While Hasnaui has not yet published a book-length collection of her original poetry, her verse appears in many different Saharaui anthologies, including *Aaiún: gritando lo que se siente; Um Draiga; Treinta y uno; Don Quijote, el azri de la badia Saharaui;* and *La primavera saharaui.*

8. Martin-Márquez goes on to mention Afghani women in particular: "Thus, the Saharawi women, who are represented as uniquely receptive to Westernization, and as engaging in a common struggle for gender equity, may be considered the true sisters of Spanish women – unlike, for example, those inscrutable Afghani women, who shocked Western Feminists when they resumed wearing the burka after their 'deliverance,' as Lila Abu-Lughod wryly reminds us. Abu-Lughod has analyzed these ongoing forms of feminist neo-imperialism, posing a question that is equally pertinent for the Saharawi context: 'Can we only free Afghan women to be like us?'" (334).

9. Galia has published several individual works, including *Lágrimas de un pueblo herido: poemario por un Sahara libre* (1998), *La henna y sus maravillas* (2001), *Pueblos de sabi@s, pueblos de pocas necesidades: cultura oral de los nómadas* (2004), *Poemas saharauis para crecer: Nada es eterno* (2009), and *La dignidad: una corona de oro* (2013).

10. Zunes and Mundy describe Luali as one of the liberation movement's key founders, a "charismatic and tireless organizer" who was "born of impoverished nomads" and eventually founded the Polisario (104–5). Luali was raised as a nomad in Western Sahara until economic problems forced his family to settle in Morocco, where he completed his education and received scholarships for university study, distinguishing himself in, among other things, constitutional law.

11. Luali's efforts were successful against the Spanish, as the colonial government withdrew from the region in 1975 under pressure from the Polisario front. When the conflict with Morocco and Mauritania ensued, Luali led Saharaui refugees towards camps in Algeria, seeking escape from bombardment by Moroccan forces. Luali was subsequently killed in battle (June 9, 1976) while attempting to sabotage water sources in Morocco.

12. As Martin-Márquez notes, "The Saharawis have become equally practiced at fomenting alternative notions of brotherhood and sisterhood with Spaniards that do not imply acceptance of presumably Western feminist values, or of the language of colonization. These forms of alliance are in fact dramatically counterposed to the neo-imperialist rhetoric that subtends much of the more mainstream Spanish support for the nationalist struggles in Spain and the POLISARIO's fight for political independence" (335).

Works Cited

Aaiún, gritando lo que se siente. Universidad Autónoma de Madrid y Editorial Exilios, 2006.

Ahmed, Sara. "A Phenomenology of Whiteness." *Feminist Theory*, vol. 8, no. 2, 2007, pp. 149–168.

Saharaui Women Writers in Spain   65

Amigos del Pueblo Saharaui en Aragón. *Um Draiga: Poesía Saharaui Contemporánea*. Um Draiga, 2006.

Bollig, Ben, and Pablo San Martín, eds. *Treinta y uno: Thirty-One: A Bilingual Anthology of Saharawi Resistance Poetry in Spanish*. Ediciones Sombrerete, 2007.

Boulila, Stefanie C. *Race in Post-Racial Europe: An Intersectional Analysis*. Rowman & Littlefield, 2019.

Campoy-Cubillo, Adolfo. *Memories of the Maghreb: Transnational Identities in Spanish Cultural Production*. Palgrave Macmillan, 2012.

Galia, Fátima. *Lágrimas de un pueblo herido: poemario por un Sahara libre = Herri zaurituaren malkoak: Sahara askearen aldeko poemak*. Servicio Editorial Universidad Del País Vasco, 1998.

———. *La henna y sus maravillas*. S.n, 2001.

———. *Pueblos de sabi@s, pueblos de pocas necesidades: cultura oral de los nómadas*. F. Salem, 2004.

———. *Poemas saharauis para crecer: Nada es eterno: Antología de 1989 a 2009*. Lankopi, 2009.

———. *La dignidad: una corona de oro*. F. Salem, 2013.

———. "Luali." *Mil y un poemas saharauis II*, edited by Xabier Susperregi, Biblioteca de las grandes naciones, ISSUU.com, junio 2013, p. 26, issuu.com/xjibe/docs/mil_y_un_poemas_saharauis_libro_ii.

Hartman, Saidiya. "The Anarchy of Colored Girls Assembled in a Riotous Manner." *South Atlantic Quarterly*, vol. 117, no. 3, 2018, pp. 465–490.

Hasnaui, Zahra. "Se me olvidó." *Mil y un poemas saharauis II*, edited by Xabier Susperregi, Biblioteca de las grandes naciones, ISSUU.com, junio 2013, p. 13, issuu.com/xjibe/docs/mil_y_un_poemas_saharauis_libro_ii.

Huete Machado, Lola. "Poetas castellanos del Sáhara." *El País Semanal*. Ediciones El País SL, 27 Mar. 2013, https://elpais.com/elpais/2013/03/27/eps/1364409377_080491.html.

La primavera saharaui: los escritores saharauis con Gdeim Izik. Bubok, 2011.

Lewis, Reina, and Sara Mills, eds. *Feminist Postcolonial Theory: A Reader*. Routledge, 2003.

Martin-Márquez, Susan. *Disorientations*. Yale UP, 2008.

McSweeney, Anna, and Claudia Hopkins. "Editorial: Spain and Orientalism." *Art in Translation*, vol. 9, no. 1, 2017, pp. 1–6.

Mil y un poemas saharauis I. Edited by Xabier Susperregi. Biblioteca de las grandes naciones. ISSUU.com. Febrero 2013, issuu.com/xjibe/docs/03_-_mil_y_un_poemas_saharauis_digi.

Mil y un poemas saharauis II. Edited by Xabier Susperregi. Biblioteca de las grandes naciones, ISSUU.com, Junio 2013, issuu.com/xjibe/docs/mil_y_un_poemas_saharauis_libro_ii.

Mil y un poemas saharauis III. Edited by Xabier Susperregi and Ana Patricia Santaella, Diciembre 2013. Biblioteca de las grandes naciones. ISSUU.com, issuu.com/xjibe/docs/025-_mil_y_un_poemas_saharauis_iii.

Mil y un poemas saharauis IV. Edited by Fátima Nascimento. Diciembre 2014, en.calameo.com/read/004070991a8bb7a0fb5d0.

Mil y un poemas saharauis V. Edited by Xabier Susperregi. Trans. Fátima Nascimento, Marzo 2015, en.calameo.com/read/0040709916755844cdced.

Mil y un poemas saharauis VI. Edited by Xabier Susperregi. Trans. Fátima Nascimento, Marzo 2015, en.calameo.com/read/004070991d484ae8d183d.

66 *Debra Faszer-McMahon*

Mil y un poemas saharauis VII. Edited by Xabier Susperregi and Fátima Nascimento, Abril 2015, en.calameo.com/read/0040709910e06a2802277.

Mil y un poemas saharauis VIII. Edited by Xabier Susperregi and Fátima Nascimento, Julio 2015, en.calameo.com/read/0040709910fa1cb7f21f7.

Mohamed, Darak. "Amor mío no me dejes." *Mil y un poemas saharauis II.* Edited by Xabier Susperregi, Biblioteca de las grandes naciones, ISSUU.com, junio 2013, pp. 130–131, issuu.com/xjibe/docs/mil_y_un_poemas_saharauis_libro_ii.

———. "Gritos por el Sahara." *Mil y un poemas saharauis II.* Edited by Xabier Susperregi, Biblioteca de las grandes naciones, ISSUU.com, junio 2013, pp. 102–103, issuu.com/xjibe/docs/mil_y_un_poemas_saharauis_libro_ii.

Rigoni, Isabelle. "Intersectionality and Mediated Cultural Production in a Globalized Post-colonial World." *Ethnic and Racial Studies*, vol. 35 no. 5, May 2012, pp. 834–849.

Robbins, Jill. "Celebrity, Diplomacy, Documentary: Javier Bardem and *Sons of the Clouds: The Last Colony.*" *African Immigrants in Contemporary Spanish Texts: Crossing the Strait*, edited by Debra Faszer-McMahon and Victoria L. Ketz, Ashgate, 2015, pp. 115–130.

Said, Edward W. *Orientalism.* 1st ed., Pantheon Books, 1978.

———. *Orientalismo.* 2nd ed., Random House Mondadori, 2002.

Salem Iselmu, Alí et al. *Don Quijote, el azri de la badia saharaui*, edited by Bahia Mahmud Awah, Conchi Moya, and Garcés C. Valero, Universidad de Alcalá de Henares, 2008.

Sandoval, Chela. "US Third-World Feminism: The Theory and Method of Oppositional Consciousness in the Postmodern World." *Feminist Postcolonial Theory: A Reader*, edited by Reina Lewis and Sara Mills, Routledge, 2003, pp. 75–102.

Small, Stephen. "Theorizing Visibility and Vulnerability in Black Europe and the African Diaspora." *Ethnic and Racial Studies*, vol. 41 no. 6, 2018, pp. 1182–1197.

Sons of the Clouds: The Last Colony = Los hijos de las nubes: La última colonia. Dir. Alvaro Longoria. Prod. Javier Bardem, Lilly Hartley, and Elena Anaya. Morena Films, 2012.

Zunes, Stephen, and Jacob Mundy. *Western Sahara: War, Nationalism, and Conflict Irresolution.* Syracuse UP, 2010.

4 Sex, Identity, and Narration in the Equatoguinean Diaspora

Mahan L. Ellison

The Spanish publisher Sial Pigmalión has a reputation for publishing high-quality literary works; I was, therefore, surprised when the bookseller dismissed a new work by a young Equatoguinean author by remarking that "that's the book that is only about sex." Indeed, the author of this particular book, O'sírima Mota Ripeu, does not hide the fact that erotic fiction had a significant role in her development as an author; on the book jacket, she cites V. C. Andrews' *Flowers in the Attic* and the Spanish romance novelist Lena Valenti as her earliest influences. But while Mota Ripeu openly acknowledges that her 2017 novel, *El punto ciego de Cassandra* [*Cassandra's Blind Spot*],[1] draws on romance and erotic literary influences, her writing focus parallels that of other young Afro-Hispanic authors such as Guillermina Mekuy and Trifonia Melibea Obono. This younger generation of authors (all three were born after 1980) is producing texts that differ in theme and focus from their literary Equatoguinean predecessors. In fact, the esteemed Equatoguinean poet Justo Bolekia Boleká wrote the prologue for *El punto ciego de Cassandra*, and he concludes by saying that

> Estamos ante una sociedad de los nuevos jóvenes españoles en la que destaca la influencia de la imagen, con descripciones directas y sinceras, sin la censura mental e indirecta de la sociedad de los adultos . . . no existe el rubor ni los tabúes culturales . . . [y] los adultos estamos invitados a aguantar hasta el final . . .
>
> (14)

> [We stand before a society of the new Spanish youth in which the influence of the image stands out, with direct and sincere descriptions, without the mental and indirect censorship of the society of adults . . . there is no blushing or cultural taboos . . . [and] we adults are invited to endure until the end . . .]

Bolekia Boleká does not dismiss her work but rather situates her as a part of a new "contexto demográfico [en España] . . . donde se refleja la

DOI: 10.4324/9781003245117-6

68   *Mahan L. Ellison*

España diversa y multiétnica de hoy" [demographic context in Spain . . . where today's diverse and multiethnic Spain is reflected] (14). And Mota Ripeu's novel – like the work of Mekuy and Melibea Obono – engages with contemporary questions of identity, sexuality, and community in new and sometimes shocking ways.

While creating works that are distinct from the previous generation of Equatoguinean authors such as Donato Ndongo Bidyogo, Juan Tomás Ávila Laurel, María Nsué Angüe, or Justo Bolekia Boleká, these younger authors of Equatoguinean descent are writing works that address social issues within more popular narratives and genres. Mota Ripeu, Mekuy, and Melibea Obono are creating provocative literary works that cross generic lines and ignore distinctions between high and low art, and their works evince an important approach to sexuality and identity in the Equatoguinean diasporic space in Spanish literature.

As Michel Foucault elaborates on in *The History of Sexuality*, sexuality can be understood as a discursive and cultural construct that is built on complex relations of power (94–95), and a Foucauldian discourse analysis can help to contextualize and understand the "polymorphous techniques of power" on display in the literary works of this diasporic generation of authors (11). Through my analysis here, I consider how these three authors engage with themes of sexuality and identity in the context of diasporic identity and space.

To consider these three authors together in the context of diaspora and diasporic identities, Avtar Brah's conceptualization of *diaspora space* is useful and necessary. While each author has a unique biography and relationship to Equatorial Guinea and Spain, Brah's concept of diaspora space is inclusive enough to account for each of their experiences because

> as a conceptual category [diaspora space] is 'inhabited' not only by those who have migrated and their descendants but equally by those who are constructed and represented as indigenous. In other words, the concept of *diaspora space* (as opposed to that of diaspora) includes the entanglement of genealogies of dispersion with those of 'staying put'.
>
> (181)

Brah further describes *diaspora space* as one "where multiple subject positions are juxtaposed, contested, proclaimed or disavowed; where the permitted and the prohibited perpetually interrogate; and where the accepted and the transgressive imperceptibly mingle" (208), and this space of multiple subjectivities and transgressions is a useful framework for considering the work by Mota Ripeu, Mekuy, and Melibea Obono.

At the center of Brah's understanding of diasporic identities and diaspora space are the "myriad processes of cultural fissure and fusion that

Sex, Identity, and Narration in the Equatoguinean Diaspora   69

underwrite contemporary forms of transcultural identities" (209), and it is evident that these authors' diasporic Equatoguinean identities add important nuances to their engagement with cultural power dynamics. There are residual colonial and postcolonial power structures that are on display in their works. In colonial Spanish Guinea, Spanish colonial rule was not only a political exercise but a "sociocultural affair" that meant "Hispanicization in every sense of the word: linguistic, cultural, social, and moral" (Allan, *Silenced Resistance* 68). The cultural imposition preceded and made possible the subsequent economic exploitation (Allan, *Silenced Resistance* 68). In her book, *Silenced Resistance: Women, Dictatorships, and Genderwashing in Western Sahara and Equatorial Guinea* (2019), Joanna Allan notes how Christian sexual morality was imposed upon preexisting Fang mores; she writes that

> The Spanish import of Christianity . . . impacted negatively on women's sexual freedoms, especially in the Fang case. Unlike other Guinean ethnicities, Fang girls were allowed to explore their sexualities before they were married. Yet the arrival of Christianity converted female sexuality into a terrible and dangerous force to be tamed in and outside of marriage.
>
> (70)

Elsewhere, Allan further examines resistance to

> El modelo de mujer que trajo España . . . el de ama de casa: las metas en la vida de la mujer ideal falangista eran casarse, tener hijos, educarlas bien según la ideología de la falange y cocinar para su marido. La Sección Femenina de la Falange Española fue un instrumento que usaron los colonos y la élite guineana para adoctrinar a las guineanas a obedecer el modelo del patriarcado falangista.
>
> ("El colonialismo y el patriarcado" 145)[2]

> [The model of the woman that Spain brought . . . the housewife: the life goals of the ideal Falangist woman were to marry, have children, educate them well according to the ideology of the Falange, and to cook for their husband. The Women's Section of the Spanish Falange was an instrument that the colonizers and the Guinean elite used to indoctrinate Guinean women to obey the Falangist patriarchal model.]

These Western, heteronormative sexual mores served as colonial power structures, and their influence continues to persist and reappear in literature by Equatoguinean authors.

For the authors under consideration here, a diasporic identity and existence further nuances the construction of identity and sexuality. Fataneh

70   *Mahan L. Ellison*

Farahani considers this added layer in her book *Gender, Sexuality, and Diaspora*, as she examines the Iranian community in Sweden, noting that

> The processes of migration and displacement have further compli-cated the already gendered and racialized dichotomy of self/other by making the 'otherness' of these women visible in the dominant white context as well as . . . patriarchal and colonial racialized structures that urge to keep women in their traditional place.
>
> (153)

These competing societal forces place migrant and diasporic women in a position where their identity and sexuality become a "construct of simul-taneous resistance and incorporation of (selective) mixes and matches of identity markers" (153). As minorities in Sweden, the alterity of these women is on display, and with it comes assumptions and realities of cul-tural and sexual identity. Melibea Obono, in an interview with the Span-ish newspaper *ABC*, discusses her complicated identity by saying that

> Yo ya no sé lo que soy hace mucho. He nacido y he crecido en Guinea, pero luego he sido de España. Cuando vengo a España me siento mentira. Siento que España es mentira. Pero lo mismo me ocurre en Guinea. Cuando estoy en España me llaman "la negra", pero cuando estoy en Guinea me llaman "la españolita". Lo que siento allí y aquí es que ninguna de las dos comunidades sienten [sic] que forme parte de ella. Pero yo sí me siento parte de las dos comunidades.
>
> (Armada)

> [It's been a while since I've known what I am. I was born and I grew up in Guinea, but later I was from Spain. When I come to Spain, I feel like a lie. I feel that Spain is a lie. But the same thing happens to me in Guinea. When I am in Spain, I'm called "la negra," but in Guinea, I'm called "the little Spaniard." I feel there and here that neither of the communities felt that I form a part of them. But I do feel like a part of both communities.]

Melibea Obono clearly articulates how her sense of identity is formed through a constant state of alterity and from "where multiple subject posi-tions are juxtaposed, contested, proclaimed or disavowed" (Brah 208).

In his study of Equatoguinean authors in exile, Michael Ugarte consid-ers the "double consciousness" of many of these exiled authors (29).[3] For them, Spanish is a "tool of liberation" that provides a certain level of inte-gration into Spanish society, but it also produces "certain ambivalences among the Guineans who use it" (29). And Moha Gerehou – author, reporter, and second-generation Gambian immigrant to Spain – in his memoir *Qué hace un negro como tú en un sitio como este* [*What Is a*

Sex, Identity, and Narration in the Equatoguinean Diaspora 71

Black Man Like You Doing in a Place Like This] (2021) – writes that "Lo que realmente me carcomía de forma constante era la confluencia entre identidades y culturas que me colocaba en posiciones incómodas y me ponía ante decisiones que marcaron mi camino" [What really gnawed at me constantly was the confluence between identities and cultures that put me in uncomfortable positions and placed me before decisions that marked my path] (60–61). Gerehou describes life in Spain as the child of African immigrants as "Crecer con África en casa y Europa en la calle" [Growing up with Africa at home and Europe in the street] (66); highlighting the constant cultural crossings that the diasporic subject experiences, and echoing the sentiments of Melibea Obono, but with a slightly different nuance.

Furthermore, Gerehou directly examines the confluence of race and sexuality by reflecting on the many times he had been asked "Y a ti, ¿te gustan blancas o negras?" [And you, do you prefer white girls or black girls?];

> Además de presuponer la heterosexualidad, es llamativo que se plantee como una dicotomía ante la que solo hay una respuesta posible. O unas u otras, pero ambas no pueden ser. . . . Sin embargo, lo curioso es que nunca oí esa pregunta dirigida a personas blancas.
>
> (143)

> [On top of assuming heterosexuality, it's striking that it is planted as a dichotomy before which there is only one possible answer. Either this one or the other, but it can never be both. . . . Nevertheless, what is curious is that I never heard this question directed towards white people.]

As a diasporic subject, he finds himself in a double bind of stereotypes and expectations that he constantly must ignore or actively resist but which he can never seem to escape. Farahani echoes the impact that this cultural labyrinth can have:

> 'sexuality' is considered to be one of the central organizing principles of identity and identity formation. It covers a wide spectrum of elements and includes questions regarding gender and identity, femininity (and masculinity), embodied practices, emotion, desire, fantasy, body language, clothing norms, and moral values, among others, which have a significant impact on the construction of identity.
>
> (2)

And so, with the myriad influences at play for the diasporic subject, it is clear that there is, as Foucault asserts, "a multiplicity of discursive elements that can come into play in various strategies" (100). And Farahani,

72   Mahan L. Ellison

drawing on Paul Gilroy, writes that the diasporic subject must constantly navigate "*cultural routes* [that] challenge fixed, cohesive, ethnic, and cultural origins" recognizing "persistent border crossings and women's sexuality as a construct of simultaneous resistance and incorporation of (selective) mixes and matches of identity markers" (153).[4] The diasporic subject experience, then, is often interstitial as they live between the various cultural forces that surround them, but it is, perhaps, more appropriate to understand them as nexuses that connect, link, and interact with the "polymorphous techniques of power" swirling around them (Foucault 11).

The three authors that I consider here – Trifonia Melibea Obono, Guillermina Mekuy, and O'sírima Mota Ripeu – were all born after 1980, and all have different diasporic experiences, but they are all united by their relative youth, their use of Spanish as their chosen language of literary expression, and their inclusion of sexuality as a major theme in their works.[5] Their works are, at times, provocative, and they cross generic lines and ignore distinctions between high and low art; just as the authors are the products of multiple cultural influences, so does their artistic production reflect myriad influences.

María del Carmen O'sírima Mota Ripeu, whose provocative erotic novel first inspired this analysis, was born in Madrid in 1989. She published her 500-page novel in 2017 with Sial Pigmalión Casa de África. Over those 500 pages, she develops the story of 16-year-old Cassandra, a gaditana whose mother is from Cape Verde and whose father is from Equatorial Guinea. The plot focuses on Cassandra's romantic and social relationships, especially her sexual awakening. It has not received much critical or academic attention yet – perhaps because of its erotic, melodramatic tone – but it does share much in common with other authors included here as well as authors such as Lucía Etxebarría or José Ángel Mañas.[6]

Guillermina Mekuy was born in Evinayong, Equatorial Guinea, in 1982 and is the author of three novels. Her books have received some critical attention, both positive and negative. Mekuy's work has been criticized through a comparison to melodramas, telenovelas, and popular movies (Nistal in Lewis 90), and Marta Sofía López Rodríguez described her as

> literariamente huérfana, hija apócrifa del exilio, y que su novela ha nacido por tanto (des)madrada: desvinculada de la tradición literaria de las mujeres negras, de la cultura origen de la escritora, de la oratura africana no menos que de la narrativa escrita del continente y la diáspora, e indiferente a la trágica historia de [Guinea Ecuatorial].
>
> (10)

> [literarily orphaned, an apocryphal daughter of exile, and her novel has been born out of this motherlessness: disconnected from the literary tradition of black women, from the culture of origin of the

Sex, Identity, and Narration in the Equatoguinean Diaspora 73

author, from African orality and also the written narratives from the continent and the diaspora, and indifferent to the tragic history of Equatorial Guinea.]

While this critique is valid in many ways, it overlooks some of the subtle connections to Fang tradition that Mekuy's erotic focus at first glance ignores,[7] and Mekuy's work is a valuable example of the treatment of sexuality in the Equatoguinean diasporic imagination.

Trifonia Melibea Obono – born in 1982 in Evinayong, Equatorial Guinea – has received some significant attention in recent years with her books *La bastarda* (2016)[8] and *Las mujeres hablan mucho y mal* [*Women Talk a Lot and Badly*] (2018), along with an English translation of *La bastarda* published in 2018 that establishes her as the first female Equatoguinean author translated into English. The former Spanish diplomat to Equatorial Guinea, Luis Melgar Valero, writes that Melibea Obono's explicit engagement with LGBT issues "Es un hito, algo sin precedente" [is a milestone, something without precedent] (11), and Arturo Arnalte favorably describes her as "una decidida vocación feminista y militante a favor de la emancipación de la mujer de las costumbres tradicionales que la subordinan al varón en muchas culturas subsaharianas" [a fighting voice that erupts in the regional literary panorama with a strong feminist and militant vocation in favor of the emancipation of women from the traditional customs that subordinate women] (17).

Each of these authors has written books that, in some way – as Joanna Boampong writes about Mekuy – "desecrate the sacred subject of sex and the erotic that most African writers feel obliged to avoid" (106). Each of these authors includes non-heteronormative sexual encounters as an integral part of their narratives, and their discursive treatment of this sexual diversity echoes Foucault's assertion that "we must not imagine a world of discourse divided between accepted discourse and excluded discourse . . . but as a multiplicity of discursive elements that can come into play in various strategies" (100). These authors each reimagine interpersonal relations of power through sexual expression, and their works have a consistent theme of a struggle for identity and sexual awakening. But while the erotic content is primarily titillating and provocative at first glance, the contextualized narration engages with power dynamics present in the diasporic experience.

Melibea Obono's *La bastarda* and *Las mujeres hablan mucho y mal* both directly confront the Fang cultural expectations for a heteronormative conceptualization of sexuality. While her narrative in *La bastarda* focuses on the sexual awakening of the protagonist Okomo and her realization that she is a lesbian, the text also emphasizes how cultural sexual expectations are damaging to both women and men. And, as noted previously (in Allan), these expectations are a product of the diaspora space that developed out of Spanish colonialism and the imposition of a Falangist

74 *Mahan L. Ellison*

patriarchal model onto Fang culture. In *Las mujeres hablan mucho y mal*, Melibea Obono directly addresses this dual influence: "España, que fortaleció a su manera mi identidad de mujer libre, también me esclavizó con el obligado proceso de cubrir las rodillas si quería ser educadora" [Spain, that in its own way taught me how to be a free woman, also enslaved me with the obligatory process of covering my knees if I wanted to be an educator] (*Las mujeres* 160). Melibea Obono's protagonists must contend with a matrix of power dynamics that emanate from cultural gender roles (*Las mujeres* 165–169), Spanish colonial social (*Las mujeres* 160) and religious (*Las mujeres* 158) mores, traditional Fang customs (*Las mujeres* 37–39, 168), and linguistic limitations (*La bastarda* 96), among others. At each attempt to act independently, Melibea Obono's protagonists are confronted with an external expectation that limits their individual autonomy.

Melibea Obono further explores the personal pursuit of pleasure, fulfillment, and autonomy in her book *La bastarda*, as the protagonist of this work realizes that she is a lesbian and leaves behind the communal expectations that she marry and settle with a man. In a conversation between the protagonist and her gay uncle, Melibea Obono examines how the restrictive language about sexuality intertwines with cultural beliefs and how it dehumanizes individuals:

> – . . . Pero en el pueblo dice que un hombre normal no se deja hacer eso, hacer el amor como una mujer. Por esa razón os llaman hombres-mujeres. Nosotras no tenemos nombre.
> – ¿Y no crees que es mucho más grave vuestra situación? Si no tenéis nombre, sois invisibles, y si sois invisibles, no podéis reivindicar ningún derecho. Además, el apelativo ofensivo hombre-mujer encierra desprecio hacia la mujer, la convierte en un objeto sexual y una persona subordinada: no toma la iniciativa en el acto sexual.
> (*La bastarda* 95–96)

> [". . . But in the village, they say that a normal man would never do that, make love like a woman. For that reason, they call you all men-women. We don't have a name."
> "And don't you think that your situation is much worse, then? If you all don't have a name, you are invisible, and if you're invisible, you can't claim any rights. Also, the offensive term man-woman also conveys disdain for women, it turns them into a sexual object and a subordinate person: they don't take the initiative in the sexual act."]

Melibea Obono highlights the problematic terminology for non-heteronormative sexualities, emphasizing that there is not even a word for lesbianism. This lack of vocabulary culturally and socially marginalizes individuals that do not conform to communal ideals for sexuality. Melibea

Sex, Identity, and Narration in the Equatoguinean Diaspora 75

Obono's protagonist finds that the only solution is to go and live in the forest with her gay uncle and her lover, concluding that "El bosque de mi pueblo constituía el único refugio de las personas que no encontraban sitio en la tradición fang como yo" [The forest of my village was the only refuge for people that could not find a place in the Fang tradition like me] (*La bastarda* 116). The protagonist is unable to reconcile her sexuality with her Fang community and must literally live in a peripheral space to find personal sexual fulfillment. The peripheral linguistic existence that gay and lesbian individuals face in Fang culture is also made into literal peripheral existence. In the introduction to the book, Arturo Arnalte notes that Melibea Obono employs "la homosexualidad como metáfora de la libertad" [homosexuality as a metaphor for liberty] (26), and it is possible to interpret the protagonist's sexual identity as the deciding factor that enabled her to escape from an oppressive social paradigm, but it is also necessary to recognize that the lesbian protagonist is forced to move to a peripheral space in order to gain personal autonomy. Within the narrative, there is not a space for non-heteronormative sexuality within the village's social sphere. Melibea Obono's protagonist finds (sexual) fulfillment and autonomy, but she is forced to leave society and live in the jungle to achieve it.

While Melibea Obono considers how societal and cultural discourse about sexuality marginalizes non-heteronormative sexual expression, Guillermina Mekuy has a parallel yet distinct approach to sexuality. In *Las tres vírgenes de Santo Tomás*, Mekuy's protagonist is the daughter of a very religious father who seeks to protect his three daughters' virginity at all costs. The Equatoguinean father, in his religious fervor, changes his name to Tomás because of his adoration for Thomas Aquinas "que consideraba a las mujeres seres biológicamente inferiores a los hombres" [who considered women to be biologically inferior beings to men] (16). The father's religious obsession with female sexuality prioritizes the virginity of the three daughters above all else, so much so that the protagonist's mother pleads with her that

> – Sólo te pido una cosa: puedes ofrecer tu cuerpo a la lujuria, emular a todas las mujeres del mundo que se han prostituido . . . sólo tienes que prometerme una cosa: seguirás siendo virgen. Serás deseada, acariciada, lamida, sojuzgada, pero nadie penetrará en ti, ni aun cuando estés en medio de una orgía de hombres que te quieran poseer y a los que les darás todo menos una cosa: el húmedo tesoro de tu virginidad.
> (110)

> [I only ask one thing of you: you can offer your body to lust, emulate all of the women of the world that have prostituted themselves . . . you only have to promise me one thing: you will stay a virgin. You will be desired, caressed, licked, subjugated, but no one will penetrate

76   *Mahan L. Ellison*

you, not even when you are in the middle of an orgy of men that want to possess you and you will give them everything except for one thing: the humid treasure of your virginity.]

Mekuy's protagonist is surrounded by "patriarchal and colonial racialized structures that urge to keep women in their traditional place" (Farahani 153–154), similar to that of Melibea Obono's protagonist. And yet her response to these "monolithic heteronormative notions of sexuality" (Farahani 155) is distinct.

Where Melibea Obono's protagonist must live on the margins of society to experience fulfillment, Mekuy's protagonist attempts to exploit heteronormative structures while still operating within them. Her protagonist seeks out sexual power and fulfillment without penis-in-vagina penetration, explaining herself in this manner:

> Cuando uno se propone conseguir sus metas y realmente siente lo que cree y sigue el camino correcto, es digno de admiración. Yo quería ser puta pero sin perder la virginidad, quería disfrutar dando placer, pero sin que nadie me penetrara. Sabía que el placer era algo momentáneo y efímero, pero sentía que me gustaba proporcionar a los hombres momentos inolvidables de felicidad a cambio de algo que no tenía: dinero.
>
> (133)

> [When someone sets out to achieve their goals and really believes in them and follows the correct path, that is worthy of admiration. I wanted to be a whore, but without losing my virginity, I wanted to enjoy giving pleasure without anyone penetrating me. I knew that pleasure was something momentaneous and ephemeral, but I felt that I enjoyed giving men unforgettable moments of happiness in exchange for something that I didn't have: money.]

The penetration-free sex act is a financial exchange, but it is one that the protagonist engages in for her own benefit and empowerment and for reasons that the protagonist believes are "worthy of admiration." In the narrative context, it is an empowering act that enables the protagonist to exert her autonomy and experience personal fulfillment. The protagonist's approach to sex allows her to exert control over the patriarchal framework that structures her life: "me daba la capacidad de dominar [los hombres]" [it gave me the capacity to dominate the men] (125). Mekuy's protagonist exploits the confining moral structure in ways that empower and satisfy her sexual (and financial) needs.

Mekuy's approach has garnered sharp criticism. Marta Sofía López Rodríguez criticizes Mekuy's lighthearted treatment of sex work in her other book *El llanto de la perra*, concluding that "debería hacer que los

Sex, Identity, and Narration in the Equatoguinean Diaspora   77

huesos de Nora Zeale Hurston, Bessie Head, Mariama Bâ y tantas otras luchadoras por la dignidad de las mujeres negras se revolvieran en sus tumbas" [it should make the bones of Nora Zeale Hurston, Bessie Head, Mariama Bâ and all of the other fighters for the dignity of black women turn over in their graves] (9). But Joanna Boampong argues that "Mekuy's female African protagonist does break the mould in which African women have traditionally been cast" (107) and that she "desecrate[s] the sacred subject of sex and the erotic that most African writers feel obliged to avoid" (106). Mekuy's protagonist works within the patriarchal paradigm to find ways to desecrate and subvert the power that her protagonists are subjected to. As Avtar Brah theorizes, Mekuy operates in the diaspora space where "the permitted and the prohibited perpetually interrogate; and where the accepted and the transgressive imperceptibly mingle" (208).

If Melibea Obono's protagonist must leave the sphere of cultural influence to find fulfillment, and Mekuy's protagonist must find ways to subvert from within, then O'sírima Mota Ripeu's narrative offers an alternative that ignores these constraints. Mota Ripeu's protagonist, the titular Cassandra, a mother from Cape Verde and a father from Equatorial Guinea. Her father is a dentist and her mother a sexologist, and both support Cassandra's development of a safe and healthy sexual identity; for example, her mother slips condoms into her purse before her first date and often checks in with her daughter (74). In comparison with the works of Melibea Obono and Mekuy, there is a conspicuous absence of strict religious or traditional cultural dogma; the narrative presents sexuality as a frontier to be explored and not as a subversive act of resistance. In its own way, this approach is subversive in that it circumvents the religious and social mores that would control sexual expression, and Mota Ripeu's response is to ignore their existence and power.

Mota Ripeu's novel explores the pleasures of sexual intimacy explicitly and imaginatively. For the protagonist, the pursuit of sexual fulfillment and pleasure is a personal journey that is supported by her community. Her friends help her overcome her shyness with a new love interest; her mother slips condoms into her purse; her brother gives her advice, and when the big Christmas Eve party arrives, Cassandra feels prepared and supported to lose her virginity: "Todos sabíamos que había llegado el momento de perderla" [We all knew that the moment had arrived to lose it] (37). Within this narrative, Cassandra's cultural sphere is affirming and inclusive. Due to the diverse constituency of her social and familiar spheres, there is acceptance of difference, and Cassandra does not have to directly confront "patriarchal and colonial racialized structures that urge to keep women in their traditional place" (Farahani 153). In this novel, the diaspora space permits Cassandra a great deal of autonomous liberty.

There are, however, still strong cultural pressures at work. These pressures are not explicit or dogmatic, but they exert a clear influence on the

78 Mahan L. Ellison

protagonist. Cassandra's peer group is multi-racial and multi-cultural but is clearly influenced by global media trends such as television, music, and the internet. The characters reference Queen Latifa and her film *Beauty Shop* (2005) (58) and Frank Miller's *Sin City* (2005) (244). They listen to musical artists such as the Cape Verdean-Dutch singer Nelson Freitas (63), and then there are the repeated references to the influence of pornography (51, 59, 112, 463). It is no surprise that Justo Bolekia Boleká, in the prologue, categorizes the book as "[una] proyección sociofílmica" [a sociofilmic projection] (14). Unlike the negative cultural pressures in Mekuy and Melibea Obono's work, Mota Ripeu's cultural influences are instructional and inspirational. The narrative is not focused on subverting or escaping them but rather on exploring the possibilities that they create. In this sense, Mota Ripeu's narration of sexuality is significant; it displays what Brah describes as a core characteristic of the diaspora space:

> the infinite experientiality, the myriad processes of cultural fissure and fusion that underwrite contemporary forms of transcultural identities. . . . These emergent identities . . . are inscribed in the late twentieth-century forms of syncretism at the core of culture and subjectivity.
> (208)

While an initial read of Mota Ripeu's work might dismiss it as little more than popular erotic fiction, a consideration of the work as a product of the diaspora space – especially in comparison with its peers – reveals important dynamics of identity culture at play.

As members of the younger generation of Equatoguinean authors, Melibea Obono, Mekuy, and Mota Ripeu all display distinct approaches to sexuality in their works. Through differing strategies, they each confront the discursive societal forces that structure cultural sexual norms. On display in their works are cultural forces that arise from traditional Fang norms, Spanish colonial mores, modern Spanish trends, and other global and multicultural influences. These Foucauldian "polymorphous techniques of power" highlight the constant pressure that the diasporic subject faces in the process of forming and articulating identity, and the responses from these authors are distinct. To summarize succinctly, these three authors' approaches could, perhaps, be summarized as escape, exploit, or explore.

Melibea Obono's protagonist in *La bastarda* must escape the societal forces that demand heteronormative compliance; Mekuy's protagonist chooses to exploit the limiting moral structure for her own empowerment, and Mota Ripeu explores the possibilities of community and sex-positivity in her narrative. Each of these strategies (directly or indirectly) confronts the myriad cultural influences that the diasporic subject faces and considers alternatives that lead to sexual fulfillment and personal empowerment. The diversity of the strategies offered also

Sex, Identity, and Narration in the Equatoguinean Diaspora 79

highlights the fact that the diasporic experience is not monolithic but contextually unique in every case. These works by Melibea Obono, Mekuy, and Mota Ripeu are valuable examples of a new generation of diasporic Equatoguinean authors who are charting new territory with their exploration of sexuality and identity, and while they may be dismissed, at times, for their direct approach to sex, their works are contextually important for understanding Equatoguinean literature in the twenty-first century.

Notes

1. Unless otherwise noted, all translations from Spanish to English are my own.
2. This is also clearly portrayed in the film *Palmeras en la nieve* [*Palm Trees in the Snow*] (2015), which was based on the novel of the same name by Luz Gabás.
3. Ugarte draws from Paul Gilroy's *The Black Atlantic: Modernity and Double Consciousness* (1993) for this, applying it to the Equatoguinean context. Gilroy, in turn drew from W. E. B. Du Bois's articulation of the term in *The Souls of Black Folk* (1903).
4. Farahani draws on Gilroy's articulation of *cultural routes* in *The Black Atlantic*, a term that plays off of the homonym between "roots" and "routes" (133).
5. What Ngũgĩ wa Thiong'o would call "Afro-European literature," as opposed to "African literature" in an African language (102). Thiong'o's theorization of "colonial alienation" through the language of literary expression highlights another identity structure that the diasporic subject must confront.
6. Mota Ripeu's treatment of sex and sociality reminds me at times of Etxebarría's *Cosmofobia* (2007), Ángel Mañas' *Historias del Kronen* (1994), and other authors of the Generación Kronen.
7. I examine these in a chapter on Mekuy in my book *African in the Contemporary Spanish Novel, 1990–2010* (2021), and Joanna Boampong has also closely examined Mekuy's work in her book chapter "Reconfigurations of the Female Protagonist in Hispanophone African Literature."
8. "La bastarda" translates as "The Bastard," but the 2018 English translation by Lawrence Schimel maintains the original Spanish title.

Works Cited

Allan, Joanna. "El Colonialismo y el patriarcado en la literatura afrohispana: Los Escritos de resistencia de Lehdia Dafa y María Nsué Angüe." *Trans-afrohispanismos: Puentes culturales críticos entre África, Latinoamérica y España*, edited by Dorothy Odartey-Wellington, Brill Rodopi, 2018, pp. 137–151.

———. *Silenced Resistance: Women, Dictatorships, and Genderwashing in Western Sahara and Equatorial Guinea*. U of Wisconsin P, 2019.

Andrews, V. C. *Flowers in the Attic*. Simon & Schuster, 1979.

Armada, Alfonso, and Trifonia Melibea Obono. "Entrevista: Trifonia Melibea Obono: 'En España me llaman 'La negra', en Guinea Ecuatorial 'La españolita'." *ABC*, 15 Dec. 2016, www.abc.es/cultura/cultural/abci-trifonia-melibea-obono-espana-llaman-negra-guinea-euatorial-espanolita-201612121313_noticia.html?ref=https%3A%2F%2Fwww.abc.es%2Fcultura%2Fcultural%2Fabci-trifonia-melibea-obono-espana-llaman-negra-guinea-euatorial-espanolita-201612121313_noticia.html.

Arnalte, Arturo. "Introducción: Viaje iniciático hacia la libertad." *La bastarda.* Flores Raras, 2018, pp. 17–27.

Boampong, Joanna. "Reconfigurations of the Female Protagonist in Hispanophone African Literature." *In and Out of Africa: Exploring Afro-Hispanic, Luso-Brazilian, and Latin-American Connections*, edited by Joanna Boampong, Cambridge Scholars Publishing, 2012, pp. 96–108.

Bolekia Boleká, Justo. "Prólogo." *El punto ciego de Cassandra.* Sial Ediciones Casa de África, 2017, pp. 13–14.

Brah, Avtar. *Cartographies of Diaspora: Contesting Identities.* Routledge, 2003.

Du Bois, W. E. B. *The Souls of Black Folk*, 1903. Penguin Books, 2021.

Ellison, Mahan L. *Africa in the Contemporary Spanish Novel, 1990–2010.* Lexington Books, 2021.

Farahani, Fataneh. *Gender, Sexuality, and Diaspora.* Kindle ed., Routledge, 2018.

Foucault, Michel. *The History of Sexuality, Volume I: An Introduction.* Translated by Robert Hurley, Vintage Books, 1990.

Gabás, Luz. *Palmeras en la nieve.* Planeta, 2013.

Gerehou, Moha. *Qué hace un negro como tú en un sitio como este.* Ediciones Península, 2021.

Gilroy, Paul. *The Black Atlantic: Modernity and Double Consciousness.* Verso, 1993.

Lewis, Marvin. *Equatorial Guinean Literature in Its National and Transnational Contexts.* U of Missouri P, 2017.

López Rodríguez, Marta Sofía. "(Des)madres e hijas: De *Ekomo* a *El llanto de la perra.*" *Afroeuropa*, vol. 2, no. 2, 2008, pp. 1–12.

Mekuy, Guillermina. *El llanto de la perra.* Plaza Janés, 2005.

———. *Las tres vírgenes de Santo Tomás.* Suma de Letras, 2008.

Melgar Valero, Luis. "Prólogo." *La bastarda.* Flores Raras, 2018, pp. 11–14.

Melibea Obono, Trifonia. *La bastarda.* Flores Raras, 2016.

———. *La bastarda.* Translated by Lawrence Schimel, Feminist Press, 2018.

———. *Las mujeres hablan mucho y mal.* Sial Ediciones Casa de África, 2018.

Mota Ripeu, O'sírima. *El punto ciego de Cassandra.* Sial Ediciones Casa de África, 2017.

Palmeras en la nieve. Dir. Fernando González Molina, performances by Mario Casas, Adriana Ugarte, Macarena García, Berta Vázquez, and Djédjé Apali, Nostromo Pictures, 2015.

Thiong'o, Ngũgĩ wa. "Decolonising the Mind." *Diogenes*, vol. 46/4, no. 184, 1998, pp. 101–104.

Ugarte, Michael. *Africans in Europe: The Culture of Exile and Emigration from Equatorial Guinea to Spain.* U of Illinois P, 2010.

5 Mothering, *Mestizaje* and the Future of Spain

Anna Tybinko

Throughout her autobiographical essay, *Más allá del mar de arena: una mujer africana en España* (Beyond the Sea of Sand: An African Woman in Spain, 2005), Agnès Agboton denounces the intolerance and xenophobia with which West African migrants are treated in Spain. With the onset of a new "migration crisis" as her starting point, she takes the opportunity to remind her two sons, Axel and Didac: "Sois el ejemplo inmediato y palpable, desde que nacisteis, de que el mundo es variado y de que nadie puede reclamar la exclusiva del bien, de la cultura y de la verdad" [You [plural] are the immediate and palpable example, since you were born, that the world is diverse and that no one can claim an exclusive right to what is good, to culture and to the truth] (Agboton 75).[1] In doing so, she pins her hopes for a more just, racially diverse, and equitable society on future generations of racialized Spaniards. Writing as a mother speaking to her children, this chapter will not only assess *Más allá del mar de arena*'s potential as a "narrative of migration" but as an act of empowered mothering as well. Finally, it will consider Agboton's text in relation to more recent production by writers, artists, and activists of African descent in Spain to bring nuance to the terminology of diaspora in the Spanish context.

Más allá del mar de arena weaves past with present as it follows Agboton's trajectory from Porto Novo, Benin, to Bingerville, Ivory Coast, and finally to Barcelona, Spain, where she moved with her Catalan husband, Manuel Serrat Crespo, at the age of 18. Given its blended temporalities, *Más allá del mar de arena* is what we would call a *libro de memorias* – or memoir – in Spanish, although it was clearly written in response to the uptick in immigration that Spain witnessed at the start of the new millennium. But rather than dwell on historical fact, Agboton offers her own life story as an entry point from which to examine how the African diaspora, and specifically the movement of people from the Gulf of Guinea to the Iberian Peninsula, has shaped contemporary Spain. While the country passed its first unified immigration law in 1985, the most significant demographic impact of the *Ley de Extranjería*, or Foreigner's

DOI: 10.4324/9781003245117-7

82 *Anna Tybinko*

Law as it is casually known, was not seen until the early 2000s. According to the Instituto Nacional de Estadística (National Statistics Institute), in the year of *Más allá del mar de arena*'s publication, the number of registered, foreign-born residents reached almost 4 million, representing about 8.5% of the total population of Spain. With this percentage growing by 1–2 points per year, in absolute terms, Spain was second only to the United States among the OECD (Organization for Economic Cooperation and Development) countries, regarding the sheer volume of migration received during the first decade of the twenty-first century (Muñoz Comet 24).

The 1990s saw the erection of massive barrier fences surrounding the Spanish-held territories of Ceuta and Melilla in North Africa. The fences made this once-porous border region emblematic of "Fortress Europe" and had a significant impact on migratory flows from Africa in particular, sending more and more migrants to sea. Due to increased patrols in the Mediterranean, the media spectacle of sub-Saharan migrants arriving via the more dangerous route to the Spanish Canary Islands reached its zenith in 2006 (Andersson 21) – even though no more than 1% of migrants to Spain come by boat, this perilous mode of transport is indelibly etched in the Spanish imaginary. As Silvia Bermúdez explains, the circulation of images displaying dark-skinned individuals resorting to increasingly desperate measures to enter Europe reflects "in an acute manner the shock with which Spain experiences the influx of people of the Third World as people of color" (178). By highlighting the perils of the journey, this focus on those ensnared in barbed wire or left adrift at sea also turns migration into a spectacle; it reifies preconceptions of what constitutes a border and distracts attention from the challenges that migrants face upon arrival.

Agboton addresses this tense political environment in her very first chapter:

> en estos últimos tiempos, las noticias que dan por televisión nos bombardean con episodios e imágenes de gente que arriesga su vida embarcándose en las costas africanas, en condiciones muy precarias, para llegar hasta aquí, hasta la mítica Europa, en busca de un futuro mejor.
>
> [Recently, the television news bombards us with episodes and images of people that risk their life departing from the African coasts, in very precarious conditions, in order to arrive here, to mythical Europe, in search of a better future.]
>
> (Agboton 18)

At first, Agboton positions herself among the "us" – the residents of "mythical Europe" who watch this tragedy from a mediated distance. However, she quickly switches tack.

5 Mothering, *Mestizaje* and the Future of Spain

Anna Tybinko

Throughout her autobiographical essay, *Más allá del mar de arena: una mujer africana en España* (Beyond the Sea of Sand: An African Woman in Spain, 2005), Agnès Agboton denounces the intolerance and xenophobia with which West African migrants are treated in Spain. With the onset of a new "migration crisis" as her starting point, she takes the opportunity to remind her two sons, Axel and Didac: "Sois el ejemplo inmediato y palpable, desde que nacisteis, de que el mundo es variado y de que nadie puede reclamar la exclusiva del bien, de la cultura y de la verdad" [You [plural] are the immediate and palpable example, since you were born, that the world is diverse and that no one can claim an exclusive right to what is good, to culture and to the truth] (Agboton 75).[1] In doing so, she pins her hopes for a more just, racially diverse, and equitable society on future generations of racialized Spaniards. Writing as a mother speaking to her children, this chapter will not only assess *Más allá del mar de arena*'s potential as a "narrative of migration" but as an act of empowered mothering as well. Finally, it will consider Agboton's text in relation to more recent production by writers, artists, and activists of African descent in Spain to bring nuance to the terminology of diaspora in the Spanish context.

Más allá del mar de arena weaves past with present as it follows Agboton's trajectory from Porto Novo, Benin, to Bingerville, Ivory Coast, and finally to Barcelona, Spain, where she moved with her Catalan husband, Manuel Serrat Crespo, at the age of 18. Given its blended temporalities, *Más allá del mar de arena* is what we would call a *libro de memorias* – or memoir – in Spanish, although it was clearly written in response to the uptick in immigration that Spain witnessed at the start of the new millennium. But rather than dwell on historical fact, Agboton offers her own life story as an entry point from which to examine how the African diaspora, and specifically the movement of people from the Gulf of Guinea to the Iberian Peninsula, has shaped contemporary Spain. While the country passed its first unified immigration law in 1985, the most significant demographic impact of the *Ley de Extranjería*, or Foreigner's

DOI: 10.4324/9781003245117-7

82   Anna Tybinko

Law as it is casually known, was not seen until the early 2000s. According to the Instituto Nacional de Estadística (National Statistics Institute), in the year of *Más allá del mar de arena*'s publication, the number of registered, foreign-born residents reached almost 4 million, representing about 8.5% of the total population of Spain. With this percentage growing by 1–2 points per year, in absolute terms, Spain was second only to the United States among the OECD (Organization for Economic Cooperation and Development) countries, regarding the sheer volume of migration received during the first decade of the twenty-first century (Muñoz Comet 24).

The 1990s saw the erection of massive barrier fences surrounding the Spanish-held territories of Ceuta and Melilla in North Africa. The fences made this once-porous border region emblematic of "Fortress Europe" and had a significant impact on migratory flows from Africa in particular, sending more and more migrants to sea. Due to increased patrols in the Mediterranean, the media spectacle of sub-Saharan migrants arriving via the more dangerous route to the Spanish Canary Islands reached its zenith in 2006 (Andersson 21) – even though no more than 1% of migrants to Spain come by boat, this perilous mode of transport is indelibly etched in the Spanish imaginary. As Silvia Bermúdez explains, the circulation of images displaying dark-skinned individuals resorting to increasingly desperate measures to enter Europe reflects "in an acute manner the shock with which Spain experiences the influx of people of the Third World as people of color" (178). By highlighting the perils of the journey, this focus on those ensnared in barbed wire or left adrift at sea also turns migration into a spectacle; it reifies preconceptions of what constitutes a border and distracts attention from the challenges that migrants face upon arrival.

Agboton addresses this tense political environment in her very first chapter:

> en estos últimos tiempos, las noticias que dan por televisión nos bombardean con episodios e imágenes de gente que arriesga su vida embarcándose en las costas africanas, en condiciones muy precarias, para llegar hasta aquí, hasta la mítica Europa, en busca de un futuro mejor.
>
> [Recently, the television news bombards us with episodes and images of people that risk their life departing from the African coasts, in very precarious conditions, in order to arrive here, to mythical Europe, in search of a better future.]
>
> (Agboton 18)

At first, Agboton positions herself among the "us" – the residents of "mythical Europe" who watch this tragedy from a mediated distance. However, she quickly switches tack.

Mothering, Mestizaje *and the Future of Spain* 83

In a sort of literary *vaivén* [back and forth], Agboton continues by confirming her common bond with those who are portrayed by the Spanish news media as part of a mass phenomenon or invasion: "estas imágenes me conmueven y nunca puedo mostrarme indiferente ante esos dramas. Porque sé de dónde proceden los hombres de las pateras, sé lo que los mueve; pero también porque sé adónde van y cuál será el terrible final de sus sueños" [these images move me and I can never express indifference to those dramas. Because I know where the men on the *pateras* come from, I know what moves them; but also, because I know where they are headed and what the terrible end of their dreams will be] (Agboton 18).[2] In a move typical of Agboton's writing, she both exposes much of the brutality undergirding the construction of contemporary Spain as part of the supranational conglomeration that is the European Union but never directly indicts Spanish racism. She ultimately concludes that: "África no es una tierra fácil, pero Europa también puede ser un lugar terrible" [Africa is not an easy homeland, but Europe can also be a terrible place] (Agboton 18). Echoing her earlier "terrible final de sus sueños," she reminds us once again that, while life in Africa may be complicated and often difficult, Europe – and by extension, Spain – can be truly "terrible." Despite her insistence, there is no further explanation of this more sinister designation. She crafts a purposeful informational lacuna and, in doing so, entices the attentive reader to fill the gap.

To understand this approach, we might also consider *Más allá del mar de arena* within her larger body of work. Agboton has published numerous cookbooks on African and West African cuisines, several collections of myths and legends from the continent, and two volumes of her own poetry – both of which speak to her experience as an intercultural agent. She also spent years working as a cultural mediator in Barcelona, offering storytelling sessions through various educational institutions. Critics such as Julia Borst, Mar Gallego, Maya García de Vinuesa, M'bare N'Gom, and Raquel Vega-Durán dedicate ample attention to these activities and deserve much credit for underscoring the importance of Agboton's oeuvre as what can tentatively be termed "Hispanic African Literature" or "Afro-Spanish" letters (N'gom 103; Borst 170). However, as I argue elsewhere and will expand upon here, the significance of the subject position Agboton chooses for herself as a Black woman writing explicitly for her multiracial children cannot be overlooked.[3]

Many of her other works are instructional in nature, but *Más allá del mar de arena* is written with the explicit intent of helping her sons – and by proxy, her readership – navigate Spain's rapidly changing social landscape. Borrowing from Elaine Showalter's term "gynocentric," feminist theorist Andrea O'Reilly draws heavily on the idea of a "matrifocal narrative" as developed by Marianne Hirsch, Brenda O. Daly, and Maureen T. Reddy to envision a matricentric feminism. Told from a mother's perspective and attending specifically to what "mothering" (Rich) or

84   *Anna Tybinko*

"motherwork" (Collins, "Shifting the Center") meant for her transition from Bingerville to Barcelona, Agboton's narrative epitomizes a text in which the maternal is structurally central. As Inmaculada Díaz Narbona astutely points out in her introduction to *Más allá del mar de arena*, Agboton manages to translate the lively oral traditions from the Gulf of Guinea – or what she calls "the ritual of orality" – onto the written page.[4] A key facet of this ritual is the interaction with one's audience; in this case, the frequent use of the second person, as if she is engaging her sons in conversation. Much like the West African griots, or bards, who played an edifying role in their communities, Agboton sets out to inform Axel and Didac of their origins through a lengthy genealogical tale. It seems important to recognize that from the very first line, "Hijos míos, os lo diré como cuando erais pequeños, como me lo decían a mí hace ya mucho, mucho tiempo" [My sons, I will tell it you like when you were young, like they told it to me a long, long time ago now], Agboton's memoir emanates from her role as a mother.

In her first chapter, Agboton gives a folkloric account of Benin's origins; a story of how the landless sons of a princess and a leopard (Los hijos del leopardo or *agasuvi*), set off in search of somewhere to call home. A brief aside interrupts the narrative to remind us: "Hay muchas leyendas africanas que comienzan así, con un éxodo, pero también las europeas están llenas de pueblos que buscan un lugar para vivir. También en eso las leyendas se hermanan" [There are many African legends that begin this way, with an exodus, but European legends are also full of people in search of a place to live. In this respect, the legends are related] (Agboton 15). From there, she goes on to describe how the sons of the leopard chanced upon the kingdom of Dan and took advantage of his African hospitality to establish themselves. They eventually engaged in a bloody battle with the monarch, took over his lands and built their house over his cadaver. The famous Kingdom of Dahomey, which resisted French colonial rule until 1904, got its name from this violent act: "*Dan-homè huégbé*, 'la casa sobre el vientre de Dan'" [the house on top of Dan's stomach] (17). As Agboton points out, colonization at least served to preserve this name (and therefore origin story) in the Western archive.[5] This gruesome story is presented in a matter-of-fact tone. Compared to the type of children's entertainment prevalent in the occidental world, it seems particularly brutal – and could therefore be misinterpreted as confirming stereotypes of African barbarism. However, Agboton strategically introduces an important parallelism by presenting the foundational tales of Africa and Europe on the same symbolic level. She thus insinuates that one version of history is no more or less accurate than the other (Gallego 72). In doing so, she makes clear that human mobility, conflict – and even conquest – have shaped both civilizations and, furthermore, that they will continue to shape their futures.

Mothering, Mestizaje *and the Future of Spain*   85

Agboton is not the only African-born author who engages with epistolary autobiography or memoir as a means of intergenerational communication. I will also point to Saïd El Kadaoui's *Cartes a meu fill. Un català de soca-rel, gairebé* [Letters to My Son. A Born and Bred Catalan, Almost, 2011] and Najat El Hachmi's *Jo també soc catalana* [I am also Catalan, 2004].[6] Both El Kadaoui and El Hachmi are originally from Morocco but migrated to Catalonia as children, and both write for their own sons, claiming a Catalan identity in the process. Miguel Pomar-Amer reads the two works in unison not only for their formal similarities (which parallel Agboton's in terms of a disregard for chronology) but also for messaging. In consideration of what enunciation from the parental position denotes, Pomar-Amer observes that:

> the ultimate goal of merging the private and public spheres is to turn their own intimacy into a politically charged tool that voices the migrant, who is otherwise uncritically perceived as a distant and unknown reality to most of their readership.
>
> (43)

He adds: "the figure of the son works in both cases as a mediator between the authors and their readers and allows them to use a patroni[s]ing and authoritative voice that would be discouraged otherwise" (Pomar-Amer 45). Critics of *Jo també soc catalana*, Michelle Murray and Cristián H. Ricci, underscore El Hachmi's relationship with what could be described as a Spanish-Moroccan borderlands identity; one that engages Catalan and Tamazight as minority languages (in Spain and Morocco respectively) to subvert traditional notions of transnational migration – and a resulting hybrid subject. Thinking specifically about this maternal role, and with an eye to the power dynamics that Pomar-Amer brings to light, we ought to consider how Agboton's choice of Axel and Didac as addressees and mediators between her and a Spanish readership similarly allows her to claim a unique position of authority.

A vital difference between Agboton's memoir and that of either El Hachmi or El Kadaoui is the way it speaks to the specificities of anti-Black racism. For, as Dani McClain insists (albeit in the American context), "Black mothers haven't had the luxury of sticking our heads in the sand and hoping that our children learn about race and power as they go. Instead, we must act as a buffer and translator between them and the world, beginning from their earliest days" (McClain). While El Hachmi and El Kadaoui attempt to navigate Spanish prejudice against people from the Maghreb by considering their children's belonging as demonstrative of their own, Agboton conceives of her children as the amalgam of two worldviews, Black and white, which European colonialism framed as "antipodal" (Agboton 64). At a distance from the maternal figures she refers to as *maestras* (teachers), she reminisces about having fearlessly

86 *Anna Tybinko*

formed her own methods of care regardless of whether "esos conocimientos adquiridos resultaban exóticos y extraños en la sociedad donde ahora vivía" ["this acquired knowledge seemed exotic and strange in the society where I now lived"] (Agboton 93).[7] These included singing lullabies in her native Gun to foster contact with the language and, most prominently, strapping the boys to her back so that she could go about her own work:

> Yo era muy joven, es cierto, y estaba en un país que me resultaba extraño, pero vosotros erais mestizos; África corría también por vuestras venas, y digámoslo todo, resulta mucho más cómodo y mucho más cálido, también en Europa, ocuparse de las cosas de casa, ir de un lado a otro con tu hijo bien pegado a tu piel, en vez de tenerlo siempre agarrado a tus faldas o dejarlo aparcado, en un rincón de la casa, en uno de esos 'parques' para niños.
>
> [I was young, it's true, and I was in an unfamiliar country, but you two were *mestizos*; África coursed through your veins too, and to be frank, it's so much more comfortable and warm-hearted – in Europe as well – to do things around that house or move around with your child firmly glued to your skin, instead of always clinging to your skirts or left parked in a corner of the house, in one those "play pens."]
>
> (Agboton 93)

This practice, she insists, was not only freeing; it helped her form a special bond with her sons. While she seems to feel it was an especially appropriate way of caring for Axel and Didac given their African heritage, she also casts it as more pragmatic. Could it therefore signal an important departure from the presiding Spanish model of mothering?

One of Andrea O'Reilly's principal contributions to the field of maternal scholarship is to highlight how the cultural construct of institutional motherhood has always stemmed from the presiding economic model. From the "Cult of True Womanhood" that produced the nineteenth century "Angel in the House " model (*ángel del hogar* in Spanish) to the 1950s housewife and the more recent "helicopter mom," the pressures on women to perform a certain role as mother have been determined by capitalist patriarchy.[8] In particular, O'Reilly focuses on the notions of sacrificial motherhood that emerged in the second half of the twentieth century as women were first forced to give up their wartime employment and then had to elbow their way back into the workforce during the following decades. The difference between the postwar period and today is that the stay-at-home-mom was more of a custodial approach in which childrearing was one of many household demands, whereas the recent privatization and government deregulation of social services like education, healthcare, recreation, and so on "downloaded" those responsibilities to mothers (O'Reilly 24). While normative discourses about motherhood have always banked on gender essentialism and the false biological assumption that women are somehow natural caregivers, this neoliberal iteration insists that "good mothers" spend quality time with their children – that they practice "intensive mothering," as O'Reilly calls it – all while balancing full-time employment. In the previous quote, Agboton does not shy away from remarking on the difficulties that becoming a mother at such a young age – and in a foreign country – imposed. In other instances, she exclaims about the financial burden, the stress of trying to obtain permanent residence,[9] or running home between classes to nurse as she tried to finish her degree in Spanish literature. At the same time, she expresses the satisfaction gleaned from the maternal bonds formed with her children and offers traditional African methods as an empowering alternative to Spain's predominant neoliberal model.

Central to O'Reilly's notion of empowered mothering is the idea that maternal practice is inherently an intellectual activity (O'Reilly 21). In *Más allá del mar de arena*, Agboton mothers through the act of writing, making her efforts legible to a much wider audience. For this reason, her memoir is perhaps better read in line with the intersectional figure of "community othermother" as described by Patricia Hill Collins. Collins insists that "the cooperative nature of child-care arrangements among bloodmothers and othermothers in Caribbean and other Black diasporic societies gives credence to the importance that people of African descent place on mothering" (*Black Feminist Thought*, 181). Collins is interested in how "fictive kin" can act as "othermothers" offering networks of care and support to "bloodmothers" and their children. However, she also explores how this extends into "mothering of the mind relationships" wherein Black women (in Collins' definition, although we could now apply this to anyone who identifies with the mother role regardless of their gender identity) seek to foster Black children, students, and protégés from the community at large (Collins, *Black Feminist Thought* 191). For Collins, "mothering of the mind" is core to Black women's political activism throughout the diaspora. I, therefore, argue that Agboton's memoir intentionally merges the intimacy of the maternal with her commitment as a public intellectual in a politically motivated act of othermothering. Indeed, as Collins elucidates elsewhere (and again, speaking to the specificities of the United States):

> Racial ethnic women's mothering and work experiences occur at the boundaries demarking these dualities. "Work for the day to come" is motherwork, whether it is on behalf of one's biological children, children of one's racial ethnic community, or children who are yet unborn.
>
> ("Shifting the Center" 372)

To better understand the implications of Agboton's motherwork, we must parse out exactly what she means by *mestizaje* (or racial mixing) – precisely

88 *Anna Tybinko*

because of her affinity for contradiction. The chapter "Ser o no ser . . . distinto" [To Be or Not To Be . . . Different] provides some clarity as she discusses her sons' experiences with racism in Spain, rather than her own. In the case of Didac, she stresses his observative nature and distanced, almost theoretical approach to his identity formation:

> A menudo me has dicho que el mestizaje no sólo supone una mezcla de sangres sino, también, un cúmulo de influencias tan heterogéneas que ni siquiera se puede intentar catalogarlas. Aunque tampoco es necesario. Estoy de acuerdo contigo cuando dices que, de hecho, te hacen mestizo los ojos de los demás.
>
> [Frequently you've told me that mestizaje is not just the mixing of blood, but also an accumulation of such heterogenous influence that they can't even be catalogued. Even though it's not necessary to try. I agree with you when you say that, in fact, you're made *mestizo* in the eyes of others.]
>
> (Agboton 104)

In this sense, *mestizaje* is relative and dependent on context. It's about being identified as different from those around you while also adapting to – or "appropriating" (as Agboton puts it) – the norms of your present environment.

In contrast, Axel is described as a gregarious child who more easily accepts "being educated between two cultures" (Agboton 106).[10] Agboton recalls an incident during a visit back to Benin when Axel was still small: "me comentaste muy extrañado que todo el mundo te llamaba *yovó*, 'blanco' en lengua gun, y que, en cambio, en Barcelona eras el *negritu*" [you mentioned to me, totally shocked, that everyone called you *yovó*, 'white' in Gun, and that, conversely, in Barcelona you were the *negritu*] (Agboton 106). While this is clearly an intimate moment shared between mother and son, it is also one of the few instances where Agboton reveals she is not just reviving this memory for Axel's sake. In the original Spanish, the word *yovó*, for white in Gun, and the word *negritu*, for black (or worse, "darkie") in Catalan, are written in italics, indicating that they are not Castilian Spanish. Yet, while the Gun (that Axel clearly understood at the time) is accompanied by a definition, the Catalan is not. It is through these small details that, while discussing Axel and Didac's multicultural background, it becomes clear that Agboton's anecdotes are also aimed at capturing the imagination of a Peninsular audience for the sake of vivifying the experience of miscegenation.

At one point, Agboton asks directly of her sons: "¿Soy una madre africana que vive en Barcelona? ¿Soy una madre barcelonesa de origen africano? No lo sé, y si queréis que os diga la verdad, me es indiferente. Soy una madre, eso sí. Vuestra madre" [Am I an African mother that lives in Barcelona? Am I Barcelonian mother of African origin? I don't know, and if you want me to tell you [plural] the truth, it's irrelevant to me. I'm

Mothering, Mestizaje *and the Future of Spain*   89

a mother, that's for sure. Your mother] (Agboton 99). These are anything but rhetorical questions; Agboton intentionally includes Axel and Didac in her own process of self-definition; the act of producing knowledge out of hybridity is a project that spans multiple generations.

Recent years have seen an outpouring of cultural production by Afro-diasporic Spaniards, many of them millennials like Axel and Didac. While some may have migrated to Spain in their lifetime, and others are the children of those who migrated earlier – others have no relationship with contemporary migration. It is, therefore, far from the unifying theme of this corpus. Instead, we can observe a collective effort to reimagine the politics of representation. This is at stake in an ever-growing number of non-fiction, autobiographical, or semi-autobiographical works such as Moha Gerehou's testimonial *¿Qué hace un negro como tú en un sitio como este?* [What's a Black Person Like You Doing in a Place Like This?] (2021) and Rubén H. Bermúdez's photobook *¿Y tú, por qué eres negro?* [And You, Why Are You Black?] (2019). The titles of these two works alone gesture towards the same sort of interrogation of race and belonging that Agboton underwent in her day, that Axel experienced as well, and that she turns back on her sons in the previous quotation. Bermúdez, for example, recalls being confronted about his racial identity, much like Axel: "La primera vez que alguien me llamó negro estaba en un mercado con mi abuela. Fue otro niño pequeño. Utilizó la palabra 'negrito'. Nadie me dijo nada; yo tampoco." [The first time someone called me "black," I was at a supermarket with my grandmother. It was another little boy. He actually used the word "darkie." Nobody said anything, neither did I] (14).[11] This piercing question (or microaggression) and the silence following it clearly serve as the impetus for Bermúdez's visual exploration of Blackness in Spain which, as he explains in the dedication, is composed of images that are either drawn from the "collective imaginary" or his own personal archive. We should also turn to the women artists and authors who are part of this boom in Afrodiasporic cultural production in Spain. While they are far from the only examples, two recent works by Lucía-Asué Mbomío Rubio and Desirée Bela-Lobedde are particularly pertinent here because they stress the importance of cultural referents for the process of identity formation. Mbomío Rubio's novel *Hija del camino* [Daughter of the Road] (2020) tells the fictional tale of Sandra Nnom, daughter of a Black Equatoguinean father and white Spanish woman (not unlike Mbomío Rubio), whose journey to self-discovery takes her from the Alcorcón area of Madrid to Malabo, Lisbon, and London. In a moment of reckoning, Sandra realizes that all the Black writers (many of them recommended to her by her father Antonio) that "han contribuido a llevarla hasta su yo actual" [had lead her to current self] are men and that she is desperately in need of Black women as role models (Mbomío Rubio 50). Bela-Lobedde's *Ser mujer negra en España* [Being a Black Woman in Spain] (2018) is autobiographical in nature and dedicates a chapter to this same

90 *Anna Tybinko*

issue. This chapter, "Referentes" [Role Models] discusses potential that possible venues and platforms for the diffusion of African and Afrodiasporic knowledge in Spanish. These range social media accounts and blogs to cultural spaces and dedicated bookstores like Deborah Ekoka's United Minds Libros in Valencia. As Bela-Lobedde concludes:

> Es nuestra obligación como madres y padres afrodescendientes conectar a nuestros peques con eso porque, tal y como reza el dicho: "Hasta que los leones no tengan sus propios historiadores, las historias de cacería seguirán glorificando al cazador".
>
> [It is our obligation as mothers and fathers of African descent to connect our kids with this [these resources] because, as the saying goes: "Until lions have their own historians, hunting stories will continue to glorify the hunter."]
>
> (Bela-Lobedde 141)

Neither woman cites Agboton directly but their work and that of Gerehou, Bermúdez, and more continues Agboton's "mothering of the mind" tradition, that is her mission to uphold Black life in contemporary Spain. At the same time, this next generation of cultural practitioners must refute designations like "mestizo" to claim belonging in Spain regardless of their family history or proximity to migration.

Notes

1. Unless otherwise noted, all translations into English are my own.
2. "Patera" refers to the small fishing boats or other unseaworthy vessels such as rafts that are used by migrants for clandestine transport across the Mediterranean or from the coasts of West Africa to the Spanish-held Canary Islands, although the word *cayuco* is also used in this instance.
3. I am using this designation in English a gesture toward Agboton's own choice of "mestizo/a" ("mixed race" or "multiracial") to describe her identity and that of her children.
4. Inmaculada Díaz Narbona says "Como no podía ser de otra manera, Agnès Agboton emprende el hecho de contarse en este libro de memorias, siguiendo el ritual de la oralidad: en primer lugar se dirige a su público (sus hijos), les muestra la utilidad de lo que les contará (parte de sus orígenes) e inicia su relato, el relato de su vida por donde lo hacen los griot, por la genealogía" [Since it couldn't be any other way, Agnès Agboton takes on the act of narration in these memories, following the ritual of orality: in the first place she addresses her public directly (her sons), she shows them the utility of what she will tell them (it's part of her origins) and she starts her story, the story of her life as the griots do, with a genealogy] (Díaz Narbona 11).
5. "Y mi país se convirtió en una colonia llamada Dahomey: el vientre de un rey había entrado en los atlas de geografía" [And my country became a colony called Dahomey: the stomach of a king managed to make it onto the geographical atlases] (Agboton 17).
6. These are Pomar-Amer's translations of the two titles, neither has been published in English.
7. "Os he llevado a ambos atados a la espalda, pegados a mi piel, como lo hacemos las madres en África, aunque eso, en una Barcelona que no era la ciudad de inmigración que es hoy, despertara cierta sorpresa cuando los amigos venían a visitarnos a casa" [I carried you both strapped to my back,

Mothering, Mestizaje and the Future of Spain 91

adhered to my skin, like we mothers do in Africa, even though, in Barcelona, which was not yet the city of immigration that it is today, that caused certain surprise when friends came to visit us at home] (93).

8. "Ángel del hogar" [angel of the hearth] refers to the idealized Spanish homemaker. The evolution of these stereotyped gender roles is different in Spain than in the Anglophone context O'Reilly is speaking to and has generated its own body of research in Spanish literary and cultural studies. For example, Bridget Aldaraca's *El Ángel del Hogar: Galdós and the Ideology of Domesticity in Spain* explores the emergence of the term in the nineteenth century in terms of the spiritualization of women's labor by the Catholic Church. Moving into the twentieth century, Gabrielle Miller addresses the uneven transition from the figure of "ángel del hogar" to the supposedly liberated "nueva mujer moderna" under the Second Spanish Republic (1931–1936) in her reading of empowered mothering in Mercè Rodereda's *La plaza del diamante*.

9. See sections like:"De hecho, las únicas preocupaciones que teníamos eran de tipo económico. ¡Cómo nos costaba llegar a fin de mes!" ["In fact, the only worries we had were of the economic sort. It was so difficult to make it to the end of the month!] (Agboton 79). And in regards to the legal processes: "El asunto del permiso de residencia era también un dolor de cabeza, y cuando se acercaba el momento de renovarlo, sólo con pensar en las inmensas colas que se formaban en la Jefatura de Policía de Via Laietana y, más tarde, en la comisaría de la Plaza España, se me revolvían las tripas. Eran días muy penosos, para mí y para mis compañeros de infortunio" [The issue of attaining permanent residence was also a headache, and when the time neared to renew my permit, just thinking about the immense lines that formed outside police headquarters on Via Laietana and, later, at the station in the Plaza de España, made my stomach turn] (Agboton 79).

10. It can seem as though Agboton greets Axel's outlook with more approval: "De todos modos, te resultó mucho más fácil que a tu hermano admitir que habías crecido entre dos formas de vida, que tenías un padre blanco y una madre negra, y que eso te hacía una persona distinta ante los ojos de los demás" [Anyway, it was much easier for you than for your brother to admit that you had grown up between two lifestyles, that you had a white father and a black mother, and that this made your different in other people's eyes] (Agboton 106). To this she adds: "Presumes de sentirte educado entre dos culturas, de sentirte al mismo tiempo occidental y africano. Y me gusta que eso te enorgullezca porque, aunque las circunstancias del nacimiento no deben ser motivo de orgullo, cierto es que has tenido la suerte de ser el heredero de un patrimonio de culturas muy distintas" [You boast of feeling educated between two cultures, about feelings Western and African at the same time. And I like that this makes you proud because, even though the circumstances of one's birth shouldn't be a cause of pride, it's true that you've had the fortune of being the heir of the cultural patrimony of two very different cultures] (Agboton 106).

11. Both quotations are from *¿Y tú, por qué eres negro?/And You, Why Are You Black?* which is captioned in Castilian Spanish and English.

Works Cited

Agboton, Agnès. *Más allá del mar de arena*. 2nd ed., Verbum, 2018.

Aldaraca, Bridget A. *El Ángel del Hogar: Galdós and the Ideology of Domesticity in Spain*. University of North Carolina Press, 1991.

92 Anna Tybinko

Andersson, Ruben. *Illegality, Inc.: Clandestine Migration and the Business of Bordering Europe*. U of California P, 2014.

Bela-Lobedde, Desirée. *Ser mujer negra en España*. Penguin Random House Grupo Editorial, 2018.

Bermúdez, Rubén H. *¿Y tú, por qué eres negro?/And You, Why Are You Black?* Phree & Motto Books, 2019.

Bermúdez, Silvia. "Rocking the Boat: The Black Atlantic in Spanish Pop Music from the 1980s and the '90s." *Arizona Journal of Hispanic Cultural Studies*, vol. 5, 2001, pp. 177–193.

Borst, Julia. "Tropos de transculturalidad en la obra de Agnès Agboton." *Transafrohispanismos: puentes culturales críticos entre Africa, latinoamerica y españa*, edited by Dorothy Odartey-Wellington, Brill Rodopi, 2018, pp. 169–189.

Collins, Patricia Hill. "Shifting the Center: Race, Class, and Feminist Theorizing about Motherhood." *Representations of Motherhood*, edited by Donna Bassin and Margaret Honey, Yale UP, 1994, pp. 371–389.

———. *Black Feminist Thought: Knowledge, Consciousness, and the Politics of Empowerment*. Taylor & Francis, 2000.

Díaz Narbona, Inmaculada. "Presentación." *Más allá del mar de arena*. Lumen, 2005.

Gallego, Mar. "Gender, Migration and Identity: Agnès Agboton's *Canciones del poblado y del exilio*." *Migrations and Gendered Subjects: Colonial and Postcolonial Representations of the Female Body*, edited by Silvia Castro Borrego and Maria Isabel Romero Ruiz, Cambridge Scholars Publishing, 2011, pp. 75–98.

———. "On Both Sides of the Atlantic: Hybrid Identity and the Spanish Speaking Diaspora in Agnès Agboton, Monica Carrillo and Eulalia Bernard." *Migration, Narration, Identity: Cross Cultural Perspectives*, edited by Peter Leese et al., Peter Lang, 2012.

———. "Integración e hibridez en *Más alla del mar de arena de Agnès Agboton*." *Afroeuropean Cartographies*, edited by Dominic Thomas, Cambridge Scholars Publishing, 2014, pp. 71–82.

———. *A ambas orillas del Atlántico: Geografías de hogar y diáspora en autoras afrodescendientes*. KRK Ediciones, 2016.

García de Vinuesa, Maya. "Agnès Agboton: Self-Translation and Intercultural Mediation." *Afroeurope@n Configurations: Readings and Projects*, edited by Sabrina Brancato, Cambridge Scholars Publisher, 2011, pp. 210–222.

———. "Autotraducción literaria de una orilla a otra del Mediterráneo: Agnès Agboton Entrevistada por Maya G. Vinuesa." *VERTERE: Monográficos de La Revista Hermēneus*, edited by Ingrid Cáceres Würsig and María Jesús Fernández-Gil, vol. La traducción literaria a finales del siglo XX y principios del XXI: hacia las disolución de fronteras, no. 21, 2019, pp. 281–292.

Gerehou Gerewu, Moha. *¿Qué hace un negro cómo tú en un sitio cómo este?* Ediciones Península, 2021.

El Hachmi, Najat. *Jo també soc catalana*. Columna, 2004.

El Kadaoui Moussaoui, Saïd. *Cartes al meu fill: Un català de soca-rel, gairebé*. Ara Llibres, 2011.

Mbomío Rubio, Lucía Asué. *Hija del camino*. Penguin Random House Grupo Editorial, 2019.

McClain, Dani. "As a Black Mother, My Parenting Is Always Political," Mar. 2019, *The Nation* www.thenation.com/article/archive/black-motherhood-family-parenting-dani-mcclain/.

Miller, Gabrielle. "Institutionalized Motherhood and Maternal Practice in Mercè Rodoreda's *La plaza del Diamante.*" *Revista de Estudios Hispánicos*, vol. 53, no. 3, 2019, pp. 855–878, https://doi.org/10.1353/rvs.2019.0070.

Muñoz Comet, Jacobo. *Inmigración y empleo en España: de la expansión a la crisis económica*. CIS, Centro de Investigaciones Sociológicas, 2016.

N'gom, M'bare. "Writing, Migration and Identity in African Hispanic Literature." *Afroeurope@ns: Cultures and Identities*, edited by Marta Sofía López Rodríguez, Cambridge Scholars, 2008, pp. 79–107.

O'Reilly, Andrea. "Maternal Theory: Patriarchal Motherhood and Empowered Mothering." *The Routledge Companion to Motherhood*, edited by Lynn O'Brien Hallstein and Andrea O'Reilly. Routledge, 2020, pp. 19–35.

Pomar-Amer, Miquel. "Voices Emerging from the Border. A Reading of the Autobiographies by Najat El Hachmi and Saïd El Kadaoui as Political Interventions." *Planeta Literatur: Journal of Global Literary Studies*, Jan. 2014, pp. 33–52.

Ricci, Cristián H. "African Voices in Contemporary Spain." *New Spain, New Literatures*, edited by Luis Martín-Estudillo and Nicholas Spadaccini, Vanderbilt UP, 2010, pp. 203–231.

———. "The Reshaping of Postcolonial Iberia: Moroccan and Amazigh Literatures in the Peninsula." *Hispanófilo*, vol. 180, 2017, pp. 21–40.

Rich, Adrienne. *Of Woman Born: Motherhood as Experience and Institution*. Bantam Books, 1977.

Tybinko, Anna. "Decolonizing the Metropole: The Born-Translated Works of Najat El Hachmi and Agnès Agboton as Literary Activism." *Studies in 20th & 21st Century Literature*, vol. 46, no. 1, Jan. 2022, https://doi.org/10.4148/2334-4415.2210.

Vega-Durán, Raquel. *Emigrant Dreams, Immigrant Borders: Migrants, Transnational Encounters, and Identity in Spain*. Bucknell UP, 2016.

Part II
Portugal

6 Black Migration, Citizenship, and Racial Capital in Post-Imperial Portugal

Daniel F. Silva

Much critical attention to Black artistic and literary work in Portugal since the 1980s has importantly shed light on how such interventions challenge ongoing narratives of Portuguese imperial history shaped by claims to racial exceptionalism, most notably those synthesized and expounded upon by Gilberto Freyre, such as Lusotropicalism (*O Luso e o Trópico*). Beyond, yet still attentive to, these narratives and dominant historiographies, Black cultural producers in Portugal have gauged these while situating their experiences of systemic racism in Portugal into longer histories of coloniality and racial capitalism. In the process, these producers – and as such, theorists and activists – propose radical revisions of the interwoven matrices of Portuguese nationality-making and anti-Blackness – while laboring toward and situating themselves within broader Black diasporic epistemologies and world-making. To this end, this chapter will put in conversation works from distinct cultural genres such as Telma Tvon's novel, *O preto mais português* [The Most Portuguese Black Man] (2018) and rap artist Valete's "Quando o sorriso morre" ["When the Smile Dies"] (2012).

These works propose alternate and emerging counter-hegemonic historiographies of Portuguese colonialism and coloniality more broadly that contextualize postcolonial African migration to the metropolis into a longer history of the transatlantic slave trade and the Portuguese state's dominant role in it, the trafficking of enslaved African people into the metropolis, and the long-durée mechanisms of colonial extraction. In this regard, we can understand the works to be examined as placing the contemporary economic and cultural structures of anti-Blackness in Portugal as part of what Cedric Robinson theorized as "racial capitalism" (2–3). Here, Robinson argues: "The development, organization, and expansion of capitalist society pursued essentially racial directions, so too did social ideology. As a material force, then, it could be expected that racialism would inevitably permeate the social structures emergent from capitalism" (2). Through this framework, racial capitalism is both a system of racialized micro and macroeconomic relations, as well as, in

DOI: 10.4324/9781003245117-9

98 *Daniel F. Silva*

the intellectual hands of historians and theorists, a theorization of global power relations ushered in through the processes of European consolidation and expansion. In modern world systems, participation in racial capitalism has become a global phenomenon across nation-states, as Jodi Melamed surmises, underscoring "the complex recursivity between material and epistemic forms of racialized violence which are executed in and by core capitalist states with seemingly infinite creativity" (77).

In his tome on the emergence of Black radical traditions, Robinson also carefully charts the emergence of capitalism as an always-already racialized endeavor spanning European feudalism and the forced labor of religiously and ethnically minoritized groups and communities within Europe. In this regard, and making Melamed's theorization ring true, the emergence of racial categories as epistemological ways of differentiating peoples as exploitable was always a fluid mechanism, with racializing processes developed and deployed at different stages of capital and empire. In this process of becoming an economic center in an ever-expanding world system based on imperial expansion, the concept of Europe emerged as a geopolitical, cultural, religious, and ultimately racial entity. Robinson pays particular attention to these processes at work in the emergence of Portuguese statehood and, later, its expansion into the Al-Gharb and eventually into Africa. Portuguese imperial expansion beyond the imagined borders of Europe, as well as the imperial projects of other European states, concomitantly usurped lands, markets, and bodies, and in the process, reified racial divisions between Europe, Africa, Asia, and the Americas – divisions that simultaneously ascribed labor roles in the burgeoning of capitalism and laid the groundwork for settler-colonial societies around the globe.

Following the dissolution of colonial settler societies in Africa and Asia following World War II, the racial rhetoric and imperial epistemologies surrounding Europeanness continue to circulate in the contemporary moment of capital. The formation of the European Union, the opening of borders in the Schengen Area, and especially African and Asian migratory patterns into Europe have accompanied and sustained the recycling of such discourses equating whiteness with Europeanness. The influx of African and Asian migrants in Europe, spurred on by the material legacies of colonialism and neocolonial political destabilization in the Global South, has been the catalyst of conservative and wider mainstream proclamations of the European crisis – threatening the phantasmatic fixity of European whiteness. This has translated into European Union political pressures to either oblige southern European states to impose more robust border controls along the Mediterranean (acting as Fortress Europe) or revoke the Schengen agreement, which integrated southern Europe into the borderless European economic zone.

In light of these imperial legacies of European anti-Blackness, Black bodies are seldom posited as Portuguese, but as an outside other – occupying

Black Migration, Citizenship, and Racial Capital in Portugal 99

the hegemonically articulated site of "migrant" – situated within a particular imperial spectrum of racialized power and division of labor; a continual binary opposition to the centuries-long historicization of Portuguese nationhood. The Portuguese nation-building process has been based on expansion and the discourses of alterity that have underpinned it in overlapping periods of Portuguese continental consolidation and transcontinental occupation – anti-Castilianness, anti-Arabness, anti-semitism, anti-blackness, and the envisioning of Europeanness as a geographic, philosophical, cultural, institutional, and political embodiment of these. These can be found in a wide breadth of cultural and political artifacts foundational to Portuguese imperial nation-building up to current waves of literature of colonial nostalgia and contemporary visual media.

In this regard, Portuguese race relations continue to be informed by the imperial circuitries and mediated histories of national identity that operate via a long material, textual, political, and corporal field of meaning in which Black bodies have served as objects of particular forms of national production. Moreover, within this everyday discursive and historical fabric, Black bodies, and non-European bodies more broadly, are signified, surveilled, and consumed in post-imperial race relations; while liminally integrated into fraught narratives of contemporary multicultural nationhood. The disparate meanings surrounding Black bodies in European societies lay bare the various textualities and imageries that have been latched onto these bodies throughout the development and reproduction of Portuguese imperial narratives – which continue to render Black people in Portugal as ambivalent citizens of the nation-state. In this sense, the term "migrant" – often applied to, or implied for, second or third-generation immigrants – speaks to the space occupied of flexible in/exclusion that envelops such bodies as well as the experience of stripped citizenship lived through institutional violence, barred access to the neoliberal webs of social mobility, and myriad forms of cultural marginalization (from stadiums to literature).

Within the imperial continuities that mark metropolitan society, full access to citizenship is quotidianly denied as the Black body has historically been a central corporal object over which the notion of Portuguese (and European) citizenship has been produced through empire. Through many roles and facets, Black bodies have served as objects of production for the imperial schema of Portuguese nationhood and citizenship within the development of racial capitalism. These include the economic and cultural instrumentalization of Black bodies as labor tools of accumulation, as labor-driven commodities in the Atlantic slave trade (which was a central focus of Portuguese imperial endeavor on a market level as well as colonial settlement). Related, and indeed intrinsic to these, the production of Portuguese Europeanness and national claims to whiteness have been imperially contingent upon the constructed inferiority and colonizability of African bodies, lands, and commodities. Throughout the different epochs of Portuguese imperial nation-building, Black bodies have been sites of not only economic pleasure (accumulation) but also of intertwined corporal fantasies and pleasures for imperialist subjects and audiences – sexual, sporting, culinary, among others – tied to the varied discourses of excess and deficit that have been placed on such bodies.

In her illuminating critical ethnography of African migrant life and labor in the late twentieth and early twenty-first century Lisbon, Kesha Fikes theorizes the consumption of Black migrant labor in Portuguese society (guided by a migrant/citizen dichotomy and racial paradigm of power) as rendering their bodies as "migrants for citizens" (7). According to Fikes's analysis, this racialized consumption of migrant bodies and labor (especially Cape Verdean female fishmongers, "peixeiras") is grounded in recent processes of Portuguese Europeanization following the formal end of empire, specifically its entrance into the European Economic Community in 1986. The racialization of Cape Verdean female labor, despite operating in proximity to white Portuguese female laborers, "had assumed a 'rightful,' socially productive role as appendages to Portuguese civilians and thus as catalysts for appearances of European modernity" (7). This post-imperial Portuguese Europeanness thus implied revised paradigms of white European subjectivity – "the ideal of the Portuguese citizen became synonymous with a picture of middle-classness" (7) and with greater participation in neoliberal modes of consumption. More broadly, the post-imperial influx of low-wage racialized labor – one that signals a new stage of racial capital and colonial relations – came to stage Portuguese nationhood's shift, as Fikes crucially underscores, "from an *e*migrant to an *im*migrant nation" (8), from one whose economic marginality in the world system at the turn of the twentieth century obliged its (white) citizens to enter racialized divisions of labor abroad in complex ways (Almeida, Bastos, Castelo) to a national economy based on white middle-class life. Migrant bodies are thus corporal sites against which neoliberal bourgeois national life is imagined after empire, as well as material sites of economic exploitability to be extracted for an emerging national system of accumulation.

Fikes's critical study sets us on an urgent theoretical track in the critical examination of racial power and racialization in contemporary Portugal, one that urges us to consider the relationships between anti-Black discourses pertaining to African migrants, the racial idea of Europe, and the global flows of postcolonial labor forces into metropolitan Europe. Piecing these together will help us elucidate today's misrecognized machinery of racial capitalism and coloniality and how they operate in metropolitan Portugal and Europe decades after the settler-colonial empire. In this regard, anti-Black discourses, violence, and surveillance exercised by the state or sanctioned by its white supremacist culture is directly tied to the ongoing colonial operation of rendering exploitable surplus labor; thus reproducing accurate Ruth Wilson Gilmore's concise diagnosis that

Black Migration, Citizenship, and Racial Capital in Portugal 101

"capitalism requires inequality, and racism enshrines it" ("Geographies," 1:40–1:41). In other words, anti-Black discourses in the political sphere and anti-Black violence on the ground must be understood in the context of the ongoing need of the Portuguese state and state-sanctioned capitalist enterprises to reproduce precarious racialized labor forces.

Valete and the Global Terrains of Racial Capital

Along these lines, several Black Portuguese cultural producers epistemologically intervene, laying bare the connections between systemic anti-Black racism; notions of a white Europe; the reinvention of colonial racial divisions of labor; and the historical continuities of coloniality underpinning, and underpinned by, migratory flows into Europe. In the process, such works reframe "post-imperial" Portugal as not merely a body politic and discursive terrain grappling with the legacies and narratives of an imperial past but more importantly as a set of material structures (economic, political, and cultural) that are grounded in the racial and gendered logics and mechanisms of coloniality.

This is especially rendered legible and knowable in the music of Portuguese rapper Valete. Born Keidje Lima in Lisbon in 1981 to Angolan and São Toméan parents, Valete makes these connections particularly clear in his 2012 song titled "Quando o Sorriso Morre" ["When the Smile Dies"]. His lyrics make the trans-temporal and trans-spatial connection between Portuguese colonial settlement in Africa, formal decolonization, post-independence economic precarity, African migration to the former metropolis, and metropolitan exploitation of this migrant labor force stripped of institutional rights. The song begins with the moment of euphoria surrounding independence:

> O colonialismo acabou
> Independência
> Os tugas já se foram, bro
> A terra é nossa.
> [Colonialism finished
> Independence
> The Portuguese left, bro
> The land is ours.]
>   (00:11–00:15)

The euphoria, though, makes way to disenchantment stemming from the crumbling of colonial infrastructure following the mass exodus of white colonial high-skilled labor, from which Black residents were barred.

> Já não há empregos
> Médicos nem professors

Não há quadros formados
Não temos doutores. (nada)
Não há comércio, não há serviços
Não há nada
Os tugas bazaram
Deixaram toda a gente condenada.

[There are no longer jobs
Doctors nor teachers
No more skilled labor
We have no doctors. (nothing)
There are no businesses, no services
There is nothing
The Portuguese left
They left us all damned.]
(00:33–00:45)

Valete dialogues here with Amílcar Cabral's warning during the anti-colonial armed struggle, thus positing the fight against colonialism as one to be carried out long after independence, that colonialism always leaves the necessary conditions for neocolonialism (*Revolution* 128). Valete goes on to highlight that the precarity left by Portuguese colonial structures of racial marginalization and exploitation has translated into an exploitable labor force in both the postcolony as well as in the former metropolis in the shape of migrant labor.

Passada história
Eles são nossos amigos agora
Emigra para Portugal
E começa uma vida nova
Aquilo é Europa
Lá todos vivem bem
Sai desta miséria
Vai e tenta ser alguém.

[That history is over
The Portuguese are our friends now
Migrate to Portugal
And begin a new life
That is Europe
Over there everyone lives well
Escape from this misery
Go make yourself into someone.]
(1:01–1:12)

Black Migration, Citizenship, and Racial Capital in Portugal 103

The promise and illusion of a better life in a prosperous Europe, packaged as such by colonial educational apparatuses, soon become a nightmare of ongoing coloniality.

Isto é Lisboa
Não há sol todos os dias
Muito cimento
Flora só em fotografias
Tens compatriotas a construirem
vilas que eles chamam ghettos
Vai viver ao pé deles
Eles têm os teus enredos

Tugas dizem que
não podes ter outro desenlace
Para além dos trabalhos precários
Porque só tens a quarta classe
[. . .]
Entras às sete horas
Sais quando o sol se ausenta
Vais para a tormenta diária
Que todo o africano enfrenta.

[This is Lisbon
Not all days are sunny
Very gray
Only flowery in photos.
You have compatriots building
villages that they call ghettos
Go live close to them
They have the script you are to follow.

The Portuguese say that you
have no other way
aside from precarious work
Because you only have a fourth-grade education
[. . .]
You start work at 7 am
You leave when the sun leaves
You go through the daily torment
That every African faces.]

(1:29–2:09)

The implied African migrant character in the song's lyrics is more than a persona but also an epistemology that revises dominant metropolitan

104   *Daniel F. Silva*

historiographies guilty of proposing facile periodizations of colonial settlement, decolonization, and independence. The song consistently repeats "o colonialismo acabou" ["colonialism has ended"] to articulate the absurdity and theoretical insufficiency of hegemonic historicization that posits colonialism as something that abruptly ends. Instead, it is a political, cultural, economic reality and series of mechanisms that are reinvented with periods building on one another rather than erasing one another.

Valete's lyrics and the implied ontology of an African migrant laborer in Portugal effectively elucidate the conditions of the current period of coloniality and capital, particularly the former metropolis's reinvention of its role in global capital via the opportunistic reproduction of labor surplus in the wake of colonial decay in the postcolony. In this sense, his musical intervention epistemologically intervenes in a Portuguese public sphere shaped and reproduced through the materiality of colonial accumulation and ongoing exploitation as well as through continued narratives of imperial exceptionalism. In the face of a societal reality that reenacts colonial logics of stripping humanity from Black life into exploitable labor, "When the Smile Dies" also leaves space for and ends with a call to everyday survival for Black lives in Portugal. The song's final appeal, "Mano, sorrie/enquanto a vida corre/porque um africano morre/quando seu sorriso morre" ["Brother, smile/while life goes on/because an African dies/when his smile dies"] reads less like a trapping into colonial stereotypes of Black joy, but rather a reclamation/reinvention of humanity in the face of dehumanizing mechanisms.

"Remixing" the Citizen/Migrant Distinction

A recent literary piece that consistently fleshes out the racialized citizen/migrant dichotomy while also enacting a reclamation of humanity in contemporary Portugal is Telma Tvon's *Um Preto Muito Português* [A Very Portuguese Black Man], published in 2018. Before the publication of this novel, her debut publication in the literary world, Tvon first pursued a musical passion as a Hip Hop artist, and she continues to be active in this realm. She was born in Luanda, Angola, in 1980 and emigrated to Portugal in 1993, settling in Lisbon where she would go on to earn a bachelor's degree in African studies as well as a master's degree in sociology from the University of Lisbon. *Um Preto Muito Português* is noteworthy not only because it is Tvon's first literary publication but mainly because of the book's close relationship to Hip Hop epistemologies. In fact, in interviews ahead of the novel's release, Tvon revealed that the book's concept initially started as a song she had begun to write and which served as an interrogation into the complexities and everyday material challenges of Black Portuguese identity (Matos, n.p.). In this regard, the novel's relationship to Hip Hop is particularly important given the emergence of the cultural movement (spanning music, art, and dance) in Portugal and

Black Migration, Citizenship, and Racial Capital in Portugal   105

beyond during the growing influx of African immigrants into Portugal following official decolonization in Angola, Cape Verde, Guinea-Bissau, Mozambique, and São Tomé and Príncipe.

The emergence of Hip Hop aesthetics and knowledge formations overlaps with the particular and "on the ground" exigencies faced by different communities of the African Diaspora in the late 1970s and early 1980s. Hip Hop emerged specifically in Afro-Caribbean and African American communities of New York City following the Civil Rights struggles of the previous decade, the urban ruination of white flight, red-lining, the transition to a post-industrial U.S. economy, and the global rise of neoliberalism. Nonetheless, Hip Hop would reverberate among Black youth cultures the world over, offering a critical lexicon and aesthetic of resistance as paradigms of colonial power and its exercise shifted following the official end of settler colonialism in Africa and Asia. In this regard, for Black youth in Portugal, largely unrepresented in the public sphere and visible in Portuguese national imaginaries mainly as formerly colonized beings and racial others, Hip Hop represented a terrain of cultural production through which Black residents in Portugal could produce meanings and knowledge formation pertaining to systemic racism in the former metropolis while partaking in Black diasporic worldmaking.

The very title of Tvon's novel signals this work, especially in reference to identitarian inquiry in the context of the relationship between Blackness and Portugueseness, and the novel is narrated by the titular character, who identifies himself as João Moreira Tavares but is known to friends and family by his nickname, Budjurra. He also refers to himself often in the third person using the latter name. Throughout the text and his life narrated therein, organized like a journal of daily vignettes written by the titular narrator, João navigates the materialities of racial capital in contemporary Portugal as a young Black man, born in Lisbon of Cape Verdean parents. More specifically, João's narrated trajectory through the social terrains of anti-Blackness in Portugal pays particular attention to a racial division of labor that situates Black bodies as working-class migrants in opposition to bourgeois whiteness as the epitome of Portuguese citizenship. He confronts these discourses and structures of racial and economic conflation as part of a lower-middle-class that achieved access to higher education and aspiring to white-collar labor. João, the narrator, makes this clear from the outset:

> Não vivo num daqueles bairros a que eles chamam de problemáticos mas eu sou um ser deveras problemático. Sou problemático porque não me enquadro em nenhum dos cenários que as estatísticas me querem meter. Eu *até* me licenciei, eu *até* falo o português conveniente. Ninguém sabe como lidar comigo, não se sabe se eu sou Preto o suficiente ou se ando a tentar por Branco inconscientemente.

106 *Daniel F. Silva*

[I do not live in one of those communities they call problematic, but I am truly a problematic being. I am problematic because I do not fit into any of the categories into which the statistics look to place me. I *even* earned my bachelor's and speak "correct" European Portuguese. No one knows how to deal with me; they do not know if I am sufficiently Black or unconsciously trying to pass as white.]

(5)

In this regard, he navigates and tries to narrate himself in relation to the racial, economic, and institutional structures of contemporary metropolitan Portugal as well as the racial discourses that surround his body, his presupposed knowledges, and his use of language.

As a result, his relationship to the citizen/migrant distinction brings its own complications that, nonetheless, lay bare the reality that birthplace is trumped by racialization when it comes to where he falls in this duality. Though he was born in self-made housing on the outskirts of Lisbon, João's parents decided to move the family (including his two siblings) to a private housing complex (8). Additionally, he is often situationally placed as separated from fellow Black colleagues and friends that were born in Africa and immigrated to Portugal. For instance, soon after entering college, following a party for first-year students, a white fellow student approaches him happily and declares, "Ó João, tu até que és bacano. Não tens nada a ver com os pretos que moram ao pé de mim" ["Oh, João, you are actually cool. You are nothing like the Blacks that live close to me"] (11).

Nonetheless, he is always interpellated by white Portuguese people as a migrant and seldom as a citizen. In this regard, he cites white nationalist rhetoric that dismisses the existence of Black Portuguese people, including those born in Portugal. He offers the following comparison that: "É curioso que ninguém diz a um português que tem pais espanhóis ou alemães que não é português" ["Interestingly, no one tells a Portuguese person who has Spanish or German parents that they are not Portuguese"] (10). He later relates coming across only one white Portuguese person that included him in the enunciation of "este é nosso país" ["this is our country"] (110) when discussing the difficulty of finding white-collar employment in Portugal and the possible alternative of moving abroad. In the face of this ongoing racial citizen/migrant distinction that structures social realities, João, despite his sometimes situationally ambiguous position, makes his racial and political stance clear from the outset and as he navigates quotidian and structural instances of state and popular aggression. When reflecting on the racial division of the school classroom in his youth, in which most Black students, migrants from Africa, would sit in the back of the class, he clarifies: "Mas eu nunca me esqueci de que o meu lugar era junto ao deles" ["But I never forgot that my place was among them"] (8).

Black Migration, Citizenship, and Racial Capital in Portugal   107

Although João tacitly believes that racism can somehow be resolved and surpassed in immediate reality, he is often confronted with the stark realization that racism is not merely a social phenomenon but a structuring force in the current terrains of capitalism. On this point, and despite his fleeting optimism, many passages read like Frantz Fanon's masterpiece on colonial discourse and the everyday psychic terrains of anti-Blackness, *Black Skin, White Masks*, published in 1952, in which he also circulates. Throughout the novel and in daily interactions, João feels the psychic and societal weight of his racialization and the impossibility of justice, from the perception that the challenges of his Black classmates born in Africa become inscribed on him to the actual institutional consequences of this racialization. This includes the quotidian challenge of finding a job as a young Black man in a job market flooded with unemployed white college graduates, as well as being caught in the infamous *arrastão* of Carcavelos beach in 2005.

As in the novel, during a summer day, as usual, the beach in the upscale coastal municipality of Cascais was bustling with beachgoers, many of whom were Black. That day, the police received reports of various thefts occurring on the beach by supposedly a large group of Black perpetrators. Chaos ensued with armed police officers evacuating the coast and detaining a large number of Black beachgoers. Panic in the media quickly followed, with various news outlets reporting on the incident in fear of a crime wave being carried out by Black populations in Portugal. The very term *arrastão*, meaning a large-scale and simultaneous coordinated robbery of many people, was profoundly racialized, having been the name given to cases of robberies on beaches in Rio de Janeiro – spaces of white middle-class and upper-class leisure coming under threat by Black bodies. It was later uncovered, through numerous interviews with beachgoers and police reports that, aside from a minor altercation on the beach, there were no robberies, and what had triggered the panic of the white population present that day in Carcavelos was the mere presence of Black youth on the beach, with some running as they played and subsequently being profiled as potential criminals. In the wake of the phantom *arrastão*, both the racialized media language surrounding the incident and the outcry of right-wing groups and politicians calling for a "Portugal para os portugueses" ["Portugal for the Portuguese"] operated through and reproduced the citizen/migrant distinction that orders labor and life in contemporary Portugal. The incident underscores, moreover, the mechanisms of racial capital in Portugal after empire, with policing and surveillance (by the state and the broader populace) informed by racial discourses of deviance and national (un)belonging, as well as numerous forms of anti-Black employment practices, especially in white-collar/high-skilled labor, operating as simple forms of reproducing surplus labor.

Against the grain of the citizen/migrant distinction, João seeks alternative ways of narrating and placing himself as Black and Portuguese

108 *Daniel F. Silva*

vis-à-vis the long history of coloniality and capitalism, as well as within histories of Black diasporic resistance and aesthetics. This is most notable in the second-to-last chapter of the novel, titled "De Cabral a Budjurra" ["From Cabral to Budjurra"]:

> Porque sou filho de Cabral pois eu sinto que "O importante não é ser forte, é sentir-se forte" e como eu me sinto forte, porque sou filho de Mandela, porque sou filho da Nzinga Mbandi, porque sou filho de Zumbi. Sou na tez, sou na aceitação do que sou, sou porque eles me querem como filho, como semente, como vida e continuação. Sou alegria de um batuque que de dia dorme na mentira duma sociedade evoluída e de noite vive e respira uma verdade entorpecida pelo nectar da ilusão que eu não escolhi para mim.
>
> [Because I am the son of Cabral, I agree that "what matters is not being strong, it is feeling oneself be strong, and I feel strong, because I am the son of Mandela, because I am the son of Nzinga Mbandi, because I am the son of Zumbi. I am this in complexion, accepting what I am because they want me as a son, as a seed, life, and continuity. I am the happiness of a batuque that sleeps during the day in the lie of an evolved society and lives during the night breathing a torpid truth through the nectar of the illusion that I never chose for myself.]
>
> (181)

By the end of his journal, João's hopes for change are dashed by an almost dystopian realization that white supremacy is more than a set of attitudes held by a portion of society.

He thus looks to anchor his future resistance and resilience in a genealogy of Black anti-colonial struggle that also serves as a cognitive temporal map through which he can articulate his Portugueseness. In the process, he delinks Portugueseness from whiteness through a critical lexicon once again influenced by Hip Hop: "Sou um remix do Carlos do Carmo com a Cesária Évora que acabou por dar num Boss AC" ["I am a remix of Carlos do Carmo with Cesária Évora that produced a Boss AC"] (181). The sentence more specifically evokes the national discourses surrounding Portuguese Fado music (in the form of singer Carlos do Carmo) and Cape Verdean Morna (in the form of singer Cesária Évora), as well as the blend and escape of these in the form of rapper Boss AC, artist name of Ângelo César do Rosário Firmino, born in Mindelo, Cape Verde and moving to Portugal as a child where he has resided since and established his career. João evokes Boss AC, therefore, as an example of imagining selfhood and aesthetics beyond both the dichotomy of Cape Verdeanness and Portugueseness and, most importantly, beyond the citizen/migrant dichotomy. As such, this particular enunciation is ultimately one of self-reinvention, both individual and collective. In the spirit of Hip Hop, this reinvention is practiced through the ruins consistently produced by racial capitalism.

Black Migration, Citizenship, and Racial Capital in Portugal   109

Like Hip Hop's improvised and inventive recycling of instruments, existing songs, scrap materials, and buildings into art forms that reclaim space, body, and community, João's fashioning of Black Portugueseness in this way recircuits the lives and trajectories of the three names evoked into his self- and worldmaking process.

Grounded in Hip Hop in this way, it is no surprise, then, that the final chapter in the novel is entirely composed of the lyrics of Black Portuguese rapper Gutto's song "Ser Negro" ["Being Black"] (2009). Gutto, born Augusto Armada in Luanda in 1972, emigrated with his family to Lisbon in 1974 following independence, and where he has resided ever since. A pioneer of Hip Hop in Portugal in the late 1980s, Gutto's song is an anthem of Black collective self-invention in the face of anti-Black discourses and histories. By closing the novel in this way, João and Tvon arguably deploy the song's lyrical content as the epistemological and ontological frame through which the ongoing dismantling of the racial citizen/migrant distinction, as well as liberatory enunciation of self, are carried out.

Rethinking the Human in Racial Capital

Both Tvon and Valete's respective works labor against what Christina Sharpe, in *In the Wake* (2016), has pointed out as racial capital and white supremacy's "calculus of dehumaning" (73), while signifying the everyday material and discursive mechanisms of this dehumaning in contemporary Portugal. Dialoguing with other important works of the Black feminist tradition such as Hortense Spillers and Saidiya Hartman, Sharpe approaches "dehumaning" as the imperial foreclosure of Blackness from concepts of the human (rather than "dehumanizing" as the stripping of humanity) in the everyday enacting of white supremacist power on Black life in terms of the different vessels through which this has occurred, both during slavery as well as in its global afterlives. In the process, she points out, among others, sites that are both physical/corporal and metaphoric, such as the hold of the slave ship and the Black woman's womb, as locales through which Blackness is signified in burgeoning and reproductive colonial imaginaries as othered labor. In the case of Hartman, in *Scenes of Subjection* (1997), she pays particular attention to the coffle as "a domestic middle passage, piracy, a momentous evil, and most frequently, a crime" (32). The term "middle passage," here transposed from the transatlantic voyage of enslaved people into the more specific controlled transportation of enslaved people chained together on land, underscores that these quotidian events of violence were always-already ones that reproduced meanings about the violability and supposed inhumanity of Black lives.

In this regard, the envisioning and practice of European colonial power required the stolen and forced physical labor as well as the symbolic labor of Black bodies in capitalist formation and the intertwined formation of

110　*Daniel F. Silva*

whiteness as identity and institutional edifice. Sharpe thus deploys a terminology of "anagrammatical blackness" (75) that looks to account for the ongoing processes of colonial meaning and value making that render particular bodies as "blackened," as well as for every day and resistant redefining of Blackness by those beings that have been objectified by racial capital. In the latter sense, Sharpe conceptualizes a space for "blackness anew, blackness as a/temporal, in and out of place and time putting pressure on meaning and that against which meaning is made" (76).

Sharpe considers and theorizes the material ways in which Blackness continues to be rendered and managed through different state and cultural apparatuses around the globe in the afterlife, or wake, of slavery. Through this critical prism, she analyzes and inscribes border control and police surveillance methods in Europe over Black bodies. Drawing on her assessment and the insights offered by both Valete and Tvon, the idea of Europe and its relation to whiteness is reproduced through these modes of violence and management of Black life and movement. As Sharpe expounds, using the example of "stop-and-frisk" protocols in New York City, but also used the world over, "the reality and the provenance of policing and stop-and-frisk language of 'furtive movement' follow a direct line from the overseer and the slave master/slave owner's and white person's charge of impudence" (86). These mechanisms of "dehumaning" build upon and operate in dialectic, of course, with the anti-Black epistemologies of empire.

In her analyses on contemporary Black arts and literatures from across the diaspora, Zakiyyah Iman Jackson underscores the work of various writers and artists in redefining not only Blackness but also notions of the "human" in a decolonial turn away from western imperial epistemes that, through "the Chain of Being's physical anthropology, using human and animal physical measurements, sealed the connection between Africans and apes as scientific fact" (8). This is evocative of Sylvia Wynter's provocation that racism "is an effect of the biocentric conception of the human" (364). Though Jackson prefers the term "bestialized humanization" over the concept of dehumanization, both she and Sharpe are concerned with the multifaceted, material, and metaphysical processes of othering in the formation of an anti-Black world and an opposing historicity of western humanism. Like the authors and artists studied by Jackson, including Octavia Butler and Toni Morrison, both Tvon and Valete enact meaningful gestures that reclaim and go beyond conceptions of the human. Arguably, this is a recourse of both survival and reinvention in and against the reproductive logics of racial capital. While Tvon's narrator/protagonist performs this maneuver through the "remixing" of Blackness and Portugueseness, Valete's formula seems to center on a radical dismemberment against the machinery of racial capital that fragments the Black worker's body. While his evoked Black migrant in "Quando o Sorriso Morre" is signified imperially as a being toward death, a systemic

Black Migration, Citizenship, and Racial Capital in Portugal   111

and prolonged dismemberment, Valete articulates the undying smile as a sort of post-human entity, an out-of-body fragment that will outlive the violence of capital.

Both works, and Valete's in particular, get to a concept of post-humanism that Justin Adams Burton identifies in contemporary Rap music as not so much ingrained in technological hybridism (the complex relationships between voice and electronic sounds), but more aligned with critical race and radical queer discourses. In this regard, Valete's undying and extra-corporal smile intervenes in the reinvention of life in the face of its gradual effacement. In the process, Valete's posthuman intervention is not merely about redefining Black diasporic humanity concerning imperial and liberal humanisms. It teaches us that any such intervention must be grounded in and address the material conditions of racial capital's dehumaning. As a result, and understood in the context of Valete's larger oeuvre, which includes calls for anti-colonial and anti-capitalist action,[1] his musical work also labors toward a certain project of reconstruction in the sense that Burton identifies in the work of Black diasporic cultural producers:

> Reconstructing systems with violent histories can be a fool's errand. One must give time and energy to a concept that means you harm, must turn toward a totalizing force and pay it the attention it craves, must busy oneself with the work always asked of women and queer people of color: explain to the dominant culture what is so patriarchal/white supremacist/heteronormative about the culture, then suggest how to do it better.
>
> (16)

Reconstruction, therefore, depends on the persistent seeking of new repertoires of human configuration and action to rethink the body – individual and collective – into sites of decolonial action.

Note

1. See songs like "Anti-Herói," "Fim da Ditadura," and "Rap Consciente."

Works Cited

Adams, Justin Burton. *Posthuman Rap*. Oxford UP, 1997.

Almeida, Miguel Vale de Almeida. *An Earth-Colored Sea: "Race," Culture, and the Politics of Identity in the Postcolonial Portuguese-Speaking World*. Berghan Books, 2004.

Bastos, Cristiana. "Unseen Diasporas: Portuguese Labor Migrants in Colonial Plantations." *Migrant Frontiers: Race and Mobility in the Luso-Hispanic World*, edited by Anna Tybinko, Lamonte Aidoo and Daniel F. Silva, Liverpool UP, 2023.

112 *Daniel F. Silva*

Cabral, Amílcar. *Revolution in Guinea: Selected Texts*. Monthly Review Press, 1972.

Castelo, Cláudia. *Passagens para África: O Povoamento de Angola e Moçambique com Naturais da Metrópole (1920–1974)*. Edições Afrontamento, 2007.

Fanon, Frantz. *Black Skin, White Masks*. Grove Press, 2008.

Fikes, Kesha. *Managing African Portugal: The Citizen-Migrant Distinction*. Duke UP, 2009. Print.

Freyre, Gilberto. *O Luso e o Trópico*. Realizações, 2010. Print. Gutto. "Ser Negro."

Hartman, Saidiya. *Scenes of Subjection: Terror, Slavery, and Self-Making in Nineteenth-Century America*. Oxford UP, 1997.

Jackson, Zakiyyah Iman. *Becoming Human: Matter and Meaning in an Antiblack World*. New York UP, 2020.

Matos, Alexandra Oliveira. "Tvon conta a história de *Um preto muito português*." *Rimas e Batidas*, 25 Jan. 2018, www.rimasebatidas.pt/tvon-conta-historia-um-preto-portugues/. Accessed 2 Oct. 2021.

Melamed, Jodi. "Racial Capitalism." *Critical Ethnic Studies*, vol. 1, no. 1, 2015, pp. 76–85.

Robinson, Cedric. *Black Marxism: The Making of the Black Radical Tradition*. Zed Press, 1983.

Sharpe, Christina. *In the Wake: On Blackness and Being*. Duke UP, 1996.

Tvon, Telma. *Um Preto Muito Português*. Chiado Editora, 2018.

Valete. "Quando o Sorriso Morre." 2012. *YouTube*. Rap Luso Vive Aqui! 13 June 2018, https://www.youtube.com/watch?v=PBYaT5xuDp4.

Wynter, Sylvia. "Race and Biocentric Belief System: An Interview with Sylvia Wynter." *Black Education: A Transformative Research and Action Agenda for the New Century*, edited by Joyce E. King, American Educational Research Association, 2005, pp. 361–366.

7 We Are Not Your Negroes

Analyzing Mural Representations of Blackness in Lisbon Metropolitan Area

Margarida Rendeiro

Planning postcolonial Lisbon as an inclusive political and social space cannot be a successful enterprise if it does not entail a discussion involving everybody, regardless of their ethnic or cultural background, and with widely acclaimed equal rights to the city. This argument concerns the concept of collective cultural memory, which needs to be understood as polyphonic. The discussion about the Portuguese collective memory in the public space has fundamentally been exclusionary; in other words, although Portuguese Black minorities have voices, their memory experience has not been integrated into the nationwide collective memory that privileges a white perspective of history. Furthermore, this hegemonic narrative has played an important role in outbound tourism promotion, especially in Lisbon, publicized as a multicultural city, though Black minorities have continuously been pushed away from the city center to underprivileged neighborhoods in the urban periphery. In addition, street art has been vital in the widespread promotion of cosmopolitan Lisbon in the international routes of the global phenomenon street art has become. Murals have been used to brighten cities and constitute a resource to depict resistance, particularly in the urban periphery. In view of a hegemonic collective memory narrative, do murals depict Black figures in the neoliberal Lisbon Metropolitan Area (LMA)? They certainly do, but a close analysis shows that Black figures are different whether murals are located in the city center or the urban periphery. This chapter discusses various street art representations of Black figures in the LMA and contends that street artists miss the opportunity to actively engage with the broader discussion on postcolonial race relations in Portugal, hitting the heart of the Lusotropicalist narrative the nation still grapples with, when they choose not to depict Portuguese Black figures and the problems that affect them in the city center. An analysis of the various murals shows that the murals in the city center depict internationally acclaimed Black icons whereas murals that depict conflictual postcolonial relations are located only in the marginalized periphery. Should these murals representations be in the city center, street artists would eventually produce potentially

DOI: 10.4324/9781003245117-10

114 *Margarida Rendeiro*

subversive art, contributing to the discussion on postcolonial Lisbon in the center of the public urban space.

Competitive Collective Memory, Street Art, and Urban Segregation

In his study that brings together Holocaust studies and postcolonial studies, Michael Rothberg (2009) expands the concept of multidirectional memory instead of competitive memory. Whereas multidirectional memory is a productive concept "subject to ongoing negotiation, cross-referencing and borrowing," constituting a polyphonic experience, competitive memory promotes a hegemonic collective memory narrative that involves "zero-sum struggle over scarce resources," blocking the participation of conflicting views of the past (Rothberg 3). The absence of diversification of voices has characterized the discussion about the collective memory of the Portuguese colonial legacy, as shown in Portuguese historian Manuel Loff's research (2015) about the public memories of the Estado Novo regime (1933–1974). The monument commissioned by the Lisbon city council to Portuguese sculptor João Cutileiro, inaugurated in Edward VII Park in 1997, is the sole celebratory memorial of the Carnation Revolution (1974) in Lisbon. This memorial conveys nothing about the contribution of the African liberation movements to the collapse of the Estado Novo dictatorship. Portuguese public memories tell us a *white* narrative about a *white* democracy.

There is no memorial to the victims of Portuguese colonialism in Lisbon yet and much less in the rest of the country, while there is a memorial in Lisbon to the soldiers fallen during the Colonial War (1961–1974).[1] Not surprisingly, it is in Belém, near the Tower of Belém and within walking distance to Jerónimos Monastery, the Imperial Square, and the Monument of the Discoveries, the latter two being remnant sites of the Portuguese Exhibition of the Portuguese World, set up in 1940 by Salazar's regime to celebrate eight centuries of Independence and three centuries of Restoration of Independence. The imperial memories of the grandeur of Portugal have not yet been challenged by the public policies of memory in Portuguese democracy. The war memorial is part of an array of ancient and modern buildings that celebrate the memory of the heyday and fading of Portugal's imperial past. Suppose it is undeniable that the Colonial War killed thousands of conscripted Portuguese soldiers. In that case, it is also true that decolonization in 1975 led to massive immigration of former Portuguese settlers and colonized Africans and caused a profound impact on the present-day ethnic composition of the Portuguese, especially the composition of the population living in the LMA. However, the postcolonial nation has had little to offer to African minorities and the Portuguese of African descent, in that nothing includes them in the public policies of memory of the colonial past, though multiculturalism has essentially been a word used in travel brochures and in Portuguese history textbooks to characterize the consequences of Portuguese maritime expansion in the 15th and 16th centuries.

The implementation of democracy in 1974 did not constitute a disruption to the long-standing effects of a four-decade-long project founded on nationalist pride and in the public memory narrative of not-so-violent colonialism, known as Lusotropicalism.[2] The policies of the most extended right-wing democratic government (1985–1995) in Portuguese democracy were also grounded on a national identity project that was not radically different from that of the Estado Novo and whose sites of memory also stem from the official narrative of Portuguese uniqueness and historical contribution to the world. The glorification of the Portuguese discoveries constituted the core of that official memory narrative, as shown in the commemorative regatta in 1988 to celebrate the 500th anniversary of explorer Bartolomeu Dias's achievement of sailing around the southernmost tip of Africa and the recreation at Expo92 in Seville of King Manuel I's Embassy to the Vatican. Moreover, the idealist and exceptionality of the Portuguese colonial legacy have constituted a reference in official speeches to this day. In 2017, the incumbent President Marcelo Rebelo de Sousa visited the island of Gorée, the largest slave-trade center on the African coast between the 15th and 19th centuries, during a state visit to Senegal, and there he stated that when Portugal introduced limited abolitionist laws in 1761, it recognized the injustice of slavery. Unlike other leaders, such as Pope John Paul II and Brazilian President Lula da Silva, the Portuguese president chose not to issue apologies on Gorée; consequently, 50 outraged Portuguese intellectuals signed an open letter to complain against the fact that the President's words revived the whitewashed vision of colonial oppression.

The population of the LMA represents around 26,6% of the Portuguese resident population and has changed significantly, mostly since 1974. In the 1950s, rural migratory flows were set up in Lisbon's urban periphery, expanding the capital's boundaries. After decolonization in 1975, the immigration flows of former white settlers and Africans were particularly intense, especially in the metropolitan area. Many Africans and fewer Asians from the former colonies started living together with the rural migrants and Cale and Romani ethnic groups in informal, self-built neighborhoods, such as 6 de Maio and Bairro do Alto da Cova da Moura along the Military Road that delimitates the city of Lisbon.[3] Official statistics indicate that Africans are mainly concentrated in the LMA; statistics also show that immigrants rocketed from 31,983 to 437,126 between 1975 and 2006 (Taviani 61). The largest group of immigrants came from the Portuguese-speaking African countries due to the political, economic, and social instability that followed African independence processes. For example, in 1996, 56% of the foreigners with residence permits were from these countries and Brazil (Taviani 73). The 1980s and 1990s were

116 *Margarida Rendeiro*

also the decades with profuse public construction projects; for example, in the late 1990s, part of the east side of Lisbon was rebuilt to host the World Exhibition Expo98.

The urban evolution of the LMA resulted in ethnic segregation regarding the labor market: immigration from African countries has been overrepresented in precarious, semi-skilled, and unskilled jobs (public construction sites, cleaning services, and catering businesses), whereas the less representative immigration from European countries and the United States have been better qualified and paid (Batalha 2008, qtd. in Taviani 66). In addition, changes introduced into the law of citizenship after 1975 left a significant number of citizens of African descent in a vulnerable situation because they could not have access to Portuguese citizenship.[4] Hence, there is still a significant number of citizens who are considered African for administrative purposes (Cape Verdean, Angolan, Guinean). However, they were born in Portugal and have never been to Africa.

When African families came to Portugal, most of them built their own low-cost houses in abandoned and inexpensive areas in the urban periphery with access to public transportation to go to work in the city center. The solidarity practice *djunta-mon* (Guinean and Cape Verdean Creole for "hand-joining") brought together these families and enhanced communitarian relations (Silva, Correia & Malheiros 2019; Sousa & Guterres 2021). Ties of solidarity and communion contrast radically with the neighborhoods' public image. As shown in Peter Anton Zoettl's published research (2013) on 6 de Maio neighborhood (now demolished), the residents' overall perception is that they do not belong to Lisbon. Their belief is enhanced mainly by the neighborhood's public image, primarily influenced by social problems, such as drug trafficking and violence, that depict informal neighborhoods' residents in the media as a potential external danger to the city. A significant case is the street demonstration to decry police violence, organized by hundreds of Africans and Portuguese of African descent, violently repressed by the police in the city center on January 23, 2019. The online edition of the daily *Diário de Notícias* (Ferro) reported that "*the periphery* walked down Av. da Liberdade to decry daily police brutality" (n.p.), quoting José 'Sinho' Baessa de Pina, member of the Portuguese Black Consciousness movement, who was brought up in Fontaínhas neighborhood (now dilapidated).

Furthermore, Ana Rita Alves's research on the demolition of Santa Filomena neighborhood, within the broader Dedicated National Rehousing Plan, the PER (Programa Especial de Realojamento), initiated in 1984 and still running nowadays, shows that in many ways ethnic segregation is hardly different from that promoted in colonial cities (Alves 67). Although the televised demolition of informal neighborhoods and subsequent rehousing of its residents were shown as a success by the standards of this program, this process has also constituted a traumatic experience for those subjected to it because it destroyed communitarian relations when those rehoused had to live in social housing neighborhoods even farther from the city center (Sousa & Guterres 2021). Luso-Angolan visual artist Mónica de Miranda's exhibition *Contos de Lisboa/Tales of Lisbon* held in Arquivo Municipal de Lisboa in 2020, involving image and sound installations, depicting some of these demolished neighborhoods built along the Military Road, shows the extent to which activism can convey dilapidation as a painful process of alienation of entire communities.

Street art has thrived in Portugal since the early years of 2000, with legislation introduced in 2013 to regulate graffiti art, making it a criminal offense when done without permission in public places and property, but empowering city councils to provide free walls for street artists. This phenomenon is quite different from the mural painting spree following the Carnation Revolution when murals were used to encourage popular support for the uprising. Street art has impacted the broader process of gentrification of urban neighborhoods. When the Urban Art Gallery was set up under the responsibility of the Department of Cultural Heritage of Lisbon City Council in 2008, its primary goal was to preserve the cultural heritage of deteriorated downtown Bairro Alto neighborhood and raise awareness of street art (Costa & Lopes 2). Other city councils have followed similar strategies in the LMA to promote "regeneration" of the public image of some of the "problematic neighborhoods" but often without the contribution of residents in matters involving what to paint and where. This has essentially been a decision between city councils and commissioned street artists, as shown in Otávio Raposo's research on Quinta do Mocho (Raposo 127). Tour guides from communities have been essential, but few have been involved in these decisions (Raposo 139). On the 40th anniversary of the Carnation Revolution, in 2014, celebrations included mural painting, many commissioned by city councils, including Lisbon's Urban Art Gallery, media groups, and social activists; for example, *25 Abril, 40 Anos 40 Murais* (April 25, 40 Years 40 Murals) was activist António Alves's project, committed to painting 40 murals, mainly in the LMA, with the participation of professional and amateur artists of all ages.[5]

However, the effect of a hegemonic collective memory narrative has often been shown in various (un)commissioned murals. In 2013, the ARM Collective, a team composed of street artists Miguel Caeiro a.k.a. RAM and Gonçalo Ribeiro a.k.a. MAR, was commissioned by *Visão*, a weekly magazine, to paint a 100-meter-long mural in the area of Belém, representing five Cantos of Luís Vaz de Camões's epic poem *Os Lusíadas* (1572) that celebrates Portuguese explorer Vasco da Gama's discovery of the sea route to India. This mural was painted for the celebrations of *Visão*'s 20th anniversary, including ten books, each one focusing on one Canto, with short stories written by Portuguese author José Luís Peixoto.

118 *Margarida Rendeiro*

Furthermore, the memory of the Portuguese maritime expansion has nurtured the creativity of street artists. Noteworthy recent examples are Brazilian street artist Nunca's mural (2014) in Chelas, in the east side of Lisbon, representing Pedro Álvares Cabral, explorer credited with the discovery of Brazil in 1500, commissioned for the Underdogs Gallery's Program of Public Art; Nark's *Novas Descobertas* (New Discoveries) mural (2017), on new street art achievements on the Hall of Fame Amoreiras, in Lisbon city center, depicting Adamastor, the mythological character created in *Os Lusíada*'s 5th Canto to symbolize the dangers of the sea and the formidable forces of nature ultimately overcome by Portuguese navigators; Vile's "Afonso de Albuquerque" mural (2018), depicting the second viceroy of Portuguese India in the 16th century, commissioned by the municipality of Alhandra, São João dos Montes, and Calhandriz for the celebrations of the "European Heritage Days" event in Alhandra; and AkaCorleone's *Conquista o Sonho* (Conquer the Dream) mural (2018) in Covilhã, showing various symbols of the Portuguese maritime expansion, for a more comprehensive street art project organized by the Portuguese Football Federation, in partnership with several Portuguese city councils and eight Portuguese street artists, to encourage the national football team for the FIFA World Cup.[6]

Street artists have used their art to take stances on global political and social problems; examples include Fidel Évora's and Tamara Alves's mural (2012) in downtown Lisbon, raising awareness of female genital mutilation (FGM) survivors; Vanessa Teodoro's mural on gender equality (2017) commissioned by Almada City Council on the Tagus south bank; and Kobra's mural depicting Brazilian indigenous leader Raoni Metuktire (2017) in Marvila, in the east side of Lisbon and the latest open-air street art gallery, to amplify solidarity with the indigenous peoples' cause. Nevertheless, the fact that street art has transformed a few deprived neighborhoods into tourist-presentable open-air urban street art galleries, within an overall process of urban gentrification, makes street artists less memory transgressors than art creators in the age of neoliberal urbanization, making visual consensus on global issues a tourist attraction. Martin Irvine's essay on visual culture claimed in 2011 that street art "thrives on the paradox of being the mural art of the *extramuros*, outside the institutional walls" (239). This metaphor is productive because it draws attention to the art on street walls as genuine art democratization. I propose, however, to take this metaphor one step further ten years later: in the age of neoliberal urbanization, where street art is an established and consensual phenomenon, it contends that the *intramuros* corresponds to the gentrified city center and the open-air street art galleries, while the *extramuros* is the marginalized neighborhoods whose issues are regarded as alien in the *intramuros*. This metaphor is a fecund concept to understand how street art interacts with ethnic segregation in the LMA.

Intramuros Cosmopolitan Street Art

This section of the chapter draws particular attention to street art murals that depict well-known Black figures. This decision is tied up with the fact that when street artists choose to iconize celebrities to the detriment of others, they convey internalized systems of social and cultural (de)valuation. At the same time, they engage with the dynamics of the city through visual art. Hence, these murals are essential contributions to shed light on street artists' engagement with the Portuguese hegemonic collective memory narrative.

Although contemporary graffiti is linked to the emergence of hip-hop, it has gradually become an autonomous manifestation of resistance, driven by specific motivations (Campos & Vaz 131). In Portugal, the hip-hop phenomenon expanded during the 1990s is associated with the Africans and Portuguese of African descent living in the LMA who reacted against social and ethnic marginalization. Graffiti also emerged in Portugal during that period and was essentially an illegal activity, though less motivated by ideological, political, or ethical reasons than street artists' self-motivation to become well known. Furthermore, graffiti has symbolically been reconfigured when public and private institutions commissioned and legitimized this art manifestation (Campos & Vaz 132). The association of graffiti with hip hop culture is still visible in a few murals painted in the LMA, as shown in Kilos Graffiti's recent murals (2021) depicting Kendrick Lamar and Jay-Z in the area of Saldanha and on the Hall of Fame Calçada da Glória, respectively, in Lisbon city center; Styler's mural (2019) with rapper Snoop Dogg in Rio de Mouro, Sintra; Spray Spotting's *Einstein meets Snoop Dogg* mural (2014); and Aspen One's *Tupac* (2013) on the Hall of Fame Amoreiras.

Apart from famous hip-hop figures, murals depicting well-known Black personalities in the LMA result from collaboration work with institutions. In this regard, three murals stand out in Lisbon city center: those that depict Nelson Mandela, Marielle Franco, and the Cape Verdean Batucadeiras (women Batuque players). In 2018, Lisbon City Council joined the annual Mandela International Day celebrations, officially declared by the United Nations. Besides inaugurating Mandela roundabout, organizing a conference and a concert in honor of Nelson Mandela, the city council also commissioned artist Nuno Saraiva to paint a mural in Campo Grande, in central Lisbon. It was painted on the blind building gable whose proprietor has family roots in South Africa. Before the inauguration of this mural, Styler had also signed another mural depicting Mandela in Cacém, Sintra, in 2016. Alexandre Farto, a.k.a. Vhils, participated in the extension activity of Amnesty International's (AI) *Brave* Campaign, a global campaign to raise awareness to human rights defenders. This extension activity results from the AI's collaboration with the worldwide street art community. For example, street artist Katerina Vononina

Figure 7.1 Nelson Mandela, Campo Grande, Lisbon
Source: Photo by Rendeiro.

painted a mural in Berlin depicting Marielle Franco, the Brazilian human rights defender who served as city councilor of the Municipal Chamber of Rio de Janeiro and was brutally killed in a so-far-unsolved crime in 2018. Vhil's mural also pays tribute to Marielle; it is at Panorâmico de Monsanto, a deserted restaurant that has gained cult status over the years,

We Are Not Your Negroes 121

situated on Monsanto's highest mountain, in Lisbon. The inauguration of this mural was at *Iminente* Festival, an international festival of urban culture, curated by Vhils and Underdogs Gallery in Lisbon in 2018.

In 2019, on the 44th anniversary of the Independence of Cape Verde, the Cultural Center of Cape Verde (CCCV) was set up in a building that

Figure 7.2 Marielle Franco, Panorâmico de Monsanto, Lisbon
Source: Photo by Rendeiro.

122 *Margarida Rendeiro*

Lisbon City Council offered to the State of Cape Verde for this purpose through a protocol signed in December 2018. For its inauguration, Frederico Draw and Ergo Bandits painted a mural entitled *Batuko* on the blind building gable of this building, depicting the Batucadeiras and thus paying tribute to the Cape Verdean women players who play this music genre and contribute to keeping this important marker of their identity alive among the Cape Verdean immigration (Ribeiro, 2010, p. 99). Despite groups of Batucadeiras, such as *Finka-Pé*, integrated into the activities of the Moinho da Juventude Cultural Association, in Bairro do Alto da Cova da Moura, in Amadora, and *Fidjos di Tera*, composed of Cape Verdean students and student-workers based in Oporto, having regular performances in the urban peripheries since their establishments, it was in 2019 that they became more well known outside the periphery. The inauguration of the Cultural Center, along with the exhibition *As Batucadeiras de Cabo Verde* at the Museum of Arts in Sintra, for the 8th edition of the international festival of performing arts *Periferias* and, particularly, the participation of the Orquestra de Batukadeiras de Portugal in singer-songwriter Madonna's *Madame X* album (2019) and documentary *The World of Madame X* (2019), filmed during her widely Portuguese media–publicized three-year stay in Lisbon, that led this group to occasional performances in RTP1, the Portuguese state-run mainstream channel, in 2020.

The mural representation of Black figures results from decisions that involved national and international institutions that essentially place cosmopolitan Lisbon in the global routes of street art. Moreover, these murals draw attention to civil rights, racism, and discrimination, but they do not depict the extent to which these problems exist in Portugal. The open-air street galleries in the city's borders hardly change this positioning of street art in the city center. An illustrative example is the latest edition of the Lisbon *Muro* Street Art Festival (2021), held on the east side of Lisbon, with the participation of over 60 various internationally acclaimed street artists. Under the motto "the wall that (re)unites," this area was divided into three thematic spaces: sustainability, urban culture, and multiculturalism. The space allocated to multiculturalism was the Casal dos Machados neighborhood. There, murals explore the relations between community, nations, cultures, and equality. Casal dos Machados is near Bairro do Condado, an underprivileged area where Bruno Candé, a Portuguese actor of Guinean descent, worked before being killed in 2019. This was the first time in the history of Portuguese democracy that a court sentenced the perpetrator, a veteran of the Colonial War (1961–1974), to imprisonment for racial hatred. No murals painted in Casal dos Machados depict anything that indicates that postcolonial Portugal has issues with multiculturalism that need to be addressed.

In 2014, however, António Alves painted a mural in Quinta do Mocho, within the *25 de Abril, 40 Anos, 40 Murais* celebration, showing the extent to which murals can challenge the collective memory narrative,

Figure 7.3 Batuko, CCCV, Lisbon
Source: Photo by Rendeiro.

even though they are painted in the periphery. It depicts Amílcar Cabral on a blind building gable of a building located on Amílcar Cabral Avenue. This avenue is the dividing line between deprived Quinta do Mocho, whose residents are primarily of Cape Verdean and Guinean descent, and the access road to the more privileged residential areas of Lisbon.

Figure 7.4 Amílcar Cabral, Quinta do Mocho
Source: Photo by Rendeiro.

By paying tribute to the Bissau-Guinean and Cape Verdean theoretician and leader of the liberation movement in the Portuguese African colonies, Alves rescues the memory of the contribution of the African liberation movements, secluded from the visuality associated with the public memory policies of the Carnation Revolution that signals the beginning of Portuguese democracy. This mural is the counter-visuality that challenges the memory of democracy as a narrative of social and ethnic justice; the silenced issues of ethnic inequality and discrimination are the elephant in the room Portuguese democratic society is still reluctant to discuss and address in the public space. This mural resists time to this day.

Extramuros Street Art of Resistance

Street art is intervention in the public space, often in specific neighborhoods; no space is neutral because zones and territories are socially constructed (Irvine, 2011, p. 238–240). In marginalized neighborhoods, what is depicted is political. When walking *through* these neighborhoods in the LMA, such as Bairro do Alto da Cova da Moura, Bairro Casal da Boba, Quinta do Mocho, and Chelas, we see various murals representing Black figures known for their engagement in civil rights; examples include Martin Luther King in Cova da Moura; Bob Marley in Cova da Moura, Quinta do Mocho, and Chelas; Malcolm X in Cova da Moura; Amílcar Cabral in Quinta do Mocho, Cova da Moura, and Casal da Boba; and Thomas Sankara in Casal da Boba. These are depictions that celebrate memories and symbols related to Pan-Africanism. Besides enhancing the residents' feeling of belonging to a particular ethnic and cultural community and thus contributing to the fabrication of the hybrid identities of many of those living in these neighborhoods (Campos & Vaz 134), mural depiction emerges as counter-visuality against the visuality of neoliberal urban order (Mirzoeff 485). The replication of these murals in various neighborhoods shows the extent to which counter-visuality is the artistic expression of an imagined community (Anderson 2006) involved in a collective act of resistance against social marginalization. These murals can be found either on the blind building gables of those buildings facing streets and avenues that delimit neighborhoods (Martin Luther King, Bob Marley, Amílcar Cabral) or on walls in the communities (Amílcar Cabral, Bob Marley, Thomas Sankara, Malcolm X). Furthermore, the fact that many of these murals were painted by members of the local communities indicates that resistance comes from *within* and is mostly *uncommissioned*. It is resistance from the *extramuros*: there have never been murals with any of the previously mentioned figures in Lisbon city center or any open-air public art galleries.

Shortly after veteran football player Eusébio da Silva Ferreira died in 2014, Odeith painted a mural on one of the walls in the outer limits of Cova da Moura to pay tribute to his memory. In 2020, an anonymous group of Sporting Lisboa and Benfica supporters painted the *Mural da Glória*, a long mural near Benfica stadium, representing the historical record of Benfica's outstanding football players: among them, several Black football players and Luso-Mozambican Eusébio, known as the Black Panther during his golden days in the 1960s and, so far, the only Black Portuguese personality transferred to the national Pantheon, was one of them; however, the technique used in this mural does not identify the ethnicity of any of the represented football players.

The success of Eusébio as a player who played for Portugal's national team in the 1960s was used by the Estado Novo regime to promote

Figure 7.5 Eusébio, Cova da Moura
Source: Photo by Rendeiro.

Portugal as a multiracial state and the end of the Indigenous Law in the African colonies. This law was abolished, but ethnic marginalization did not end by decree and continued after 1974. African minorities rarely hold publicly prominent positions in Portugal, such as anchors on the mainstream television channels, company management-level positions, political posts, or columnists in the print media. However, aligned with other postcolonial nations, sports have shown that Portugal is a multicultural nation, despite publicized episodes of racism disrupting this imagined consensus. Ironically and unintended as it may be, *Mural da Glória* does more for maintaining the Lusotropicalist memory narrative in the present than for promoting multiculturalism that integrates ethnic and cultural differences. This is particularly clear compared with Odeith's mural, whose depiction does not conceal Eusébio's ethnic origin. This aspect is even more significant when read in the context of social and ethnic segregation.

A walk through these peripheral neighborhoods is also a walk down the visual memory lane of many of those who lived in these neighborhoods and died for various causes, ranging from criminal violence, accidents to police violence. A noteworthy exception is Vhil's mural depicting San

Figure 7.6 DJ Nervoso, Quinta do Mocho
Source: Photo by Rendeiro.

Tomean DJ Nervoso (2015), the DJ from Quinta do Mocho who promoted *batida*, within the hip-hop scene, in the urban periphery.[7]

Nevertheless, this exception was involved in controversy at the time because it was a decision of the city council as part of its municipal strategy to promote the neighborhood's public image that did not involve the residents who only reluctantly agreed to see the face of one of them exposed on a mural for that purpose (Raposo 138). In Chelas, Vile's and

Odeith's murals pay tribute to Mc Snake, the rapper killed by the police in 2010; another, unsigned, to Mota Jr, the rapper abducted and murdered in 2020; and Nomen's mural depicts names of youngsters killed in accidents and criminal violence. In Quinta da Lage, Elson Sanches, a.k.a. Kuku, the 14-year-old boy shot by the police in 2009, is depicted on the wall of the house where he lived; an unsigned mural depicts Anílson João, a.k.a. Bila, stabbed to death near his home in Bairro da Serafina in 2017; in Bairro do Condado, Odeith's mural pays tribute to rapper Barbosa GQ, killed in a motorbike accident in 2012; and in Cova da Moura, Odeith's mural to Tupak Shakur (2005) also includes the names of deceased youngsters, while another, also signed by him, pays tribute to Roberto, another youngster who passed away in violent circumstances. This list is extensive, though incomplete; nearly every deprived neighborhood shows visual mural tributes to their deceased young residents. Some of these deaths made it to the news, but others did not. Most of these murals can only be seen if you walk through the neighborhoods. They are the visual manifestations of a complex problem that concerns the social conditions that have led to the imaginary of moral degradation that has shaped the public image of these neighborhoods (Raposo et al. 10). In the *extramuros,* murals restore the humanity taken away from a public image

Figure 7.7 Mc Snake, Chelas
Source: Photo by Rendeiro.

Figure 7.8 Kuku, Quinta da Lage
Source: Photo by Rendeiro.

of "problematic" neighborhoods in public media and political speeches, but their memory and sorrow for their loss, their sheer humanity, do not make it to the *intramuros*.

In 2021, Lisbon City Council commissioned a mural to pay tribute to Bruno Candé in Bairro do Condado. The mural reads the sentence "Everything could go wrong in my life, but I am Bruno Candé" [Eu tinha tudo para dar errado, mas sou o Bruno Candé] and has a plaque with the logo of Lisbon City Council that reads "It is not enough to be non-racist, you must be anti-racist." Not far from this mural, Vile also painted a mural tribute to Candé, depicting his face and the same sentence.

These mural tributes to the memory of someone whose violent death was under national media exposure also follow similar criteria that associate tributes with the places where these figures were born, raised, and

Figure 7.9 Bila, Bairro da Serafina
Source: Photo by Rendeiro.

Figure 7.10 Bruno Candé, Bairro do Condado
Source: Photo by Rendeiro.

worked but overlook the national impact this case had. It happens that their lives were led in the *extramuros*. Street art shows that these neighborhoods' problems are part of a discussion preferably held on the other side of the wall. Therefore, it does little to disrupt national apathy regarding what should constitute a core discussion in the center of the public urban space.

Final Considerations

This section contends nothing against street artists' freedom to depict specific figures in the *intramuros* and *extramuros*. Freedom is particularly relevant for any artistic expression. The point it makes here is a different one. When street art became legitimized in the Portuguese urban space, it succumbed to a visuality that does not put the hegemonic Portuguese memory narrative in perspective. The neoliberal capitalist economy also uses this narrative to thrive while being grounded upon the ethnic and social inequalities that capitalism explored. When Portuguese Black figures are depicted in the periphery only, out of the commercial circuits fostered by neoliberal urban policies, street artists reproduce the aesthetics of urban marginalization aggravated in neoliberal times and contested by many Black voices. It is not even a question of not having representations of African culture in the *intramuros*. Murals depict Black and Indigenous faces and African culture, but they are mostly artistic creations that could, at best, encourage locally unengaged discussions about multiculturalism. They contribute to the inertia that keeps a hegemonic memory narrative that has already proved an advantage for the Portuguese neoliberal economy. In November 2021, a UN Working Group of Experts on People of African descent visited Portugal to gather information on forms of racism, racial discrimination, xenophobia, and related intolerance. When interviewed by the media, they expressed their perplexity about a clear contrast between the still ongoing promotion of an idealized perspective of the colonial legacy against present-day ethnic segregation and discrimination (Lusa). By fostering a counter-visuality against the imagined consensus around the Portuguese cultural collective memory narrative and adopting visual strategies that bring what is depicted in the *extramuros* to the urban center, street art could produce subversive art and thus contribute to raising public awareness towards the need of racial equity strategies in the urban environment.

Notes

1. Lisbon will have its first memorial to slavery, but it has not been built yet. The creation of this memorial was proposed to the Participatory Budget of Lisbon in 2017 by Djass, the Portuguese association of Afrodescendants. It was announced as one of the winning projects of that Lisbon City Council initiative which included it in its budget. A sculptural installation entitled *Plantation:*

132 *Margarida Rendeiro*

Prosperity and Nightmare built by Angolan artist Kiluanji Kia Henda will be located at Campo das Cebolas, in downtown Lisbon. This place is a symbolic choice because historians have identified a slave market in this area during the 16th and 17th centuries. Following the announcement of the memorial as one of the winning projects, Henda's design received the most votes tallied over six public sessions that also showed the blueprints by four other African and artists of African descent. Djass organized these sessions across several locations around Lisbon, among communities populated mainly by Africans and Portuguese of African descent.

2. Lusotropicalism is a colonial theory created by Brazilian anthropologist Gilberto Freyre in the 1930s. According to this theory, the Portuguese had been more successful colonizers than their European counterparts because they naturally accepted miscegenation with colonized women; the reason for this acceptance, he claimed, was the fact that the Moors had occupied Portugal and the biological temperament of the Portuguese grew more suitable for the tropics than that of any other white Europeans. This theory accounted for what Freyre believed was the epitome of success in the Brazilian society and was later adopted by Salazar's Estado Novo to maintain colonial power in Africa as international pressure against the Portuguese colonial empire grew in the 1950s and 1960s.

3. The Military Road for Lisbon Defense was built at the end of the 19th century to protect Lisbon from foreign invaders and followed the city's boundaries at the time. This road was eventually abandoned for these purposes, and, ironically, history shows that (im)migratory flows of Portuguese and Africans settled along this area. At the same time, their presence was not particularly welcome in the city center.

4. In 1975–1985, only those born in Macau, Goa, and Diu kept their Portuguese citizenship. Africans could only access Portuguese citizenship if they lived in Portugal five years before 1974 or had a Portugal relative. The law change introduced in 1981 replaced birthright citizenship (*jus soli*) with the obligation of having a Portuguese parent (*jus sanguinis*) to access citizenship. This change was reverted in 2006 only, but without retroactive effects.

5. For the *25 de Abril 40 Anos 40 Murais* mural project and other murals painted for the celebrations of the 40th anniversary of the Carnation Revolution, see Rendeiro (2019).

6. Years within brackets after references to murals indicate when they were painted.

7. Art Keeps Me Alive depicted Carlão, a Portuguese rapper, on a mural entitled *The land where I was born* (2016) in a street in Almada, on the Tagus south bank. It is another rare mural depicting a Portuguese rapper in the urban periphery of Lisbon city.

Works Cited

Alves, Ana Rita. *Quando Ninguém Podia Ficar: Racismo, Habitação e Território.* Preface by Mamadou Ba. 1st ed., Tigre de Papel, 2021.

Anderson, Benedict. *Imagined Communities: Reflections on the Origin and Spread of Nationalism.* 3rd ed., Verso Books, 2006.

Campos, Ricardo, and Cláudia Vaz. "Rap e graffiti na Kova da Moura como mecanismos de reflexão identitária de jovens afrodescendentes." *Sociedade e*

Cultura: Revista de Ciências Sociais, no. 1, 2013, pp. 127–139, www.redalyc. org/pdf/703/70329744013.pdf.

Costa, Pedro, and Ricardo Lopes. "Is Street Art Institutionalizable? Challenges to an Alternative Urban Policy in Lisbon." *Métropoles*, no. 17, 2015, pp. 1–18, http://metropoles.revues.org/5157.

Ferro, Carlos. "'Não ao racismo', 'Grito à liberdade'. Novos vídeos do protesto na Avenida." *Diário de Notícias*, 23 Jan. 2019, www.dn.pt/pais/nao-ao-racismo-grito-a-liberdade-novo-video-mostra-protesto-na-avenida-da-liberdade-10476722.html.

Irvine, Martin. "The Work on the Street: Street Art and Visual Culture." *The Handbook of Visual Culture*, edited by Barry Sandwell and Ian Heywood, Berg Publishers, 2011, pp. 235–278.

Loff, Manuel. "Estado, democracia e memória: políticas públicas e batalhas pela memória da ditadura portuguesa (1974–2014)." *Ditaduras e Revolução: democracia e políticas de memória*, edited by Manuel Loff, Filipe Piedade, and Luciano Castro Soutelo, Almedina, 2015, pp. 23–143.

Lusa. "Pertos da ONU surpreendidos com relatos de brutalidade policial sobre pessoas africanas em Portugal." Online edition *Público*, 6 Dec. 2021, www. publico.pt/2021/12/06/sociedade/noticia/peritos-onu-surpreendidos-relatos-brutalidade-policial-pessoas-africanas-portugal-1987597.

Mirzoeff, Nicholas. "The Right to Look." *Critical Inquiry*, vol. 37, no. 3, 2011, pp. 473–496.

Raposo, Otávio. "Guias da Periferia: Usos da Arte Urbana Num Bairro Precarizado de Lisboa." *Cidades em Mudança: processos participativos em Portugal e no Brasil*, edited by Renata de Sá Gonçalves and Lígia Ferro, Mauad Editora LTD, 2018, pp. 127–144.

Raposo, Otávio, Ana Rita Alves, Pedro Varela, and Cristina Roldão. "Negro drama. Racismo, segregação e violência policial nas periferias de Lisboa." *Revista Crítica de Ciências Sociais*, no. 119, 2019, pp. 5–28, https://doi. org/10.4000/rccs.8937.

Rendeiro, Margarida. "Streets of Revolution: Analyzing Representations of the Carnation Revolution in Street Art." *Challenging Memories and Rebuilding Identities: Literary and Artistic Voices that undo The Lusophone Atlantic*, edited by Margarida Rendeiro and Federica Lupati, Routledge, 2019, pp. 98–120.

Ribeiro, Jorge Castro. "Migration, *Sodade* and Conciliation: Cape Verdean Batuque Practice in Portugal." *Migrações Journal – Special Issue Music and Migration*, no. 7, 2010, pp. 97–114.

Rothberg, Michael. *Multidirectional Memory: Remembering the Holocaust in the Age of Decolonization*. 1st ed., Stanford UP, 2009.

Silva, Katielle, Marcos Correia, and Jorge Malheiros. "Viajando por periferias diversas e criativas de Lisboa: os bairros da Cova da Moura e do Talude." *Revista Periferias*, Jul. 2019, https://revistaperiferias.org/materia/viajando-por-periferias-diversas-e-criativas-de-lisboa/.

Sousa, Ana Naomi de and Guterres, António Brito. "Lisbon's Rehousing Policies Lose the Life of the Neighbourhoods they Demolish." *The Architectural*

134   *Margarida Rendeiro*

Review, 6 Jan. 2021, www.architectural-review.com/essays/city-portraits/
pushed-to-the-periphery-lisbons-policies-of-demolition-and-rehousing.

Taviani, Elena. "Das políticas de habitação ao espaço urbano: Trajetória espacial
dos Afrodescendentes na Área Metropolitana de Lisboa." *Cidades, Comunidades e Territórios*, no. 38, 2019, pp. 57–78, https://journals.openedition.org/
cidades/1133.

Zoettl, Peter Anton. "Ver e ser visto. O poder de olhar e o olhar de volta." *Sociologias*, no. 34, 2013, pp. 246–277, https://seer.ufrgs.br/sociologias/article/
view/44112/27720.

8 Reclaiming an Individual Space

The Angolan Diaspora in Portugal

Sandra Sousa

In 2008, Eduardo de Sousa Ferreira, Carlos M. Lopes, and Maria João Mortágua published the only detailed study regarding the Angolan diaspora in Portugal. Their study resulted from the importance given by the *Secretariado de Estado da Cooperação* [Secretariat of State for Cooperation] to the topic of the Angolan diaspora. It aimed to provide recommendations for a better practice of cooperation between several institutions and individuals involved in migratory patterns between Portugal and Angola. Even though the study can give us some insight into this community, it is nonetheless a sociological/economic analysis based heavily on quantitative data. As such, the result and conclusions of the study do not present a complete view of the living/humane realities and experiences of the individuals that form the Angolan diaspora. Furthermore, for my purpose and concerns here, the most relevant part of the study is the description of the waves of Angolan emigration since its independence in 1975. According to Ferreira et al., in Europe, it is in Portugal that the Angolan diaspora takes on its most significant dimension and heterogeneity (46).[1] This is due to diverse factors such as a common language, current family ties, and the historical link between both countries.

In this sense, the Angolan community in Portugal has been represented by three substantial immigration waves since 1975. The first began before the country's independence, right after the 25th of April 1974, and lasted until 1977. It was composed of Angolans who joined the mass immigration of the so-called *retornados* and, after independence, Angolans (most with double nationality) who were not satisfied with the political situation in their country. The second phase occurred in the mid-80s, and it coincided with a difficult political time in Angola marked by the civil war, lack of freedom and economic austerity played the leading role in people's decision to leave. The third period was initiated at the end of 1992 with the rekindling of civil war and rendering a migratory movement that, up until recently, is still felt in Portugal.

Given the fact, as previously mentioned, that sociological studies of economic nature do not completely and satisfactorily reveal the issues related to the Angolan diaspora in Portugal; that is, they do not expand

DOI: 10.4324/9781003245117-11

136 Sandra Sousa

the human and historical thinking of the processes of interaction in the space of a post-colonial grammar, it is the aim of this chapter to look at the Angolan diaspora in Portugal through the literary works of three of its most recently acclaimed writers, Kalaf Epalanga's *Também os Brancos Sabem Dançar* [*Whites Also Know How to Dance*] (2018); Djaimilia Pereira de Almeida's *Esse Cabelo* [*That Hair*] (2015) and *Luanda, Lisboa, Paraíso* (2018); and Yara Monteiro's *Essa Dama Bate Bué* [*That Lady Beats A Lot*] (2018). Appearing on the literary scene less than a decade ago, these new Angolan diasporic voices are not only changing how post-imperial Portugal's looks at its African communities but paving the way for a space in literary circles and cultural production where African voices can be heard as well as being able to claim their place in History. It is also my aim to correlate these new Angolan diasporic voices in a broader European context by showing epistemological and corporal aesthetic forms of resistance to ongoing forms of coloniality, having in the background the insights on Portuguese identity offered by Eduardo Lourenço (*Nós e a Europa ou as Duas Razões*) and recently by Margarida Calafate Ribeiro (*Uma história de regressos: império, Guerra Colonial e pós-colonialismo*). They have emphasized that Portugal can and should be thought of within the European context and therefore connected with other European countries when grappling with its imperial discourses.

Thus, one should turn to Eric Morier-Genoud and Michel Cahen's argument that despite the influential, but obsolete, thesis on the exceptionality of the Portuguese Empire, "the fundamental dynamics of imperialism were similar in the Portuguese case to those of other European metropoles" (3). Hence the Portuguese Empire was not different from other empires. As they further state, "it is true that the economic, financial, military, and political power of Lisbon was inferior to that of London and Paris. But it is a difference of degree, not of nature" (7). Morier-Genoud and Michel Cahen dispel the possibility of whether the Portuguese Empire and its romanticized exceptionalist narratives correlated to an autonomous social space of migration for the colonial population. Still, the same argument can be made regarding the movement of formerly colonized people from Africa to the metropole. In other words, only if we consider post-imperial Portugal as exceptional and in nature radically different from other post-imperial nations can we consider the African diasporic movements that established themselves mainly in their post-imperial capitals or, more accurately, in their suburbs, as also fundamentally different from each other.

It is well established that there is no formal consensus on what a diaspora is, and it is beyond the scope of this chapter to solve that debate. Therefore, diaspora here will be taken as a loose concept as described by Robin Cohen,

> dispersal or expansion from homeland, collective memory and myth about the homeland, and idealisation of ancestral home, development

Reclaiming an Individual Space   137

of a return movement, a strong ethnic group consciousness, a troubled relationship with host societies, a sense of empathy and coresponsibility with one's coethnics, and finally, the possibility of a distinctive creative life.

(17)

As Morier-Genoud and Michel Cahen also remind us based on Soulet's concept, diasporas need historicity: "diasporas form only with time: after the first migrants pass away, their children and grandchildren need to maintain the community to be able to talk of a diaspora" (10).

In a recent study on Afro-diasporic communities, Sheila Khan affirms that Portugal received "other faces, other lives with other experiences, other narratives and other modes of being," and "these other human presences continue to be, nonetheless, socially ignored and marginalized despite the existence of a politically correct profilaxis of Portugal as a 'Lusotropicalist'" and, as such, multicultural country" (42–43). In relation to the deficit of attention toward everything that came from the former colonies, Khan states that:

> [that] deficit . . . stems from a certain Portuguese tendency of not knowing how to face and accept the Other as kin and, in a certain way, as part of its social and cultural history. In many regards, as Eduardo Lourenço (2001) observes, we forget the past, wanting to break from our African past and immediately within that imaginary excess, we direct ourselves toward another center of self-representation and identification that extended itself upon the European horizon.
>
> (76–77)

That effort to cut with the African past after the independence of the African colonies, as stressed by Khan, is apparently seamless. It did not produce the expected results because of the impossibility of stopping the flows of people coming from Africa. As Fernando Arenas reminds us,

> The fates of Portugal and various regions in Africa have been intertwined for hundreds of years as a result of Portugal's maritime-colonial expansion and the transatlantic slave trade, that also co-involved colonial and independent Brazil, with profound historical, geopolitical, socio-economic, and cultural consequences.
>
> (167)

The signs of the presence of Black Africans in Portugal go even further back in time to the Roman, Moorish, and Medieval Christian periods (Arenas 168). That presence never ceased to exist, even if present to a lesser extent in some periods. Fernando Luís Machado's article "Forty Years of African Immigration" confirms such a stance. African immigration is the oldest

138 *Sandra Sousa*

of modern Portugal – starting in the second half of the 1960s – of labor migrations to Portugal and the first to sedentarize, since the great majority of Africans, mainly from Cape Verde, but also from Angola, Mozambique, and Guinea-Bissau, stayed in Portugal permanently. According to Machado,

> Being the oldest and largest, it was also the first to expand into three 'generations' and the first to age in the host society, leading to the phenomenon of elderly immigrants. It is also the first wave to assimilate in varying degrees to Portugueseness by way of growing naturalizations of younger immigrants due to increased socialization, mixed marriages, and other processes of cultural assimilation.
>
> (135)

Formed almost only by individuals and families from Lusophone African countries, this immigration represents more than 90% of Africans residing in Portugal. In this regard, it is important to consider the Angolan diaspora in Portugal in the broader context of cultures and structures of anti-Blackness in Portuguese history. Therefore, the experiences of members of the Angolan diaspora in Portugal are marked by these very mechanisms.

Africans and their descendants living in Portuguese territory are still seen as "others." This is also attested by the fact that in the process of regularization of immigrants in 2001, the largest one in Portugal, "African immigrants represented merely 13%" (Machado 137). African immigration also showed Portugal's true colors as racial slurs against Africans were often (and are still occasionally) heard in public spaces. Statements such as, "Your ugly blackness/niggerness," "Go back to your country," "I killed blacks/niggers like you" are mentioned in Fikes's study (5). City representatives chose to ignore racist skinhead graffiti, still hiding under the premise that "'there was no place for racial hatred in Portugal'" (Fikes 5). As Fikes mentions, "the former belief that Portuguese individuals could not be racist was fading among the general public. . . . Somehow, in just over a decade, 'racism' had evolved from something effaceable and even negotiable to something incriminating" (8). As Arenas also states, in Portugal and most European countries, there is an ambivalent perspective towards the large presence of African immigrants in the national landscape, which ranges from resistance to intolerance to racism (171).

Even though one can argue that Portugal has had a relatively stable African migration as part of the broader African Diaspora for the past 50 years, the new generations of Afro-Portuguese still have disadvantages in relation to their Portuguese counterparts: they are even now, for the most part, relegated to precarious labor, engaging in meager occupations, and facing instability of work conditions; they have low representation at the university level; and the levels of poverty in their community are high, living literally at the margins of society, as the "famous" Cape Verdean "bairro" Cova da Moura, in the outskirts of Lisbon, readily attests. Machado's study sees progress in the integration of African communities in Portuguese society; nonetheless, he also affirms that the kind of racism mentioned by Fikes is a reality:

> Although perceptions vary as to the intensity, interviewed subjects generally report the existence of racism in Portugal, locating it in a variety of quotidian contexts and relating, in detailed fashion, racist episodes of which they are victims. Racism is thus, in this context, precisely the opposite of symbolic inclusion, as the expression "go back to your country," so often heard, sadly illustrates.
>
> (163)

Isabel Castro Henriques emphasizes this issue in the following manner:

> the strength of secular prejudice reemerges through the resurrection of old, absurd, and obsolete formulas and representations. These formulas and representations reinforce, in the context of new laws and new problems inherent to the globalization that formatted the world beginning with the 1980s, innumerable acts of racial and social discrimination facing the many African immigrants who are seeking within Europe a place for survival and a new way of life.
>
> (99)

The realities faced by Africans in their host countries have changed, but not so considerably that the picture is much brighter, as we will further observe.

Almeida, Monteiro, Epalanga: Three Angolan Voices

The literature of postcolonial tradition as well as the fictional work of a young generation grappling in their daily lives with situations and cultures of racialization and social isolation has brought not only autobiographic evidence but spaces of historic revindication and reparation, of the paradoxes of Portugal as a postcolonial country as well as its European counterparts. According to Khan (2022), the "post-colonial turn" focused on the critical reflection on race and racism has been enriched with the duty of post-memory, that is, the contribution of artists, writers, thinkers, and scientists who feel themselves heirs of coloniality and take from it the narrative voices expressing the urgent need to decolonize the social and cultural fabric still predominant in European and colonial settler societies.

Djaimilia Pereira de Almeida, Yara Monteiro, and Kalaf Epalanga are three Angolan narrative voices who have contributed to the re-thinking through their fictional, autobiographical, and musical works Portugal by

140 *Sandra Sousa*

questioning relevant issues such as race, language, and citizenship. The three were born in Angola during the late 1970s early 1980s, and at some period of their lives, they found themselves living in Portugal. In this country, they all received an academic education. Thus, we are in the presence of three voices of the Angolan diaspora who have been questioning the colonial past and how this past is reflected in their (and their community's) present and future as diasporic and de-territorialized citizens. Almeida, Monteiro, and Epalanga are part of a generation of 21st-century African or Afro-descendant writers living outside of Africa who, as pointed out by Margarida Calafate Ribeiro, "reaffirm themselves within a literary trajectory of European coverage – *afropean* . . . or *afropolitan* . . . of identities that have inherited colonial processes" (2). I will discuss these terms used by Calafate Ribeiro further later in this chapter. For now, I would like to take a closer look at their fictional/autobiographical work to demonstrate that the issues marking their experiences as part of the Angolan diaspora in Portugal share important commonalities with African diasporic experiences elsewhere and thus contribute to important textualities of African diasporic epistemologies and decolonial communal life.

Since her first book, *Esse Cabelo*, in 2015, Almeida has garnered national and international acclaim, with the attribution of the Oceanos 2019 award and the translation to English of *Esse Cabelo [That Hair]* by the American publisher Tin House in 2020. Tori L. Tharps, in a *New York Times* critical review, affirms that

> "That Hair" contains themes that will be recognizable to so many readers, regardless of their mother tongue, who are wrestling with their own mixed-race experience today – anyone who is attempting to make sense of hair texture, skin color, and family ties that cannot fit into little blue census boxes. Despite the label of fiction, Mila's struggle in "That Hair" is all too real.
>
> (n.p.)

Esse Cabelo dissects modern culture, unveiling layers of racism and sexism. Mila, the protagonist in *That Hair*, reveals social norms that inhibit the lives of young women, in particular Afro-Portuguese and African women in Portugal, and their battle with issues of race that affect their daily lives not only in the host countries but also in Angola. The book broaches the racial aesthetic politics of spaces structured by white supremacy, among other related topics. This presents quotidian and epistemological challenges that these women have to overcome since the expectation is not to display their natural hair but to straighten it with chemicals to fit the "white ideals" of European spaces, to be taken seriously in job interviews or as professional women. Concomitantly, *Esse Cabelo* makes us reflect on Black women's misrepresentation and the need for a better understanding of their multifaceted, differing, and common

Reclaiming an Individual Space 141

experiences at the intersection of anti-Black racism and white patriarchal power. Confronted by *Lança*'s question regarding internalized racism via hair, Almeida states:

> Sempre tive uma relação complicada com o cabelo. Não sabia como tratá-lo, nem como lidar com o que me era natural. A verdade é que ressentia o cabelo, sem que me tenha atirado para o lado oposto: nunca tive longos cabelos desfrisados, usei muito o cabelo rapado. Era como se não existisse, e quando me lembrei dele fiz tudo para o esquecer. Quando explico que acordei para certas coisas das quais passei ao lado, o cabelo é uma delas. Involuntariamente, estava sob uma amnésia a respeito não só de coisas que têm a ver com o lugar onde pertenço mas também se estendia às lembranças exteriores disso.
> (n.p.)

> [I have always had a complicated relationship with my hair. I did not know how to treat it, nor how to deal with what was natural for me. The truth is that I resented my hair; without having gone as far as straightening it, I instead shaved it often. It was as if it did not exist, and whenever I was reminded of it, I did all I could to forget it again. When I talk about awakening to certain things I had ignored, my hair was one of them. Involuntarily, I was under a sort of amnesia regarding not only things that have to do with where I belong, but this amnesia also extended to memories beyond those.]

In the novel, Mila is a semi-autobiographical female character who, through her experiences with hair and, by extension, race, shows this commonplace for women of African/Angolan origin living in Portugal. In *That Hair*, the story of Mila and that of her hair is also a collective one of Portuguese nationality and integration of people of African descent in Portugal. As the protagonist mentions: "A verdade é que a história do meu cabelo crespo cruza a história de pelo menos dois países e, panoramicamente, a história indirecta da relação entre vários continentes: uma geopolítica" ["The truth is that the story of my kinky hair traverses the story of at least two countries and, more broadly, the indirect history of the relationship between various continents: a geopolitical story"] (13). The biography of Mila's hair takes the reader on a journey of understanding a country that, over the centuries, has been silencing and marginalizing the stories of Black lives (aesthetic and political) and the epistemologies of those Black bodies who live within its borders. The story of Mila's hair is as well the history of the status of African women and non-white immigrants in Portugal. A whole history emerges through one apparently simple aspect of physical appearance, a history of human beings that occupy the Portuguese national space. Still, because they are physically and epistemically othered in the discursive matrix of capital and white supremacy, they are relegated to invisibility or caricature.

142 *Sandra Sousa*

Luanda, Lisboa, Paraíso is also a book engaging the Angolan diaspora with the African diaspora. Almeida narrates the story of Cartola and his son, Aquiles. They leave Angola at the end of the 1980s so that Aquiles, who has a malformation on his heel, is able to receive medical treatment. As Miguel Fernandes Duarte states, "In a certain way, Cartola came to Lisbon to restart, always imagining that in Portugal he would be recognized as Portuguese" (s/p). He soon recognizes that the man he was in Luanda, an accoucheur, was left behind. He now has to face a new reality in Portugal, working in construction in order to survive. Cartola and his son are soon confronted with the realities of their new life residing in a slum along the south margin of Lisbon. Their life situation turns them, as Inocência Mata affirms, into the

> paradigm of simultaneous conditions of being exiled, immigrants and minorities . . . initiating a journey through the complexities of that triple-condition, following the effects of a reality of inequality and the consequences of a monolithic and teleological understanding of identity, itself always in collision with Huntingtonian theories of "the clash of civilizations" and what are considered to be "universal values".
>
> (n/p)

His son describes Cartola as a man weakened by his reality in Lisbon, a city that forced him to lose direction and his life compass:

> Cartola parecia mais baixo ao filho desde que haviam chegado a Lisboa. O filho olhava-o como quem teme que o rei sucumba a uma conspiração. A nobreza que o porte dele lhe inspirava em Luanda dera lugar à confusão de Cartola, que lhe fazia abrir muito os olhos como se tivesse medo de ir contra as coisas. Tinha chegado a Lisboa tarde demais, depois de lhe ser possível domesticar a cidade.
>
> (37)

> [Cartola looked shorter to his son since they had arrived in Lisbon. His son would look at him as if fearing the king would succumb to a conspiracy. The nobility that his body exuded in Luanda gave way to Cartola's confusion, which would force him to open his eyes wide as if he feared resisting things. He had arrived in Lisbon too late, too late for him to domesticate the city.]

This formulation can be validated as a veiled critique to post-imperial Lisbon, which, as its past twin colonial capital, continues to exert its power over African bodies, vilifying and subjecting them to racism, discrimination, to the margins, and invisibility. In fact, Cartola becomes a ghost of himself (68). As Miguel Fernandes Duarte states,

> Cartola não era olhado enquanto português, e é omnipresente o olhar reprovador que recebe de fora, tanto pela sua etnia como pela sua

condição. Fora do seu local quotidiano, tanto ele como Aquiles são constantemente olhados de lado, tidos como pedintes, carcaças, lixo humano.

(s/p)

[Cartola was not seen as Portuguese, and that disapproving gaze that signifies him as 'outsider' is omnipresent throughout, tied to both his ethnicity and his social condition. Outside of their local quotidian life, both Cartola and Aquiles are constantly side-eyed and perceived to be beggars, corpses, and human refuse.]

That is, the phantoms of an empire, in which they blindly believed, return, this time, to diminish their hopes and illusions.

By linking migration and the lack of viable socioeconomic opportunities, the novel portrays a cosmopolitan view that intertwines the local and the national with global concerns. While the novel mainly discusses the crises of postcolonial nations, it does it in a way that looks at the nation connected to a wider world: war and corruption, which is also part of the narrative, are impactful on global levels. Nonetheless, the narrative does not envision an easy leap to a better future: the son is left with a father's disturbing legacy mirroring the struggles for radical sovereignty in post-colonial nations: "A culpa era sua. Tinha condenado o filho a não ter história por medo de que ele não se conseguisse erguer se a conhecesse" (152). ["It was Cartola's fault. He had condemned his child to historyless-ness out of fear that Aquiles would not be able to move forward had he known"]. These worlds that both father and son inhabit will continue to be crippled until history rectifies itself.

Yara Monteiro appears in the Portuguese literary scene in 2018 with the novel *Essa Dama Bate Bué!* [*That Girl Goes Hard!*]. The diasporic writer sets her novel between Portugal and Angola, spanning from colonial to postcolonial periods, including Angola's violent civil war. Monteiro's novel also lifts taboos "over traditionally silenced discourses about domestic and intimate violence" (Kalisa 3). Vitória, the main character, departs at a young age with her grandparents to Portugal to escape a devasting civil war, leaving behind a mother that she never met fighting in that same war. The book is her journey back to her roots to find her mother. In Luanda, she discovers a city permeated by chaos, violence, and cruelty. Nonetheless, in Portugal, other forms of violence also were part of Vitória's life. They are not only experiences with racism at school, but the inherent violence inscribed in any narrative of a displaced life, whatever the reason. Since Vitória left for Portugal at a very early age, she experiences something that could be described as a "double displacement," as it is observed in some of her comments upon returning to Angola: ""Sinto o comentário como se fosse uma mão abruptamente lançada à minha cara. Um lembrete áspero de que não pertenço ali. Não tenho o sotaque da terra" (71). ["I feel the comment as if it were a hand suddenly slapping

144 *Sandra Sousa*

my face. A rough reminder that I do not belong there. I do not have an Angolan accent"]. Vitória's narrative is, therefore, not only the search for her mother but also the creation of her own narrative stability through that quest. She strives for a sense of belonging that only her mother can give her.

Vitória feels displaced not only in Portugal but in Angola as well. Even though she identifies herself as Black, Angolan society does not see her as such, thus placing her in the same category as that of her Portuguese grandfather, the "middle place." Belonging to the space in-between is, for her, the second-worst place in which a woman can be: "here I am light, there I am dark, the in-between space is the second worse" (59). To complexify her identity and the violence that surrounds her, Vitória is not only a Black woman; she is also a gay black woman, a part of her identity that she has learned to hide from her family and society.

Essa Dama Bate Bué! portrays the violence of imprisonments, the hunger, the rapes, as well as other silenced forms of violence. Vitória's tale is one in which the violence of war is perpetuated in the children of these women fighters. Not having participated in the war, children have nonetheless become extensions of generally silenced war traumas. Living in the in-between place, between her past and her future, Vitória might as well keep waiting since, like Juliana, her mother's war comrade, states, "És de um povo que ainda está à espera, que espera, sempre" (206) ["You are of a people that are still waiting, that always waits"].

Kalaf Epalanga, best known as a member of the Angolan-Portuguese band Buraka Som Sistema, published in 2018 *Também os Brancos Sabem Dançar*, a semi-autobiographical novel enriched by its musical background. Epalanga was born in Angola and was sent to Portugal by his mother at 17 to escape the country's civil war. He does identify as Portuguese and sees Lisbon as "his" city. Currently living between the Portuguese capital and Berlin, he is arguably the most de-territorialized of the three writers here in question. In the sense of a transnational, multi-territorial identity, he and his novel remind us of Caryl Phillips and Johny Pitts's search through Europe of their African "tribe," rejecting monolithic identities. Despite defining Lisbon as a half-blood city, Epalanga is, nonetheless, able to identify its problems and the racism inherent to its society which produces the same type of invisibility of Afro-descendants living at its margins as in the rest of Europe.

In the 1980s, Black Kittitian-British Caryl Phillips began a European journey that resulted in his first book, controversially titled *The European Tribe*. This was not the standard touristic travel narrative, since it had a particular objective, as stated by the author: "if I was going to continue to live in Britain, how was I to reconcile the contradiction of feeling British, while being constantly told in many subtle and unsubtle ways that I did not belong?" (9). During his journey, he discovers a Europe through the lexicons of otherness projected by colonizers and white Europeans onto Africa and Africans, that is, exoticizing lands and bodies onto the margins of history. In Phillips's words, the troubles, conflicts, ethnic cleansings and so forth that he observed, "leads me to the conclusion that the very same patterns of conflict and brutality which have troubled, and continues to trouble, the Third World are alive and very much part of life in 'darkest' Europe" (132). His point is a straightforward one: "Europeans are human beings. They are subject to the same insecurities, the same inability to forget, the same prejudices, the same disturbing nationalism, the same cruelties, as any other people" (132). When it comes to racial prejudice and visibility of Black people in the "civilized" continent, 13 years after his travels, Phillips sees changes; nonetheless, they don't necessarily mean an improvement to the lives of Africans, African descendants, or immigrants in Europe. As he states:

> it remains a fact that the problem and difficulties persist across the breadth of the continent, some of which appear to be intractable. The continued and overwhelming evidence of both overt and covert racism has led many – including myself – to speculate as to just how deeply Europe is wedded to inequity.
>
> (131)

Another Afro-British writer who has speculated about the same issue is Johny Pitts, a sort of mentee of Phillips who, belonging to a different generation and almost four decades after Phillips's book, also embarks on a journey of discovery of Black Europe. It is certainly no coincidence that the assumptions made by Phillips of the intractability of racism in the continent have led Pitts to a voyage of observation across Europe in order to make sense of his own double identity. The Sheffield-born son of a white English mother and African American father, Pitts spent five months on the road in search of Africa in Europe, leading to his book, *Afropean: Notes from Black Europe* (2019). He was also searching for his "tribe" and a sense of belonging by claiming membership to a collective Black community in Europe that offers a sense of belonging more nourishing than the reductive nationalism of individual European countries. Pitts makes a breakthrough by using the concept "Afropean," which rejects an identity that is never absolute or monolithic, including a myriad of experiences, which comes, at the same time, from the need to affirm an identity that is both European and African. "Afropean," according to Pitts, "had to build a bridge over that dividing fence that says whether you're in or out and form some sort of informal cultural coalition" (5). This also means that Pitts chooses "Afropean" as "a potentially progressive self-identifier (rather than 'European') because there is something about the nature of Europe that destroys by assimilation" (24). As he travels across

146 *Sandra Sousa*

Europe, his convictions about how race and African diasporic movements are perceived in the continent become more clear:

> Various tempos reveal different realities, and very often Europe's black workforce inhabits the liminal terrain I'd just experienced, as cleaners, taxi drivers, porters, security guards, ticket sellers and night-club bouncers; they are there and not there. I knew of this world, of course; I'd been part of it in the past but had never before thought of it as an *invisible* world through which white Europe blithely passes without ever really seeing.
>
> (34)

Resembling Phillip's Europe, Pitts's nevertheless is not the same one any longer, since historicity is now a defining element of its African diasporic experiences and "Afropeans" reclaim a new "configuration of ideas, connected to Africa and Europe but transcending both" (59). Whereas in *The European Tribe*, Phillips reversed the usual narrative of the white explorer in the "developing world" by dissecting the malaise at the heart of Europe and treating white Europeans as anthropologically attractive, Pitts's focus, moreover, is on previously white spaces now occupied by Black people.

Whereas Phillips's desire for Europe at the dawning of the 21st century would be for European centers to "assume responsibility of identifying themselves as places where difference is not only tolerated, but encouraged" (133), Pitts claims that Europe's Black diaspora needs "connection and collaboration to create a climate that can sustain plurality and produce a louder voice when facing racism" (62). These aspirations are not mutually exclusive, and together they claim an interplay between Black and European cultures, something that Pitts called a "utopian vision of a black European experience" (4). The younger writer went further into Black Europe than his predecessor, visiting Lisbon and one of its most established locales of the African Diaspora, Cova da Moura. In his words, this "slum" in the outskirts of Portugal's capital,

> was indicative of a concealed narrative all over Europe: taxi-drivers, waitresses, shop assistants, cleaners and security guards were inhabiting the same spaces as consumers but living an entirely different world most of those consumers don't have to think about. And that's what Cova da Moura was; a hidden world that forced you to question identity and the structures behind the grand visions of Lisbon.
>
> (372)

Nonetheless, as he continues,

> this vision can't be upheld forever. If the West continues to vilify or close its eyes to global poverty, gross inequality, and the necessary

Reclaiming an Individual Space 147

environmental and economic migrations currently taking place, Cova da Moura is what most of Europe may look like soon enough.

(373)

Afropeans, or if we want, Afrolisbonites such as Kalaf Epalanga, are also starting to reclaim an identity that is no longer hyphenated, reclaiming a place for themselves which is at the same time *in* and *of* Lisbon, *in* and *of* Portugal, *in* and *of* Europe, and *in* and *of* the world. In *Também os brancos sabem dançar* [*Whites Also Know How to Dance*], the narrator affirms his role in redefining and reconstructing European cultural identity:

> Eu também estou aqui na qualidade de cooperante, vim para ajudar a reconstruir e redefinir a identidade cultural europeia.
> A minha identidade pessoal ganhou forma dentro destas fronteiras, sou músico, aspirante a escritor e depois, claro, também emigrante. E divirto-me quando me dizem "tu já não és angolano", o que é, no meu entender, uma forma de dizer "tu já não és negro". Como se o saber articular ideias que são correntes neste espaço me dispa automaticamente do fator que me identifica como sendo negro e me despromova da condição de imigrante.
> Sempre me recusei a aceitar que a minha condição de emigrante condicionasse os meus movimentos. Mesmo quando estive, sim, ilegal.

(67)

> [I am also here in the capacity of collaborator. I came to help rebuild and redefine Europe's cultural identity.
> My identity has developed in new ways within these borders. I am a musician, an aspiring writer, and, of course, an emigrant. It amuses me when people tell me, "you are no longer Angolan," which is, in my understanding, a way of saying, "you are no longer Black." Knowing how to articulate current ideas in this space automatically strips me of my Blackness and demotes me from my condition as an immigrant.
> I have always refused to accept that my condition as an emigrant will determine my actions. Even when I was, yes, illegal.]

By refusing to let his emigrant status, as well as the color of his skin, pigeonhole him into a specific racialized category, Epalanga chooses, as many of his diasporic generation, to encapsulate Afropeanity. This identifier encompasses fluidity and avoids rigidity.

In a century where mass migrations and the dispersion of people throughout the world are central and defining issues, it does not come as a surprise that migration and the economic, social, and cultural factors attached to this geographical movement have become a topic in

148 *Sandra Sousa*

contemporary African literature. Through his musical assets and a diasporic imagination, Epalanga's book, like himself, transposes borders, guiding the reader around the world, from Africa to Europe to America. With an eye in Europe or the United States and another in Africa, a new generation of African or Afro-descendant writers, as Almeida, Monteiro, and Epalanga exemplify, are unified by their choice of literary themes which reflect contemporary concerns with the world they live in and which affect their communities either in their country of origin or in their new home societies. On this particular front, writers and cultural producers of the Angolan diaspora, in facing entrenched economic and cultural structures of racism and concomitant realities of displacement (from the civil war in Angola to precarity in Lisbon), are at the forefront of revising Europe's borders and Portuguese national exceptionalism, all the while inaugurating radical epistemologies of Black collective life in Europe and beyond. One of the prevalent issues discussed throughout this chapter and across the fictional works in this study is race and racializing processes emanating from the long history of coloniality and Europe's ongoing investment in it, explicitly impacting how one is perceived and treated when living outside of Africa. And if we carefully engage Johny Pitts's words that "racism and prejudice are cages – a prison sentence alienating those who hold these attitudes from the beautiful diversity of the world" (50), and in the sound of music that makes the Norwegian immigration officer have more in common with Epalanga than with his coworkers, then we might have a chance of having African diasporas fully integrated in their host countries.

This project redefines Europeanness away from the monolith of whiteness in a way that Europeans may disidentify with whiteness and towards solidarity across spaces and coloniality's rigid categories.

Note

1. All translations from Portuguese, direct or paraphrased, are my responsibility.

Works Cited

Almeida, Djaimilia Pereira. *Esse Cabelo*. Teorema, 2015.
————. *Luanda, Lisboa, Paraíso*. Companhia das Letras, 2018.
Arenas, Fernando. "Cinematic and Literary Representations of Africans and Afro-Descendants in Contemporary Portugal: Conviviality and Conflict on the Margins." *Caderno de Estudos Africanos*, vol. 24, 2012, pp. 165–186.
Cohen, Robin. *Global Diasporas: An Introduction*. Routledge, 2008.
Epalanga, Kalaf. *Também os Brancos Sabem Dançar*. Todavia, 2018.
Fernandes Duarte, Miguel. "'Luanda, Lisboa, Paraíso', o espantoso regresso de Djaimilia Pereira de Almeida." *Comunidade, Cultura e Arte*, 13 Nov. 2018.
Ferreira, Eduardo de Sousa, Carlos M. Lopes, and Maria João Mortágua. *A Diáspora Angolana em Portugal: Caminhos de Retorno*. Principia, 2008.

Fikes, Kesha. *Managing African Portugal: The Citizen-Migrant Distinction*. Duke UP, 2009.

Henriques, Isabel Castro. "Africans in Portuguese Society: Classification Ambiguities and Colonial Realities." *Imperial Migrations. Colonial Communities and Diaspora in the Portuguese World*, edited by Eric Morier-Genoud and Michel Cahen, Palgrave Macmillan, 2012, pp. 72–103.

Kalisa, Chantal. *Violence in Francophone African and Caribbean Women's Literature*. U of Nebraska P, 2009.

Khan, Sheila. *Portugal a Lápis de Cor. A Sul de uma pós-colonialidade*. Almedina, 2015.

———. "Saudade, Solidão e Silêncio em *Luanda, Lisboa, Paraíso* de Djaimilia Pereira e em *Reino Transcendente* de Yaa Gyasi." *The Africas in the World and the World in the Africas: African Literatures and Comparativism*, edited by Sandra Sousa and Nazir Ahmed Can, Quod Manet, forthcoming 2022.

Lança, Marta. "Eu mesma – entrevista a Djaimilia Pereira de Almeida." *Buala*, 16 Sept. 2015.

Lourenço, Eduardo. *Nós e a Europa, ou as duas razões*. Imprensa Nacional Casa da Moeda, 1988.

Machado, Fernando Luís. "Quarenta Anos de Imigração Africana: um Balanço." *Ler Historia*, vol. 56, no. 56, 2009, pp. 135–165.

Mata, Inocência. "Uma implosiva geografia exílica." *Ípsilon*, 14 Dec. 2018.

Monteiro, Yara. *Essa Dama Bate Bué!* Guerra & Paz, 2018.

Morier-Genoud, Eric and Michel Cahen. "Introduction." *Imperial Migrations. Colonial Communities and Diaspora in the Portuguese World*, edited by Eric Morier-Genoud and Michel Cahen, Palgrave Macmillan, 2012, pp. 1–28.

Phillips, Caryl. *The European Tribe*. Vintage Books, 1987.

Pitts, Johny. *Afropean. Notes from Black Europe*. Penguin Books, 2020.

Ribeiro, Margarida Calafate. *Uma história de regressos*. Afrontamento, 2004.

———. "Luanda, Lisboa, Paraíso?" *MEMOIRS – Filhos de Império e Pós-memórias Europeias*, 14 Dec. 2019, pp. 1–5.

Tharps, Tori L. "That Hair by Djaimilia Pereira de Almeida." *New York Times*, 17 Mar. 2020.

9 Luso-Arabic Poetry
Reviewing the Concept

Catarina Nunes de Almeida

In southern Europe, the history of the Arab occupation has produced an intellectual terrain that diverges somewhat from the scenario described by Edward W. Said in *Orientalism* (1978). Here, the phenomenon could be defined as "Counter-Orientalism," after Karla Mallette, since in countries like Portugal or Spain, "modern Orientalist scholarship has had to accommodate a fact of regional history: the object of the (distancing) Orientalist gaze is the history of the nation" (19).

As far as Portugal is concerned, the discourse about the Arabs, produced throughout the 19th and 20th centuries, has taken different perspectives. While some academics have worked to reconstruct Portuguese Arab-Islamic history as part of the national heritage, using tools from philology above all (here the dominant figure was the Arabist[1] David Lopes), others ultimately rejected this theory and the spirit motivating it. For the more conservative faction (which included historians like Alexandre Herculano and Joaquim Pedro de Oliveira Martins), the Arabs did not play a significant role in Portuguese history; this was perhaps because accepting their influence would mean challenging the canonical genealogy of the intellectual heritage of modern Europe (Mallette 19). Consequently, for 19th-century Portuguese historiography, Romanization, Christianity, and the supremacy of the Arian element were given priority at the expense of the Islamic strand, which was often presented as evidence of civilizational decline and populational inferiority.

In defense of this "de-orientalization" of the Iberian Peninsula, the dominant historiographic discourse presented the Arab influence as limited to a marginal territory in the South of mainland Portugal, in particular the regions of the Algarve and Alentejo, known as Gharb al-Andalus.[2] Thus, despite the attempts of David Lopes and some of his disciples to construct a narrative that was less affected by racial and religious discourses, the idea that Arab culture was extraneous and irrelevant to Portuguese modernity gained ground.

After the military coup which, in 1933, instituted the fascist regime known as the Estado Novo, the Arab-Islamic domination of the Iberian Peninsula was presented even more categorically as an insignificant and

DOI: 10.4324/9781003245117-12

Luso-Arabic Poetry 151

somewhat inconvenient episode in the development of a Christian and westernized nation. The Moors were portrayed as cruel and backward people with no depth in school programs and literature, befitting their absurd theology and despotic Islamic law. In literary works, the *topoi* of the "Moor" or the "Turk" (an image of an enemy frequently sanctioned by punishment, defeat, or death), or the more benevolently accepted *moura encantada* (the enchanted Moorish woman), have dominated Portuguese prose and poetry since the 15th century. As the incarnation of the evil infidel, who should be forcibly crushed or converted to Christianity, they enabled the exploration in literary texts of a dichotomy between Christians and infidels, with the latter always presented as foreigners from the East rather than as legitimate inhabitants of the territory. Featuring in romances, ballads, plays, and legends as outlaws, enemies, conquered peoples, or examples of converts, they became recurrent figures of the collective imaginary, exploited to add exoticism and dramatic effect to the texts (Correia 203–208). Only the Mozarabs were, to some extent, an exception, understood as the faithful repositories of some hypothetical national feeling. The focus was firmly on the Christian matrix of a nation founded by the Reconquest, which was responsible for definitively unifying the territory and transforming it into a Catholic kingdom. Thus, for over 40 decades, the Islamic past was effectively occluded from Portuguese history and the canonical narrative of "Portugality" (*Portugalidade*).

However, after the democratic revolution of 1974, some scholars began to admit that the Arab presence in Portugal had produced some significant works of art and architecture and pointed out that some of the literary giants of Al-Andalus – such as the poets Al-Mu'tamid and Ibn Ammar – had been born on "Portuguese" soil. Historians, archaeologists, and independent researchers now contributed to reframing the medieval Gharb, particularly the city of Silves (Shilb), as a pinnacle of cultural sophistication, prosperity, and enlightenment, much as Cordoba or Granada were. Many of the works published at the turn of the millennium attempted to trace Portuguese culture back to the Islamic presence, introducing a new narrative that deconstructed the idea of an entirely hostile and barely significant relationship between Christian Portugal and its Arab "Other." In espousing a trend that some Spanish philologists had adopted for at least a century (Mallette 54–55), Portuguese academics sought to deal with the historical vacuum around the Arab question by appropriating a narrative of origins that described the Arabs from Gharb as the actual ancestors of the Portuguese and affirming "Portugality" as a concept firmly rooted in its culture. In the words of the historian António Borges Coelho:

> A generalidade dos portugueses com luzes crê ainda que a civilização árabe peninsular nos tocou apenas na epiderme. . . . É esta civilização do silêncio que pretendemos desenterrar agora do esquecimento e fazer ouvir a voz independente e autêntica.

152 *Catarina Nunes de Almeida*

[Most enlightened Portuguese still believe that Iberian Arab civilization only affected us superficially. . . . It is this civilization of silence that we now aim to retrieve from oblivion and allow its independent and authentic voice to be heard.]

(Portugal na Espanha Árabe 11–12)

This paradigm shift was brought about by a series of works that sought to overturn the idea that the medieval Arabs of Iberia represented a foreign culture that had to be observed from a distance. Now the object of research ceased to be "them" and became "us," a perspective that left an indelible mark on post-1974 generations (Barros 36). One of the most significant works of the new paradigm was António Borges Coelho's *Portugal na Espanha Árabe* [*Portugal in Arab Spain*], which encompasses historical excerpts and extracts from geographic, philosophical and literary texts about the land and figures of Gharb al-Andalus. In the prologue to the first edition, published in three volumes between 1971 and 1973 (i.e., during the fascist dictatorship), Coelho sought to contest the discourse of Christian nationalism disseminated by the regime, which perceived Portuguese heritage as resulting from the Reconquest:

Qual de nós não se sentiu alguma vez, ao estudar a história medieval, uma espécie de cruzado da Reconquista? Os acontecimentos são vistos pelo lado de cá e com os olhos ideológicos da cruzada. Quem é esse mouro com o qual, segundo nos deram a entender, só eram possíveis as relações de espada contra alfange? Qual a influência real da civilização árabe no território português, na sua população, na sua cultura? . . . A voz apostólica-romana dos vencedores apagou as marcas dos vencidos mas os seus ecos continuam a chegar até nós.

[Who amongst us has not at times experienced something of the crusading spirit of the Reconquest when studying medieval history? The events are seen from this side and through the ideological eyes of the crusade. Who is that Moor with whom, as we are led to understand, the only possible relationship is the sword versus the sabre? What was the real influence of Arab civilization on Portuguese territory, its population, and its culture? . . . The Catholic voice of the vanquisher has obliterated the marks of the vanquished though the echoes of it continue to reach us.]

(Coelho, *Portugal na Espanha Árabe* 13, 21–22)

The positioning of historians like António Borges Coelho has to be pondered in the light of the political context in which their works were published. This context favored an attitude of resistance against the system, and it explains the effects of the change of perspective on various domains of knowledge. It is archaeology, however, that brings about the decisive paradigm change regarding the Arab domination through the works which, from the end of the 1970s, would give rise to the Mértola Archaeological Site. Led by the archaeologist Cláudio Torres, these works would bring the history of the Arab-Islamic presence to a broader public, reinterpreting it and projecting it definitively onto Portuguese historiographic discourse. However, it should be pointed out that this update was not naive or ingenuous. During the dictatorship, Torres and Coelho had trod similar paths of resistance to the regime, including imprisonment or exile. This suggests that the positive discourse about the Arabs that arose in the last quarter of the 20th century was, at its source, an act of resistance to the established power and the historical narrative of Christian inspiration that nourished it.

These two authors aimed to show that, despite not having administrative autonomy under Islam, Gharb al-Andalus was perceived from early on as an individualized territory that would play an active role in all decentralizing movements (Torres 75; Coelho, *Para a História da Civilização* 8–10). Coelho argues that it was the site of many significant events and that we can connect to Gharb al-Andalus a substantial number of Iberian Islamic thinkers (Coelho, *Para a História da Civilização* 63). However, his claims are rarely supported by historical documents. In the case of illustrious Andalusians not born in present-day Portuguese territory, Coelho would cleverly try to trace an alternative ancestry that would connect them to it. For example, we are told that the poet, historian, jurist, philosopher, and theologian Ibn Hazm was from a Muladi family, from the region of Huelva, and therefore from Gharb al-Andalus (Coelho, *Para a História da Civilização* 48); that Ibn Bayya, known as Avempace, is from a family originally from Beja (Coelho, *Para a História da Civilização* 52); that Ibn Al-Arabi, one of the greatest Sufi thinkers, whom he admits was born in Seville, studied under (among others) Abu Imran al-Mertuli, who was from the Portuguese city of Mértola (Coelho, *Para a História da Civilização* 62). Borges Coelho proposes the decentralization and demystification of Iberian spaces generally recognized as capitals of power during the Islamic presence, such as the Spanish cities of Seville and Cordoba (*Portugal na Espanha Árabe* 27).

The aim of this historiographic narrative seems to be to rank the Portuguese settlements among the principal (or most important) cities of Al-Andalus, devolving to them the importance that they supposedly had in the political, social, economic, and cultural hierarchy of the time and showing that various intellectuals had praised the cultural superiority of Iberian Islam over other eastern territories. It is even argued that the foundation of Portugal occurred precisely when this civilization was at the peak of its prosperity in scientific and artistic terms; thus, its birth as a nation bore the marks of that Arab excellence, which benefitted Christian sovereignty, and of which vestiges were conserved until now.

Arguments such as these, which sought to establish a direct relationship between the borders of Gharb (or its predecessor, Lusitania) and

154 *Catarina Nunes de Almeida*

the later kingdom of Portugal, in an attempt to legitimize the Arab heritage through common geography, encountered resistance from the more canonical historiography, less dominated by emotional discourse. Today, the idea that Roman or even pre-Roman Lusitania could be identified with modern Portugal, or that the origins of the Algarve could be traced to the old Ager Cuneus and the diocese of Ossónoba, is considered spurious by critics (Oliveira-Leitão 73), who argue that territorial coincidences are not in themselves enough to trace the genealogy of the country.

While this discourse introduced important changes to historiography, it also revised the medieval literary canon. The reinterpretation and opening up of the poetic tradition acquired a new dimension in 1987 when Adalberto Alves published a collection of poems by 39 poets from Gharb al-Andalus entitled *O Meu Coração é Árabe: a Poesia Luso-Árabe* [My Heart Is Arab: Luso-Arabic Poetry]. In the following years, Alves prepared more publications dedicated exclusively to the two poets considered major within the "Luso-Arabic" lineage: one collection of poems by Al-Mu'tamid (1996) and another by Ibn Ammar (2000). These volumes, which contained lengthy impassioned introductions in addition to the translations, enabled Portuguese readers, who may have been aware of the foreign bibliography on the subject, to discover Arab-Islamic poetry from the former Gharb for the first time. Grounded in a theory that holds this poetry to be the ancestor of the medieval Portuguese lyric, these works also took up the controversial question of the Arabic influence on the forms and spirit of Iberian courtly poetry (Monroe 398–411; Boase 457–482; Zwartjies 45–54; Reckert 37–123), particularly on the Galician-Portuguese lyric.

The origins of cultured poetry in the Galician-Portuguese area tend to merge with the sources of Romanesque poetry in general – or rather, they can be traced back almost entirely to the common troubadour tradition that presided at the development of lyric poetry throughout Western Europe. Written over 150 years – between the end of the 12th century and the middle of the 14th – these medieval songs date from the dawn of Iberian nationalities and are largely contemporaneous with the Christian Reconquest.[3] For certain Portuguese scholars, who, like their Spanish counterparts, were eager to establish native origins for these poetic forms, the discovery of the *kharja* (a collaborative poetic practice that emerged at the confluence of Christian, Arabic, and Hebrew cultures, and which was interpreted as a vestige of popular Mozarab poetry) suggested that erudite Andalusian lyric might have had national "folk" origins (Tavani 141–142). They were tempted to relate the *kharjas* to the later (or even contemporaneous) *cantigas d'amigo* of Galician-Portuguese troubadour tradition (Correia 199); however, despite some significant analogies between the two forms, there are also important differences in tone and poetic substance that could not be ignored (Tavani 31).

Luso-Arabic Poetry 155

The arguments supporting the connection between Arab poetry and the troubadour lyric were taken even further. Salma Khadra Jayyusi, for example, mentions points of contact between Arab poetry and the attitudes of chivalry, courtesy, and polite address that formed the basis of the courtly love tradition, which flourished in the Renaissance throughout most of Europe; yet these attitudes, she argues, are not purely Andalusian in origin but rather belong to a vast body of Arab love literature,

> so rich both east and west of the Mediterranean, one which still needs to be discussed in modern terms, and to be seen not simply in the light of semantic and technical accomplishment, but vis-a-vis the Arab-Islamic ethos and background which underlies the erotic.
>
> (352)

She emphasizes the importance of studying the whole *corpus* of Arabic love poetry as the source of attitudes and sentiments still considered attractive today. As for the Romantic stereotypes that crystallized around the personalities and feats of certain Andalusian poets, Jayyusi has also deconstructed them, commenting on the two leading figures of the famous group of "Luso-Arabic" poets, Al-Mu'tamid and Ibn Ammar: "With Ibn Ammar (d. 479/1086) we have a poet who epitomised the Machiavellian spirit"; he "was certainly a good poet, but not a great one"; "[t]here were many poets in al-Andalus, before, after and contemporary with him, whose poetry was equal to and often greater then Ibn Ammar's" (Jayyusi 355–356). As for the well-known "poet-king" Al-Mu'tamid, Jayussi has also shown that much of his fame was based on canonical representations: he "lives in memory first and foremost because of the tragic figure he cuts, as the prince whose fall from great wealth and power produced so many poems of exile and self-lament, bewailing the vicissitudes of time and the treacherous mutability of fate" (Jayyusi 356–357).

A more "disaffected" reading comes from Maria Filomena Barros, who points out that the Portuguese "Islam 'fashion', strengthened of course by world events and the growing visibility of immigration from Muslim countries, is still based on a superficial and distorted essentialism, stemming from a multicultural Al-Andalus discourse, just like in Spain[4] as well" (Barros 37). The role that poetry from Al-Andalus occupies in Portuguese popular and academic discourses is thus characterized by a certain romantic nostalgia and a body of critical work very much dominated by feelings, opening up the way to a narrative that is essentially fictitious, especially in historiography.

In fact, with the spread of "Luso-Arabic" (or "Hispano-Arabic") as a concept, there has been an intensification of tourism associated with the Arab legacy in Portugal, particularly in the regions of the Algarve and Alentejo. The Routes of Gharb al-Andalus and the Route Al-Mu'tamid are good examples of this increasingly coordinated action between Portugal

156 *Catarina Nunes de Almeida*

and Spain in the tourism sector. The fact that, in Spain, the Al-Andalus Legacy was classified as "European Itinerary" (1997) and "Great European Itinerary" (2004) by UNESCO has contributed considerably to the growing attention given to this heritage, and a series of routes of a historical and literary nature were unveiled to establish a cross-border intercultural dialogue. It should also be mentioned that UNESCO included "The Andalus Legacy" in its *Mediterranean Programme* (2014). In creating routes and itineraries of interest to tourists, poets are frequently presented as one of the most valuable legacies of the Muslim past, particularly in Silves,[5] which has even been described as the "Baghdad of the West" (Nunes 331–347).

The significant expansion of the concept of Luso-Arabic poetry allows us to reflect on certain poetic phenomena that have marked contemporary Portuguese poetry. Declaring themselves to have been inspired by Islamic poetry and philosophy, some poets have brought to their work formal precepts, thematic obsessions, and modes of figuration taken from Sufi doctrine, for example. The subtle approximation to non-Christian contemplative practices and the adhesion to an aesthetic thought that has its roots outside the European matrix have contributed decisively to changing the idea of a literary tradition, introducing new ways of understanding poetic writing. In this respect, the most significant case is the Portuguese poet António Barahona (b. 1939). However, there are also younger authors whose work draws on the Sufi imaginary: through a dialogue with Persian poetry (Miguel Manso), or through an encounter between the written and oral traditions, which generates a prayer- or mantra-like quality, associating poetic practice to performative exercises that tend towards meditation and spiritual ascesis (António Poppe).

Since the end of the 1970s, a pluralized horizon of relations between Portuguese poetry and its *Orients* has opened up. This is not a simple symbolic or aesthetic record, dominated by a certain exoticism, but rather a complexification of postures. Some poets, publishing since the last quarter of the 20th century, have metaphorically played the role of *converts* by expressing their adhesion to distant spiritual traditions and the reception of certain ritualistic practices and teachings, which come together in their writing. As regards the Sufi tradition, the poetry of António Barahona is the one that best illustrates that *conversion*: "Canto porque sofro de não ser sufi,/guardador de rebanhos ou mendigo à porta do templo/Canto porque tenho saudades de Deus" [I sing because I suffer for not being Sufi,/keeper of flocks or beggar at the door of the temple/I sing because I long for God] (*O Sentido da Vida é Só Cantar* [The Meaning of Life Is Just Singing] 26).

Having adopted the name of Muhamad Abdur Rashid Ashraf when he converted to Islam, António Barahona lived in Mozambique and Goa in the 1970s and 1980s, a restlessness related to a spiritual quest and to the study of Sanskrit, which years later would result in the translation

Luso-Arabic Poetry 157

into Portuguese of the *Bhagavad Gita* (2007) and *Brihadaranyaka Upanishad* (2015). Barahona's poetic-spiritual posture occupies a central role throughout his whole oeuvre, though there are certain syncretic convergences in the concept of religion that develops from book to book. Already in the Preface to the first edition of the *Bhagavad Gita*, he explained that his most important purpose in translating the sacred book into Portuguese was precisely to help clarify the profoundly symbolic and providential nature of the encounter between Hinduism and Islam in India: Hinduism as the oldest integral tradition (primordial) and Islam as the most recent (terminal). He argues that the antagonisms of form do not affect the single universal Truth, given that what is explicit in the *Bhagavad Gita* is implicit in the *Koran*, and vice versa (Barahona, *Bhagavad-Guitá* 15).

Indeed, in Barahona's poetic oeuvre, the ideals that sustain an ecumenical religiosity are clear from his first books, as we can see in these lines from *Aos Pés do Mestre* (1974): "O melhor islamismo é o melhor Cristianismo,/o melhor de qualquer religião" [The best Islam is the best Christianity,/the best of any religion] (*O Sentido da Vida é Só Cantar* 27). In several poems from this work and others, rhetoric is put at the service of a synthesis of tradition; the quest for a single universal Truth expressed by Buddhism, Islam, and even Christianity: "Já não importa saber/se sou António ou Muhammad:/assino conforme o soro/Em mim não há dois poetas:/há indícios de vivida/união de duas sombras" [It's no longer important/if I'm António or Muhammad:/I sign by the serum/In me there are not two poets:/there are signs of life experienced/union of two shadows] (Barahona, *O Sentido da Vida é Só Cantar* 101).

There are two terms intimately connected to Sufi spiritual practices, which also seem to find in poetry space for interesting reflection: evocation and invocation. From the human perspective, the Islamic concept of *dhikr* illustrates both the awareness of God and that awareness through language, whether voiced or silent. As William C. Chittick points out, in Islam, "[w]e return to God by remembering Him on every level of our being. To remember Him is to make the fact of His unity, the fact of His absolute and infinite Reality, the axis of our thought, speech, and activity" (50). To follow the guidance of the prophet is to recall God in thoughts, words, and actions. The *dhikr* appeals to the conservation of the presence of God at all moments and in all places and activities, mainly through writing. In Barahona, the commitment to scrutinize God is inseparable from the craft of the poet, as we can see from passages like "O meu poema é rezar" [My poem is praying] or "preciso do Mestre-Bem-Amado/cheio de Sílabas e Céu" [I need the Well-Loved-Master/full of Syllables and Heaven] (*O Sentido da Vida é Só Cantar* 23).

But other concepts take shape in his poems. *Inverberation*, or the presence of God in the Koranic word, is another idea to take into account in the axis linking the word and the spirit. Before it materialized into the written book, the Koran began as pure orality, as a sonorous letter. This

158 *Catarina Nunes de Almeida*

is why one of the most important rituals of the Islamic tradition is the recital. While for Christians God is *incarnated* in a man, for the Islamists God *inverberates*: "Ó situação tão minha conhecida/mais que familiar e mais que íntima/integrada no gesto de surpresa/de ver Deus na sombra duma sílaba" [Oh, a situation that I know so well/more than familiar and more than intimate/involved in the gesture of surprise/of seeing God in the shadow of a syllable] (Barahona, *O Sentido da Vida é Só Cantar* 254). The believer's relationship with the holy word is based on the idea that God is contained in the word (*in verbum*), which implies that he is available for ongoing hermeneutic activity (Bárcena 83–86). In that attempt to grasp the divine through the word, the sound is a fundamental element, alongside semantics and the texture of the letter. Because it has magical value, the efficacy of ritual formulae depends on the exact enunciation of the prayers. This understanding of the sound power of the word inspires uninterrupted repetition, usually in Arabic, of some specific spiritual formulae pronounced rhythmically, synchronized with breathing; indeed, for the Sufi, breathing is a powerful means of spiritual transformation (Bárcena 144–146).

Moreover, some contemplative practices require concentrating thought into sacred syllables (such as *mantras*). To each holy monosyllable is attributed a particular vibration in a specific zone of consciousness, hence the importance of repetition (Hatherly 130–132): the insistence on a specific sound or group of sounds has an impressive incantatory effect, which induces deep listening and leads the practitioner – in the case of Sufism – to supreme union with God. The poetic work of António Poppe (b. 1968) derives precisely from this interaction between writing and orality as a means of attaining the divine. Poetry assumes a performative role, as the written signs only produce their effect when said aloud, when reunited through the voice, as can be seen here: "fulmi Camarón/ rádio fulmi oiço és é mó/fulmi Camarón/fulmi juba/fulmi morro cambiante caballo/astro nutre colo de djemi de djemi de djemi" (Poppe, *medicin* 32). The repetitions – some words, others mere syllables – which structure the poems pervade not only each book but continue to resonate from book to book as if the poet were concentrating from the outset on the composition of one single poem.

Beyond that symbolic unity that Poppe's poetry seeks to consolidate, it is also revealed as a space where the poetic subject inscribes contemplative practices. Throughout the work *come coral* (2017), the poetic subject exhibits his affiliation to the practice of conscious breathing, carved in lines like "Nada além da respiração" [Nothing beyond breathing] (Poppe, *come coral* 9), or "conheço-me reunido na respiração/da ampla essência do que não se vê" [I know myself reunited in breathing/the ample essence of what is not seen] (Poppe, *come coral* 19). Indeed, Poppe's whole poetic oeuvre since *Livro da Luz* (2012) – here allied to his trajectory as a visual artist, since this book is accompanied by collages and graphic compositions, mostly based on Asian religious iconography – proposes an idea of poetry as prayer, like a hymn, which should be integrated into a broader ritualistic activity. Both strands of Poppe's output – his poetry and visual art – complement each other through a practice intimately connected to meditation and immersion in eastern philosophies (with the public often being invited to meditate with the author inside his exhibition). In his books, too, he has developed a kind of "singable poetry," as the titles themselves announce, in "Canção persa de embalar" [Persian Lullaby] or "Melopeia" [Melopoeia] (Poppe, *Livro da Luz* 195, 198). The first corresponds to the phonetic transcription of a song in Persian, in which the semantic value of the (apparently unreadable) written signs gives way to a sound value only attainable by the reader through orality or vocal reproduction.

However, in contemporary Portuguese poetry, we can also find another example of approximation to Arab imaginary, in which poets exhibit their quality as *readers*. Through the mythification of specific natural motifs (such as the dawn and the morning, water, rivers, trees, and fruits) and certain animals (birds, horses, lions, or gazelles), Miguel Manso (b. 1979) embraces classical Arab and Persian poetry in his work through creative gestures and new ways of reading. Part of his sixth book, *Persianas* (2015), is a homage to Persian poetry, immediately evident in the choice of epigraphs (from Rumi and Omar Khayyam). As well as learning the sound power of the spoken word through this poetry – learning to "elevar a escrita à casta de leitura" [raise writing to the caste of reading] (76) – Manso makes explicit his reverence for his masters, those that "sabiam colocar no dia exacto/no instante mais animoso do ano o poema/sobre a lage ofuscada de um templo/e ver – tácita atenção – o Sol verter/as estrofes" [knew to place on the exact day/at the most spirited moment of the year the poem/on the shadowy slab of a temple/and to see – quiet attention – the sun pour out/the verses] (76–77). The images come essentially from a legendary Persia, stopped in time, where flocks graze, distances are calculated astronomically, and alchemical formulae are produced. However, despite that panegyric, some poems also carry a tone of lament by the fact that the material and immaterial legacy of that great civilization is today condemned to ruin and oblivion: "perderam-se os sussurros/as ladainhas o murmúrio indecifrável/na fala dos pássaros // as gazelas deixaram de correr à frente/dos séculos // e os leões perderam uma das duas/cabeças" [they're lost the whispers/the litanies the indecipherable murmur/in the speech of birds // the gazelles have stopped running in front/of the centuries // and the lions have lost one of the two/ heads] (75).

Though already disconnected from a Romantic-style quest for origins (boosted, as we have seen, by Adalberto Alves's translations of Andalusian poets from 1987), these contemporary phenomena may also be integrated into the context of a "Luso-Arabic" output if we accept the

160   *Catarina Nunes de Almeida*

term *Luso-Arabic* as a repository of the encounter between East and West in the Portuguese language, without restricting the timeframe. As I have tried to show previously, contemporary poetry is no longer limited to seeking in the oriental tradition exotic material with which to illustrate it or speak in its name. Literary creativity now depends on immersion in canonical texts, in original sources – Arab poetry, Persian poetry, the Koran, and so on – which stimulates the desire to relate *poetically* with alterity. This is, therefore, a voluntary *conversion* to another tradition, a kind of invisible diaspora of values, attitudes, and canonical references, which the poets accommodate in their creations.

This hybridity of values means that the poetic must now be considered on a level that can no longer be defined as purely Portuguese. Some of the works produced by the authors mentioned in this chapter – none of whom are of Arab ancestry and all of whom were born in Portugal – are the last result of a confluence of languages, styles, ideas, and points of view that do not follow the normative orientation of a school but instead reflect a choice, a reading, a personal inquiry, and, even more, an art of living that is far removed from the identity standards deemed "Portuguese." Before such a broadening, we are forced to revise the very concept of Portuguese poetry as a base that defines a particular literary heritage in its canonical uniqueness. The poets that I have discussed here assume a kind of idealized poetic globalization, to which have contributed the works of translation that some of them have produced, opening the door to other forms of writing. Thus, there has been a conscious rupture with literary history and a diversification of readings and influences. In a poet like António Barahona, we no longer find a distillation of the classical Greek and Latin authors or the canonical authors of Portuguese modernity, such as Luís de Camões or Fernando Pessoa; instead, these emblematic figures are being symbolically and unexpectedly replaced by others, like Rumi, Omar Khayyam, or Ibn Arabi. This means that a concept such as Luso-Arabic poetry needs to be extended beyond the traditional spatial-temporal boundaries, defined as medieval poetry produced in the region of Gharb al-Andalus. The specific poetic phenomena discussed here show that contemporary Portuguese literature is now a space of hospitality, where new forms, themes, and genres from the Arab tradition have begun to be accepted, blended, and reconfigured.

Notes

1. In the Iberian Peninsula, the term "Arabism" has come to refer to a field of study devoted above all to the Arab-Islamic past of the territories which, in the Early Modern period, became Portugal and Spain, thus distancing it from colonial actions which, in the Portuguese case, focused only on the territories of sub-Saharan Africa, Goa, Macau, and Timor. As Manuela Marín ("Orientalismo en España" 118) explains, this is not a purely terminological question: by avoiding the more general word "Orientalist," the Iberian Arabists

demarcated themselves from colonialist movements that supported the active intervention of the state and of science in overseas matters.

2. During the first seven centuries of Portugal's existence, the southernmost mainland region – the only one clearly defined by natural boundaries – which became known as al-Gharb, meaning "the West" (a term generally used, in the Iberian context, in correlation with al-Andalus), was known by the title of "Kingdom," showing that it was considered marginal to Portugal proper. For that reason, from the mid-13th century until the proclamation of the Republic in 1910, Portuguese monarchs styled themselves Kings of Portugal and the Algarve (and, after 1471, of the Algarves).

3. The Kingdom of Portugal was established from the County of Portugal in the 1130s, ruled by the House of Burgundy. During most of the 12th and 13th centuries, its history is essentially that of the gradual Christianization and the "reconquest" of the territory from the various Muslim *taifas* of the period. In that time, Galician-Portuguese, the western Romance variety of the ancient territory of Gallaecia, was the language used in nearly all of Iberia for lyric poetry. In 1230, the Kingdom of Galicia and Leon and the Kingdom of Castile were united permanently under a single crown. As the Christian kingdoms continued to expand their territories southward, the court and the administrative apparatus moved inland towards the center of the peninsula. The accession to the throne of Afonso III, the Boulonnais, in Portugal (1248) and Alfonso X, the Wise, in Castile (1252) breathed new life into the troubadour movement at both courts. Galician-Portuguese lyric knows its zenith in this period. In Portugal, it was predominantly an aristocratic form of poetry used to entertain the social elites at court.

4. In fact, Manuela Marín identifies a similar tendency in contemporary Spain: a phenomenon that she calls "el secuestro de al-Ándalus" ("Reflexiones sobre el arabismo español" 16), in which emotional arguments prevail over critical inquiry and scientific reflection. This "sequestration" consists of stripping that society of any characteristics it may have acquired from the medieval Arab-Islamic world, making it into a species of exception, an island of tolerance and peaceful coexistence converging with some of the expectations of our contemporaneity – or rather in selecting some significant aspects of their activity and giving them a kind of impeccable "hispanic" seal.

5. It was precisely here that Adalberto Alves founded the CELAS – Centro de Estudos Luso-Árabes de Silves [Luso-Arabic Study Centre of Silves], focusing not only on providing training in Arabic language and culture but also researching the Arab legacy in the Iberian Peninsula. The impact of Adalberto Alves's work into Luso-Arabic poetry was so significant that he was awarded the Sharjah Prize for Arab Culture by UNESCO in 2008.

Works Cited

Alves, Adalberto. *O Meu Coração é Árabe: a Poesia Luso-Árabe*. Assírio & Alvim, 1987.

———, trans. *Al-Mu'Tamid. Poeta do Destino*. Assírio & Alvim, 1996.

Alves, Adalberto and Hamdane Hadjadji, trans. *Ibn 'Ammâr Al-Andalusî – O Drama de um Poeta*. Assírio & Alvim, 2000.

Barahona, António, trans. *O Poema do Senhor. Bagavad-Guitá*. 2nd ed., Assírio & Alvim, 2007.

———. *O Sentido da Vida é Só Cantar*. Assírio & Alvim, 2008.

162 Catarina Nunes de Almeida

Bárcena, Halil. *Sufismo*. Fragmenta Editorial, 2012.

Barros, Maria Filomena Lopes de. "From the History of Muslims to Muslims in History: Some Critical Notes on 'Arab-Islamic Studies' in Portugal." *Hamsa. Journal of Judaic and Islamic Studies*, no. 1, 2014, pp. 29–40.

Boase, Roger. "Arab Influences on European Love-Poetry." *The Legacy of Muslim Spain*, edited by Salma Khadra Jayyusi, E. J. Brill, 1992, pp. 457–482.

Chittick, William C. "On the Cosmology of *Dhikr*." *Paths to the Heart: Sufism and the Christian East*, edited by James S. Cutsinger, World Wisdom, 2004, pp. 48–63.

Coelho, António Borges. *Para a História da Civilização e das Ideias no Gharb Al-Ândalus*. Instituto Camões, 1999.

———. *Portugal na Espanha Árabe*. 3rd ed., Caminho, 2008.

Correia, João David Pinto. "A literatura oral/escrita tradicional e o espaço mediterrânico: história, assuntos, poéticas." *O Mediterrâneo Ocidental. Identidades e Fronteira*, edited by Maria da Graça Mateus Ventura, Colibri, 2002, pp. 193–208.

Hatherly, Ana. *Nove Incursões*. Sociedade de Expansão Cultural, 1962.

Jayyusi, Salma Khadra. "Andalusi Poetry: The Golden Period." *The Legacy of Muslim Spain*, edited by Salma Khadra Jayyusi, E. J. Brill, 1992, pp. 317–366.

Mallette, Karla. *European Modernity and the Arab Mediterranean: Toward a New Philology and a Counter-Orientalism*. U of Pennsylvania P, 2010.

Manso, Miguel. *Persianas*. Tinta-da-China, 2015.

Marín, Manuela. "Orientalismo en España: estudios árabes y acción colonial en Marruecos (1894–1943)." *Hispania*, vol. LXIX, no. 231, 2009, pp. 117–146.

———. "Reflexiones sobre el arabismo español: tradiciones, renovaciones y secuestros." *Hamsa. Journal of Judaic and Islamic Studies*, no. 1, 2014, pp. 1–17.

Monroe, James T. "*Zajal* and *Muwashshaha*: Hispano-Arabic Poetry and the Romance Tradition." *The Legacy of Muslim Spain*, edited by Salma Khadra Jayyusi, E. J. Brill, 1992, pp. 398–419.

Nunes, Natália Maria Lopes. "Shilb (Silves) no período islâmico – a 'Bagdad do Ocidente'." *Cadernos de História*, vol. 18, no. 28, 2017, pp. 331–349.

Oliveira-Leitão, André. "Do Ġarb al-Ândalus ao 'segundo reino' da 'Coroa de Portugal': território, política e identidade." *CLIO – Revista do Centro de História da Universidade de Lisboa*, no. 16/17, 2008, pp. 69–104.

Poppe, António. *Livro da Luz*. Documenta, 2012.

———. *medicin*. Douda Correria, 2015.

———. *come coral*. Douda Correria, 2017.

Reckert, Stephen. *Para Além das Neblinas de Novembro. Perspectivas sobre a Poesia Ocidental e Oriental*. Fundação Calouste Gulbenkian, 1999.

Tavani, Giuseppe. *A Poesia Lírica Galego-Portuguesa*. Editorial Comunicação, 1990.

Torres, Cláudio. "O Garb Al-Andaluz." *História de Portugal*, edited by José Mattoso, vol. 1, Círculo de Leitores, 1992, pp. 363–415.

Zwartjes, Otto. "The Andalusi *Kharjas*: A Courtly Counterpoint to Popular Tradition?" *Scripta Mediterranea*, vols. XIX–XX, 1998–1999, pp. 45–54.

10 Portugal Against the Moors in the 21st Century

Invisible Diasporas and the "Mediatic Romanticism" of a Contemporary Opera[1]

Everton V. Machado

Portugal contra os mouros [*Portugal Against the Moors*] is the title of a work of historical vulgarization written by an important Arabist, David Lopes, published during the second decade of the 20th century in a popular book series called *Os Livros do Povo* [*The Books of the People*]. The literary works that founded Portuguese romanticism in the previous century already shared the Orientalist paradigm of the "clash of civilizations" with nationalist historiography.[2] Lopes's book begins by claiming that "gentes estranhas, vindas da África do Norte" [strange people from North Africa] had invaded the Iberian Peninsula in the 8th century (3). It was only after the Carnation Revolution of April 25, 1974, and the end of Salazar's dictatorial regime (*Estado Novo*) that the Arab-Islamic presence in Portugal began to be studied with eyes other than those of the "ideológicos de cruzada" [ideologists of crusade], to use the words of António Borges Coelho (13), one of the intellectuals responsible for this change of paradigm (Correia 170).

The impressive staging of *Geraldo e Samira: Uma ópera para Évora* [*Geraldo and Samira: An Opera to Évora*][3] – an open-air show of 2019, seen by a thousand people in the historic Portuguese-Arab city of Yabura (as Évora was called in Arabic) and sponsored by the local government – featured the Portuguese version of *Cid Campeador*, Geraldo Sem Pavor [Geraldo the Fearless], who conquered many territories of al-Andalus in the wake of the so-called *Reconquista* carried out by the Christian kingdoms around the 12th century. The territory now occupied by Portugal corresponds to the western part of al-Andalus ("Gharb"). Arab-Islamic dominance on the peninsula effectively ended in 1492, with the conquest of the Kingdom of Granada by the Catholic Monarchs of Spain, but the Portuguese had already achieved outright victory in its territory in 1249, with the capture of the city of Faro. Geraldo captured Évora from the Almohads (a caliphate that originated in Morocco) in 1165. Lopes himself contributed to the historical prestige of this legendary character, in contrast to his predecessors, who saw the Portuguese knight just as an ordinary mercenary.

DOI: 10.4324/9781003245117-13

164 *Everton V. Machado*

Through analyzing *Geraldo e Samira*'s discourse on the Other, this chapter will explore the possible connections between a persistent "mediatic romanticism" (Silva 33) (riddled with Orientalism) and the cultural and political "invisibility" of those who are today the "Moors" of Portugal: the Muslim diaspora communities from former Portuguese colonies (especially those from Mozambique and Guinea Bissau), as well as those from other former European colonies (especially those from Pakistan, Bangladesh, and Senegal).[4] Contrary to what has been happening across Europe in recent years, Portugal is seen as an example of how to deal with Muslim immigration due to an alleged promotion of multicultural coexistence. This chapter aims to question this vision of the phenomenon, insomuch as the idea of integrating the Other into the national community does not fail to meld with long-standing civilizational stereotypes. Here is a previous problematization of this situation:

> In viewing the phenomenon of Islam in present-day Portugal, the interest of what we see lies in what we do not see: no demonstrations against opening mosques; no controversial issues in parliament, in local administration, or in the media; no 'headscarf affair;' no debates on official recognition or standards of secularism. . . . One must ask why this is so. . . . [T]he fact that Muslims, who represent the largest non-Christian religious minority in Portugal, are few in number is not the one and only explanation for the relatively encouraging state of socio-religious co-existence. . . . To prevent misunderstandings, one must note that the silence surrounding the Muslim minority in Portugal means neither that they have been ignored, nor that they have been privileged. It appears rather that they have been overlooked in various contexts and for a variety of reasons.
>
> (Tiesler 71–72)

Could literary, historical, and artistic discourses help us with these reasons? I will first seek to explore how the figure of Geraldo[5] has been presented over the course of history before being featured in the opera, which shares with 19th-century literary products not only the paradigm of the *invention of the Orient* (Said 1978) but also romantic nationalism. Finally, by way of conclusion, I will propose an analysis of that which a European report described as the "apparent ambivalence" of the Portuguese government "towards the Muslim community" (Allen and Nielsen 26), since it may be linked to the ambivalence present in the discourses on the historical relationship between Portugal and Islam, thus helping to explain the existence of *invisible diasporas* in the territory today:

> a relação de Portugal com o Islão remonta à fundação da nacionalidade, e essa tão apregoada longa história, bem como os usos dessa

história, não são sem consequência quer para o olhar português sobre o Islão, quer para os muçulmanos em Portugal.

[Portugal's relationship with Islam dates back to the founding of the nation, and this much-touted long history, as well as the uses of this history, are not without consequence, be it for the Portuguese vision of Islam, or for Muslims in Portugal.]

(Vakil 283)

A Controversial Political Object

The figure of Geraldo is all the more interesting for a discussion concerning identity constructs and Orientalism because – despite the secondary role that he played in the history of Portugal (not to mention the much-debated theories about the exact nature of his contribution) – he has been transformed into a "hero" identified with an ideal of the Portuguese people or nation. It is certain that "um simples ladrão não se atreveria a tomar Trujillo, Évora, Cáceres, Montanchez, Serpa e Juromenha e ir pôr cerco a Badajoz" [a simple thief would not dare to capture Trujillo, Évora, Cáceres, Montánchez, Serpa, and Joromenha, and go and lay siege to Badajoz], but men like Geraldo, who operated in *frontier zones* – the actions of the character in question played out essentially in the area today known as the Portuguese Alentejo and Spain's Extremadura – "limitavam-se a oferecer os seus préstimos aos diversos reinos peninsulares, mouros . . . ou cristãos" [restricted themselves to offering their services to the various peninsular kingdoms, whether Moorish . . . or Christian] (Barata 368–371).

In any case, albeit with somewhat debatable characterization, Geraldo appears as a certified hero in the Portuguese national epic, Camões's *Os Lusíadas* [*The Lusiads*] (1572).[6] Camões was part of a trend through which "the topos that Islamic presence was an intrusion into Portuguese history" came to be established:

> it was necessary to make visible the differences, not only religious, but also political, social, and cultural. These differences justified the fact that Islam was to be expelled from the Portuguese historical memory just as Muslims were physically expelled from the kingdom.
>
> (Xavier and Zupanov 12)[7]

The eighth Canto of *Os Lusíadas* invokes the famous motif of the attack on the watchtower from the legend of Geraldo. The hero returns from the tower with two Moorish heads, then lures the Muslims out of Yabura, leaving the gates of the city open. The knight and the decapitated Moorish heads became the official symbol of the Municipality of Évora in 1987 and are now featured in its coat of arms. Camões could have taken the

166   Everton V. Machado

episode (along with many other details relating to Évora and the Middle Ages) from the works of the humanist André de Resende (Soares Pereira 845), one of the most important figures responsible for the change in tone in the treatment given to Geraldo. Indeed, although Geraldo's name ended up being passed down before the sixteenth century, it was not without a certain "laconismo" [curtness] or "suspeitosas reservas" [suspicious reserve] (Sousa Pereira 24). Resende gave substance to the character of Geraldo,[8] despite basing his account on somewhat disjointed information or simple conjectures. Even so, the legacy that he left to posterity "trata-se da apresentação e interpretação dos factos que tem sido repetida até à exaustão, sobretudo ao nível da história local. Tal a sua força identitária" [consists in the particular presentation and interpretation of the facts that have been repeated ad nauseam, especially at the level of local history, such is its strength in terms of identity] (Sousa Pereira 28).

In the 19th century, Alexandre Herculano, the father of modern Portuguese historiography, refused to take Geraldo seriously, relegating his circle to the status of "bandos de salteadores . . . indiferentes à luta do predomínio das duas raças, e atentos só a saciar a própria crueldade e cobiça nas suas correrias e assaltos sem objecto político" [bands of brigands . . . indifferent to the struggle for dominance being fought between two races, and interested only in satisfying their own cruelty and greed in their raids and attacks, which had no political objective] (551). Finding little relevant information in documents from the period, Herculano concludes by asserting that the silence surrounding this character "poderia até fazer suspeitar o sucesso de fabuloso" [could even make us consider the event as a fable] (552).[9] Oliveira Martins, another prominent figure in Portuguese culture in the 19th century, accuses Geraldo and his companions of not having "noção de pátria a que pertencessem, nem de religião que seguissem" [notion of a homeland to which they might belong or of a religion that they might follow] (93–94).

As can be easily inferred, the disdain of Herculano and Martins arises from the fact that someone like Geraldo was not inspired to act by a necessity or a *patriotic* logic (in accordance with the ideology of the 19th century) of expelling the Moors from the territory. Ultimately, however, it was the fanciful attack on the watchtower which – in the imaginary and through the symbology that it conjures up – ended up becoming a "political object," carrying the "notion of a homeland." In order to understand not only the image of the knight that will serve as the basis for the opera but also the diegetic alteration of the motif of the watchtower, here is the account of the episode in a reasonably well-circulated 19th-century historical monograph, where the attack on the watchtower is narrated as a decidedly truthful fact:

> [L] ogo que anoiteceu, [Geraldo] sahiu acompanhado de todos [os seus companheiros], a quem mandou occultar em certo sitio perto da

entrada do castello. Em seguida dirigiu-se sósinho á torre da Atalaya, onde estava por sentinella um mouro e uma sua filha. Não tinha esta torre porta de entrada, mas apenas uma janella por onde só se podia penetrar por meio de uma escada de corda. Intemeratamente, espetando lanças de ferro nas juntas das pedras, subiu até á janella onde estava a moura, que precipitou abaixo da torre, onde entrou, degolando em seguida o mouro que ainda dormia, levando as cabeças do pae e da filha aos seus, em signal de bom annuncio.

(Pinheiro Chagas 61)

[As soon as night fell, (Geraldo) set out with all of (his companions), telling them to hide in a particular place near the entrance to the castle. He then went alone to the watchtower, where a Moor was stationed as a sentinel with his daughter. This tower had no door as an entrance, just a window through which one could only pass using a rope ladder. Righteously, he drove iron spears into the joints between the stones to climb to the window, where he found the Mooress and threw her down from the tower, which he then entered, decapitating the still-sleeping Moor and taking the heads of father and daughter back to his men as a sign of the good news.]

This is the *imagery* that stuck. Here one must recall what was said previously concerning the dual movement of the expulsion of the Moors: this is an *imagery* that symbolizes an evident "construção identitária que prefigura o renascimento de Évora, sob o signo de uma criação descontaminada de qualquer vestígio anterior" [identity construct which prefigures the rebirth of Évora, in the guise of a creation decontaminated of all previous vestiges] (Barros 11). It is indeed in the sense of an *identity construct* that the author himself of *Portugal contra os mouros* comes to contradict his master, Herculano:[10] Lopes express irritation with the fact that the former only "aceita[r] a custo a historicidade de Giraldo" [begrudgingly accepts Giraldo's historicit] (*Os Arabes* 104). He cites Arab historians from the period to demonstrate that "a personalidade histórica de Giraldo é incontestável; elle foi um verdadeiro heroe, não de romance, mas de epopeia" [the historical nature of Giraldo is incontestable; he was a real hero, worthy not of a romance, but an epic] (96). Here Lopes undoubtedly echoes Camões but also invests Geraldo with a necessary patriotic halo. He even writes a study entirely dedicated to the knight (1940) and considers him on equal terms with Spain's Rodrigo Díaz de Vivar, the famous *Cid Campeador*.[11]

In any case, it appears that there is now little doubt among specialists that Geraldo "actuava por sua própria conta e risco, à margem de qualquer autoridade" [acted to his own ends and at his own risk, outside of any kind of authority], not to mention that he was "mais próximo do mercenário que da fidelidade vassálica dos romances de cavalaria e das histórias patrióticas eivadas de anacronismos" [more like a mercenary

168 *Everton V. Machado*

than the faithful vassal depicted in chivalric romances and patriotic histories littered with anachronisms] (Sousa Pereira 53). The opera *Geraldo e Samira* can very much be counted among the latter. Despite suggesting a love story (and, consequently, tolerant intercultural coexistence), its title alone immediately sets up the antinomy of Occident/Orient, which is underscored by the use of the Hispano-Arabic and Galician-Minhoto languages by the piece's Muslim and Christian characters, respectively. Indeed, the reasoning behind this choice was that it would "highlight the two different cultures of the characters" (Musicamera Produções 9).

From Coexistence to Its Failure

If, on the one hand, "the nineteenth and twentieth centuries witnessed a flourishing of European scholarship, literature, and art that focused on the Orient," on the other, "many Orientalists, however, developed images of Muslim and Arab peoples that . . . perpetuated medieval stereotypes" (Green 79–80). Furthermore, "the image of the Saracen pagan lives on in the European imagination," as demonstrated, for example, by the "festivals of Moors and Christians [taking] place to this day in small towns throughout contemporary Spain," in which participants celebrate "Christian victories over the Moors, or Muslims of North African origin, during the Reconquista" (Green 47). Portugal also has its share of journeys into the past, in the form of medieval festivals that transform locations such as Santa Maria da Feira or Óbidos into attractive tourist destinations ("Viagens ao passado" 82), although in smaller numbers than in Spain and without reflecting, as in the latter, a "cultural trauma" (Flesler 12–13).[12]

The so-called *Mértola effect* is what gives to the case of Portugal a particular character. This phenomenon is named after the project led since late 1970 by Cláudio Torres, founder and director of the archaeological site of the municipality of Mértola. Here,

> os estratos arqueológicos dos diferentes períodos romanos, paleocristãos e muçulmanos parecem ali sobrepor-se harmoniosamente, ilustrando facilmente a possibilidade de uma multiculturalidade sucessiva e menos conflituosa que a apresentada pela visão heroica salazarista dos manuais escolares.
>
> [the archaeological strata of the different Roman, Paleochristian and Islamic periods appear to overlap harmoniously, neatly illustrating the possibility of a continuous multiculturality less characterized by conflict than is suggested by the heroic Salazarist vision offered by school textbooks.]
>
> (Silva 29)

Not only did Mértola become "em vinte anos, o grande baluarte das origens árabes de Portugal" [the great bastion of the Arabic origins of

Portugal, within twenty years], but its reverberations in the media in the 1990s promoted it "como modelo de desenvolvimento local, o que levou à sua imitação (ou tentativa disso) noutros pontos do país. E, no pacote desenvolvimentista seguiram, também, os árabes, e a sua promoção" [as a model of local development, which led to imitations (or attempts at imitations) in other locations around the country. And wrapped up in this development-focused package were the Arabs, as well as their promotion] (Silva 30). Since 2001, Mértola has organized an Islamic Festival involving music, gastronomy, crafts, exhibitions, and conferences, which attracts thousands of visitors when it takes place every other year. Regarding historical representations in music and dance shows, whether in the context of festivals such as Mértola's or at independent events, they ultimately conform to a single paradigm in Portugal:

> Por um lado, a figura do mouro emerge num tom grotesco claramente como candidato à derrota. . . . [E]sta posição decorre, creio, do confronto de representações de natureza política, ética, moral e religiosa. . . . Por outro lado, quando se procura retratar uma ambiência civilizacional e introduzir elementos performáticos como a música, a dança ou certo tipo de acções espectaculares . . ., aí intervêm outras categorias, positivizadas, na construção da imagem do oriente. . . . No contexto dos projectos de dança e de música de inspiração árabe e oriental . . ., é claramente visível este enfoque no belo civilizacional, positivizando a imagem do outro, ainda que manipulando estereótipos de natureza semelhante aos que sustentaram os olhares e representações do árabe e do Oriente desde o Iluminismo na Europa.
>
> (Raposo 69–70)

> [On the one hand, the figure of the Moor is presented in a grotesque light, as a clear candidate for defeat. . . . [T]his position, I believe, is the result of the confrontation of representations of political, ethical, moral and religious natures. . . . On the other hand, when re-enactments seek to present a civilizational ambiance and introduce performance elements, such as music, dance, or a certain kind of spectacular action . . ., other positive categories intervene in the construction of the image of the Orient. . . . In the context of Arab and Oriental-inspired dance and music projects . . ., this focus on civilizational beauty is visible, making the image of the Other positive, albeit while manipulating stereotypes similar in nature to those which have sustained perspectives on and representations of the Arab and the Orient since the Enlightenment in Europe.]

In *Geraldo e Samira*, we find similar ways of dealing with the Moor and performative exoticism. But the ambivalence which constitutes my principal interest arises from the very paradigms that underlie the conception of the opera. The script's paratext even contains contradictory discourses from the

170 Everton V. Machado

show's creators. The words of its producer and artistic director, Luís Pacheco Cunha, not only reflect the myth of *convivencia* that was belatedly fostered in the 20th century but also indicate that Cunha is not comfortable with the fact that the controversial figure of Geraldo is a representative of Évora:

> Geraldo não será, talvez, o herói que a cidade merece. A sua acção, em plena Reconquista . . . veio interromper a pujança cultural da cidade, o seu cosmopolitismo, fundado na tolerância que a civilização árabe promovia e permitia a todas as raças e credos viver em harmonia à sombra das suas muralhas, embalados no manso fluir do tempo e da história.
>
> (Musicamera Produções 11)

> [Geraldo is not, perhaps, the hero that the city deserves. His action, amid the Reconquista . . . interrupted the city's cultural vigor, its cosmopolitanism, which was founded on the tolerance that Arab civilization promoted and that allowed all races and creeds to live in harmony in the shade of the city's walls, softly rocked by the gentle flow of time and history.]

Indeed, here one can see "the idealization of the 'convivencia,' or peaceful coexistence between diverse faiths living under benign Muslim rule," which "serves diverse rhetorical purposes" (Tolan 303). It is no coincidence that the *Mértola effect* triggered "formas de islamofilia e arabismo num processo político de reconfiguração identitária de traços culturais minoritários e invisibilizados pela história ibérica" [forms of Islamophilia and Arabism in a political process of identity reconfiguration regarding traces of minority cultures and cultures rendered invisible by Iberian history] (Raposo 82). However, in the words of the opera's scriptwriter, Helena da Nóbrega, there is not exactly an idea of *convivencia* or Islamophilia, as one can see in her insistence on a supposed *just cause* motivating the actions of the mercenary. In the citation that follows, it is worth noting the historical mishmash presented by her. Well, in the 12th century, the Almoravids had been replaced in the control of the territory by the Almohads (who did not arrive at the same time as the former, nor did they act similarly to them in terms of politics), and the Mozarabs were actually the Christians who remained in the peninsula under Islamic rule (and Arabized themselves), without being prohibited from practicing their religion:

> [no] século XII . . . a ameaça do reino de Portugal ao Gharb Al-Andaluz era cada vez maior e a chegada de tribos almorávidas e almôhadas ao sul da Península Ibérica configurava então as primeiras políticas de exclusão e intolerância, obrigando judeus e moçárabes a procurar refúgio nos reinos cristãos ao norte da península.
>
> (Musicamera Produções 12)

Portugal Against the Moors in the 21st Century 171

[(in the) twelfth century, the threat presented by the Kingdom of Portugal to Gharb al-Andalus was ever more significant. The arrival of Almoravid and Almohad tribes in the south of the Iberian Peninsula led to the first policies of exclusion and intolerance, which forced Jews and Mozarabs to seek refuge in the Christian kingdoms to the north of the peninsula.]

Although acknowledged as a controversial figure, Geraldo is totally romanticized. It is not difficult to see that the scriptwriter justifies Geraldo's actions either because of religion or the nation's formation. He is presented as "rejeitando a cultura 'andaluzi'" [rejecting "andalusi" culture] (Musicamera Produções 12), even though today historians almost unanimously agree in affirming that men like him were driven by personal gain. He will certainly not have been a "herói pátrio e intrépido servidor de uma causa nacional e religiosa" [patriotic hero and intrepid servant of a national and religious cause] (Sousa Pereira 86). The scriptwriter of *Geraldo e Samira* continues:

[ele] tem características – psicológicas e sociais – do anti-herói, e/ou um determinado carisma através do qual obtém a aprovação dos seus seguidores, mesmo praticando actos ilícitos. Os seus objectivos são considerados justos ou, pelo menos, compreensíveis. Séculos de narrativas populares podem ter ajudado a transformá-lo numa personagem lendária da história de Portugal em que os fins justificam os meios.

(Musicamera Produções 12)

[(he) has psychological and social characteristics of the anti-hero and/or a certain charisma through which he obtains the approval of his followers, even while carrying out illicit acts. His objectives are considered just or, at least, understandable. Perhaps centuries of folk tales have helped to transform him into a legendary figure in the history of Portugal, where the ends justify the means.]

As for the Moorish woman, Samira appears to be "habituada a conviver com pessoas e culturas diferentes" [accustomed to living alongside different people and cultures] (Musicamera Produções 12). The same is true of her maid, Yasmina, who even "mostra conhecer a liturgia cristã praticada pelos moçárabes" [shows that she knows the Christian liturgy practiced by the Mozarabs] (Musicamera Produções 12). This *convivencia* is therefore present in the opera, but it is ultimately the very reason for the downfall of the Moors, seeing as it is "nesta abertura de comportamentos que Geraldo vê uma oportunidade para tirar proveito da sua relação com Yasmina e raptar Samira, filha do alcaide de Yabura, usando-a depois como moeda de troca para tomar a cidade" [in this

172 *Everton V. Machado*

openness of attitudes that Geraldo sees an opportunity to take advantage of his relationship with Yasmina to kidnap Samira, daughter of the mayor of Yabura, and use her as a bargaining chip to capture the city] (Musicamera Produções 12).

Along with various other characters, both Samira and Yasmina are invented figures, absent from all versions of the legend of Geraldo. As can be perceived immediately from the opera's plot, the events that reportedly led to the capture of Yabura have been completely changed. The reinterpretation of the motif of the attack on the watchtower is quite creative: instead of Geraldo climbing up to the window and throwing the Moorish woman down, Samira – who has been taken captive and has fallen in love with her kidnapper – dies after throwing herself from the tower of her own free will, due to the impossibility of this love.[13] Ultimately, the opera inserts itself in "the large field of Medievalism" in its "creative" aspect, although it would not be incorrect to classify it within the "political-ideological" field, in light of the ambivalences that this chapter has pointed out in discourses. In the case of the former, "topics, works, themes, and also authors of the Middle Ages, are used for new works creatively." In the latter, they "are used for political purposes to legitimate or denounce (for example the ideology of 'crusade')" (Müller 853).

As is already well known, "interest in the Middle Ages arose and has intensified since the end of the 18th century as a result of Romanticism and the beginnings of European patriotism and nationalism" (Müller 854). The opera shares with creative Portuguese works of the 19th century not only the reproduction of the motif of captivity seen in Medieval romances and Renaissance novellas but also the topos of conversion through love and marriage (see Teo 2012). Naturally, this topos is interpreted in quite different ways: in both Almeida Garrett's *Dona Branca ou A conquista do Algarve* [Dona Branca or The Conquest of the Algarve] (1826) and Alexandre Herculano's *Eurico, o Presbítero* [Eurico, the Presbyter] (1844), for example, the captives are white/Christians. Furthermore, in the former, the love between Dona Branca and the Moor, Aben-Afan, results from a magical spell which is subsequently broken, while in the latter, Hemengarda energetically defends herself against her kidnapper, Abdulaziz. It is nevertheless significant (as a transposition of established narrative themes) that the romantic relationship (or desire of one) between Moors and Christians is doomed to utter failure in *Dona Branca*, *Eurico*, and *Geraldo e Samira*: it seems that, in order to preserve a pure ethnic foundation for the nation, the two races cannot be allowed to mix.

In addition, both the protagonist of the opera, Samira, and her maid, Yasmina, are the object of that which – in diegetic, scenographic, and musical terms – fundamentally sustains the opera, or at least makes it appealing to the eyes of the public. That is, the characterization of these women drifts towards the so-called "re-presentation of canonical material" in the context of Orientalist production (Said 177): the

Portugal Against the Moors in the 21st Century   173

exoticization/eroticization of Arab women, not to mention the idea that they easily submit to white men, seeing as both Samira and Yasmina fall in love with Geraldo, even though he is deceptive. In the first act, the "sweet dark girl," Yasmina, invites her "Christian friend" into her bed ("lie down naked") (Musicamera Produções 16): "historical facts of domination" that authorize the possession of the Oriental woman by the Western man (Said 6), if not the stereotype of her natural willingness. Although she has been kidnapped, Samira goes so far as to help Geraldo capture Yabura. And, as is to be expected, belly dancing – the Oriental dancing girl is, after all, a colonial invention (Bracco 2017) – is front and center in the show. At their core, these artistic clichés conceal a heavy ideological weight: "são justamente estas fantasmagorias do desejo e da volúpia mas também do mistério e do exótico oriental que se propagam no contexto [destas] recriações históricas" [it is precisely this phantasmagoria of desire and sensuality, but also of mystery and oriental exoticism, that are propagated in the context of (these) historical re-enactments], with the Muslims becoming the object of "um pastiche cultural sobre o qual se pode fantasiar conceptualmente sem risco ameaçador" [a cultural pastiche about which one can fantasize conceptually without taking any threatening risks] (Raposo 74).

Concluding Remarks: Underlying Political Struggles

What I am ultimately calling into question regarding this opera – and it is a consideration that should be extended to other historical representations, even those that are purportedly purely for entertainment – is if the "very fictiveness of artworks" does not end up serving "to disguise or make palatable some demonstrably prejudicial portrayals of other peoples and places" (Locke 22), or, more specifically, if "the romance of 'Oriental' operatic Works" (and other artistic media) does not actually hide "underlying political struggles" (Mabilat 12). By creating a kind of *mediatic romanticism* – through the "musealização e a patrimonialização . . . de um passado oprimido" [museumification and heritagization . . . of a suppressed past] which gained extensive media coverage – the *Mértola effect* seems to have set a precedent both for the "reificação de uma certa imagem essencialista dos 'árabes' e dos 'muçulmanos'" [reification of a certain essentialist image of 'Arabs' and 'Muslims'] and for "sua apropriação pelas retóricas e paisagens da política nacional" [its appropriation by the rhetoric and landscape of national politics] (Silva 33–36). Mértola is presented as "o lugar onde pode repousar o multiculturalismo" [the place where multiculturalism can rest] with the "discurso da tolerância e da integração que se instalou em largos sectores da vida pública portuguesa" [discourse of tolerance and integration that has inserted itself into broad sectors of public life in Portugal] (Silva 34). And, as already discussed, the media attention that the project received has turned it into a template for

174 *Everton V. Machado*

other Portuguese municipalities and regions, stimulating the generation of activities that extend beyond the field of archaeology.

It is all the more important to analyze cultural products such as the opera *Geraldo e Samira* when one considers that creative medievalism can actually be speaking to us about our own present. One must not only remember that "the Middle Ages have often served as an imaginary object used to vaunt the present by casting the medieval Other in its shadow" but also recognize that "any contradictions are the result of a socially conditioned and malleable idea", which makes "it is easier to understand how and why they so readily become a collective cultural myth, and why they are not dead yet" (Elliott 32). This could well explain the "apparent ambivalence" detected in Portugal in the *Summary Report on Islamophobia in the EU After 11 September 2001*. Could this *ambivalence* (to which literary, historical, and artistic discourses all make their contributions) be responsible for the existence of *invisible diasporas* in Portugal?

> The overall picture was one of reconciliation between both Muslim and non-Muslim. . . . [T]he extremely low levels of hostility experienced following the attacks on the US were due to the historical relationship between Portugal and Islam, the integration of Portuguese Muslims into wider society and their "invisibility." . . . However, most of the political debate was connected to national security and immigration, particularly by those on the right. The leader of the Portuguese Muslim community later criticized the government for its apparent ambivalence towards the Muslim community in the aftermath of events.
>
> (Allen and Nielsen 26)

In turn, the results of a survey of expressions of Islamophobia[14] could help us to understand how, by promoting the banalization of historically conditioned *topoi*, literary and artistic works hide *underlying political struggles*, thereby revealing the nature of the aporias in discourse concerning Portugal and its relationship with Islam: "o ódio antimuçulmano é politicamente subestimado e sub-participado às autoridades" [anti-Muslim hate is underestimated politically and under-reported to authorities], it being the case that "o incentivo às denúncias de islamofobia perturbariam a lógica de despolitização que caracteriza o debate público sobre discriminação étnico-racial e religiosa no contexto português" [the incentive to denounce Islamophobia would disrupt the logic of depoliticization that characterizes public debate about ethno-racial and religious discrimination in the context of Portugal] (Araújo 28–29). The "narrativas da islamofobia identificadas como mais comuns" [narratives of Islamophobia identified as the most common] in the previous survey (ten of which were highlighted) allow us to focus on "duas questões basilares" [two fundamental questions] (Araújo 30), which are none other than those that shape not only the canonical representation of Geraldo but also the global message of the opera of 2019:

> Em primeiro lugar, os muçulmanos são percebidos como estando na Europa, mas não sendo da Europa. Como tal, tornam-se uma "presença intrusiva" que perturba uma narrativa da Europa que se baseia num espaço homogéneo e num tempo linear, segundo a qual Portugal seria um país fundacional e naturalmente homogéneo (isto é, branco e cristão) – e tornado diverso apenas pela imigração recente decorrente de processos de globalização. Nesse sentido, a formação de uma oposição binária entre Ocidente/Europa/Portugal, e o Islão/Oriente, constrói a figura do muçulmano como uma exterioridade à nação – ao mesmo tempo que invisibiliza como a história do Islão é constitutiva de Portugal.
>
> (Araújo 30)

> [First of all, Muslims are seen as being in Europe, but not from Europe. As such, they become "an intrusive presence" which disrupts a narrative of Europe which is based on a homogenous space and a linear conception of time, according to which Portugal is a country that is fundamentally and naturally homogenous (which is to say, white and Christian) – and that has only been made diverse by recent immigration resulting from the processes of globalization. In this way, the formation of a binary opposition between West/Europe/Portugal and Islam/Orient constructs the figure of the Muslim as something exterior to the nation – while simultaneously rendering invisible how the history of Islam is a constituent part of Portugal.]

In light of what has been discussed here, I am moved to agree with both Edward Said, when he highlights the "durability" and "strength" of Orientalism (7), and with Evelyn Alsultany and Ella Shohat, who point out the possible differences than can exist in different places around the world in the "interface between diasporic communities and the hegemonic society," as well as the occurrence of a "(shared) colonialist and Orientalist intertext" (5–6). In the case of Portugal, this interface is distinct in the sense that it is sustained, as it is in Spain, by a "domestic Orient" (López García 20) concerning the memory of the Arab-Islamic presence in the Iberian Peninsula and its articulations with the construction of national identity.

Notes

1. Translated from Portuguese by Robin Driver and revised by the author.
2. This is what I have sought to demonstrate (principally with reference to Almeida Garrett and Alexandre Herculano, who will be discussed in the following) in my current research project, "The Orientalisation of the Muslims

176   *Everton V. Machado*

from Alexandre Herculano (1810–1870) to David Lopes (1867–1942): Imagination, Science and Politics in the Geoculture of the Modern World-System."

3. Available to view with Portuguese and English subtitles at www.youtube.com/watch?v=OY4o_rk5Ze4.

4. The 2011 Census reported the presence of just over 20,000 Muslims in Portugal (Observatório das Migrações 8).

5. Also spelled "Giraldo" by several authors.

6. Geraldo is reminded in Cantos III and VIII.

7. The Moors were expelled along with the Jews by D. Manuel I in 1496–1497.

8. In *História da Antiguidade da Cidade de Évora* (1553).

9. The capture of Évora by Geraldo as it is told.

10. David Lopes's career as an Arabist was indebted to the historiographic and fictional work undertaken by Herculano.

11. Later, Américo Castro, who is quite well reputed in Spain, affirmed that he considered this comparison absurd, going so far as to say that he viewed Geraldo's "Sem Pavor" as an interpolation with the "Sans Peur" of Richard I of Normandy (932–996). See also González 2020: "Although Geraldo Sem Pavor did not generate such a torrent of heroic literature and subsequent mythifications as Rodrigo Díaz, both characters certainly have similarities."

12. On the other hand, and to a certain extent, one could speak of the same dialectic between *visibility* and *invisibility* that occurs in Spain if we consider other immigrant populations in the case of Portugal: "the logic of excessive visibility of the exotic Moor on which the festivals are predicated betrays the desire to relegate Moorish presence to a remote past and to distant lands, thus predetermining the invisibility of the real Moroccan immigrant of today" (Flesler 114).

13. In the legend that explains the name of another Portuguese city, Moura ("Moorish"), the princess who ruled the city (Salúquia) threw herself from a tower after being tricked by the Christians who killed her beloved, also a Moor (Bráfama). They dressed as Muslims and, thinking that the entourage that was approaching was that of her beloved, she ordered the doors of the fortress to be opened, and the city was captured.

14. A survey carried out in Portuguese cyberspace between 2001 and 2017 (in academic, political, mediatic, and social contexts).

Works Cited

Allen, Christopher, and Jorgen S. Nielsen. *Summary Report on Islamophobia in the EU after 11 September 2001*. European Monitoring Centre on Racism and Xenophobia, 2002.

Alsultany, Evelyn, and Ella Shohat. "The Cultural Politics of 'the Middle East' in the Americas: An Introduction." *Between the Middle East and the Americas: The Cultural Politics of Diaspora*, edited by Evelyn Alsultany and Ella Shohat, U of Michigan P, 2013, pp. 3–41.

Araújo, Marta. *A islamofobia e as suas narrativas em Portugal: conhecimento, política, média e ciberespaço*. Centro de Estudos Sociais, 2019.

Barata, Filipe Themudo. "A actuação de Geraldo Sem Pavor no Quadro da Sociedades de Fronteira do Século XII." *Actas 2º Congresso Histórico de Guimarães*, vol. 2, Câmara Municipal de Guimarães, 1997, pp. 359–374.

Barros, Maria Filomena de. "Prefácio." *Geraldo sem pavor: um guerreiro de fronteira entre cristãos e muçulmanos c. 1162–1176*, edited by Armando de Sousa Pereira, Fronteira do Caos, 2008, pp. 11–12.

Portugal Against the Moors in the 21st Century   177

Borges Coelho, António. *Portugal na Espanha árabe.* 5th ed., Editorial Caminho, 2008.

Bracco, Carolina. "La invención de las bailarinas orientales. Un artefacto colonial." *Journal of Feminist, Gender and Women Studies,* no. 6, 2017, pp. 55–64.

Camões, Luís de. *Os Lusíadas.* Itatiaia and Universidade de São Paulo, 1980.

Castro, Américo. *The Spaniards: An Introduction to Their History,* translated by Willard F. King and Selma Margaretten, U of California P, 1971.

Correia, Fernando Branco. "Al-Andalus en la historiografía portuguesa (del siglo XIX a inicios del XXI): Un breve intento de sistematización." *Al-Andalus/España. Historiografías en contraste: Siglos XVII–XXI,* edited by Manuela Marín, Casa de Velázquez, 2009, pp. 163–181.

Elliott, Andrew B. R. *Medievalism, Politics and Mass Media: Appropriating the Middle Ages in the Twenty-First Century.* D. S. Brewer, 2017.

Flesler, Daniela. *The Return of the Moor: Spanish Responses to Contemporary Moroccan Immigration.* Purdue UP, 2008.

Garrett, Almeida. *Dona Branca ou A conquista do Algarve.* J.P. Aillaud, 1826.

González, David Porrinas. "Geraldo Sempavor, el Cid português." *Desperta Ferro Ediciones,* www.despertaferro-ediciones.com/2020/geraldo-sempavor-el-cid-portugues/.

———. "La actuación de Giraldo Sempavor al mediar el siglo XII, un estudio comparativo." *II Jornadas de Historia Medieval de Extremadura: ponencias y comunicaciones,* edited by Julián Clemente Ramos and Juan Luis de la Montaña Conchiña, Editora Regional de Extremadura, 2005, pp. 179–188.

Green, Todd H. *The Fear of Islam: An Introduction to Islamophobia in the West.* Fortress Press, 2015.

Herculano, Alexandre. *Eurico, o Presbítero,* 1844.

———. *História de Portugal: Desde o Começo da Monarquia até ao Fim do reinado de Afonso III,* vol. 1, Livraria Bertrand, 1980.

Locke, Ralph P. "Cutthroats and Casbah Dancers, Muezzins and Timeless Sands: Musical Images of the Middle East." *19th-Century Music,* vol. 22, no. 1, 1998, pp. 20–53.

Lopes, David. *Os Arabes nas obras de Alexandre Herculano: notas marginaes de lingua e historia portuguesa.* Imprensa Nacional, 1911.

———. *Portugal Contra Os Mouros.* Livraria Profissional, 1916.

———. "O Cid português: Geraldo Sempavor (novas fontes árabes sobre os seus feitos e morte." *Revista Portuguesa de História,* vol. 1, 1940, pp. 93–111.

López García, Bernabé. *Orientalismo e ideología colonial en el arabismo español (1840–1917).* EUG, 2011.

Mabilat, Claire. *British Orientalism and Representations of Music in the Long Nineteenth Century Ideas of Music, Otherness, Sexuality and Gender in the Popular Arts.* Durham University, 2006. Durham E-Theses Online: http://etheses.dur.ac.uk/2703/.

Martins, Oliveira. *História de Portugal.* 14th ed., Guimarães Editores, 1964.

Müller, Ulrich. "Medievalism." *Handbook of Medieval Studies: Terms, Methods, Trends,* vol. 1, edited by Albrecht Classen, De Gruyter, 2010, pp. 850–865.

Musicamera Produções. *Geraldo e Samira: Uma ópera para Évora.* Câmara Municipal de Évora, 2019.

Observatório das Migrações. *Destaques Estatísticos "Sabia Que . . . ": Migrações e religiões.* Alto Comissariado para as Migrações. www.om.acm.gov.pt/documents/58428/403009/Migra%C3%A7%C3%B5es+e+Religi%C3%B5es.pdf.

178　*Everton V. Machado*

Pinheiro Chagas, Manuel. *História de Portugal, popular e ilustrada*. 3rd ed., Empreza da Historia de Portugal, 1899.

Raposo, Paulo. "Mouros, Ventres e Encantadores de Serpentes: Representações do mundo árabe nas recriações históricas em Portugal e Espanha." *Castelos a Bombordo: Etnografias de patrimónios africanos e memórias portuguesas*, edited by Maria Cardeira da Silva, Etnográfica Press, 2013, pp. 64–84.

Said, Edward W. *Orientalism: Western Conceptions of the Orient*. Pantheon Books, 1978.

Silva, Maria Cardeira da. "O sentido dos árabes no nosso sentido. Dos estudos sobre árabes e sobre muçulmanos em Portugal." *Castelos a Bombordo: Etnografias de patrimónios africanos e memórias portuguesas*, edited by Maria Cardeira da Silva, Etnográfica Press, 2013, pp. 19–42.

Soares Pereira, Virgínia. "Resende, André de." *Dicionário de Luís de Camões*, edited by Vítor Aguiar e Silva, Editorial Caminho, 2011, pp. 841–845.

Sousa Pereira, Armando de. *Geraldo sem pavor: um guerreiro de fronteira entre cristãos e muçulmanos c. 1162–1176*. Fronteira do Caos, 2008.

Teo, Hsu-Ming. *Desert Passions: Orientalism and Romance Novels*. U of Texas P, 2012.

Tiesler, Nina Clara. "No Bad News from the European Margin: The New Islamic Presence in Portugal." *Islam and Christian – Muslim Relations*, vol. 12, no. 1, 2001, pp. 71–91.

Tolan, John. "Islam: Both Foreign and Integral to Europe." *The European Way Since Homer: History, Memory, Identity*, edited by Étienne François and Thomas Serrier, vol. 1, Bloomsbury Academic, 2021, pp. 291–304.

Vakil, Aldool Karim. "Do Outro ao Diverso. Islão e Muçulmanos em Portugal: história, discursos, identidades." *Revista Lusófona de Ciência das Religiões*, vol. 3, no. 5/6, 2004, pp. 283–312.

"Viagens ao passado." *Visão História*, no. 67, 2021, p. 82.

Xavier, Ângela Barreto, and Ines G. Županov. *Catholic Orientalism: Portuguese Empire, Indian Knowledge (16th–18th Centuries)*. Oxford UP, 2015.

Part III
Latin America

11 Chilestinians and Journalism

Heba El Attar

Introduction

In 2007, Faride Zerán won the Chilean National Prize in Journalism for her "crónica" in *La guerrilla literaria: Huidobro, de Rokha, Neruda* [*The Literary Guerilla: Huidobro, de Rokha, Neruda*]. The book was first published in 1992 and then appeared in five editions, the most recent, in 2018, under a slightly different title: *La guerrilla literaria y otras escaramuzas: Pablo de Rokha, Vicente Huidobro, Pablo Neruda* [*The Literary Guerrilla and Other Skirmishes: Pablo de Rokha, Vicente Huidobro, Pablo Neruda*]. The Chilean National Prize in Journalism was established in 1953 by law decree 11.479. Until 1975, it was conferred on an annual and then a biennial basis to distinguished national talents in each one of the following areas: essay writing, chronicle writing (crónica), and sketching. After 1975, the prize became even more competitive, as it began to pay tribute every two years to superlative talents in only one of these three areas.

In 2014, Zerán received another prestigious award in recognition of her role in the history of Chilean journalism. This time it was the Amanda de la Barca award established in 1976 by the University of Chile to honor women with exceptional contributions to their professional fields. Indeed, Zerán, a university professor, is the founder and director of the Communication and Image Institute; Vice-Chancellor of the University of Chile; a former board member for Chilean National TV; author and editor of many books; a contributor to newspapers and magazines, such as *La Época* and *Pluma y Pincel*; and founder and editor of *Rocinante*, a magazine that attracted worldwide acclaim for its critical approach to culture and politics.

Thus far, however, Zerán's profile would not be considered unusual were it not for the race/ethnicity, gender, and religious intersectionality that she brings to bear. She is the granddaughter of Arab immigrants, Syrian and Palestinians who migrated to Chile in the nineteenth century. Unlike most other Latin-American countries, except for Honduras, the largest Arab-immigrant population in Chile is of Palestinian descent rather than Syrian-Lebanese. Palestinian migrations to Chile and Honduras came mainly from the Christian towns of Bethlehem, Beit Sahour, and

DOI: 10.4324/9781003245117-15

182 *Heba El Attar*

Beit Jala. Therefore, the majority of these Palestinian immigrants were (are) Christian Orthodox, and today, not only do they make up approximately 90 percent of the Arab population in Chile, but they also constitute the largest Christian Palestinian diaspora outside of the Middle East. The case of Faride Zerán's family, though, differs in a way that places their granddaughter into a triple minority of gender, religion, and race/ethnicity; her paternal grandparents, the Zeráns, were Druze Palestinians, and her maternal grandparents, the Chelechs, were Sunni Syrians:

> bajo el título de emigrantes árabes instalados en cada pueblo de este país . . . existe otra cara que se devela tal cual es: la del exilio. . . . Mi abuela materna, siria, de ojos grandes y nariz afilada, bella aún en la aridez de su rostro de surcos, me contaba de su pueblo, de sus hermanas, de su madre. Mi abuelo paterno, palestino, pequeño y de ojos claros, lloraba frente a mi infancia recordando su aldea drusa. No sé si en esos momentos los entendí en sus nostalgias. Sin embargo, hace algunas décadas, viviendo yo mi propio exilio, los comprendí en toda la dimensión de sus penas.
>
> ("Migraciones Árabes . . ." 144)[1]

underneath the immigrant status of every Arab established in each town across this country . . . there is a story – that of exile. . . . My maternal grandmother, a Syrian, with big eyes, a sharp nose, and a beautiful face despite arid wrinkles, used to tell me stories about her people, sisters, and mother. As a child, I also watched my paternal grandfather, a Palestinian, with a tiny body and clear eyes, breaking into tears as he remembered his Druze village. At the time, I may not have fully understood the dimension of their nostalgia. Decades later, however, when I experienced exile in my own skin, I realized the magnitude of their memories.

Even though Faride Zerán wrote exclusively in Spanish, engaged primarily with mainstream Chilean journalism, and was deeply involved in the political activism of the Chilean Left, her awareness of/commitment to her Arab and Palestinian heritage remained strong to the point of exposing her, at times, to profiling. She recalls that when President Ricardo Lagos named her to the board of the Chilean National Television, several newspaper headlines read as follows: "The Intifada arrived at the Chilean Public Television" (El Attar 13:11–13:43). Similar challenges, however, have never prevented Faride Zerán from continuing to use her pen and voice to defend free speech and democracy within Chile and to seek truth in her news coverage of the Middle East. She did so primarily by relying on the crónica style in many of her books and newspaper writing, for the crónica, as a hybrid genre, provides generous room for testimonials and reconstruction of memory.

Chilestinians and Journalism 183

With all this in mind, this chapter will look at two examples of Zerán's work, *La guerrilla literaria: Huidobro, de Rokha, Neruda* [*The Literary Guerilla: Huidobro, de Rokha, Neruda*] (1992), and *Tejado de vidrio. Crónicas del malestar* [*Glasshouse. Chronicles of Malaise*] (2007), to trace how she was shaped by Chilestinian's communal press and how she continued to carry out one of the chief goals of that communal press to the broader public after conquering Chilean mainstream journalism.

Chilestinians' Communal Press

Zerán's grandparents belonged to the early generations of non-European immigrants who, like their counterparts across Latin America, dealt with prejudice and racial discrimination before they were finally able to succeed financially and academically, ascend in social strata, gain political visibility, and contribute to all walks of Chilean life, including the communal press. The latter was widely cultivated by Arab immigrants across the continent to facilitate Arab immigrants' integration into the host societies, advertise the business of Arab immigrant entrepreneurs, and update the immigrant community on the most recent news and trends in the Middle East. In Chile alone, the total number of newspapers and magazines published by Arab immigrants between 1912 and 1950 reached 16 publications that appeared first in Arabic before becoming bilingual, then switching exclusively to the Spanish language. The most distinguished Chilestinian communal newspaper was *al-Islah/La Reforma* [*Reform*]. Jorge Sabaj Zurob established it in the 1930s when the Arab immigrant community was still in the process of integrating into Chile; while in the Middle East, the Arab world was facing colonialism, and the question of the partition of Palestine was at its peak. At the time, Arabic was still spoken among the first and second generations in Chile. However, as could be inferred from the bilingual title, the newspaper itself offered bilingual content that focused on Middle Eastern politics, the Chilean national economy, the Arab community's business in Chile, and the culture of both the Arab- and Spanish-speaking worlds. In the 1940s, the newspaper was blacklisted by the United States and Great Britain for its coverage of the Palestinian question. Later, in 1947, it resumed its work under a new title, *Mundo Árabe* [*Arab World*], and remained active until the second decade of the twenty-first century. Therefore, it is considered one of the oldest – if not the oldest – communal newspapers published by Arab immigrants in Latin America. Since the year 2000, in the wake of the second Palestinian Intifada, another Arab communal publication, *Al Damir* [*Conscience*], began to compete with *Mundo Árabe*, and then took over when the latter closed in 2015.

The Arab communal press's commitment to preserving the Arab cultural identity and heritage language allowed Faride Zerán and other third- and fourth-generation Arab immigrants in Chile to achieve successful

184 *Heba El Attar*

integration into Chilean society without risking total assimilation. Precisely, the Arabic language has survived in the first and second generations and beyond. Although newspapers such as *al-Islah/La Reforma* started using Spanish, they still long maintained their sections published in the Arabic language and continued to incorporate sections on Arabic literature, a feature that helped the community to preserve its heritage. Moreover, when these publications began to appear exclusively in Spanish, they were keen to include Spanish translations of excerpts from classical and modern Arabic literature and often promoted the teaching/learning of the Arabic language among the third and fourth generations of Arab Chileans.

Not only did the Arab communal press in Chile continually update the community on the political situation in the Middle East, but it also gave voice to anticolonial activism among the Arab diaspora, especially during the 1930s and 1940s, when the press in the Middle Eastern homeland was subject to censorship by British and/or French mandates. Specifically, *Al-Islah/La Reforma* played a substantial role in voicing political resistance from Chile to the Partition of Palestine and extensively covered the Great Palestinian Revolt (1936–1939). In doing so, the newspaper became one of the most instrumental communal publications in shaping Arab Chileans' political consciousness regarding the Middle East in general, and the Palestinian heritage and cause in particular. Such awareness is evident in Faride Zerán's own words:

> Alrededor de 400 mil chilenos-palestinos asentados en más de cien años de emigración conforman esta numerosa corriente dispersa a lo largo de la loca geografía chilena, la que nos remite a una diáspora poderosa que en más de un siglo se ha fundido con la tierra y el destino de Chile, pero conservando sus raíces e identidades. Fundamentalmente, en torno al sueño de una patria Palestina soberana, de un Estado Palestino independiente como parte de una nación árabe sacudida de los resabios del colonialismo y del imperialismo de occidente, y cuyos rasgos físicos y culturales aún marcan a varias generaciones de chilenos-árabes.
>
> ("Migraciones árabes . . ." 138)

> For over a hundred years, more than 400,000 Chilean-Palestinian immigrants spread and settled far and wide across the crazy Chilean geography, which makes us a powerful diaspora that was able, over the period of one century, to merge with the land and the destiny of Chile, while still preserving its roots and identities, for the dream of a sovereign Palestinian homeland, of an independent Palestinian state as part of an Arab nation that would finally be able to shake off the remnants of colonialism and Western imperialism, still marks the physical and cultural traits of several generations of Chilean-Arabs.

Thus, it could be inferred that, like many other Chilestinians, Faride Zerán was shaped by that communal press, and she could have opted to contribute to Arab communal newspapers and magazines in Chile, especially as they welcomed diverse contributors. By the late 1920s, for example, *The Orient* witnessed strong contributions by Arab-female journalists such as Mary Yanni de Atalah and Constancia Abusleme Hacle, as well as Chilean-female poets, such as Rosario Sansores. In the 1930s and 1940s, *Al-Islah/La Reforma* encouraged contributions, particularly in their literary sections, from Arab and non-Arab male and female authors, be they from Chile or the rest of the world. One of the most prestigious figures to publish with them was Gabriela Mistral (1889–1957) (del Amo 15, 26). Nonetheless, the reason Faride Zerán sought a different path was probably because as Arab-Chilean male and female journalists became more integrated into the host society, they were keen to reach out to a broader readership and therefore sought out opportunities in the mainstream Chilean press. Zerán was one of those journalists, and she was able to carve a name for herself in Chilean national media. She did so not only by committing herself to the defense of free speech but also by documenting Chilean cultural memory and making significant contributions to one of the most important journalism sub-genres in Latin America: the crónica, be it in her books, such as *La guerrilla literaria*, or in her newspaper and magazine contributions, such as *Tejado de vidrio*.

A Boom(ing) Genre

A collage of interviews, testimonies, biographies, and pop culture, the crónica, extremely popular in Latin America, is an elusive genre (Aguilar Guzmán 20–23) that falls on the borderline between journalism and literature (Urzúa-Opazo 131). According to Juan Villoro, it is a canvas of subjectivity that often distinguishes novel writing, data preciseness that usually characterizes reportages, dialogues that are best generated by conducting interviews, the analytical discussion of different themes that generally mark essay writing, and the (auto)biographical tone that is typically identified with writing on memory (qtd. in Darrigrandi 132).

In Latin America, the crónica, as a genre, evolved through three stages. The first one developed between the fifteenth and seventeenth centuries when conquerors and discoverers of the Indies used chronicle writing as testimonial descriptions of the wonders of the New World to validate the conquest and lay out an archival foundation in support of colonial ruling of the newly conquered lands (Poblete 4). The second stage developed in the late nineteenth century and early twentieth century, when modernist authors discovered that the crónica was the perfect genre to enable them to document the modernization of urban centers (Darrigrandi 124–125). According to Rotker, it was ideal for writing on national history in a fashion that would be appealing and accessible to the masses, as it was usually published in newspapers and magazines, a medium that allowed the crónica to modernize Latin American prose in general (qtd. in Ursúa-Opazo 131). Also, during that second stage, the genre was significantly shaped by Costumbrism with its pictorial representations of customs and its line-blurring between the objective and subjective, the factual and non-factual, and the individual and collective, especially in Latin America (Rotker 106–110). The third stage spans from the mid-twentieth century, the 1960s, until the present, and became known as New Journalism and/or Literary Journalism (Darrigrandi 134, 136). The latter focuses on social reality either through ethnographic realism or cultural phenomenology. Ethnographic realism, widely practiced in the Anglo-Saxon world, assumes that a journalist/reporter would be able to discern and explain reality. However, the cultural phenomenology approach, commonly practiced in Latin America, acknowledges the human limitations of any journalist/reporter, hence the impossible task of discerning any reality with precision (Aguilar Guzmán 65–70).

In Latin America, this form of hybrid writing, with the crónica as its primary unit, has been used to elicit the particularities of the continent's identity as opposed to the Anglo-Saxon world (Darrigrandi 134, 136). Importantly, it was used to criticize, challenge, and subvert official narratives and political systems (Poblete 5). In Chile, for instance, crónicas from the nineteenth century like the ones written by José Joaquín Vallejo, Joaquín Díaz Garcés, or Joaquín Edwards Bello focus on the drastic changes in Chilean society at the turn of the century, the Chilean ruling classes, elections, and so on, whereas those from the twentieth and twenty-first centuries, like the ones written by Pedro Lemebel, Rafael Gumucio, and Francisco Mouat, among others, focus on the dictatorship and/or post-dictatorship times and the official version of history (Ursúa-Opazo 132; Poblete 6; Aguilar Guzmán 29–30).

It should be noted that over the first two decades of the twenty-first century, there has been a consensus about the existence of a new "Boom" in Latin America. Unlike the Boom of the 1960s, whose core unit was the novel, this new Boom is grounded in the crónica. The claim of a Latin American Boom in the crónica genre was substantiated, among other things, by a stellar number of publications covering the crónica, an increasing number of institutions that devote training to that particular genre of writing, and numerous literary prizes dedicated to promoting or honoring the genre (Aguilar Guzmán 36–37, 109; Poblete 2).

Whether or not there is a Boom of Latin American crónica, and whether or not it has exceptionalism that separates it from the European and/or Anglo Saxon, the Latin American crónica remains a popular genre par excellence in the continent. And such is the relevance of the genre which Faride Zerán relies on in *La guerilla literaria* and in many texts of *Tejado de vidrio*.

La guerrilla literaria

Faride Zerán uses the crónica in *La guerrilla literaria* to explore a scandalous feud which erupted and lasted for a lifetime among three prominent Chilean poets: Vicente Huidobro (1893–1948), Pablo de Rokha (1894–1968), and Pablo Neruda (1904–1973). Within the literary tradition of the Spanish-speaking world, this feud is surely comparable, though more aggressive, to the one between Góngora and Quevedo (Rodríguez Gutiérrez 186). Also, it resembles similar feuds in the Anglo-Saxon world, such as that between Edmund Wilson and Vladimir Nabokov or between Gore Vidal and Truman Capote, to name a few. Most of these feuds are often triggered by disagreements over literary issues or are purely personal. Regardless of what prompts them, however, the relevance of these feuds is that they can provide insight into the social and intellectual history of the times during which they erupt (Arthur 5–20).

The feud between the three Chilean poets encompassed the aesthetic, the political, and the personal. In Zerán's view, it was an unconventional war that bore similarity, in terms of ferocity though not in terms of impact on national politics, to the one unleashed between the allies of O'Higgins and Carrera during the Chilean War for Independence (*La guerrilla literaria y otras escaramuzas* 30). Gabriel Cortiñas also deems it a war; particularly a war whose cultural dimensions are comparable to the Cold War between the United States and the U.S.S.R., and territorial in nature, as the two Pablos, de Rokha and Neruda, competed at the continental level to be viewed exclusively as *the* poet of America (90). On her part, Milena Rodríguez-Gutiérrez also deems it a war with trans-Atlantic reach, given its impact on the versification of poetry in the Spanish language on both sides of the Atlantic (187).

To reconstruct the intricacies of such an unconventional war, Zerán had to piece together textual and testimonial sources. The textual ones comprised letters, diaries, essays, poems, and anthologies written by the three poets, as well as articles in Chilean newspapers and magazines covering their work, their controversies, and their mutual attacks during that era. Among the texts that Zerán examined was a love poem by Neruda about a woman called Helena who turned out to be Pablo de Rokha's sister, with whom Neruda was denied marriage, and according to Zerán, seems to have been one of the root causes for the feud between Neruda and de Rokha. Another important text that Zerán examined was de Rokha's article, published in *La Opinión* in 1934, in which he accused Neruda of plagiarizing Rabindranath Tagore's poetry. Zerán traces the fact that Neruda would explain in 1937, in the fifth edition of his *Veinte poemas de amor* [*Twenty Love Poems*] that he had paraphrased from the Indian poet's work (*La guerrilla literaria y otras escaramuzas* 82).

188 *Heba El Attar*

The testimonial sources in Zerán's book consist of interviews that she conducted with the three poets' circles of relatives and friends. According to some of the interviewees, Huidobro's children and grandchildren (i.e., Vladimir Huidobro Amunátegui and Vicente García Huidobro), the feud among the three men was mainly aesthetic in nature and fueled by each discrediting the others' styles; de Rokha would claim his poetry to be more balanced than that of Huidobro and Neruda, because, in his view, Huidobro was only concerned with form and Neruda only with content. According to this group of interviewees, the feud among the three poets was further fueled by the public's reaction to each one of them, such as the public's selective dismissal of the fact that Huidobro had been nominated for the Nobel Prize in Literature in 1925 – decades before Neruda received it in 1971. However, the testimony of other interviewees (i.e., José de Rokha and Lukó de Rokha) deemed the feud among the three poets was mainly political in nature, given their respective roles within the Communist Party, though Huidobro would end up distancing himself ideologically from communism, de Rokha would get expelled from the party, and Neruda would gain notoriety in it (*La Guerrilla Literaria y Otras Escaramuzas* 30–31, 81–82).

Importantly, by using textual and testimonial resources to capture the nuances of that feud in *La guerrilla literaria*, Zerán was mapping a cultural cartography of Chile during the first half of the twentieth century, an era during which national and international events rocked Chile. At the national level, Chile was still negotiating its national identity while working on integrating all factions: creoles, mestizos, Mapuche, and other multi-ethnic groups who migrated to the country from all over the world. It was also striving for political and economic stability, a task that proved difficult amid the constant clash and race for power between the old oligarchy on the one hand and, on the other, the masses mobilized by the socialist values heralded by the Mexican revolution in 1910 and the Bolshevik revolution in 1919. Meanwhile, at the international level, the economic crash in the United States and WWI caused further damage to the Chilean economy, already weakened by all that political unrest.

Paradoxically, the period which witnessed this grim political and economic climate is the one that generated a golden age for Chilean culture and belles-letters. Professional journalism, for example, *El Mercurio*, had already been on the rise since the late nineteenth century. Cultural magazines started opening Chile to the most recent intellectual and literary trends in Europe and Latin America (Nómez 162). Authors and poets began to experiment with different literary styles, thereby enriching the literary scenery. Vicente Huidobro, for instance, pioneered a new literary style, Creationism, and incorporated innovative techniques (i.e., cinematographic) in his poetry and novels (de los Ríos 67–68). De Rokha broke with the nineteenth-century aesthetics and found new poetic languages and revolutionary themes that were further echoed in his polemic literary criticism in cultural magazines such as *Revista Multitud* [*Masses' Magazine*] or his theoretical views on literary creativity and the social and political roles of intellectuals in support of the proletariat (Ferrada Alarcón 236). Pablo Neruda also abandoned the nineteenth-century techniques he had learned at the hands of his former teacher, Gabriela Mistral, and found a voice among the waves of the avant-garde (Bleiker 1130).

Such is the relevance of Zerán's book which maps the history, economy, politics, literature, and culture of Chilean urban centers, namely Santiago, during a time deemed to be the golden age of Chilean culture and belles-lettres. Such pertinence becomes even more critical by considering that the period covered in *La guerrilla literaria*, marked a century since the independence of Chile from Spanish colonialism in 1818.

Tejado de vidrio

In addition to using the crónica genre in several of her books, Zerán uses it also in her contributions to print media as evinced in *Tejado de vidrio*. The latter is a compilation of op-eds, articles, columns, crónicas, and so on, that had been published earlier in Chilean newspapers and/or magazines. These different pieces are thematically grouped in *Tejado de vidrio* under five different sections, each of which covers a political issue of a national or international caliber. A substantial part of each section includes op-eds that Zerán had originally published in *Rocinante*, the magazine she founded and ran for seven years until the government of President Rircardo Lagos stopped funding it thereby halting one of the most iconic voices of independent journalism in post-Pinochet Chile. A salient section of that volume is titled "Medio Oriente" [The Middle East]. It includes several of Zerán's op-eds and columns published earlier in *Rocinante*, in addition to crónicas previously published in *La Nación*. In the op-eds and columns of this section, Zerán compares and contrasts issues such as the West's double standard reaction to 9/11 and the U.S.'s ensuing war on Afghanistan, the ambiguous position of Chile and other UN members whose opposition to the 2003 war on Iraq was motivated by a fear of a global economy crash rather than a true will for peace, and the West's interest in extending back its hegemonic control over the region's natural resources since its earlier colonial project in the Middle East had been interrupted by twentieth-century Arab nationalism and Pan-Arabism (55–60).

The crónicas compiled for that section on the Middle East in *Tejado de vidrio* enabled Zerán to reconstruct the complex reality of that region through her direct observation as a journalist, critical analysis of textual resources (i.e., reports on the economy and/or academic studies on the political conditions in the region), and the inclusion of excerpts from her interviews with all stakeholders. Importantly, these crónicas constitute a testimonial of Zerán's first-hand experience with the political unrest in

190   *Heba El Attar*

the region during the first decade of the twenty-first century as well as a testimonial of how such experience was informed by/and challenging to her intersectionality:

> aquí también está la voz confrontada con las raíces de quien escribe, en un conjunto de crónicas sobre el Medio Oriente despachadas desde el Líbano, Ramallah o Belén, en instantes que la guerra de julio de 2006, me hacía testigo privilegiada de un hecho que conmocionaba al mundo.
>
> *(Tejado de vidrio* 6)

> in here, also, a face-off with my ethnic roots throughout a series of chronicles on the Middle East, which I tendered from Lebanon, Ramallah or Bethlehem, during the 2006 war which shook the world and which I witnessed first hand.

Being a Chilean of half-Syrian descent, from the maternal side, becomes part of Zerán's interview with the Lebanese President Émile Lahoud, whose collaboration with and support of Syria, as she notes, made him unpopular among many Lebanese. Conversely, being a Chilean of half-Palestinian descent, from the paternal side, facilitates her interview with Fayez Saqqa, official representative of the Palestine Liberation Organization (PLO) in the towns of Beit Jala, Beit Sahour, and Bethlehem, and who, Zerán observes, has many relatives who had migrated to Chile. Moreover, the crónicas are especially nuanced by the religious identity, Druze-Sunni, of Zerán's family, and which are relevant in some of the interviews incorporated into the body of these crónicas. This is especially the case of her interview with Walid Jumblatt, leader of the Lebanese Druze, which Zerán uses to underscore a stark difference between the Lebanese-Druze's leader's anti-Syrian views and the Lebanese President's pro-Syrian ones, for Jumblatt's obsession against the Syrian regime, she notes, disproportionately outweighed his concerns regarding the plans of the United States or Israel in the region.

Though Zerán's intersectional identity had exposed her to some racial profiling, still her crónicas about the Middle East in *Tejado de vidrio* show that such intersectionality enabled her to transcend cultural borders. This is especially true in some of those crónicas that incorporate excerpts of her interviews with leaders from Hamas and Fatah, in which she compares and contrasts their respective positions regarding secularization and government in the Occupied Territories. It is also true in other crónicas which incorporate excerpts of her interviews with Michael Eligal, counsel on Latin America at the Israeli Department of State, and Israeli researchers and/or professors at the University of Jerusalem's Turman Center, and in which Zerán aims at gauging the level of public support for the Israeli government's actions (61–69).

It's worth noting that in the introduction to *Tejado de vidrio*, Zerán shares that the different texts included in the volume embody the type of journalism she is committed to – that is, swimming upstream:

> el ejercicio del periodismo independiente en un país en el que la concentración económica de los medios determina el monopolio de la palabra, de las ideas, y de la verdad, resulta todo un desafío para quienes hemos optado por nadar contra la corriente.
>
> (*Tejado de vidrio* 5).

> practicing independent journalism in a country where the market economy imposes a monopoly of the word, the ideas, and the truth, becomes a challenge for those of us who decided to swim upstream.

Thus, her crónicas on the Middle East, originally published in *La Nación*, then later in *Tejado de vidrio*, are part of that upstream swim. Furthermore, they should be read within the context of the year 2000 – that is, the year of the Second Intifada. In Chile, this date marks the year of full re-engagement of Chilestinins with the Middle East. This re-engagement did not go unnoticed by the broader Chilean public who witnessed Chilestinians' demonstration in support of the Intifada in front of La Moneda Palace. The broader Chilean public could not miss it because such a renewed commitment was not limited to public demonstrations. Rather, it came with an organized move to reach out to the ancestral homeland with financial help and investments especially in the sectors of health services and education, hence the establishment of the non-profit Fundación Belén 2000 [Foundation Bethlehem-2000]. Moreover, this re-engagement was not limited to organizations but also included individuals' efforts. Miguel Littín, for instance, filmed the Intifada live in his *Crónicas Palestinas* [*Palestinian Chronicles*] (2001), then narrated the story of his ancestral homeland in a feature film, *La última luna* [*The Last Moon*] (2005). Not only was the film shot in the Occupied Territories, but it featured non-Arab Chilean actors and actresses speaking in the Arabic language. Thus, Zerán's crónicas which were published initially in *La Nación* and were later compiled for the section on the Middle East in *Tejado de vidrio*, aimed at providing an update on the Middle East to the broader Chilean public rather than to the Chilestinian community. In doing so, Zerán was transferring one of the chief goals of earlier Arab communal press to mainstream Chilean newspapers.

Conclusion

In her discussion of the evolution of the Arab press in Chile, Mercedes del Amo discerns several stages, one of which was *el conquistar* (conquering). In her view, it corresponds to the early 1920s when some Arabic newspapers and magazines, such as *Oriente*, opted not to use the Arabic language, though it was still pervasively spoken among first- and second-generation Arab immigrants. Instead, *Oriente* used Spanish exclusively to reach the wider Chilean public (26–27). Indeed, it may be suggested that the urge of *el conquistar* (to conquer) the broader readership is what drove third- and fourth-generation Arab immigrants to seek opportunities in mainstream Chilean press and media. Conquering may also be an acceptable description of what Faride Zerán has achieved in her writing, particularly in her award-winning book, *La guerrilla literaria*, which mapped the cultural cartography of one of the most critical moments of Chilean's cultural memory, and in *Tejado de vidrio*, which captures the complex dimensions of the political unrest rocking the Middle East since the first invasion of Iraq. Conquering can also be considered the best description for Zerán's contribution to one of the most popular writing genres in Latin America: the crónica.

Note

1. All translations into English are mine.

Works Cited

Aguilar Guzmán, Marcela Alejandra. *La era de la crónica*. Ediciones UC, 2019.

Arthur, Anthony. *Literary Feuds: A Century of Celebrated Quarrels from Mark Twain to Tom Wolf*. Macmillan, 2002.

Bleiker, Roland. "Pablo Neruda and the Struggle for Political Memory." *Third World Quarterly*, vol. 20, no. 6, 1999, pp. 1129–1142.

Cortiñas, Gabriel. "Un sismógrafo para el continente: Pablo de Rokha y el ritmo americano." *Revista de Estudios Literarios Latinoamericanos*, no. 8, 2020, pp. 88–109.

Darrigrandi, Claudia. "Crónica latinoamericana: Algunos apuntes sobre su estudio." *Cuadernos de Literatura*, vol. XVII, no. 34, 2013, pp. 122–143.

del Amo, Mercedes. "La literatura de los periódicos árabes de Chile." *MEAH, Sección Árabe-Islam*, no. 55, 2006, pp. 3–35.

de los Ríos, Valeria. "Vicente Huidobro y el cine: La escritura frente a las luces y sombras de la Modernidad." *Hispanic Review*, vol. 79, no. 1, 2011, pp. 67–90.

El Attar, Heba. *Christian Palestine in Chile*. Arab Film Distribution, 2016.

Ferrada Alarcón, Ricardo. "El proyecto teórico y crítico de Pablo de Rokha." *Revista Chilena de Literatura*, no. 99, 2019, pp. 231–252.

Littín, Miguel. *Crónicas palestinas*. Pepe Torres, 2001.

———. *La última luna*. Latido Films, 2005.

Nómez, Naín. "Literatura, Cultura y Sociedad: El Modernismo y la Génesis de la Poesía Chilena Contemporánea." *Revista Chilena de Literatura*, no. 42, 1993, pp. 157–164.

Poblete, Patricia. "Hibridez y Tradición en la Crónica Latinoamericana Contemporánea: Los Textos de Rafael Gumucio." *Textos Híbridos*, vol. 3, no. 1, 2013, n.p., https://doi.org/10.15691/textoshibridos.v3i1.35

Rodríguez-Gutiérrez, Milena. "Dos planetas poéticos: Huidobro vrs Neruda, y viceversa." *Anales de Literatura Chilena*, no. 9, 2008, pp. 185–203.

Rotker, Susana. *La invención de la crónica en México*. Ediciones Letra Buena, Argentina, 1992.

Sánchez-Prado, Ignacio M. "El Ocaso de la Comunidad: Jezreel Salazar, J. M. Servín y la Crónica Post-Monsiváis." *Hispanic Journal*, vol. 35, no. 2, 2014, pp. 115–128.

Ursúa-Opazo, Macarena. "La Loca y el Inūtil: Escritura de la Chilenidad Desde la Crónicas de Edwards Bello y Lemebel." *Chasqui, Revista de Literatura Latinoamericana*, vol. 42, no. 1, 2013, pp. 131–143.

Zerán, Faride. *La guerrilla literaria: Huidobro, De Rokha, Neruda*. Ediciones Bat, 1992.

———. *Tejado de Vidrio: Crónicas del Malestar*. LOM Ediciones, 2007.

———. *La Guerrilla Literaria y Otras Escaramuzas: Pablo de Rokha, Vicente Huidobro, Pablo Neruda*. Fondo de Cultura Económica, 2018.

———. "Migraciones Árabes, Exilios y Racismos: Escrituras del Desarraigo." *Anales de la Universidad de Chile*, no. 16, 2019, pp. 133–144.

12 Writing South, Facing East
Arab Argentine Narratives

Marcus Palmer

Muhayirun, or emigrant writers, had a profound impact on the trajectory of Arabic literature in the early twentieth century and laid the foundation for writers of Arab heritage today. Mahŷar literature emerged simultaneously in the United States and South America as émigré entrepreneurs and intellectuals penned a diverse corpus of Arabic, English, Portuguese, and Spanish language texts. To be sure, the mahŷar marked the herald of an era of renaissance in Arabic literature and created nuanced conceptualizations of culture and identity in American letters across multiple linguistic contexts. Albeit from diverse perspectives, the narratives I examine in this chapter explore the mahŷar through vignettes of Arab immigrants and first- and second-generation Arab Argentines that often espouse a "split vision" between the past and present that blurs the perceived boundaries between the hostland and homeland.[1] Innate within these texts is an intense desire to recover immigrant memory and histories from the lens of the younger generation, who, contending with the diaspora, are rediscovering their mahŷar heritage. Here, I will attend to my conceptualization of mahŷar studies and examine immigrant portraits and narrative strategies that are key to analyzing Arab heritage writing in Argentina. Later in the chapter, I further analyze narratives that confront the emotional and transnational anxieties caused by the diaspora.

Writing From the Place of Migration

When I use the word mahŷar, I refer to a diaspora and a literary history. Derived from the verb *hayara*, meaning to emigrate or abandon, the noun (mahŷar) references the place where the immigrant resides and the literature produced in the hostland. However, the scope of mahŷar literary studies potentially moves well beyond Arab immigrant and heritage writing in North and South America. Lily Pearl Ballofet's use of the term references "the combined people and territories that constitute the human spatial map of migrant worlds constructed after the massive out-migration from Ottoman Syria since the last third of the nineteenth century" (5). From present-day Syria, Lebanon, Jordan, Palestine, and

DOI: 10.4324/9781003245117-16

Israel, the ongoing diasporas demonstrate that the relevance and necessity of mahŷar studies have not diminished.

Moreover, Handi Al-Saaman promotes a global vision of mahŷar writing "by broadening the scope of gender and geographic definitions . . . shifting its focus from predominantly male writers residing in North and South American sites to women writers located in the European continent instead" (13). Syrian and Lebanese communities in the Americas have maintained transnational exchanges with the Mashriq as sites of political engagement and modes of cultural reproduction for over a century, and new hostland sites are becoming as prominent in the European continent. It would seem difficult, then, to disagree with James Clifford's belief that a longing to return to the homeland "is always a political question" (254). The extent to which the literature produced by diasporic subjects is (a) political is expressly articulated by writer aesthetics and thematic concerns, though we might argue that any representation of diaspora in some way schematizes voluntary or forced displacement.

Arriving primarily in North and South America in the late nineteenth century, Arab emigrants from Ottoman Syria formed diaspora communities, each a unique situation with its own sociocultural, economic, and political dimensions. Gabriel Sheffer's term, "ethno-national diaspora," is useful in distinguishing between Arab emigrants from the Ottoman Syria, with writers of Arab heritage, or even immigrants from contemporary diasporas,

> an ethno-national diaspora is a social-political formation, created as a result of ether voluntary or forced migration, whose members regard themselves as of the same ethno-national origin and who permanently reside as minorities in one of several host countries.
>
> (9–10)

Howsoever different the circumstances, "to be in the diaspora," argues Himradi Lahiri, "they would need to acquire legal documents, and fulfill certain criteria and then cross national borders" (4). The writers included in this chapter identify each in their own way as members of the Syrian or Lebanese ethno-national diaspora communities in Argentina. From 1900 to 1918, émigré from Ottoman Syria constituted 4 to 5 percent of the immigrant population, with estimates indicating there may be as many as 4,500,000 Arab immigrants and Argentine citizens of Arab heritage.[2] While Arabs constitute the third largest ethnic minority in Argentina, the selected authors for this chapter are full citizens residing in their country of origin and are therefore not diaspora subjects.

Immigrant Memory and the Hostland/Homeland

The grandson of Syrian immigrants, Jorge Asís's *La manifestación* [*The Protest*] is a collection of stories told from the lens of Rodolfo Zalim,

196 *Marcus Palmer*

the first fictional character-narrator of Arab heritage within the mahŷar and Argentine literary traditions. The stories primarily focus on Rodolfo's experiences as a door-to-door salesperson, his sexual pursuits, and his father's infidelity and frivolous political aspirations. Frequent references to street names, neighborhoods, and Syrian-Lebanese community organizations produce a literary mapping of Buenos Aires that narrates episodes from the life of father (Abdel) and son (Rodolfo). However, one particular story does not fit neatly within Asís's reconfiguration of the immigrant hostland and portrayal of first- and second-generation male characters of Arab heritage. Rodolfo briefly mentions his grandfather in "Como me llamo Zalim" [As my name is Zalim] and "Marionetas" [Puppets] and expresses his consciousness being a writer in "Los pasos de Julia" [Julia's Steps], "Villa Domínico," and "Vittorio." In the immigrant portrait "Abuelo Salvador," Rodolfo's assumes a narratorial role outside the text, oscillating between the report of his grandfather's inner thoughts, slow and intentional movements from one scene to the next, saying farewell to his beloved garden and wife María before passing away at home that evening.

For the most part, the immigrant homeland is inaccessible to the ethno-national diaspora community through personal memory. Accordingly, Asís reconfigures the literary space of *La manifestación* through a collage of Arabic linguistic and cultural markers, removing any references to the hostland. Drawing from memories of his grandparents, Rodolfo envisions that Salvador must have felt a premonition that he would soon die and sees him saying goodbye to his beloved garden. Getting up from his rocking chair and making his way towards the garden by leaning against the wall with every step, Salvador admires his olive tree, "Qué acetitunas grandes dará este año, pensó. Masalam – le susurró" [What big olives you will give this year, he thought – Goodbye – he whispered] and then thought to himself, "Quien diría, Salvador Zalim, enta, llorando" [Who would have thought, Salvador Zalim, you, crying] (31). Meanwhile, Rodolfo imagines his grandmother busy in the kitchen, "La abuela probablemente estaba haciendo lo mismo, en la cocina . . . para preparar el quepi crudo de la noche" [Grandma was probably doing the same as usual, in the kitchen . . . to prepare the evening's raw kibbeh]. Grandparents are symbolic and influential figures for younger generations, as they are bearers of cultural knowledge and tradition. Carol Fadda-Conrey purports that, "Reassessing the fragmented memories of home entails addressing and revising the patriarchal gender roles that are embedded in Arab immigrant perspectives" (39). We see here that by drawing on the memory of Salvador, Asís directly confronts the enactment of gender roles within the ethno-national diaspora in Argentina by shifting the portrayal of the male role in *La manifestación* from first and second-generation Arab Argentines to that of Arab immigrants.

In addition to food, language is another essential element in Rodolfo's fragmented memory of his grandparents. María and Rodolfo modify their speech through codeswitching registered in the text as transliterated Arabic with translations provided as footnotes for the reader. Sitting at the dinner table, Salvador asks if there is any wine for dinner, "¿Fí vino?" to which María responds, "Para enta ma fi" [there is none for you] (32). Salvador tenderly insists that María serve him wine [Attine vino], and to her surprise, he offers a toast to their marriage and nine children. Having finished their meal, Rodolfo, from his narrative lens, observes: "De inmediato se levantó a ayudarla a levantar la mesa, y hasta secó un plato sin romperlo" [He immediately got up to help her clean the table and even dried a plate without breaking it] (35). As Salvador and María retire for the evening, he asks María to wait for him, using a term of endearment "Vieja, esperame" [Honey, wait for me] and commenting, "Cincuenta y tres años aguantándote" [Fifty years, putting up with you] to which María replies in Arabic, "Ana, ana" [Me, me] (33). Salvador and María walk together for the last time, "La tomó del hombro y fueron juntos caminando hacia la pieza. Él miraba las baldosas del patio; ella a él. Al llegar a la pieza la besó en la mejilla" [He took her by the shoulder and walked towards the bedroom together. He was looking at the tiles in the patio, and she was looking at him. Arriving in the bedroom, he kissed her on the cheek] (33). Through symbolic yet straightforward gestures of affection, Rodolfo's memory of Salvador is centered on his grandfather's attentiveness to María and his overwhelming desire to subdue the intense feelings of nostalgia.

Salvador successfully maintains his stalwart intention of hiding his fears by not shedding tears in front of María. Fraught with the fear that he would urinate on himself, he waits until María is asleep before making his way to the bathroom on the other side of the outdoor patio. The sight of thick blood in his urine confirms the suspicion that he will soon die, and ensuring that any visible traces are erased, he flushes the toilet multiple times. Described by Rodolfo as a "viejo caprichoso" [stubborn old man] (33), Salvador attempts to return to bed with María without signs of distress, and despite his efforts, Rodolfo observes, "Pero igual lagrimeaba él y las baldosas y las macetas cuando lentamente esta vez volvió a cruzar el patio" [But still, he, the tiles, and pots were crying]. Alerted by his absence, María waits for him, "Roj shjojj" [I went to pee], Salvador clarifies, and to assure María that everything is fine, he adds: "Nada, nada, rezá, rezá, dormí y rezá, masalam" [Nothing, nothing, pray, pray, sleep and pray, goodbye] (36). "Abuelo Salvador" ends as foreshadowed, and in stark contrast to the sexist views of Abdel and Rodolfo, the memory of Salvador evokes the figure of an uprooted immigrant – who, although physically weakened by age, embodies strong sentiments of nostalgia and cultural sensitives that has been lost in the second and third generations. From this lens, Asís draws on immigrant nostalgia to express the loss of family unity and wholesome traditional values in the hostland.

198 *Marcus Palmer*

Indeed, not all writers of Arab descent in Argentina actively participate in their local ethno-national diaspora communities, nor should we expect to take up themes related to the diaspora, migration, or ethnic identity in their writing solely based on their Arab ethnicity. Steven Salaita reminds us that "Arab American Literature, like other ethnic or national literary traditions, is not a singular or even unified entity" (133). Nonetheless, the portrayal of Arab immigrants and first- and second-generation Arab Argentines in *La manifestación* has since developed into a thematic pattern for heritage writers in the twenty-first century, and within the genre of the short story, Elsa Serur Osman's *Hal-Lhuzz y la lámpara de Kehtrín* [*Hal-Lhuzz and Ketrin's Lamp*] evidences the strong connections between narrative voice, memory, and mahŷar family histories. Osman weaves childhood and immigrant memories into the chronological narrative as mother (Millie) and daughter (Hal-Lhuzz) travel to visit Millie's ailing sister Elena in Larroque, a town located in the northeastern province of Entre Ríos, Argentina where the author was born. *Hal-Lhuzz* shares narrative strategies with *La manifestación*, as Millie's status as a character-narrator of Arab heritage and frequent portraits of family members produces a similar intratextuality found in Rodolfo's stories. Millie, however, deals more directly with the nostalgia of home and homeland upon returning to Larroque and recovering cultural knowledge and immigrant memories accompanied by her daughter Hal-Lhuzz. In terms of linguistic choices, Osman incorporates transcribed Arabic with translations in parenthesis or as footnotes, representing speech errors to denote a character's immigrant status or difficulty speaking the hostland language. Even though each story in the collection can be read independently, the collection is truly an extended narrative replete with analepses that highlight the role of memory in transmitting knowledge about family history and cultural traditions. In (perhaps) an adaptation of the prologue in Domingo Fausto Sarmiento's *Recuerdos de provincia*, Osman includes a helpful diagram of Millie's family tree that contains the names and family relationships across four generations. In this way, Osman schematizes *Hal-Lhuzz* as a family history record that offers a multilayered vision of the hostland and immigrant homeland that brings to bear the connectedness between the diaspora, cultural assimilation, and identity formation in ethno-national diaspora communities.

In the opening narrative, Millie and Hal-Lhuzz, having left Buenos Aires hours before, are waiting for the train's arrival that will finally take them to their destination. Millie returns to her hometown for the first time in 30 years, and Hal-Luzz is anxious to meet her aunt and other relatives. Forced to confront this nostalgia, Millie must negotiate immigrant memory and notions of fatherland, reconfiguring and transmitting the concept of home and homeland for Hal-Lhuzz. According to Femke Stock, "at the core of the concept of diaspora lies the image of a remembered home that stands at a distance both temporally and spatially" (24).

Writing South, Facing East 199

For Avtar Brah, the concept of diaspora intrinsically "embodies a subtext of home" (190). The narrative premise of *Hal-Lhuzz* seeks to reclaim the temporal and spatial distance between Millie's childhood home and the immigrant hostland from a lens that renders the concept of homeland rather unstable. In this respect, William Safran's statement on "home" and "homeland" is quite helpful: "Whether that home is necessarily the 'original' homeland is a matter of controversy. It may, in fact, not be the ancestral homeland at all but rather the place where one was born and raised but that was originally a hostland, that is, a diaspora" (13). Thus, the conflation between home/hostland for members of an ethno-national community does not dismiss the "original" homeland in representations of diaspora, nor is the immigrant homeland forgotten.

As Millie and Hal-Lhuzz await the next train, a station employee begins to make casual conversation with them, and to Hal-Lhuzz's surprise, purports to know perfectly well who her aunt is, adding that Doña Elena's husband was known to be a "turco bravo" [ill-tempered Turk]. Conscientious of her story-telling role, Millie intervenes by observing, "a la gente le gusta inventar historias" [people like to make up stories], and assures her that she will tell her everything, adding: "Quiero ir recordando a medida que pasan las horas, como si de nuevo yo fuera joven y todo estuviera ocurriendo ahora" [I want to continue remembering as the hours go by, as if once again I were young and everything was happing now] (14–15). Memory here, as with all the analepses in Osman's stories, can be distinguished from the chronological narrative through double-spacing and italicized font. What follows is a dialogue between Elena and the "turco bravo," who asks his wife where she has been, insinuating that he knows for a fact that that she was not really at her brother's house. Don Nula adds, "*la han visto subir un carro*" [they saw you get in a car] (15). Perhaps having previously dealt with similar accusations, Elena stands her ground,

> – *¿Qué gente?*
> – *¡Yo, yo la he visto! – se animó a decir el marido!*
> . . . *menteroso, menteroso! – gritó ella mientras lo aferraba del cuello.*
> *Él era un hombre muy bajito. Ella una mujer grande y buena moza*

> – What people?
> – Me, I saw you! – the husband dared to say.
> . . . liar, liar, she shouted while grabbing him by the neck.
> He was a very short man. She was a big and very beautiful woman.
> (15)

Don Nula proceeds to implore Elena's sympathy, "*¡Suelte, suelte!, quería saber nomás*" [Let go, let go! I just wanted to know] (15), and after a few slaps to the face, Elena asserts, "¡Tomá, tomá! ¡para que otra vez no

200   *Marcus Palmer*

hables de gusto" [Take that, and that! So next time you don't run your mouth for the sake of it] (16). Once released from Elena's grasp, Don Nula proclaims: "*¡Es fuerte usted . . . qué poder, Dios mío*" [You are strong . . . my God, what power!] (16). Osman's use of memory as a stylistic intervention highlights the importance of oral histories in recovering immigrant memory and tracing familial connections across generations. With each story, Millie recovers her youthful sentiments of family and belonging, while Hal-Lhuzz becomes aware of her family's legacy of hard work and significant sacrifice and loss.

Although immigrant mahŷar expressions of the homeland often articulate a desire to return or a longing for loved ones that remained abroad, the family members that stayed in the fatherland undoubtedly lived a similar experience. Millie's recreation of a dialogue between Elena and Don Nula provides Hal-Lhuzz with an alternative perspective of her uncle's perceived ill temperament. In the first-person account in "Elena," Hal-Lhuzz is able to construct a complete portrait of the loneliness felt by her ancestors that emigrated from their fatherland. The account in "Elena" provides insight into the reality families confronted as their loved ones left for America one by one. Beginning with the question, "*¿Por qué me dejaste solo ia omme?*" [Mother, why did you leave me alone?] (109), the text reads like a monologue or personal reflection on the precarious day-to-day conditions in the homeland as Millie struggled to survive. Indeed, Elena's account of her family's diaspora to Argentina is quite extraordinary. Her mother, Mariana, was the first to leave for America, not her father. The reader is left to infer that Elena stayed to care for her father due to his old age, as she recounts the gracious assistance received from friends and family, though they, too, soon left her alone. In developing the sense of abandonment that Elena felt as a result of the diaspora, we see how these emotions transformed into hatred for the fatherland, "Sola con mi Kaleb (perro), que un día me quitaron los soldados mientras se reían de mí, que era muy chica y los odiaba, y odiaba los barcos que un día te llevaron con Jalil, mi hermano querido" [Alone with my Kaleb (dog), whom one day was taken away from me, meanwhile the soldiers laughed at me because, that I was very tiny and I hated them, and I hated the ships that one day took you and my dear brother Jalil] (109). Configured as the locus of loss, the homeland for Elena becomes a space of violence and hunger, whereas the hostland is constructed as home: "América, Argentina. Allá había paz, comida, familia, yo no tenía nada" [America, Argentina. Over there was peace, food, family, I had nothing] (110). Elena's uses the term "turco" as a marker of this violence and loss, of tyrants and murderers, "Pero nunca pude comprender ni perdonar el dolor. . . . Que me causaron los turcos. . . . Se llevaron todo. Hasta al pobre Sejja lo llevaron como traductor y nunca más lo dejaron volver" [But I never could understand or forgive the pain. . . . What the Turks caused. . . . They took everything. They even took poor Sejja as a

Writing South, Facing East 201

translator and never let him return] (110). In the last century, the term "turco" has predominantly been used in derogatory and orientalist portrayals of Arab immigrants and Argentines of Arab heritage. However, that the term in "Elena" is used as an identifier to protest the embodiment of loss and loneliness in the fatherland calls into question its proper use in the hostland, particularly within ethno-national diaspora communities.

Immigrant memories and the representations of the diaspora in Osman's collection of stories explore the nostalgia of home and the homeland, enabling Millie to reconnect with her childhood and for Hal-Lhuzz to establish familial connections to the mahŷar. Diaspora inherently involves transnational matters dealing with topics such as migration and displacement. Paul Jay observes that common narrative techniques in transnational writing include "multiple intersecting stories that often unfold in a non-linear way and are narrated from different voices or different perspectives" (79). We have examined how character-narrators of Arab heritage use memory to portray Arab immigrants and ethno-national diaspora communities in Argentina as strategies to reconceptualize notions of homeland and hostland. Vignettes of Arab immigrants in "Abuelo Salvador" celebrate the successful cultural assimilation to the hostland while maintaining linguistic and cultural manifestations of the homeland. Moreover, the immigrant histories narrated by Millie and Elena bear records of the feelings of solitude and loneliness, in addition to the anxiety first- and second-generation Arabs can experience when they move away from their hometowns and local ethno-national diaspora communities. In the final section, I examine how Juana Dib's narratives take-up of these thematic patterns to foreground the physical dangers and emotional traumas related to the mahŷar.

Arrival and Assimilation

Juana Dib, the daughter of Syrian émigrés, examines the assimilation processes and cultural misunderstandings in the hostland through narratives that portray the immigrant vulnerabilities that resulted from the diaspora. While centered on the emotional and physical violence enacted on the immigrants, Dib's writing promotes a vision of the diaspora that celebrates individual valor and the collective efforts of ethno-national diaspora communities.[3] Contrary to the protagonist-narrator voices discussed in the work of Asís and Serur Osman, Dib cultivates a narratorial voice outside the stories and privileges character dialogue and inner thoughts to create literary spaces that reflect the diversity of immigrant perspectives and voices. In the introduction to a collection of poems titled *Uno mismo* [One's Self], Carlos Duguech describes his parents as "emigrantes de dolor" [emigrants in mourning] who, leaving Lebanon after the First World War, arrived in Argentina with a French passport and found themselves among "inmigrantes de esperanza," [immigrants with hope] (37).

202 *Marcus Palmer*

Duguech highlights the many difficulties involved in migration and arriving at the hostland, which for Avatar Brah, brings "sites of hope and new beginnings" (193). In this vein, we will see that the narratives in Juana Dib's *Las invitadas* [*Those Invited*] and *Destino: La Argentina* [*Destination: Argentina*] recount stories that reveal this juxtaposition of mourning and hope in histories that protest the social injustice endured by the Arab immigrants and celebrate the solidarity within Argentina's ethno-national diaspora communities.

"El tesoro de la abuela" [Grandmother's treasure] incorporates biographical and empiric data points to protest the unequal legal treatment and justice of crimes committed against Arab immigrants. The narrative voice oscillates between the figure of Father Kassab and a group of immigrants en route to Buenos Aires. As the story begins, the Reverend is saddened by the reported massacre of 130 Arab immigrants by plains Indians in the Pampa and wishes he could sing a *maual* or sad song to accompany the pain and loss of the family members they left behind in the homeland. At the same time, Father Kassab is mindful of the that hundreds of Lebanese and Syrian immigrants are on their way to Argentina and will arriving shortly, "El barco no tardará en llegar, ¡Cuánta gente lo espera!" [The ship will not delay in its arrival, So many people will be waiting for him!] (86). He is hopeful that the natural beauty and kind people of the Province of Misiones, where they will reside, offers them the freedom and peace they are earnestly seeking, "Y cuando conozcan a sus gentes, tan generas y nobles, que nos enseñan su lengua, la que hasta tiene palabras casi iguales a las de nosotros" [And when they meet its people, so generous and noble, who teach us their language, which has many words similar to ours] (86). Meanwhile, on the ship, Lebanese and Syrian families are playing traditional music and dancing to entertain themselves and celebrate the liberties and opportunities awaiting them in Argentina. Dib uses gendered immigrant memory to describe the migrants' activities, explaining that the women typically oversaw the transportation of religious objects, the hookah, and *támbac* (white tobacco), while the men primarily took care of carrying money or other valuables. Among the dangers involved in traveling by ship were sickness and robbery, and this group of immigrants became the latter's target. The story's narrative voice shifts from the portrayal of the Syrian and Lebanese immigrants to two male passengers that were looking for the opportunity to prey on vulnerable passengers, "Los muchachos habían observado que la abuela de los Majul . . . guardaba una bolsita bajo su blusa oscura, que trataba de proteger cruzando las manos sobre su pecho" [They boys had observed that grandmother of the Majul family . . . carried a small bag under her dark blouse which shed tried to protect by crossing her hands on her chest] (89–90). The two men attacked the grandmother, one of them stabbing her with a stiletto in the back, piercing a lung, as she desperately fought the second to guard her treasure. Although the criminals were caught and jailed, sadly, the grandmother died that afternoon. Arriving in Buenos Aires, the ship has brought joy and sadness to the hostland, "Todos bajan contentos, aunque miran con tristeza la pena de los Majul" [Everyone happily disembarks, though they feel sorry for the loss of the Majul family] (91). Father Kassab must now meet with the ship's captain, the victim's family, and local police authorities to view the contents of the stolen item. Reverend Kassab can only embrace and sob with the Majul family as the hand-sewn bag is opened – revealing a *mancash* or wooden tool to decorate bread and a smaller white cloth bag containing *majlab* (ground seeds), which are added to give the bread dough its special flavor. The value of Grandmother Majul's treasure is clearly not monetary; rather, it is symbolic of the simple objects that were transported as fragmented pieces of the homeland and are emblematic of immigrants' traditional values.

Historical documents demonstrate that many immigrants arrived as complete families and with significant financial resources. However, the reality is that all too often, young single and married men left their homes and families in search of a prosperous and peaceful future, arriving with very little. "Los pañuelos al aire" [Handkerchiefs in the Air] tells the story of how Farah emigrated to Argentina and followed in his family's legacy of personal sacrifice and solidarity. Farah's uncle returns to visit his family in Syria and gifts him enough gold coins to buy passage to Argentina. This new opportunity, however, is met with immediate feelings of loss through the personification of nature the evening before his departure, "Hay tristeza en la brisa que arranca gemidos de los olivares" [There is sadness in the wind as it tears away groans from the olive grove] (11). Farah's family expressed sentiments of nostalgia as he said his goodbyes, each offering a unique gift for him to treasure. Though Farah's mother laments not having anything of material value to give him, she offers her prayers for him and Argentina. Despite Farah's own dreams, his father reminds him of his cultural and family responsibility to his sisters who will be awaiting him to return and take care of them. Lastly, his grandmother sings her farewell in silence, tracing the verses in the sky, "La abuela también tiene su cancion, la escribió en el aire y la guarda en su corazón" [Grandmother also has her own song, she wrote it in the sky and keeps in her heart] (12). Such expressions of love and support motivate Farah to confront the challenges of the diaspora while simultaneously establishing familial and cultural expectations.

As Farah begins to assimilate to the hostland, there is a concerted effort to cultivate his homeland culture. Farah is able to quickly start working as an ambulant salesperson and live independently thanks to the guidance and generosity of his uncle. The support he receives from his relatives is not only monetary, as his uncle mentors him in Arabic and insists on a standing invitation to share a meal at his home on Sundays. At the same time, Farah remains in awe of the consumer goods available to the public

204 *Marcus Palmer*

and reflects what he might buy for himself and each of his family members. Having saved enough money to purchase a new suit and bicycle, he hurries to store, "dispuesto a gastar su dinero" [willing to spend his money] (14). As Farah views himself in the mirror, his head drops and feels heavy with tears, "Ve en el espejo las necesidades de su familia" [He sees his family's needs in the mirror] (14). Farah hurriedly leaves the shop and passes the bicycle shop without even looking. Feeling relieved with every step, he offers all his savings to his uncle, who exchanges the money for thirty gold coins. Beside himself with excitement, Farah sends the gift home to his family from Argentina, "la tierra de promisión" [the promised land] (14). Having arrived with very little monetary means, Farah's immigrant experience is greatly enriched through the emotional and spiritual support he received from the homeland. Through his uncle's mentorship, Farah learns to negotiate the cultural and transnational anxieties involved in assimilating to the hostland and cultivate his family's tradition of generosity and self-sacrifice.

Acts of solidarity are the hallmark of ethno-national diaspora communities. The story "Un grito en el camino" [A Scream on the Path], describes the loss a young Palestinian immigrant suffered in her homeland and the difficulty of coping with the trauma of her forced diaspora. Sheila attends a social gathering at the Arrieta household, where they celebrate their oldest son's birthday with an *asado* [barbeque], but her haunting screams interrupt the festive atmosphere. At first, the family fear something has happened to their grandmother, but soon thereafter, the men begin to run after Sheila as she continues to yell and frantically flee. Unsympathetic to Sheila's distress, the younger attendees appear to be bothered by the unexplained outburst and drama. Recognizing this as a teaching moment, it is the grandmother, Doña Elisa, who relates Sheila's tragic story: "No recuerda cuánto tiempo vagó por la arena cálida, con sus padres, hermanos, parientes, y río seco de gente expulsada de su tierra, con hambre, con sed, con frío, descalzos, ni cuántos quedaron en el camino" [She doesn't remember how long Sheila roamed the hot sand with her parents, siblings, and relatives, along with a dry river of people thrown out of their lands, hungry, thirsty, cold and barefoot, or how many were left on the way] (17). Doña Elisa recalls that Sheila was only 16 when she fled to the refugee camp in Chatilla, Beirut with her family,[4] leaving behind her childhood home and dreams of marriage to Yalil, who repeatedly reassured his fiancée that once they return to Palestine, "te haré, amor, una casa blanca con ventanas al norte . . . un huerto de colores . . . te compraré imshajlah de plata" [I'll build you, my love, a white house with windows facing the North . . . a colored garden . . . I'll buy you a silver necklace] (18). Overcome with the loss, Sheila "enterró para siempre su alegría, sus sueños de enamorada . . . se castiga por ser la única sobreviviente de sus seres queridos" [forever buried her happiness and lover's dreams . . . she blames herself for being the only survivor of her loved ones] (18). With tears in their eyes, Doña Elisa pauses her storytelling as the young generation finally understands that the smell of the barbeque brought back the memory of the human pyre at the refugee camp.

Conclusion

Writers of Arab heritage are enacting a revisionary approach to mahŷar writing that intervenes in the construction of diasporic identities and ethno-national diaspora communities, and the role of language to impose hierarchies informing belonging and exclusion cannot be overstated. Linguistic juxtapositions reveal the complexity of identity and evidence how "discursive conditions of dominance," as expressed by Homi Bhabba, can be made to function as the "grounds of intervention" (160). The narratives of Jorge Asís, Elsa Serur Osman, and Juana Dib mark the emergence and development of Arab heritage writing in Argentina that expresses an evident thematic concern for the mahŷar and employ writing strategies that recover immigrant memory and stories in celebration and protest of the mahŷar experience. Undoubtedly, the first-person accounts of character-narrators of Arab descent are unique in the Argentine mahŷar and national canons, revealing multilayered perspectives of the diaspora – and in the wake of continuous flows of migrants from the Mashriq, there remains a significant amount of scholarly work to be performed in mahŷar studies that trace the development of emerging writing trends.

Notes

1. Suhair Majaj, Luisa. "New Direction Arab American Writing Today": Eds. Ottmar Ette and Friederike Pannewick. *ArabAmericas: Literary Entanglements of the American Hemisphere and the Arab World*. Iberoamericana, 2016.
2. Reference: www.atlanticcouncil.org/blogs/menasource/viva-los-arabes-underreported-stories-of-the-arabs-of-the-americas/.
3. Juana Dib has published numerous collections of poetry that are concerned with questions of cultural and linguistic identity, and take up thematic concerns and aesthetics promoted by immigrant mahŷar writers throughout the Americas. See: "Juana Dib y el mahyar árabe americano."
4. The Chatilla refugee camp was originally set up for Palestinians in 1949 and has continued to house emigrants as civil war erupted in Lebanon (1982) and Syria (2011).

Works Cited

Al-Samman, Hanadi. *Anxiety of Erasure: Trauma, Authorship, and the Diaspora in Arab Women's Writings*. Syracuse UP, 2015.
Asís, Jorge. *La manifestación*. Talleres Gráficos, 1971.
———. *Don Abdel Zalim*. Corregidor, 1972.
Balloffet, Lily Pearl. *Argentina in the Global Middle East*. Stanford UP, 2020.

206 *Marcus Palmer*

Bhabha, Homi K. *The Location of Culture*. Routledge, 2012.

Brah, Avtar. *Cartographies of Diaspora: Contesting Identities*. Routledge, 1996.

Clifford, James. *Routes: Travel and Translation in the Late Twentieth Century.* Harvard UP, 1997.

Dib, Juana. *Las invitadas*. Ediciones el Robledal, 2000.

———. *Destino: La Argentina*. Fondo Editorial de la Provincia, 2015.

Duguech, Carlos. *Uno Mismo*. De Los Cuatro Vientos, 2013.

Fadda-Conrey, Carol. *Contemporary Arab-American Literature*. New York UP, 2014.

Jay, Paul. *Transnational Literature*. Routledge, 2021.

Lahiri, Himradri. *Diaspora Theory and Transnationalism*. Orient Black Swan, 2019.

Mishra, Sudesh. *Diaspora Criticism*. Edinburgh UP, 2006.

Osman, Elsa Serur. *Hal-Lhuzz y la lámpara de Khetrín*. Lumen, 1997.

Palmer, Marcus. "Juana Dib y el mahyar árabe-americano." *Transmodernity*, vol. 9, no. 4, 2020, pp. 103–18.

Safran, William. "Deconstructing and Comparing Diasporas." *Diaspora, Identity and Religion: New Directions in Theory and Research*, edited by Waltraud Kokot, Khachig TöLölyan and Caroline Alfonso, Routledge, 2004.

Salaita, Steven. *Modern Arab American Fiction*. Syracuse UP, 2011.

Sarmiento, Domingo Faustino. *Recuerdos De Provincia: Precedido De Mi Defensa*. Sur, 1962.

Sheffer, Gabriel. *Diaspora Politics: At Home Abroad*. Cambridge UP, 2003.

Stock, Femke. "Home and Memory." *Diasporas: Concepts, Intersections, Identities*, edited by Kim Knott and Seán McLoughlin, Rawat, 2011.

13 Chronicling "the Death of the Arab" in Colombian Literature

Angela Haddad

The Colombian author Luis Fayad, whose work often takes city life and urbanization as a problematic to be explored, is one of several authors considered to have moved the nation's literary production away from magical realism and the shadow of Gabriel García Márquez through his realist novels and short stories. A descendant of Arab migrants who came to the South American country at the turn of the previous century and settled in Bogotá, Fayad never treated the migrant community as substantially in his earlier works as he did in *La caída de los puntos cardinales* [*The Fall of the Cardinal Points*] (2000). In this text, scenes replete with the tastes and aromas of new foods, language acquisition, the loss of contact with friends and family "back home" and becoming economically and socially situated in new regions put on display migrant processes of acculturation. While his exploration of migrant experiences can be thematically read as a literary account of integration, this chapter argues that the work critiques historically accepted representations of Arabs within the Colombian and greater Latin American sphere. In particular, it critiques the trope of Arab silencing, often via death, and the in-text chronicling of the migrant community by non-Arab characters that are portrayed in now-canonical fictions built on a long legacy of and engagement with Hispanic-American Orientalism. Through close readings, I propose that the author, reformulating the function of death along intertextual frames as an aperture for dismantling Orientalist tropes, re-chronicles the Arab presence within literature as an authoritative producer of knowledge on the migratory community and their descendants. As "La caída" ["The Fall"] of commonly accepted markers of space – along with the putative ontologies that have mapped onto their directionality – paratextually suggests, Fayad rearranges inherited narratives about Arabs that have circulated in distinct ways before and since their arrival to the Americas.

In the last decades of the nineteenth century and early decades of the twentieth century, hundreds of thousands of Arabic-speaking migrants from the Eastern Mediterranean, formerly the Syrian provinces of the Ottoman Empire and later regions of European colonialism and Arab

DOI: 10.4324/9781003245117-17

208   Angela Haddad

nationalism in the Levant, came to the Americas and collectively constituted what is known in Arabic as the *mahjar* (literally, "the site of emigration"). Reflecting their early arrival from Ottoman-controlled regions
and affiliated travel documents with the Ottoman Empire, migrants
across Latin America were often collectively, and misleadingly, classified
as "turcos," a term whose connotative associations have added derogatory undertones to the label over time (Civantos, *Between Argentines
and Arabs* 6). To varying degrees and at different times, migrants were
additionally called "sirio-libaneses" or qualified as "levantinos," markers
that created a sense of collective identity abroad despite internal differences (Moore and Mathewson 295–6), and, later, "libaneses," "sirios"
and "palestinos," marking the process by which Arab nationalism on
the other side of the Atlantic influenced categories of identity in Latin
America. Though exact numbers of the *mahjar* and their descendants in
Colombia are unknown, scholars analyzing port registers and census data
have placed the number at 50,000 in the 1990s, a relatively low figure
compared to other areas of the Americas, particularly Brazil, Argentina
and the United States and due to factors like civil wars, inefficient and
later restrictive migration structures and economic concerns (Fawcette de
Posada 10–14). Yet scholars and cultural producers continue to point to
the significance of this community within socio-political, economic and
literary contexts.

While studies from social history and political economy have emphasized
the integration of migrants and their descendants in the country from such
disciplinary views to the exclusion of cultural explorations,[1] Odette Yidi
David has underscored the importance of analyzing the literary contributions of descendants (217). Writers who are descendants of Colombia's
mahjar include Meira Delmar (1922–2009), Giovanni Quessep (b. 1939),
Raúl Gómez Jattin (1945–1997), Luis Fayad (b. 1945), Juan Gossaín
(b. 1949), Jorge García Usta (1960–2005) and Mario Mendoz Zambrano
(b. 1964). While some have opted not to include elements from their heritage in their works, others have. For Yidi David, the work of Delmar, born
Olga Isabel Chams Eljach, and those affiliated with the *Unión* magazine
published by a diasporic Arab organization provide self-representations
of the Arab-descendant community amid a literary scene of representation
by non-heritage authors, particularly Gabriel García Márquez (210). To
this seminal name in the literary sphere of the late twentieth century, we
may add his contemporary Álvaro Mutis, who, though writing his fictions
in exile in Mexico, is another Colombian author who represented the figure of the Levantine Arab in his novels. Though I analyze Fayad's work in
relation to these authors as they operate within the field of the novel, texts
across various genres by authors whose parentage is not of Arab heritage
have codified individuals and descendants from the region into recogniz-
able figures within Colombian and greater Latin American literary spheres
long before García Márquez's and Mutis's entry into public letters.

Hispanic-American Orientalism and the Writing of the Arab Into Canon

A phenomenon that has been treated as Hispanic-American iterations of Orientalism, representations of individuals, objects, places and ideas deemed "Oriental" have circulated within various Latin American textual productions. These have included early travel writings, newspaper articles and modernist literature ranging from poetry to the journalistic and literary form of the *crónica*, which often focused on local urban development or distant travel. While Edward Said's formulation of Orientalism emphasizes the way the Orient was geographically and conceptually mapped to differentiate it from French, British and U.S.-American selves in paradigms of domination, Hispanic Orientalism, as Susan Martin-Márquez points out, is problematized by Spain's Arabo-Maghrebian past when the Iberian Peninsula was under Muslim rule (711–1492). In the age of Western European empire and later nationhood, this history positioned Spain "on both 'sides' of Orientalism – as simultaneously 'self' and 'other,'" or, in a word, a "disorientation." Spaniards, though also "'locat[ing]' the Orient (namely North Africa) as 'over there,'" departed "from the rigorously differentialist logic of ostensibly Western constructions of subjectivity" (Martin-Márquez 8–9). In recent years, scholars have considered this "disorientation" from the periphery of Latin America and the Caribbean, many of whose regions have been, through their colonization by Spain, in early contact with the discourses and cultural topoi regarding Muslim Iberia. From the imposed association of Amerindian populations with Muslims and the "ideological continuity between the Reconquista and the Iberian conquest of America" to the lexical mapping of "Moorish" space onto "New World" architecture (Taboada 35–42), the exploratory and conquistadorial movements of Iberian subjects in the early modern period ensured the migration of the "cultural and literary situation in the Mediterranean" (Fuchs 3).

However, such displacements established a repository of Hispanic Orientalist topoi that, once unhinged from their original cultural and textual artifacts or intercommunal relations and in citational contact with other European Orientalisms,[2] took on abundant afterlives. The excesses of a putative "Orient," ranging from North Africa to West and East Asia, for example, saturate Latin American modernist texts in ways that range from exoticism to "emancipatory projections" in the envisioning of "alternative cultural space" (Schulman 105). It is what allows the canonical Cuban figure José Martí, for instance, to affectively identify with the figure of the resistant "Moor" when articulating a Cuban identity apart from the Spanish empire despite his previous experimentations in representational exoticization (Rodriguez Drissi 93) or other foundational writers such as Enrique Gómez Carillo to implement far-ranging Orientalist tropes in travel *crónicas* written from places like Fez, Cairo, Jerusalem

210 *Angela Haddad*

and Damascus – cities where the Orientalist discourses of various European traditions also proliferated and cross-pollinated.

Analyzing the works of canonical Latin American authors in the generations after Martí and Gómez Carillo, Julia Kushigian's *Orientalism in the Hispanic Literary Tradition* (1991) – one of the first studies of Hispanic American Orientalism – argues that "the Orient" thematized in work by authors like Jorge Luis Borges, Octavio Paz and Severo Sarduy "is drawn away from the role of silent partner to that of 'cultural contestant,' which offers more than the indifference of a static Other" and allows for a plurality of voices to mark the identity and hybridity of a Latin American self (109). However, later scholarship has called for sustained analyses of the socio-historical impact of Arab migration to Latin America on the permutations and treatments of the discourse. In the case of Argentina, Christina Civantos has demonstrated the dialogical encounter between nationalists of European background and Arabic-speaking migrants in articulating national identity. Whereas European-descendant authors represented the "Orient" and "Orientals" both abroad and domestically at the turn of the century to establish difference within positivist discursive hierarchies, migrants also engaged in auto-Orientalism by which they promoted the "essentialization of the self based on preexisting archetypes" that at times functioned as discursive violence and at others as "part of strategies of resistance" (Civantos, *Between Argentines and Arabs* 22, 210). In the Colombian context, some scholars have highlighted the xenophobic tones of the press ranging from initial complaints about new arrivals' poverty and illiteracy to the Orientalist ethnification of crime and fears about migrant economic activity as one of predatory competition (Viloria de la Hoz 27–28; Mosquera Paternina 60–70). Others have begun to explore the representational reverberations of such xenophobia and/or Orientalist imagery in canonical literature, especially García Márquez's *Crónica de una muerte anunciada* [*Chronicle of a Death Foretold*] (1981), which is at times critically aware of representations of Arab Otherness (El Attar 919–923) and which at other times engages such representations (Ette 226–240; Civantos "Orientalism and the Narration of Violence . . ." 169–175). Joining these scholars and broadening the discussion to include the canonical author Álvaro Mutis, I am interested in how structuring devices, in addition to thematic references, have codified the Arab subject in Colombian novelistic letters and how Fayad engages these structures along counterhegemonic lines.

Though Edward Said's formulation of Orientalism excludes Hispanic-American specificity, the methodologies of strategic location, "a way of describing the author's position in a text with regard to the Oriental material he writes about" and strategic formation, "a way of analyzing the relationship between texts and the way in which groups of texts, types of texts, even textual genres, acquire mass, density, and referential power among themselves and thereafter in the culture at large," remain relevant (20).

Chronicling "the Death of the Arab" in Colombian Literature   211

Through this pattern-yielding lens, readers become privy not only to the repetitions of banal Orientalist tropes but also narrative structures that place Orientalized figures within specific narrative spaces of silence.

In the context of late twentieth-century Colombian literary production, such methodologies allow for readings of the relationship between Arab figures and the production of knowledge as it is represented in fictional works after the *mahjar* was well under way. Implementing the entangled discursive histories of Orientalist representation and drawing from the presence of migrant communities in the Caribbean regions of Latin America, García Márquez and Mutis popularized the figure of the Levantine Arab within their novels in the late 1900s in ways that constitute a strategic formation. The contours of this formation hinge on the representation of Arab death and mediated authorship, a phenomenon which Fayad manipulates to re-write the Arab presence in Colombian letters. Though Heba El Attar draws attention to the silencing of Arab characters via death in García Márquez's *Crónica* and *La Turca* by the Honduran author Jorge Luis Oviedo in her article "El orientalismo hispanoamericano" as one way of understanding societal cognitive dissonance that opts for the elimination of the migrant Other rather than adapting to the new social reality (917), it is also important to observe how the structuring trope revolves around questions of authorship and the ability to be a knowledge-producing subject.

While numerous references to the Arab migrant community punctuate his oeuvre, García Márquez' *Crónica* especially centers on an Orientalized figure in the character of Santiago Nasar, a descendant of an Arab migrant and fatal victim of an honor killing who was accused of taking the virginity of Ángela Vicario, a *criolla*, or European-descendant, woman. Ángela, asked by the judge to elucidate her relationship with Santiago, ironically states, "[f]ue mi autor" [he was my author/perpetrator] (García Márquez, *Crónica* 98). In his analysis of this idiom, Jorge Olivares states that Ángela "equates the sexual act with the creative act" and thus places Santiago at the metafictionally "generative core of the novel" that renders the former character as an imagined text to be read (486). Though Olivares treats the work as a "dramatic gloss" of Roland Barthes' concept "the death of the author" (489), we may ask what it means that this death belongs to an Arab within the literary history of authorship and how, subsequently, this form of absent authorship relates to Orientalism.

The double meaning of the Spanish word "autor," which casts onto Santiago the role of criminal authorship (and recalls previous attempts to ethnicize violence at the turn of the century), authorizes Ángela's twin brothers to fatally carry out the code of honor to which they socially adhere. The two characters bury him as a deceased subject within the text while their own violent act allows them, "clutching the *knives wrapped in newspapers* to their chests," to author a new discourse of "honor" (García Marquez, tr. Rabassa 15, *Chronicle*, my emphasis). The swaddling of

212   *Angela Haddad*

the weapons in newsprint and the clutching of the ink-laden parcels close to their bodies suggest ownership over a discourse that would unfold in the narrated era's means of mass communication. In an overarching attempt at authorship, however, the narrator, who maintains a number of biographical similarities with García Márquez, attempts to present a chronicle of the event. Ultimately, though, the narrative teems with contradictory information and temporal incoherence in line with the author's post-modern ascriptions, and no definitive evidence points to Santiago's culpability, though readers are repeatedly confronted with his Otherness.

As Civantos concludes concerning other genealogical aspects of ambivalent Orientalism in *Crónica* ("Orientalism and the Narration of Violence . . ." 170–1), this metaphorical burying of the Arab author within the frame of a self-proclaimed "chronicle" or representation of history can be traced to the paramount work of Hispanic letters, Miguel de Cervantes' *El ingenioso hidalgo don Quijote de la Mancha* [*Don Quixote*] (1605–1615), whose ninth chapter famously establishes the Arab historian Cide Hamete Benengeli as the author of the original text. Here, it is also revealed that the manuscript undergoes a translation by a Morisco boy from Arabic into Spanish and a subsequent transcription by an overarching narrator (Cervantes 201–5). While scholars have pointed to the "discovery" of an Arabic manuscript and its subsequent "translation" or the reference to an Arab "source" as structuring narrative devices in Spanish letters prior to and contemporary with Cervantes (Riley 38; Bahous 18–20), they have also pointed to Cervantes's paradigmatic divergences. Specifically, Cide Hamete is treated as an authorial figure whose voice increasingly punctuates the text but is also perceived and evaluated by both the overarching narrator and the characters about whom he writes as they discover his writings in the space of the narrative (El Saffar 174). In the early modern work by Cervantes, then, the figure of the Arab already occupies a position vacillating between "author" and "character." While this ambiguity reappears in *Crónica*, García Márquez's description of the *autor* Santiago at the time of his death further situates the descendant of Arab migrants to Colombia into the frame of Hispanic modernity and its ties to the Reconquista which ended with the acquisition of territory from Muslims, the forced conversions or exile of non-Christians and the consolidation of the Christian Castilian empire. Dripping with blood and holding his entrails, Santiago, as Ottmar Ette points out, is described by a neighbor during "his public execution and death" as a "Saracen," despite Santiago's given name and conspicuous practices of Christianity (238–9). If *Don Quixote* displays an authorial paradox between literary indebtedness to the "Moors" and the overwriting of Iberian society into a Castilian "idiom," *Crónica*'s interpolation of Santiago into the role of an absent, originary author whose text is variously mediated draws on a narrative device that has historically allotted to the figure of the Arab an ambivalent ability to narrate society.

Chronicling "the Death of the Arab" in Colombian Literature   213

In an altogether different style, Mutis' multi-novel saga *Empresas y tribulaciones de Maqroll el Gaviero* [*The Adventures and Misadventures of Maqroll*] (1993), which details the quixotic wanderings of a man named Maqroll el Gaviero over land and sea, also highlights the figure of the Levantine Arab in the character of Abdul Bashur, Maqroll's fellow traveler, confidant and co-lover of the mistress Ilona. Though not a migrant himself, his family's profession in ship construction and business dealings in the Caribbean nevertheless reflect a *mahjar* presence in the region.[3] In the novel *Abdul Bashur, soñador de navíos* [*Abdul Bashur, Dreamer of Ships*] (1991) primary attention is allotted to this character whose life's story, after a fatal plane crash, is ultimately relayed by an unnamed narrator assuming the self-proclaimed role of "cronista" [chronicler] (Mutis 977). While narrative mediations permeate each of the novels, they are done with varying degrees of intervention. In the first novel, for example, the narrator stumbles upon the diary of Maqroll written on commercial receipts stored in the back fold of a book on the assassination of Louis I, Duke of Orléans, and reproduces it verbatim with the addition of a title and an addendum of previously written material relating to the life of the Maqroll. However, when Fatima, the deceased Abdul's sister, gives the narrator a trove of documents penned and collected by Abdul in the work bearing this co-protagonist's name, he opts for unconventional narrative structures due to the putative unreliability of the texts:

> this narrative of mine has to be written within a framework that in no way conforms to the conventions of how a story should be told. It is absolutely impossible to give it chronological unity. When there are any dates on the papers in my possession, they are not reliable. In most cases, their absence makes it impossible to determine precisely when events occurred. In addition to these documents, which are partial and not always rich in details, I have been obliged to turn to the written accounts of Maqroll himself and to my memory of our numerous conversations.
>
> (Mutis, tr. Grossman 475)

Recalling the early modern text, Mutis reformulates Cervantes' narrator's words that

> [i]f any objection can be raised regarding the truth of this [history], it can only be that its author was Arabic, since the people of that nation are very prone to telling falsehoods, but because they are such great enemies of ours, it can be assumed that [Cide Hamete Benengeli] has given us too little rather than too much.
>
> (Cervantes, tr. Grossman 204)

Despite the clear resonances with Cervantes' work with regard to Arab authorship (in their simultaneous privileging and deprivileging of the

214   Angela Haddad

identity) and non-Arab narrative imposition, the twentieth-century works' insistence on Arab death[4] presents a strategic formation of definitive silencing after the establishment of Arab migrants in the country and region. However, because a hegemonic culture representing another "is necessarily one that makes possible allegories of counterhegemonies and resistance" (Lowe 5), we will see how one descendant of the *mahjar* re-works the trope of Arab death as an aperture to deconstruct the multivalent forms of Orientalism circulating in the Colombian literary sphere in the close readings that follow.

Luis Fayad's *La caída de los puntos cardinales* [*The Fall of the Cardinal Points*]

La caída registers the arrival of a group of men and women – a heterogeneous mixture of Maronite, Shiite Muslim and Druze identities from varied socio-economic backgrounds – at the turn of the twentieth century to Colombia in a predominantly realist mode. The first part, spanning the time frame of two months, relates the steamship journey of these migrants, who are summarily labeled "turcos" upon arrival (Fayad 84). Dahmar Abderrahud, an upper-class Shiite Muslim school instructor, is married to Yanira, the daughter of sayid (sir) Yanirahi, whose family begins experiencing the pressures of a troubled economy. Muhamed Ibn Muhamedin, a lower-class stable worker employed by sayid Yanirahi but also a friend of the Abderrahuds through his membership in a freemason lodge, accompanies the couple on their journey to South America, and, once aboard, they meet the Kadalani brothers Jalil and Hichán, two Maronite men who work in tailoring.

A third-person, omniscient narrator provides a seemingly objective voice to the chronicled events, which are sometimes punctuated by flashbacks opening up a window to the characters' lives in Beirut and Colombia's Caribbean coast before their move to Bogotá. This narrative device renders readers privy to the innocent flirtations between Yanira and Muhamed before her betrothal and marriage to Dahmar; a pre-marital affair between Hichán and a woman named Hassana that results in their swift marriage and forced departure, along with Jalil, to America; and Dahmar and Muhamed's involvement in planning an attack on representatives of the Ottoman authority. The next two sections, spanning increasingly longer time frames, chronicle individual members' daily lives and activities in the country, which include their move from the Caribbean coast to Bogotá, their business projects (from dry goods importing and the local capitalization on natural food resources like grape leaves to, even, the contemplation of entering into the oil industry), participation in the Thousand Days' War between Liberals and Conservatives and the migrants' social relations with local community members involved in professions like law, shipping, social activism, prostitution and housekeeping.

Chronicling "the Death of the Arab" in Colombian Literature   215

Noticeably, the novel contains no central plot and reads, instead, as a series of migrant happenings ending with the death of Dahmar.

The narrative placement of his death, inverting the traditional model in which the Arab passes before the story even begins, presents readers with an alternative interpretation of the novel through its intertextual structure that weaves the Arab migratory presence into literary accounts of Colombian urban modernity. Fayad's crafting of Muhamed and Yanira's relationship, whose love is only physically consummated in old age after the former's multiple sexual exploits and the death of the latter's prosperous, prosaic husband Dahmar toward the end of the novel, closely resembles the drama between Florentino Ariza, Fermina Daza and Dr. Juvenal Urbino in García Márquez' *El amor en los tiempos del cólera* [*Love in the Time of Cholera*] (1985). While Fernando Urueta has read this and other intertextual moments as literary homages to García Márquez, I am interested in ways Fayad employs canonical works as means toward critique. Published after *Crónica*, *El amor* contains, contrary to its predecessor, only a passing reference to Arabs and, specifically, their mourning practices (García Márquez, *El amor* 194). This is despite the narrative time's close overlapping with the historical onset of Arab migration to the country, signaled by the use of the telegraph, the background conflict between Liberals and Conservatives, the inaugural use of travel methods like hot-air balloon rides and motorized vehicles and, in this vein, references to Charles Lindbergh which also appear in *La caída* (García Márquez, *El amor* 376; Fayad 287). Yanira's involvement with both men, I suggest, rewrites the canonical love triangle and presents a transatlantic allegory of Colombian modernity whose coordinates include Arab elements as much as European. Significantly, Dahmar's elite background and lifestyle as well as his engagement in the public sphere uncannily resonate with Dr. Juvenal Urbino. However, while the Paris-educated man of science hopes to "modernize" Colombia through medical knowledge, Dahmar's attempt at "modernizing" Colombia is found capitalistically in his vast establishments and ever-expanding business networks. Fayad's crafting of Dahmar places him as a co-articulator of modernity alongside those with access to state bureaucracy, a relation signaled throughout the novel by highly charged metaphors of card-playing that previously represented Oriental excess in *Crónica*.

The opening scene of *La caída* throws readers into a high-stakes poker game between Dahmar and Jalil on a steamship to the Americas. As the two players, surrounded by engrossed onlookers, increase the stakes, they seem to confirm the narrator's characterization of Arabs in *Crónica* as migrants whose "only driving passion" is "playing cards" (tr. Rabassa 81), an intertext furthered by the port agent's xenophobic inquiry into the presence of an "Ibrahim" or any "delincuente" [criminal] (Fayad 86–7). As Santiago's father in *Crónica* is named Ibrahim and Santiago is accused of committing a crime of honor, the agent stands in the text as the

216   *Angela Haddad*

criollo-nationalist iteration of Hispanic-American Orientalist discourse. However, Fayad challenges these Orientalist iterations by entangling *criollo* subjects into the world of cards and bets throughout the work. The border agent, for example, "[b]arajó los pasaportes sobre la mesa y los soltó como si no supiera qué hacer con ellos" [shuffled the passports on the table and put them down like he didn't know what to do with them] before engaging in a heated exchange about the migrants' religion. Ultimately, though, the official "jugó otro rato con los pasaportes golpeándolos sobre la mesa y los ordenó a su lado y abrió el libro de registro de inmigración" [played with the passports again, throwing them down on the table, and, arranging them on the side, opened the immigration register] (86). Though at first hesitant, *criollo* nationalists in the text later become collaborators in Arab migrant business endeavors; at the Palacio de los Ministerios, Dahmar tells an agent from whom he seeks an importing permit, for example, that he "'le v[a] a hacer una apuesta'" [is going to make him a bet], which becomes code for a bribe that is accepted to hasten the request's approval (160). Treating the excess of betting and card playing in the text, Rigoberto Menéndez Paredes sees the ludic not as "el llano entretenimiento o la devoción irreprimible del jugador" [the player's simple pastime or irrepressible devotion] but "un símbolo, un código cultural generalizado para todo inmigrante árabe o al menos para la mayoría de los hombres que emprendieron el camino migratorio" [a symbol, a generalized cultural code for every Arab migrant or at least the majority of the men who embarked on the migratory path] (143). While elements of risk are always present in migrant experiences, the excess of card-playing metaphors throughout the text both mocks *Crónica*'s narrator's characterization of migrants and draws in *criollo* members of the community as facilitating agents for what becomes the trope and stereotype of the Arab migrant as a late nineteenth- to mid-twentieth-century economic threat and conqueror of the Americas.[5]

The co-existing alternative to Dahmar, personified by Muhamed, posits a romantic vision of modernity, albeit anachronistically, vis-à-vis the Arab subject. Like Florentino, Muhamed moves and operates at the margins (physically in spaces like bars and brothels, socially with those racialized into lower positions and behaviorally outside the confines of sanctioned sexual relations) in his long wait for true love and, specific to his case, an ideal political struggle. An anarchist figure who militates against Ottoman rule but also joins nation-specific struggles such as those in Colombia during the Thousand Days' War or the independence movements against French rule in the Levant during a brief return stint, Muhamed is depicted as a Third-World militant figure *avant la lettre*. The saturation of intertextual references surrounding Muhamed, who has the greatest proclivity for reading and is seen with Arabic, Spanish and Pan-Arab-American texts like those by "Kahlil Gibrán" (Fayad 269) registers the novel's attempt to insert the Arab not only into the historical literary fabric of

Chronicling "the Death of the Arab" in Colombian Literature 217

the region but also into transnational forms of sociality and solidarity. When Muhamed ventures into the Thousand Days' War, for example, the narrator explains that "presenció el momento en que iban a fusilar al coronel Aureliano Buendía y no lo fusilaron" [he witnessed the moment when they were going to shoot Colonel Aureliano Buendía but didn't] (Fayad 136). Having ventured into Venezuelan territory, he meets a muleteer who left "México a pelear en la guerra de Colombia" [Mexico to fight in Colombia's war] and claims to be the son of Lucas Páramo (Fayad 136–8). Further, when Muhamed is later found alone in a forest by armed men, he absurdly claims to be "consejero Kuranosuké, vengador de infamias" [councillor Kuranosuke, avenger of infamies] to feign madness and escape (Fayad 141). The succession of allusions from García Márquez' *El amor* and *Cien años de soledad* (1967) [*One Hundred Years of Solitude*] to Juan Rulfo's *Pedro Páramo* (1955) and Jorge Luis Borges's short story "El incivil maestro de ceremonias Kotsuké no Suké" ["The Insulting Master of Etiquette Kôtsuké no Suké"] in *Historia universal de la infamia* [*A Universal History of Infamy*] (1935) – a canonically referential mapping ranging from Colombia and Mexico to Argentina – re-situates these works in relation to an unexpected interlocutor, an Arab migrant. These intertexts invite readers to more closely examine Fayad's literary weavings as disruptive of ordering systems of knowledge. Chronicled in this fashion, Dahmar and Muhamed enter into the imagined space of the nation and region as articulators of distinct visions rather than remaining outsider "turcos." Though each represents a different strand of entry into modernity, their shared union to Yanira promotes a national allegory of transatlantic proportions within a migrant framework.

In the novel, though, Dahmar's passing constitutes only one of the text's engagement with Arab death and literary re-mappings, as the deaths of Jamil and Hichán's father and Dahmar's father further open Orientalist space to critique. Prior to their departure to South America, the Kadalani brothers discover their deceased father's *taule* – a regional backgammon game in which the winner advances to and passes through the opposing player's starting quadrant via a series of spatial occupations – in their uncle's possession. Devising a plan to re-possess it before their departure, the brothers parodically stand in for an Iberian paradigm of domestic reconquest before their turn to "the New World," especially as their uncle exclaims "[a]labado sea Dios que les abrío a mis sobrinos el camino para conquistar otras tierras" [praise be to God who opened the way for my nephews to conquer other lands] while also insinuating that certain religious communities, particularly the Maronites, have been forced to "desamparar" [abandon] their lands due to Ottoman religious violence (Fayad 50). While the uncle's comment confirms xenophobic economic suspicions arising in the press of the period, the mise en abyme of conquest (from the uncle's comment to the repossession of the *taule* and the game's own internal logic), throws various layers of Orientalism into disarray. Dismissing

218 *Angela Haddad*

the providential undertones of the statement, Jalil recalls the cause of their hurried departure to the Americas, which, far from the uncle's narrative construction, is Hichán and Hassana's perceived transgression of the premarital chastity code of honor and the latter's equally Maronite father's making their union subject to the condition of expulsion to the Americas.[6] This fact of the fiction, so to speak, is used to deconstruct a form of auto-Orientalism in which the "endless tales of oppression, injustice, and maltreatment at the hands of the Ottoman government and their Muslim fellow citizens," as Kemal Karpat observes, "were aimed at arousing sympathy and support among Christians in Europe and the Americas" (179). Returning to the ludic, the brothers' attempt to recover the game before their departure can be read as an attempt to gain control over (auto-)Orientalist discourse.

In a final observation of death in the novel, Dahmar and Yanira receive a letter announcing the death of sayid Abderrahud, the former's father, in the homeland after their settling in Bogotá. After a week of gloom and marital "dejadez" [neglect] Dahmar "oyó la voz de su padre" [heard the voice of his father] who "pronunció su nombre con claridad" [clearly uttered his name] and, approaching and embracing his son, "[l]e dijo que ahora tenía otras obligaciones" [told him that he now had other obligations] such as tending to his wife and home (Fayad 103–4). As sayid Abderrahud waits for Dahmar to return to sleep, the narration is unambiguous about the perceived reality of this otherworldly moment, which brings Dahmar's father, deceased in a far-off land, into the intimate quarters of his present life to end his exilic grief. Working with the theme of integration, the migrants' induction into magical realism occurs only after their arrival in Colombia. However, it also re-writes the style's mode as it relates to the figure of the Arab.

In *Crónica*, which is a precursor for the way Arab migrants representationally relate to the quintessentially Latin American literary style, the narrator opens his account with Santiago's recurring dreams about passing through tree groves. The details of two dreams are shared with not only the reader but also the absent victim's non-Arab mother who has "a well-earned reputation as an accurate interpreter of other people's dreams" (García Márquez, tr. Rabassa, *Chronicle* 3). However, Plácida Linero does not notice "any ominous augury in those two dreams of her son's, or in the other dreams of trees he'd described to her on the mornings preceding his death" (4). Ultimately, the mother's usual precision in interpretation does not extend to Santiago, whose fate is bereft of both societal and supernatural interventions. The functionality of magical realism in *La caída*, then, appearing again when a lightning bolt sets fire to the migrants' dry goods shop after poor ventilation and humidity destroy all the goods, which saves the group from committing insurance fraud by setting their establishment on fire (Fayad 225), is one of repeated assistance rather than working toward the elimination of the text's Arab elements.

Chronicling "the Death of the Arab" in Colombian Literature   219

The father's passing, further, presents metatextual modes of newsprint representation focused on – and authored by – the figure of the Arab that are not reduced to xenophobic and reactionary accounts against migrants:

> El anuncio de Dahmar invitando a una misa por el alma del sayid Abderrahud apareció en el mismo periódico en que los hermanos Hichán y Jalil Kadalani ofrecían la mercancía de su almacén. Anunciaban paños para trajes de hombre traídos del exterior y la muselina y los encajes para vestidos de mujer que ya se exhibían en sus vidrieras. Jalil vio ambos anuncios mientras esperaba detrás del mostrador la entrada de clientes y recortó el suyo y lo guardó en un cajón del escritorio con la colección que le hacía publicidad a su negocio.
>
> (Fayad 108)

> [Dahmar's notice announcing a mass for the spirit of sayid Abderrahud appeared in the same newspaper in which the brothers Hichán and Jalil Kadalani publicized their store's merchandise. They advertised imported fabrics for men's suits and muslin and lace for women's dresses that were already in the display window. Jalil saw both announcements while he waited behind the counter for customers to come in. He cut out his and placed it in one of the desk's drawers with the collection that advertised his business.]

By entering into the marginal space of newsprint (death announcements and advertisements), Fayad points to ways Arab migrants have "authored" Bogotá in the early 1900s. These writings are not the privileged columns of economic and political articles or other written "happenings of the time" like *crónicas*, which expressed "a critical consciousness directly related to the Spanish American experience of modernity" (Reynolds 10). And yet, the inclusion of these "snippets" in a work whose totality resembles a series of urban and travel *crónicas* expands understandings about the people – and the multiple regions with which they are affiliated – that constructed experiences of late modernity and the period of modernization. Ultimately, Fayad presents a transatlantic Arab-Colombian national consciousness that invites readers to re-evaluate the various texts, and their authors, that have written the social imaginary.

To close, *La caída* integrates Arab migrants into the literary field as figures that navigate the layered history of Hispanic-American Orientalism and author their own relation to society and textual production. By re-writing the structuring trope of death and its link to authorship and discourse, Fayad occupies an opposing strategic location that critiques ways Arab migrants have been traditionally represented since their arrival to Colombia and Latin America more broadly. While this chapter has focused on *La caída*, I would like to suggest that an opposing strategic formation may appear with the exploration of other texts by descendants

220 Angela Haddad

of the *mahjar* (e.g. Juan Gossaín Abdallah's *La balada de María Abdala* [*The Ballad of María Abdala*], whose title also signals the re-ordering of knowledge with its nestled anagram and whose intertextuality further re-writes the function of "Arab death"). Indeed, by moving beyond the representations of Arabs in works by García Márquez and Mutis, readers encounter alternative narratives about migrant experiences and what the practice of "integration" may entail.[7]

Notes

1. See, for example, Louise Fawcett de Posada's *Libaneses, palestinos y sirios en Colombia* (1991); Fawcett de Posada and Eduardo Posada-Carbó's "Árabes y judíos en el desarrollo del Caribe colombiano, 1850–1950" (1998); Massimo Di Ricco's "Filling the Gap: The *Colombo árabes* Emergence as Political Actors in Barranquilla and the Caribbean Region" (2014); and Pilar Vargas and Luz Marina Suaza's *Los árabes en Colombia: del rechazo a la integración* (2007).
2. Here, it is worthwhile to draw on the work of Lisa Lowe in her *Critical Terrains: French and British Orientalisms* (1994). In it, she argues "for a conception of orientalism as heterogeneous and contradictory" that not only consists "of an uneven matrix of orientalist situations across different cultural and historical sites" but also is "internally complex and unstable" (5). Though her work focuses primarily on the heterogeneity of French and British Orientalisms in the paradigm of domination, the instability and intersections of space, culture and discourse resonate with studies on Hispanic-American Orientalism, which was not only in contact with multiple French and British iterations of the discourse but also replete with its own set of variables, including the mass migration of Arabic speakers to Latin America.
3. Newspapers from the Caribbean region throughout the 1920s and 1930s are replete with Arab migrants' advertisements for steamship travel. The agency Gebara & Co., managed by Arab migrants, for example, ran advertisements in Haiti's newspaper *La Presse* for Colombian Steamship Co., Inc. that announced the itineraries of steamships and liners that widely traversed the Caribbean and made trips to New York (Colombian Steamship Co., Inc.).
4. The contemporary crime fiction *Muerto, vendido y desaparecido para siempre* (2005 by Fernando Iriarte Martínez) is another work drawing the figure of the Arab, in this case, an Egyptian, into frames of death and absence and points to the lingering presence of the narrative structure in Colombian literature in the twenty-first century.
5. The fear of economic conquest appeared in many newspapers across the Americas where migrants had settled, especially in regions of the Caribbean basin. In Haiti, for instance, an entire newspaper first called *Le Devoir* that was later renamed *L'anti-syrien*, registered in a national's name but edited by a European, frequently warned of a "Syrian" economic invasion and deployed anti-Semitic tropes that berated both Arabic-speaking migrants and Jews (Gayle Plummer 529).
6. Resonating with this early scene of expulsion, Yanira and Dahmar's daughter and the son of a Jewish family named are threatened with expulsion from school for their perceived misbehavior alone in a room late in the novel (Fayad 297). Explaining that they were praying in a way that differed from their presumably Catholic peers, the daughter creates a parallel between their impending removal and the expulsion of Muslim and Jewish communities from early modern Spain. The trope of al-Andalus and the shadow of *convivencia*,

however, quickly disintegrate into national geo-political affiliations as señor Blumenkranz donates to the newly established state of Israel and Dahmar plans to contribute funds to the newly independent Lebanon, whose politics, he hears, is now influenced by Syrians on the border and Palestinians seeking refuge from Israelis (308).

7. I would like to thank Christina Civantos, Fan Fan, Rebekah Smith, Sylvia Gorelick and Natalia Aguilar Vasquez for commenting on previous versions or segments of this chapter.

Bibliography

Bahous, Abbes. *The Novel and Moorish Culture: Cide Hamete "Author" of Don Quixote*, PhD dissertation. U of Essex P, 1990.

Cervantes, Miguel de. *Don Quixote*. Translated by Edith Grossman, First Ecco paperback edition. Ecco, Harper Collins, 2005.

Civantos, Christina. *Between Argentines and Arabs: Argentine Orientalism, Arab Immigrants, and the Writing of Identity*. State U of New York P, 2006.

———. "Orientalism and the Narration of Violence in the Mediterranean Atlantic: Gabriel García Márquez and Elias Khoury." *The Global South Atlantic*, edited by Kerry Bystrom and Joseph Slaughter, Fordham UP, 2018, pp. 165–185.

El Attar, Heba. "Orientalismo Hispanoamericano En Crónica de una muerte anunciada de Gabriel García Márquez y La Turca de Jorge Luis Oviedo." *Hispania*, vol. 91, no. 4, Dec. 2008, pp. 914–924.

El Saffar, Ruth Snodgrass. "The Function of the Fictional Narrator in Don Quijote." *MLN*, vol. 83, no. 2, Johns Hopkins UP, 1968, pp. 164–177.

Ette, Ottmar. "Chronicle of a Clash Foretold? Arab-American Dimensions and Transareal Relations in Gabriel García Márquez and Elias Khoury." *ArabAmericas: Literary Entanglements of the American Hemisphere and the Arab World*, edited by Ottmar Ette and Friederike Pannewick, Vervuert Verlag; Iberoamericana, 2006, pp. 215–260.

Fawcett de Posada, Louise. "Libaneses, Palestinos y Sirios En Colombia." *Documentos*, vol. 9, 1991.

Fayad, Luis. *La caída de los puntos cardinales*. Editorial Planeta Colombiana, 2000.

Fuchs, Barbara. *Mimesis and Empire: The New World, Islam, and European Identities*. Cambridge UP, 2001.

García Márquez, Gabriel. "Alguien desordena estas rosas." *La increíble y triste historia de la cándida Eréndira y de su abuela desalmada*. Mondadori, 1987.

———. *Chronicle of a Death Foretold*. Translated by Gregory Rabassa, Vintage Books, 2003.

———. *Crónica de Una Muerte Anunciada*. 1st Vintage International ed., Vintage International, 2003.

———. *El amor en los tiempos del cólera*. Primera edición, Vintage Books, 2003.

Gebara & Co., "Colombian Steamship Co., Inc." *La Presse*, NYPL Microfilm, 11 Feb. 1931.

Gossaín Abdallah, Juan. *La balada de María Abdala*. Editorial Planeta Colombiana, 2003.

222 Angela Haddad

Kushigian, Julia. *Orientalism in the Hispanic Literary Tradition: In Dialogue with Borges, Paz, and Sarduy.* 1st ed., U of New Mexico P, 1991.

Lowe, Lisa. *Critical Terrains: French and British Orientalisms.* Cornell UP, 2018.

Martin-Márquez, Susan. *Disorientations: Spanish Colonialism in Africa and the Performance of Identity.* Yale UP, 2008.

Menéndez Paredes, Rigoberto. *Árabes de cuentos y novelas: el inmigrante árabe en el imaginario narrativo latinoamericano.* 1st ed., Huerga & Fierro Editores, 2011.

Moore, Aaron, and Kent Mathewson. "Latin America's Los Turcos: Geographic Aspects of Levantine and Maghreb Diasporas." *Nóesis: Revista de Ciencias Sociales y Humanidades*, vol. 22, no. 43, Jan. 2013, pp. 290–310.

Mosquera Paternina, Sandra Elena. *La Prensa y La Inmigración Sirio-Libanesa En Cartagena 1912–1930.* Universidad de Cartagena, 2010.

Mutis, Álvaro. *Empresas y tribulaciones de Maqroll el Gaviero.* RM Verlag, S.L.; Ciudad de México, México, 2019.

Olivares, Jorge. "García Márquez's *Crónica de una muerte anunciada* as Metafiction." *Contemporary Literature*, vol. 28, no. 4, 1987, pp. 483–492.

Plummer, Brenda Gayle. "Race, Nationality, and Trade in the Caribbean: The Syrians in Haiti, 1903–1934." *The International History Review*, vol. 3, no. 4, Oct. 1981, pp. 517–539.

Reynolds, Andrew. *The Spanish American Crónica Modernista, Temporality, and Material Culture: Modernismo's Unstoppable Presses.* Bucknell UP, 2012.

Riley, Edward C. *Cervantes's: Theory of the Novel.* Clarendon, 1968. Print.

Rodriguez Drissi, Susannah. *Between Orientalism and Affective Identification: A Paradigm and Four Case Studies Towards the Inclusion of the Moor in Cuban Literary and Cultural Studies.* UCLA, 2012.

Said, Edward. *Orientalism: Western Conceptions of the Orient.* Penguin Classics, 2003.

Schulman, Ivan. "Narrating Orientalisms in Spanish American Modernism." *Orientalism and Identity in Latin America: Fashioning Self and Other from the (Post)Colonial Margin.* U of Arizona P, 2013, pp. 95–107.

Taboada, Hernán G. H. "The Mentality of the Reconquest and the Early Conquistadors." *Orientalism and Identity in Latin America: Fashioning Self and Other from the (Post)Colonial Margin.* U of Arizona P, 2013, pp. 35–43.

Urueta, Fernando. "La caída de los puntos cardinales." *Narrativa colombiana contemporánea*, 13 May 2014, Departamento Literatura Unal. Lecture, www.youtube.com/watch?v=mdZ4POFfGq4.

Viloria de la Hoz, Joaquín. *Los "turcos" de Lorica: presencia de los árabes en el Caribe colombiano, 1880–1960.* Proceditor, 2004.

Yidi David, Odette. "From Khalil Gibran to Meira Delmar: Reflections on the Literature of the Colombian Mahjar." *Los Rostros Del Otro: Colonialismo y Construcción Social En Medio Oriente y Norte de África.* Universidad Externado de Colombia, 2019.

14 The Otherness That Remains. The Past From The Future

Cuaderno de Chihuahua [*Chihuahua Notebook*] by Jeannette Lozano Clariond

Rose Mary Salum

Mexico, to this day, has not been officially recognized as a country of immigrants. In the eyes of the international community and within its society's own narrative, it is a country with a homogeneous identity whose population is made up of "mestizos," a product of combining the indigenous with the Spanish. Claudia Dávila Valdés claims that Mexico has never been characterized as a major recipient of foreign migration (104). That is, in rough terms, the way the country has been portrayed or, in short, how it has been stereotyped. But nothing could be further from the truth: its shores have welcomed waves of immigrants that have shaped the country as we know it today. From Mexico's independence in 1821 until the present, migratory processes have been highly influential in the making of the nation. There is still much to discover about these migratory movements: the extent of their assimilation, how they have been welcomed, and how they are currently perceived.

The main objective of this chapter is to focus and analyze the nature of Lebanese migration to Mexico as seen through the book of memoirs *Cuaderno de Chihuahua* [*Chihuahua Notebook*] (Fondo de Cultura Económica, 2013) by Jeannette Lozano Clariond, a descendant of immigrants from Lebanon. She was born in Chihuahua, but her family arrived from Beirut "con el fin de procurarse un mejor modo de vida" [with the purpose of obtaining a better way of life.] (*Cuaderno*, 14). Lozano Clariond is one of many Mexican authors whose roots may be traced to the Middle East and whose ancestors left home in order to launch a transatlantic migration to hacer la América [to make the Americas], as they used to say. Through their work, these writers have unveiled all sorts of stories that soon became part of Mexican literature and history. They include Bárbara Dian Jacobs, Héctor Azar, Gabriel Zaid, and Carlos Martínez Assad, just to name a few. They have written fiction and non-fiction and are part of a robust literary movement in Mexico. On this occasion, I will be studying Lozano Clariond's memoir.

DOI: 10.4324/9781003245117-18

224   *Rose Mary Salum*

In addition, this chapter will act as a vindication and a reclamation of a very specific historical phenomenon, one that is rarely found in non-fiction books and can be neatly dated between the 19th and 20th centuries. Second, I will examine how these immigrants were received through their interactions with the local population, as the circumstances they encountered and the ones we will talk about later in this chapter created a culture of descendants that has transcended time. Even now, in the 21st century, its members self-identify as Lebanese. The chapter's goal is to acquaint the reader with the nature of this Levantine migration using the voices of its descendants as its basis, despite the fact that this chapter of Mexico's migration was officially considered over by 1930. This migratory phenomenon was unique in that it had such a lasting effect. Hence, my gaze towards that influx of people will be fixed between the second and third generations of migrants. As such, descendants of this migration are separate from their ancestors, yet their self-conceived notion of origin has become pivotal to their identity. This heritage was assimilated to such a degree that the feeling of otherness remains, determining not only the character of the group but the identity of its resulting members. That is the peculiarity that will serve as the starting point for this chapter.

A Country of Immigrants

While it is true that the most important waves of migration to Mexico in terms of numbers and contributions to the country have been Spanish, U.S.-American and Latin American, roughly 100,000 migrants from the Middle East entered the country between the late 19th century and the 20th. Lebanese migration in Mexico was a phenomenon that took place at a specific time and due to very specific political, economic, and social circumstances.

Carlos Martínez Assad indicates that the Archivo General de la Nación places the arrival of the first Lebanese immigrant to Mexico in 1867 ("Los libaneses inmigrantes y sus lazos culturales en México,"135. Also qtd. in Belloni), though the Lebanese community, whose majority was of the Christian-Maronite religion, is more inclined to identify the genesis of Lebanese immigration to Mexican territory with the time of entry into the country of the priest Boutros Raffoul in 1872. Moreover, Camila Pastor states that 1878 was when official records registered the first migrants in Veracruz, one of the most important ports of entry of Middle Eastern migration (*The Mexican Mahjar*. Loc. 27 of 269). It was not until 1930 that legislative changes slowed the flow of immigration. Industrialization and a need to protect the labor force from foreign newcomers created complex economic circumstances in Mexico. Octavio Rebolledo Kloques divides the history of Mexican migration into two parts: "la primera, caracterizada por el interés manifiesto y urgente de atraer inmigrantes; la segunda, marcada por limitar su entrada y reducir su presencia de la

The Otherness That Remains. The Past From The Future   225

vida nacional" [The first, characterized by the manifestation of an urgent interest in attracting immigrants; the second, marked by limiting their entry and reducing their presence in national life] (162).

Following these policy modifications, Lebanese immigrants' flow stopped and was thus limited to the past century. It was a brief episode in the country's history that had an official beginning and end, a phenomenon which has not been witnessed since. Therefore, to study Lebanese immigrants in the 21st century is solely possible through the voices of their descendants. One might even say that the repercussions of that historical event can still be felt up to the time this chapter is written. Its consequences are evident both in Mexico and among these descendants. In other words, the effects of the migratory wave that arrived from the Middle East are still being studied in real time. Even though Lebanese descendants consider themselves a minority group, they exert significant influence over a myriad of aspects nationwide despite having, somehow, assimilated.

I adopt, hence, a dual perspective. On the one hand, Mexico regards itself as a place where miscegenation took place exclusively between Spaniards and indigenous people, and on the other, we see migrants who bear names that, at least linguistically, exclude them from national identity. In the case of the group that concerns this chapter, these immigrants were first distinguished as Turks because they arrived with passports from the Ottoman Empire. Later on, they would be recognized as Lebanese, though the term included Syrians, Palestinians, and other minority groups who arrived from that same geographic area. To date, the dichotomy about self-perception is so marked that they do not consider themselves to be entirely Mexican, even though subsequent generations were born there.

The Mexican society at large that received these immigrants has been complicit in this distinction, perpetuating it even in the present. Otherness is perceived among the descendants of migrants and repeated even through language. Carlos Martínez Assad affirms that in Mexico,

> la condición de extranjería nunca se cura, así pasen tres generaciones y entonces un descendiente de inmigrantes seguirá siendo siempre "el judío" o "el japonés" o "el argentino" y hay quien considera que están "étnicamente imposibilitados para ejercer el patriotismo."
>
> [the condition of foreigner is never healed, even after three generations have passed, thus a descendant of immigrants will always continue to be a "Jew" or "Japanese" or "Argentinean," and there are those who believe that they are "ethnically unable to exercise patriotism."]
>
> (*La ciudad cosmopolita de los inmigrantes*, 385)

In the specific case of descendants from the Levantine zone, Kevin Smullin Brown observes that, among public figures with this ethnicity, the adjective "Lebanese" is attributed to them despite having been born in

226   *Rose Mary Salum*

Mexico and being of Mexican nationality (20). Their relationship with the past – that is, with the 19th or 20th century – may still exist within the person's memory. Their identification as Lebanese, even though a portion of that specific migration could also be attributed to Syria or Palestine[11] (let's not forget that when they left, in reality, they were abandoning the Ottoman Empire), persists in the way they portray themselves to their communities and the rest of the world. Thiago Henrique Mota has identified part of this phenomenon as race relations: "This finding leads to the realization that the success of the Syrian/Lebanese community in Latin America cannot be dissociated from the context of race relations lived on the continent" (825). As Pastor points out, members of the Lebanese community in Mexico presented themselves as racially superior to the local Indigenous population, seeking a shared identity with the Hispanic-descendant *criollo* elite. Theresa Alfaro-Velcamp's thesis is that "Eastern immigrants and their descendants have drawn on an imagined Phoenician past to create an elite Lebanese Mexican class in modern Mexico" (10). Simultaneously, natives form Mexico did not like Middle Easterners because they behaved, dressed, and sounded different. In addition, Mexicans feared for their jobs.

Therefore, to provide another perspective in the study of migrations to Mexico, it is necessary to keep in mind the concept of race because the interaction between Lebanese communities and those already established as citizens became an essential part of how and why these people were also discriminated against, beyond their customs or attire. According to Thiago Henrique Mota, within this context,

> Syrians/Lebanese were incorporated into the white sector of the Latin American population and were not subjected to structural obstacles to their social ascension, despite the xenophobic prejudice expressed in the term Turk. The local condition of being white made it possible for them to maintain the established opposition to those already excluded in domestic scenarios: Indigenous and Black peoples.
>
> (825)

The scientific basis the population employed to privilege Eurocentrism favored Middle Eastern migrants because, as Camila Pastor puts it, at that precise moment, they were protégés of France, and that fact translated into their whiteness (*The Mexican Mahjar*, Loc. 70 of 269).

Cuaderno de Chihuahua [Chihuahua Notebook]

The book opens in a genuinely poetic style; its first chapter is titled "Memoria y poesía" ["Memory and Poetry"]. Memories become the narrator's companion, who approaches her subject through metaphors

The Otherness That Remains. The Past From The Future 227

related to Lebanon: its mountains and deserts, landscapes that remain idealized as an unreachable paradise created by the ancestors' stories.

Since this migratory event began, its presence in the collective memory has remained relevant to such a degree that even to date, trips to Lebanon are experienced as a return to the homeland. The stories drag across the decades like a wagon loaded with recollections. In the first chapter, there is a passage that sums up the story of so many Lebanese migrants:

> Mi madre, tres de sus hermanas y Jorge, el mayor, nacieron en Chihuahua, a donde llegaron mis abuelos al salir de Beirut con el fin de procurarse un mejor modo de vida. Paulus Ayub, mi abuelo, para nosotros Gito Bulus – recuerdo su foto en el muro de la sala – salió del Líbano en 1895, un joven que vendría a América con el fin de probar fortuna y formar un hogar. Mi abuela María salió de Dourma, un año después y, con apenas nueve años, la pusieron en un barco para hacerles casa a sus hermanos mayores. Antonio y Salomón. Mis abuelos eran cristianos ortodoxos. Paulus y María se casaron en 1901: ella con catorce años, él, con treinta y dos, un hombre recio y violento, según lo recordaba mi madre las ocasiones en que, encorvada, llegó a a hablarme de él. Mi abuela trajo consigo su fuerza, su miedo. Su desierto y, en su lengua, la estriada raíz de su linaje.
>
> (14)

> [My mother, three of her sisters, and Jorge, the eldest of them, were born in Chihuahua, where my grandparents arrived after leaving Beirut in search of a better way of life. Paulus Ayub, my grandfather, Gito Bulus to us – I can still remember his photo hanging on the living room wall – left Lebanon in 1895, a young man who would come to America to try his fortune and make a home. My grandmother María left Dourma a year later, after being put on a boat when she was just nine years old to serve as housekeeper for her older brothers, Antonio and Salomon. My grandparents were Orthodox Christians. Paulus and Maria were married in 1901. She was fourteen, he was thirty-two: a violent and foolish man, as my mother remembered him, shrugging when she told me the stories. My grandmother had brought her strength, fear, desert, and the striated root of her lineage on her tongue.]
>
> (14)

At the end of the 1870s, the arrival of Porfirio Díaz to the government created the need for manual labor to fulfill his vision of opening trade channels to the rest of the world, thus becoming a nation of exports. There was indeed a surplus of labor, but the prejudices that the Mexican society had inherited from 300 years as a Spanish colony had left the country with a mentality predisposed toward discrimination. That

228   *Rose Mary Salum*

way of thinking had been conceived during the colonial era, and it was believed at the time not only that there were races less apt for progress than others but that mere contact with them could set society back. Hence, those deemed inferior were expected to submit to subjugation. According to these beliefs, Mexicans of indigenous and mestizo origins did not possess the intellectual capacity to work at the rate that the new administration demanded. There was even a specific motion to prohibit the entry of Semitic races in order to halt the expansion of a miscegenation process that would supposedly degenerate the race.[2] The motion was passed as law in 1926. In 1927, most migrants from Syria, Lebanon, Armenia, Palestine, and Turkey were denied entry. In fact, this law reversed the 1886 Alien and Naturalization Law that granted citizenship if the period of residence exceeded two years.

Initially, the promotion of European migration resulted in the desired boom in development. Still, despite immigration policies that openly facilitated immigration and whose participants were rewarded with land, tax exemptions, and a prosperous future, Mexico was still seen as a port of entry to the United States. Few immigrants arrived, and even fewer stayed. According to María Cáceres Méndez and Fortuny Loret de Mola, some of those who left Lebanon had no idea where they would end up, but there were others who, upon leaving Lebanon, knew that their final destination would be the United States. In the end, many of them were denied entry into the United States, so they stayed in Mexico (252). This, in part, was the case of Jeannette Lozano Clariond's family who, after living in Mexico for some time, moved their children to the United States, only to bring them back to Mexico afterward. Indeed, the language and the education they received in the United States would stay with the author and her siblings for the rest of their lives. To this day, Jeannette Lozano Clariond has received numerous recognitions for her work as a translator. "Al trasladarse a El Paso, la familia Ayub Shallhoup hizo del inglés su segunda lengua. . . . La estadía de la familia en El Paso coincide con la difusión de la cultura árabe en los Estados Unidos." [Upon moving to El Paso, the Ayub Shallhoup family made English their second language. . . . The family's stay in El Paso coincides with the spread of Middle Eastern culture in the United States] (*Cuaderno* 43–44).

Yet the new migrants did not set out to work in the fields, even though many of them had been peasants in their country of origin. Instead, they opted for informal commerce at markets and fairs. According to Camila Pastor, French merchants in the Mexican Republic had been protesting Syrian competition for some time, and, towards the late 1920s, coalitions of small storeowners and pressure groups accused the Arabs of practicing unfair competition and smuggling ("Lo árabe y su doble," 299). This attitude exacerbated the rejection they had already received upon arrival. In addition, the idea that they had come to enrich themselves at Mexico's

The Otherness That Remains. The Past From The Future 229

expense, as well as their physical appearance and the way they dressed and spoke, generated animosity towards them.

Nostalgia for the Lost Paradise

"En arte, el dolor es puerta" [In art, pain is a door], says Jeannette Lozano Clariond (18). And later, she adds: "toda puerta es azar. . . . Pero el poeta, como los muertos, camina mirando hacia atrás" [every door is fate . . . . But the poet, like the dead, walks looking backward] (19). And that is just what would happen a century after the arrival of the first Lebanese in Mexico. To this day, this looking to the past continues to take place, driven by pain and destiny along the path the author illuminates: their descendants will continue to identify themselves as Lebanese.

Lozano Clariond's grandparents arrived to Chihuahua in an area originally inhabited by Concho Indians, but when the mines of Santa Eulalia (now Aquiles Serdán) were discovered, it became a settlement for the Spanish. Like so many immigrants, they came to a country convulsed by the Revolution of 1910. For some of them, this was enough to trigger a return to their longed-for place of origin or even deemed the perfect reason to leave the country, as shown in one of the author's chapters:

> La mayoría de los libaneses de Chihuahua establecieron comercios en el centro, sobre la calle Libertad. El de Ángel Ayub, primo de mi madre, se llamaba La ciudad de Constantinopla. Solía atenderlo su mujer, Munira, quien había llegado del Bled y quien nunca superó la distancia: fue ella quien motivó al tío a abrir el negocio y ella misma la que más tarde lo convencería de regresar (recuerdo la vitrina semanas antes de su partida: "Nos vamos, nos hundimos: liquidación total"). Delineaba sus labios en forma de un rojo corazón y los ojos con khol negro. Leía el periódico de Beirut sentada en una mecedora blanca, atenta a lo que sucedía en su país.

> [Most of the Lebanese in Chihuahua established their businesses downtown, on Libertad Street. The one that belonged to Ángel Ayub, my mother's cousin, was called The City of Constantinople. His wife, Munira, who had arrived from Bled and never got over being homesick, used to tend to them: she motivated him to start the business and would later convince him to return home. (I remember the display case weeks before her departure: "We're leaving, we're bankrupt: clearance.") She would outline her lips in the shape of a red heart. Her eyes, lined with black kohl, would read the Beirut newspaper as she sat in a white rocking chair, attentive to what was happening in her country.]

(59)

230 *Rose Mary Salum*

For most of the author's family and others, these things happened just as they were becoming settled in Mexico, and political events affected the lives of her family. As Jeannette Lozano Clariond describes it:

> La tierra elegida por mis abuelos nunca fue una Tierra Santa. Ellos hicieron germinar su sabiduría y, en medio de la turbulencia revolucionaria, supieron reconciliarse con su destino. Así se nace a la historia, con unos cuantos retazos de verdad y algo de comprensión hacia lo que parecía no tener ningún sentido.
>
> The land chosen by my grandparents was never a Holy Land. They sowed their wisdom and, amid the revolutionary turbulence, they learned how to reconcile themselves with their fate. That is how history is born, with a few shreds of truth and some understanding of what seemed to make no sense at all.
>
> (28)

That kind of resignation and perception of their new reality would soon be subverted. The conditions of migratory freedom during the Porfirian era, when the Lebanese arrived along with other immigrants from the Middle East and Asia, were to be transformed as the 20th century progressed. Little by little, the gateways were closed to foreigners who wanted to settle in Mexico. The author still remembers the conversations in her house about the 1911 massacre of the Chinese immigrants in Torreón who were accused of being in cahoots with Porfirio Diaz. Over 300 died, including adolescents, women, and children. Such a slaughter exemplified the collective rejection of foreigners that was emerging at the time. Approximately two years later, between 1913 and 1914, Pancho Villa was elected interim governor of Chihuahua. He decreed the departure of Chinese and Arabs from Chihuahuan territory.

Subsequently, those who wanted to enter had to be first considered prone to assimilation in order to gain entry authorization. As Daniela Gleizer points out,

> La política inmigratoria mexicana, que había surgido en el siglo XIX con un espíritu liberal, durante las primeras décadas del siglo XX, atravesó por un fuerte proceso de constricción y rigidización que conllevó a la integración de un número cada vez mayor de criterios de exclusión.
>
> [Mexican immigration policy, which had emerged in the 19th century with a liberal spirit, underwent a strong process of constriction and rigidification during the first decades of the 20th century that led to the integration of an increasing number of criteria of exclusion.]
>
> (qtd. in Dávila Valdés, 100)

Thus, since 1927, an attempt was made to find a way to exclude from the national project those elements considered "undesirable," such as,

The Otherness That Remains. The Past From The Future 231

according to their perspective at the time, workers of Syrian, Lebanese, Armenian, Palestinian, Arab, and Turkish origin (104). These measures of control had an international impact, stopping the flow of people from the Middle East and changing the perception of those who had previously entered. The reality that was brewing spawned gossip and resentment among the migrants themselves, as Lozano Clariond tells us:

> Los árabes callaban su destierro como si se tratara de algo ocurrido en un sitio irreal: no lo podían nombrar, ni recordar, ni soñar. El destierro llenó de terror todos los muros, el miedo se percibía en el rincón de cada casa en los gestos, en los ojos de los inmigrantes. Fue así como se conformó la colonia libanesa.
>
> [The Arabs kept silent about their exile as if it were something that had happened in an imaginary place: they could not name it, remember it, or dream of it. Exile filled the walls with terror; fear could be felt in every corner of every house, in the gestures and eyes of the immigrants. That is how the Lebanese colony was formed.]
>
> (30)

A settlement arose from that pain, much like a swinging door opened to usher in not only opportunities but misfortunes as well. Perhaps it was that suffering, that feeling of rejection stemming from knowing that one is not welcome, that formed a schism in their concept of identity that, even a century later, cannot be amended, as shown in this passage about Lozano Clariond's mother:

> Reservaba el árabe para sus hermanas, el español para mi padre, y el inglés para nosotras, incluso frente a nuestras amigas, algo que me perturbaba. . . . Años más tarde entendí que lo hacía para esconderse, para que ni siquiera los padres de mis amigas se enteraran de que era una desterrada, que su origen estaba marcado por la doble expulsión y que el desasosiego había clausurado su infancia. Su silencio se fue convirtiendo en inmovilidad, en un gran miedo a todo lo que no pudiera controlar; era la niña amenazada por la guerra del diario vivir, presa de una insalvable, desparramada melancolía. La amé en su dolor; quise cambiar su sino, sus ojos, sus pasos. Ella no. . . . El exilio es consustancial a toda alma que elige el movimiento interior por compañía.
>
> [Arabic was reserved for her sisters, Spanish for my father, and English for us, even in front of our friends, which was something that disturbed me. . . . Years later, I understood that she did it to hide, so that not even the parents of my friends would find out that she was an exile, that her origin was marked by a dual expulsion, and that unrest had put an end to her childhood. Her silence became paralysis, a great fear of everything she could not control. She was

232 *Rose Mary Salum*

that same girl, threatened by the battle of everyday existence, prey to
an insurmountable, diffused melancholy. I loved her when she was
enduring her pain; I wanted to change her fate, her eyes, her steps. She
didn't. . . . Exile is essential to every soul that chooses inner movement
for a company.]

(47–48)

The kind of isolation some immigrants experienced helped conceal an
identity that would become an impenetrable fortress later on. On the
other hand, language was a limitation to them, alienating their experience
in a way very unique to this "new world." Simultaneously, the discrimination they faced upon arrival forced them to adapt to new experiences
that made them lose their native tongues along the way, tongues that were
hard to recover due to their own nature and difficulty. With a compro-
mised language, identity was elusive. Author Jeannette Lozano Clariond
beautifully expresses:

Mi padre decía que teníamos sangre mitad árabe, mitad mexicana.
A él, taita le preparaba enchiladas rojas y frijoles refritos. Ni de un
lado ni del otro el matrimonio de mis padres había sido bien visto:
¿Cómo Olga Ayub Shallhoup se casaría con un mexicano? ¿Cómo mi
padre con una árabe a quienes los Lozano no conocían bien? . . . Ni
judíos ni palestinos: en casa de mi abuela María remarcaban siempre
que éramos libaneses.

[My father used to say that we had half Arab, half Mexican blood.
Taita prepared red enchiladas and refried beans for him. Neither side
of the family had welcomed my parents' marriage. How could Olga
Ayub Shallhoup marry a Mexican? How could Father be with an
Arab whom the Lozanos did not know well? . . . Neither Jews nor
Palestinians: within my grandmother Maria's house, it was always
emphasized that we were Lebanese.]

(63)

This vital and linguistic separation was made visible in constructing the
discourse that differentiates subjects. The division between Us (Mexicans)
and the Others (Arabs) was based first on economic and later racial differences: variations in physical traits to which a social significance would
be ascribed, regardless of whether the language had been learned since
childhood. This separation originated in their customs, the food they ate,
their way of seeing the world. It was independent of genetics or society's
disqualification through the concept of race. It was created as a social
construct, stemming from perceptions accrued during its participants'
day-to-day. But it also relied on cultural and educational considerations,
among other distinctions. Thus, the feeling of otherness did permeate into
how people were socially identified. To this day, any prominent figure

The Otherness That Remains. The Past From The Future 233

with Lebanese ascendance will be properly named as such, highlighting the ethnic dissimilarity. For example, artist Salma Hayek; businessman Carlos Slim Helú; soccer player Manuel Gibrán Lajud Bojalil; investor Alfredo Harp Helú; poet, translator, and writer Jeannette L. Clariond; playwright Héctor Azar; journalist and political commentator Pablo Majluf; and author Bárbara Dian Jacobs, just to mention a few, are all labeled as Lebanese descendants by their community.

Differentiation was introjected by most of the migrants. Despite the fact that this community had already been baptized as Lebanese, they continued to re-affirm their own differences from others, and in doing so, they created new doubts. As Lozano Clariond expresses, "Desde entonces empecé a preguntarme si se pertenece a un país" [Ever since then, I started wondering whether you can truly belong to a country] (63–64). That self-doubt worked two ways; on the one hand, it affirmed a sense of foreignness; on the other, it provided a sense of agglutination, of belonging, even if it was to a distant land. Even now, as Luis Alfonso Ramírez Carrillo points out,

> En la charla íntima de la tradición familiar están presentes dos tipos de elementos: los que se refieren a la posición minoritaria y al rechazo cultural de los primeros migrantes – es decir, la aceptación de haber ocupado una posición étnica subordinada culturalmente – y la pobreza de los abuelos o de los padres, con la construcción de imágenes en las que es evidente su reciente ascenso social y su temor a la miseria, de la que se guardan dolorosos y vividos recuerdos.
>
> [In intimate conversations belonging to family traditions, two topics are generally present: those that refer to a minority position and cultural rejection of the early migrants – that is, the acceptance of having occupied a cultural and ethnically subordinate position – and the poverty of parents or grandparents, with the construction of images in which their recent social ascent and their fear of misery are evident, and in which painful and vivid memories are stored.]
>
> (478)

These images continue to endure, acting as a reminder of a difference implicit in many familiar settings. Thus, one is Lebanese not because of one's language but because of an identity created at the turn of the 20th century, given the specific circumstances of the Mexican Mahjar, as explained throughout this chapter. Furthermore, the Lebanese identify themselves as such because the remainder of society functions as a chorus that supports how they present themselves to the world.

Conclusion

Studying Lebanese migration from the perspective of the 21st century invariably takes us back to the 19th and early 20th centuries, where we

234 *Rose Mary Salum*

learn that although it came to an end historically, it has not ended as a concept. One hundred years later, their experience can still be studied through the voices of their descendants. Jeannette Lozano Clariond is one such voice that expresses memories of what took place and reaffirms, through the recent publication of *Cuaderno de Chihuahua*, that otherness remains. Her identity as a Lebanese-Mexican writer emerges in this memoir and presents us with a setting that, albeit intimate, exposes the historical characteristics of the Levantine exodus. The book incorporates other aspects beyond tragic family events to show the reception, the assimilation process, and the racism that migrants from the Middle East faced. Lozano Clariond opens the door to her most intimate thoughts regarding her family and her mother throughout these memoirs. These personal reflections are woven amid a social and political subplot that is situated during a country's transitioning period and its remnants.

One of Clariond's principal themes that touches from the personal to the universal is the idea of otherness that is transmitted through the country's prejudiced views. Racist narratives, particularly those relevant to Middle Eastern migrants, increased from both sides and perpetuated the divisiveness and threats in society.

This mental construct of the migrant as a menace incited dread and rejection of immigrants. They were feared, isolated, and attacked because deep down, "we" did not understand the differences between "us" and "them." These racist discourses ultimately led to the Lebanese being relegated into a minority status based on the perceived inferiority of their racial differences. Ultimately, racism stemming from both immigrant and national groups was the motivating factor that generated said differentiation. Reflecting on the pattern of Levantine migration in Mexico, we may conclude that, despite how they were received and their struggles to find a place and an identity within the country that opened its doors to them, their migratory panorama positively transformed the nation. While these contributions are most easily measured in the area of economics, in their wake, they are migrants who have successfully influenced the fields of politics, gastronomy, industry, science, the arts, and, as in Lozano Clariond's case, literature.

Notes

1. Alfaro-Velcamp traces the beginning of the coalescence of "Lebanese" to 1922 (142).
2. In 1908, the first legislation was created to regulate immigration in Mexico. Its purpose was to continue attracting citizens from other countries while at the same time adding sanitary restrictions to their arrival.

Works Cited

Akmir, Abdeluahed, et al. *Los árabes en América latina. Historia de una emigración*. 1st ed., Biblioteca de Casa Árabe-Siglo XXI, 2009. Print.

The Otherness That Remains. The Past From The Future 235

Alfaro Velcamp, Theresa. *So Far from Allah, so Close to Mexico: Middle Eastern Immigrants in Modern Mexico*. 1st ed., U of Texas P, 2007. Print.

Belloni, Benedetta. "La voz de los descendientes. El horizonte cultural libanés en la novelas *Las hojas muertas* de Bárbara Jacobs y *En el verano la tierra* de Carlos Martínez Assad." *Ras segna Iberistica*, vol. 39, no. 105, 2016, pp. 55–68.

Cáceres Méndez, María and Fortuny Loret de Mola, Patricia. *La migración libanesa a Yucatán*. [Tesis de licenciatura en antropología] UADY, Mérida, 1977.

Cánovas, Rodrigo. "La ciudad cosmopolita de los inmigrantes de Carlos Martínez Assad(ed.)." *UNIVERSUM*, vol. 1, no. 28, 2013, pp. 261–267.

Clariond, Jeannette. *Cuaderno de Chihuahua*. 1st ed., Fondo De Cultura Económica, 2013. Print.

Dávila Valdés, Claudia. "La aplicación de la política migratoria restrictiva y controlador en Mo tul. El caso de libaneses y coreanos." *Península*, vol. 10, no. 2, 2015, pp. 97–116.

———. "Socio-Economic Trajectory and Geographical Mobility of Lebanese and Koreans. From Motul to Mérida." *Migraciones internacionales*, vol. 8, no. 2, 2015, pp. 103–131.

Díaz de Kuri, Martha and Lourdes Maccluf. *De Líbano a México: Crónica de un Pueblo Emigrante*. 1st ed., El Centro Libanés, 1995. Print.

Kaufman, Asher. *Reviving Phoenicia: The Search for Identity in Lebanon*. 1st ed., I.B. Tauris, 2004. Print.

Martínez Assad, Carlos (ed.). "Los libaneses inmigrantes y sus lazos culturales desde México." *Dimensión antropológica*, vol. 44, no. 15, 2008, pp. 133–155.

———, et al. "Los libaneses maronitas en México y sus lazos de identidad." *Contribuciones árabes a las identidades iberoamericanas*. 1st ed., Biblioteca de Casa Árabe-IEAM, 2009, pp. 93–114.

Mishima, María Elena Ota, et al. *Destino México: Un estudio de las migraciones asiáticas a México, siglos XIX y XX*, 1st ed., El Colegio de México, 1997. Print.

Mota, Thiago Henrique. 2020. "Muslims, Moriscos, and Arabic-Speaking Migrants in the New World." *Latin American Research Review*, vol. 55, no. 4, 2020, pp. 820–828.

Pastor, Camila, et al. "Lo árabe y su doble: imaginarios de principios de siglo en México y Honduras." *Contribuciones árabes a las identidades iberoamericanas*. 1st ed., Biblioteca de Casa Árabe-IEAM, 2009, pp. 287–347.

———. "La creación de un ámbito público transnacional (Primera parte)." *Estudios de Asia y Africa*, vol. 47, no. 3, 2012, pp. 485–520.

———. *The Mexican Mahjar: Transnational Maronites, Jews, and Arabs*. 1st ed., e-book ed., U of Texas P, 2017.

Ramírez Carrillo, Luis Alfonso Ramírez. "De buhoneros a empresarios: la migración libanesa en el sureste de México." *Historia Mexicana*, vol. 43, no. 3, 1994, pp. 451–486, www.jstor.org/stable/25138912.

Rebolledo Kloques, Octavio. *Extranjeros nacionalismo y política migratoria en el México independiente, 1821–2000*, Tesis doctoral. Repositorio Universidad de Granada, 2016, p. 162.

Sam, Dagher R. "Leaving Mideast Behind; Lebanese Find Success In Mexico: [Broward Metro Edition]." *South Florida Sun – Sentinel*, 23 Oct. 2001, p. 16A.

ProQuest, www.proquest.com/newspapers/leaving-mideast-behind-lebanese-find-success/docview/388079880/se-2?accountid=41021.

Smullin Brown, Kevin. *The Lebanese of Mexico, Identifications in Aspects of Literature and Lite Rary Culture*, Ph.D. thesis. U of London P, 2010.

Yankelevich, Pablo. "La arquitectura de la política de inmigración en México." *Nación y extranjería. La exclusión racial en las políticas migratorias de Argentina, Brasil, Cuba y México*. 1st ed., Universidad Nacional Autónoma de México, 2009.

15 The Idea of Translation in *Ancient Tillage*, by Raduan Nassar

Nazir Ahmed Can

The material and symbolic boundaries between literature and translation have been the subject of numerous reflections in the last decades. Intensified by western expansion, the circulation of people, goods, and ideas made translation a fundamental presence in world exchanges. Therefore, it is not surprising that the translator and the interpreter have established themselves as characters in literary fiction. However, in this chapter, I will focus on another type of representation. Indirectly used as both a theme and a method, translation becomes a "contemporary metaphor"[1] (Ribeiro 77) in several 20th- and 21st-century Lusophone narratives and, particularly, in *Lavoura Arcaica* (1975) [*Ancient Tillage* (2016)] by Raduan Nassar. The most important Brazilian writer of Lebanese origin is also one of the leading voices in Portuguese-language literature, as confirmed by the extensive number of critics who have analyzed and valued his work since then. His novel has a very particular impact on the 21st century. Translations into several languages, including English in 2016, have made *Ancient Tillage* known to a wider audience. The 2016 Camões Prize, the most renowned literary recognition of lusophone countries, consecrates the novel in this linguistic community. In Brazil, this award also has a political dimension: the author is today one of the sharpest critical voices of the far-right populist government led by President Jair Bolsonaro. Far from being a political manifesto, *Ancient Tillage* is currently one of the most-read and revisited books by Brazilian readers and academics. Thus, Raduan Nassar has inscribed his name in the history of Brazilian literature despite having published only three books: *Ancient Tillage*, which marked his literary debut in 1975; the novella *Copo de cólera* (1978) [*A Cup of Rage* (2016)]; and, finally, *Menina a caminho* (1997) [*Girl on the Way*], a volume of short stories bringing together narratives written between 1960 and 1970.

Naturally, writers of Arab origin have been part of the diaspora literature in Brazil for decades. Names such as Chaquif Maluf, Salim Miguel, William Agel de Mello, and Miguel Jorge and, more recently, Milton Hatoum, Alberto Mussa, or Michel Sleiman reflect in their works on

DOI: 10.4324/9781003245117-19

238   *Nazir Ahmed Can*

the Lebanese presence in Brazil. Mixing Western and Arab influences, they contribute to expanding the thematic and aesthetic horizons of the Brazilian literary field. Most of them maintain intense literary activity and have published several fiction books in the 20th and 21st centuries. One way or the other, they revisit forms and themes inaugurated by Raduan Nassar in *Ancient Tillage*. Indeed, to understand the Arab impact on Brazilian literature and culture in the 21st century, a reading of *Ancient Tillage* becomes imperative.[2] Milton Hatoum underlines the importance of *Ancient Tillage*:

> Por isso, o romance de Raduan me impressionou tanto. E também por outros aspectos que eu chamaria de afinidades temáticas ou laços de uma cultura comum: o Líbano, com suas ressonâncias islâmicas, bíblicas e orientais que Raduan incorpora ao topos da volta do filho pródigo em *Lavoura Arcaica*. Raduan talvez seja o primeiro ficcionista brasileiro de origem árabe a evocar de maneira tão densa e lírica certos temas da cultura oriental, mas num ambiente brasileiro e 'tradicional.'
>
> (Coutinho 13)

> [the human dimension of *Ancient Tillage* impresses me a lot. And also for other thematic affinities or ties of a common culture: Lebanon, with its Islamic, biblical and oriental resonances that Raduan incorporates to represent the classical topic of the return of the prodigal son. Raduan is perhaps the first Brazilian writer of Arab origin to evoke in such a dense and lyrical way specific themes of oriental culture, but in a Brazilian and 'traditional' environment.]

The life of Raduan Nassar is intimately linked to the complex history of Lebanon and the migratory processes that led his parents to settle in Brazil in 1920. There are few concrete records of the flow of Lebanese to Brazil, especially when compared to other communities that came from Europe during the same period and were processed through an institutional apparatus upon arrival. As Priscilla Coutinho states in her doctoral thesis on Raduan Nassar, unlike most foreigners who arrived in São Paulo in the first decades of the 20th century, the Lebanese were not processed through the "Hospedaria de Imigrantes" (Immigrant Inn), the main registration and reception center in São Paulo at the time. As such, national lists and archives do not allow names or the exact number of entries that occurred at the time to be checked (Coutinho 42). Nevertheless, it is estimated that around seven million Syrians and Lebanese settled in Brazil between the end of the 19th century and the first decades of the 20th century. The Nassar family most likely left Lebanon for similar reasons to those of their compatriots in the first wave: the difficult situation in a land of numerous conflicts dynamized by foreign forces and the regular persecution of Christian

The Idea of Translation in Ancient Tillage, *by Raduan Nassar* 239

communities in a territory, at the time, dominated by Ottoman forces. As Coutinho demonstrates, most of these immigrants left a rural world, fostered a patriarchal social organization, and considered the family the main identity element (41). Anchored in religion and agriculture, this model is internalized in the structure of *Ancient Tillage*. Also implicit in the novel is the fear that the family structure, so strong in the Lebanese context, runs the risk of weakening in foreign lands. Therefore, it is up to the patriarch of the home to strengthen the memory, reiterate a conservation model of ties, and reinforce the pillars of its composition (Coutinho 41). In addition to this legacy, time and space confirm the impression of immobility that surrounds characters' lives: the Brazilian dictatorship, which, between 1964 and 1984, was also structured on the premises of home, family, God, and national body, and the interior of São Paulo, one of the wealthiest and most conservative provinces in Latin America. Despite that, time and space are not explicitly inscribed in *Ancient Tillage*. The narrative presents the classic dispute between father and son on one level. The incestuous passion between the narrator André and his sister Ana constitutes the novel's main conflict. From this foundational tension, the narrator examines the great contradictions of the model of family organization designed by the father. On a second level, *Ancient Tillage* indirectly contemplates the opposition between two regimes of truth: the untranslated world of the colonial regime of representation (Ribeiro, "Traduzir e ser traduzido" 67), embodied in the family patriarch, and the world of "hospitality" to the difference that characterizes translation (Ricoeur 30), represented by André.

This story of universal scope, in effect, anticipates a set of questions that would mobilize the theory of translation in the decades that followed. Appropriating a conservative interpretation of the Bible (the Old and New Testaments) and of the Qur'an (which differs from the biblical text in that it does not have a new version), the narrator refuses the idea of transparency that structures the imaginary and offers an unusual density to the Portuguese language. In addition to emerging as a theme, Arabic languages, religions, and cultures penetrate the dominant discursive code (Portuguese language). Aware of the difference, Raduan Nassar recognizes that the semantic fields represented cannot always harmoniously overlap and, through different processes, expands the aesthetic code of the Brazilian literary field. Operating with instruments like those of the translator, the author inscribes the "other" as an antidote against autophagy (Campos, *Galáxias*), the untranslatable as a driver of reflection (Ribeiro, "A tradução"; Ribeiro, "Traduzir e ser traduzido"; Large *et al.*, *Untranslatability*), betrayal as a practical alternative (Ricoeur, *Sobre a tradução*), and creation as an expression of a desire (Berman, *L'épreuve de l'étranger*; Berman, *La traduction*; Carvalho, *a câmara, a escrita e a coisa dita*).

The religious statement and the moralizing reprimand, also synthesized in Portuguese as the term "sermão" (sermon), are merged in the words of the head of this family of immigrants from the Mediterranean coast.

240 *Nazir Ahmed Can*

From the transfiguration of the same material based on the lexicon of the body, the house, and the land, André, one of the sons, elaborates a kind of profane prayer that reveals the open wound of the family. In that house, the time for sermons was also mealtime. The metaphor of autophagy, that is, of thought that consumes itself and leads to dangerous proximity to totalitarian regimes, could not be more literal. The description of the setting, on the other hand, reinforces the idea of a universe closed around moral rigidity: the old, "solid, heavy" table (85); the immaculate white tablecloth laid out at one of the heads of the table; the light that makes the clean forehead of the motionless patriarch's thick body; and the antique clock hung off the wall behind him, "each and every one of his words weighted by the pendulum, with nothing distracting us more at that time than the deep bells marking the passing of the hours" (28). Interweaving the regimes of religious and political domination, these symbols seek to attenuate the division that time has forged in the family and that, ironically, is manifested in the arrangement of the seating at the table: the father at the head and, on the right, in order by age, Pedro, Rosa, Zuleika, and Huda; on the left, the mother, André, Ana, and Lula, the youngest of all. Thus, if the "right branch [were] a spontaneous growth off the trunk, starting from its roots" (87), the left branch "bore the stigma of a scar, as if Mother, from where the left side started, were an anomaly, a morbid protuberance, a graft on the trunk, perhaps even fatal, it was so weighed down with affection" (87). Finally, at the opposite head of the table, the empty place of the deceased grandfather, an old immigrant who represents the passage of time, the transit in space, and the displacement of the Arabic language by Portuguese. However, the movement is damned since the imagery remains. The difference between father and grandfather is merely formal: while the former expands the vocabulary of austerity in a litany that confiscates the hidden meaning of the world, the latter, with a "coarse belch" (52), determines the order of things: "Maktub" ("it is written"). To the narrator André, the grandfather was just a silent, old ascetic, a stalk of bone in which nothing shone "besides the chain of his terrible, golden, oriental hook" (26). But to the father, who carries on his project, he is the model of moral rigidity, "the patriarch whose mineral cleanliness of thought was never disturbed by the convulsions of nature" (34). Therefore, for the narrator, "it would be an exaggeration to say his chair remained empty" (87).

The father's message is based on keywords that bring together different religious traditions, such as Christianity and Islam, and it is founded on the idea of transparency: the veneration of blood ties, work, austerity, self-control, and a sense of duty. As described in the Biblical and Qur'anic texts, the house is also an offshoot of a healthy body. Indeed, the metaphor of the protected home/body endows the father's discourse with force: only houses with "strongly built foundations, strongly erected walls and a strongly supported ceiling" (35) and delimited by "our fences" (32) can

The Idea of Translation in Ancient Tillage, by Raduan Nassar   241

ward off the imbalance caused by the "malignant tremor" (32) that seizes the hands of lovers; corrupts the "blessed strength of the arms" (32); spreads "throughout the pure regions of their bodies"; and penetrates through the head, "clouding their eyes with turmoil and darkness" (32). In this line of reasoning that values the retreat built around well-sealed boundaries, preventing the invasion of external impure shadows, "build a fence around your body or simply shield it" (33) are the two faces of a world without translation. According to António Sousa Ribeiro, no translation theory can be based on a perspective such as the one expressed in this way, built on a logic of mutual exclusion and a definition of the border as a dividing line ("A tradução" 81). In the same article, Ribeiro reminds us that this model is designed for simple corroboration of the starting point references and thus is destined to silence everything that is presented in the Other as discrepant to those references. In this conception, for Ribeiro, a simultaneously partial and universal world is built, within which the Other and its differences are reduced to the same (84–85).

Therefore, the playbook of principles is based on the cliché of the cleanliness of the body and the protection of the home. In both cases, the "dead metaphor" binds the diversity around a commonplace and, focusing on the most intimate and political space of all (the body), removes the possibility of movement. It has nothing to do with the transit between different worlds, which mutually enriches each other by producing the negotiation of difference. Remember that, for Paul Ricoeur (*A metáfora viva*), the "living metaphor" combines style and perception to construct new knowledge (22). Far from the characteristic *transposition*[3] of this poetic and translational procedure analyzed by the French theorist, the father's words are fixed in a *position*. His grammar is oriented toward the division between "us" and "them" and towards the linkage between notions of race ("our blood") and geography ("our house"). Used in all eras for the purpose of conservation of power and/or as a defensive attitude, communitarianism is the first effect of racial hierarchization based on spatial criteria (Mbembe 174). This combination also gives rise to formulations of a primordialist nature (Appadurai 15), that is, based on essentialist arguments: backed by the invention of an ancestral purity, selects information, erases difference, produces new forms of universalism for its own benefit, and, ultimately, consolidates fascism in the world without translation. Colonial in nature, this vision is therefore bound to the conviction of self-sufficiency. Deprived of contact with the "foreigner," it disables translation; feeds the legitimacy of sovereignty; and justifies, in the symbolic plane, the emergence of "deadly identities" (Maalouf, *Les Identités meurtrières*). It is a conception remarkably close to the theory of "the clash of civilizations," which was advocated in the field of ideas by Samuel Huntington (Ribeiro, "A tradução" 86) and put into practice by some of the most violent governments of yesterday and today.

As a reaction to the archaic and "indefatigable tillage" (23) of the father, André takes refuge in the room of a boarding house, from where he begins to visualize the "ancient sky" (72). The narrator becomes the full subject of translation from the moment he expresses the tense coexistence among the family members and, consequently, between two or more cultural and ideological reference frames that inhabit the same space. André questions the values that structure the father's imagery, refuses the fate of uncritical assimilation, and surrenders to the conflict – a central problem of translation. Aware that the light projected in his house during the father's sermons was burning his eyelids, André is nourished by a speech composed of "moss, mud, and mire" (50), "good surplus manure" (70), and the shadows that live with the family. That is, from his temporary refuge, in the tense dialog he has with his eldest brother, who is trying to bring him back home, he conceives the space in a different way (now fertilized) and tempers his saliva with time (now circular). André knows that to demolish the body of the old house, he needs to get to a symbolic border and settle there as a translator who "goes into virgin forest and stays there overnight, like when someone penetrates a circle of people instead of circling it timidly from afar" (50). From this precarious and dialectic place, he evaluates the difference, examines and puts back together the shards strewn across the floor, dissects the most secret intricacies of the family, and redesigns the vessel of his old identity "from the clay of my own hands" (24).

As happens in any process of matter transformation or of transition from tradition to translation, André adds to the evaluation of the context (and its resources of a historical, geological, and metaphysical nature) a poetic investigation of the lexical, phonic, and rhythmic substances of ancient texts that expatriate, now in a different way, to the Portuguese language: "which startling, hot breath suddenly lifted up my eyelashes? Which abrupt, restless colt was carrying my body off in galloping levitation?" (29). Therefore, there is also an issue of translation at the core of his existence. Born of agony and moved by desire, André's expression combines language and communication. Just like that, as stated by Carvalho, the expression navigates the agitated waters of the confluence of the cold current of language with the hot current of speech (62).

Ancient Tillage, in effect, uses the method of translation and simultaneously anticipates a series of questions that would occupy the theorists of this science for the next five decades. In the first place, André is aware of the limits in the house and the limits of his own resistance. He knows it's not enough to reverse the world since it would remain static in doing so. This is not just an ethical and moral issue but also a political and contextual one. Unlike Lula, the youngest brother who dreams of breaching the border without considering his own dispersion, André prepares an expression closer to music. Familiarity with the instrument is decisive in an undertaking of this nature:

> in strumming the string of a lute – stretched to the limit – a highly tuned note would resonate (was assuming that it would be no more

The Idea of Translation in Ancient Tillage, *by Raduan Nassar* 243

than a melancholy, shrill twang), yet it would be impossible to draw any note at all from the same string were it to be stretched until broken
(96)

This passage contains perhaps one of the most beautiful definitions of translation. Sensitive to the need for harmony, the narrator faces the conflict and the tumult of his silenced pain, disdains the ruler that measures the apparently solid world of the family, accepts the risk of "[taking up] the hammer and saw and [rebuilding] the silence of the house and its corridors" (39) and the challenge of placing oneself in the solitude of the border. From this complex center of operations, he removes "the nectar of my dagger from the fringes of these tender words" (63) and begins his transposition. And this happens even in those moments when the narrative moves on to secondary issues, such as when he recalls an episode from childhood. The narrator remembers when he unintentionally hunted and crushed a dove at his bedroom window. There, he is confronted with the responsibility and the mistakes characteristic of the two activities. Pursuing animals and searching for the exact word are ancient sciences that intertwine wakefulness and movement, the instant and agility, contact with the sordid solidity of order, and with the living matter that subverts this order. In André's voice, these dimensions are on a porous border:

which terrible instant marks the leap? Which gale and spatial depth conspire, toying with the limit? The limit where all newly vibrationless things no longer simply make up life in the day-to-day current, but have become life in the subterranean memory.

(56)

He knows that in the hunt and the expression there can be "one kernel too many, or one second less . . .; no rapture, no jerking while pulling the string, not one extra second in the weight of the tense arm" (56–57). This awareness becomes sharper after the narrator recognizes the irreconcilable distance between his father and the carnal passion for his sister Ana. André, deep down, is faced with the oldest problem of translation: the relationship with the unspeakable, the untranslatable. As António Sousa Ribeiro says, like Walter Benjamin, Antoine Berman, Lawrence Venuti, or Paul Ricoeur, because languages and cultures are incommensurable by definition, the entire theory of translation must start by confronting the problem of untranslatability (Ribeiro, "Traduzir e ser traduzido" 62). From this confrontation also arises the need to fill the gaps left open by that contact. In other words, the relationship with the hidden dimension of family discourse and the carnal passion for his sister, which is established like two sides of the same and deep-seated untranslatable situation, far from blocking the narrator's undertaking, allows it to be practiced effectively. André retrieves the father's lexicon but pours it out profanely. To this end, he integrates categories into his discourse that are

244　*Nazir Ahmed Can*

challenging for any translator for reasons of meaning, effect, and equivalence: the murmuring, the dark omen, the secret, and the poetic virtuality that they safe keep. Finally, from the smallness of the boarding house room, the voice will circulate a broad memory in an uninterrupted flow, and, in this itinerary in which each syllable is calculated, the paradoxes of family tradition are revealed. Moreover, the narrative begins with an emphasis on the same type of lexical overlap, space/body, but now under another regime of interpretation:

> My eyes on the ceiling, nudity in the room; pink, blue or violet, the impenetrable room; the individual room, a world, a cathedral room, where, during the breaks of my anguish, I gathered a rough stem in the palm of my hand, the white rose of desperation, since, among the objects the room had sanctified, the objects of the body came first.
>
> (7)

First, the new notation is marked by the group of colors, which refutes the fallacy of purity, and by the conjunction "or" that indicates the alternative and, simultaneously, the ordeal of nonfulfillment. The room's environment is compared to a cathedral because a person lives alone with their own pain. Also, in conjunction with the space, the body becomes the main subject of the enunciation, and it is the object of a detailed cartography, the borders of which are of a different nature. Endowed with a language or with an "infralanguage" (Gil 32), the body recovers the lost complementarity of the world and converts into the main "operator of recollections" (Carvalho 60) of André's translation of the world. In the tense dialog with Pedro, who assimilates the principles of tradition from the father, André contrasts an in-depth reading of the home space with the traces left there by the bodies with the paternal syntax. Thus, against the rhythmic linearity of the world without translation architected by the father, the narrator addresses the "confused hallways" (25) of the house and proposes the imaginative exercise of removing the lid of the bathroom laundry basket to his brother. For André, it sufficed to put his hands in there to hear better "all of our cries" (26) and "the guarded silence of the intimate articles thrown in there" (26). It was possible to "realize how ambivalently they were used, the men's handkerchiefs, which had been extended like trays to protect the purity of the sheets" (25), to "gather up the wrinkled sleep of the nightgowns and pajamas and to discover, lost in their folds, the coiled, repressed energy of the most tender pubic hair" (25), to feel "the stains of loneliness . . ., many of them aborted, greased by imagination" (26). André's invitation, therefore, was to suspend the alienating time of the wall clock while the house slept to return "the roots" of his feet "to their origins" (53) and, "among gray rats" (52), to feel "the creaking wood, the cracks in the walls, the slack windows, the darkness of the kitchen" (53). With this gesture, he intends to scrutinize the vibration of the nervous

The Idea of Translation in Ancient Tillage, *by Raduan Nassar*   245

foundations, to hear the palpitations of the doors, to relive "the squalid whispers and spiderwebs dangling from the rafters" (53), to paw at the "red-dust-covered sanitary napkins, as if they were an assassin's rags" (25). It is, in fact, a literal and metaphorical movement that helps André to relate to the "vinegary, rotten smell of the cold, vein-ridden walls of a dirty clothes hamper" (26), and investigate the dough from which the restrained scream of the millenary family rituals is made. In short, in his rereading of the world, André proposes the replacement of religious guilt with individual responsibility. To this end, he precipitates language along pathways never suspected within the confines of that house. From his boarding house room, he celebrates the body in all its thickness: the markings of the filthy body of the disheveled, the intense smells, the spilled remains, the mites that impregnate the pores, the wound and the turgid bone, the cancer, the delirium, and the blood clots that spill out to release "the nauseating words that had been forever locked away in silence" (62), the anger and its text(ure). André also describes the murmuring that wanders among the rubble, probes the lime, the salt, and the "sand-filled pain of the desert" (107) contained in the bitter words of his mother and her "ancient lament that to this day can still be heard along the poor Mediterranean coast" (107). Through the body, a greater order, metonymized in the house's objects, is also profaned: "scratching into the softness of the lilies in their vases, leaving my fingerprints on their chaste parchment leaves, combing the alcoves for lascivious saints" (76).

A reflection on culture and the ways of reading it is at play throughout this process. For Ribeiro ("Traduzir e ser traduzido"), in line with what Stuart Hall proposed in the 1990s, cultures are dynamic and conflictual processes and not simply established canons. According to this definition, culture is less a question of tradition (represented in the father's narrative) than translation (incarnated in André). As such, it must be thought of as not originating from an immobile center but from a position within a relational network: "to be in translation" is not an incidental trait but an essential, defining characteristic of any culture (63). Questioning the ambiguities, disheartened by restful ideas, impatient with the clotted faces of his family, André does not disregard the history of an origin in his speech. But he also knows the very idea of origin – linguistic, religious – resulting from long-term exchanges. Therefore, he opposes the imagery of linearity and the notion of the immaculate house/body that drives the father. Attentive to porosity, he scrutinizes the "turgid bones" (76) or the "shavings of bone" of each family member, the "skeleton of my thoughts" (93) that hides them, the mother's "calcified womb" (19), Ana's feet with their "soles aflame" (20), and the "soft stomach of the moment" (20) in which everything is revealed. The narrator seeks to restore the lost complementarity of the world somehow. Imperfection plays a decisive role in this endeavor. Therefore, he celebrates the physical defects that organize the animal world: "the graceful, wobbling teal, the ducks, flat

246 *Nazir Ahmed Can*

from their beaks to their webbed feet, the puffed-up turkeys, as well as the adventure-seeking, ornery guinea hens, bearing their sickly lump as if it were a crest" (69). The figure of God is rewritten based on the same type of procedure:

> carefully removing the webs covering the ancient light of Your eyes . . .; I will also remove the corrupt dust suffocating Your terrestrial hair, and zealously remove the lice that have left tracks on Your scalp; I'll clean Your dark fingernails with mine, and will eliminate, one by one, the dragonflies laying eggs in Your pubis.
>
> (59)

Ironically, what is proposed in the entire narrative is a one-on-one with the sacred. André investigates the religious universe from where he desecrates "the family shrine at the top of [his] lungs" (78). He in no way ignores the body of tools that must be used in his solitary task. For the world he imagines by the side of his sister-lover, he foresees scrutinizing "the hammer claws, the level vial, and the saw teeth . . . so they're always ready, for I'm well aware that no one cuts without a blade" (69). Thus, using stylistic devices like the oxymoron, the ellipsis, personification, and the metaphor, which, here, favor the broadening of philosophical thinking and the application of a poetic rhythm anchored in orality, André's holy fury contemplates the demands of artistry and unity with the goal of transfiguration.

To gather together the material dispersed in this calculated dialectic, the narrator devours other texts and confirms an indispensable element in the production of knowledge: ethical responsibility. And this happens implicitly, as we have seen, or explicitly, as when he reacts to his father's reading of the tale of the starving man from the Arabic classic *Arabian Nights*: "how could a man with bread, meat and wine on his table, and salt for seasoning, tell a story about hunger? How could Father, Pedro, have left out so much every time he told that oriental tale?" (48). By focusing on the underprivileged of yesterday and today, André blows his father's hypocrisy wide open with the invention of aphorisms: "it was the apposite prerogative of gluttons to test the virtue of patience with other people's hunger" (63). In this synthesis, the teenager also indirectly presents a definition of translation processes: "It's a strange world, Father, which only unites by dividing; built up on accidents, there is no self-sustaining order" (91). The narrator's proposal, in short, encompasses a vast network of relationships that starts in the universe of religious figuration, passes through literary representation, and culminates in the sociopolitical plane. As for translation, which condenses all these phenomena, it emerges as a metaphor, method, and vehicle of a desire.

As a translator moved by an ethical sense, André fills gaps, creatively and harmonically transfigures the context, dares to use the exact word for that which until then had been silenced. I also underscore, within this

The Idea of Translation in Ancient Tillage, by Raduan Nassar 247

architecture, the game that he establishes between lexical extension and repetition. As we have seen, the former allows the breaking in of a new statement about the body and, with it, transposition to a new regime of interpretation of the sacred text. Repetition, in turn, occurring in a functional manner as in the stories of the oral tradition, allows articulation between digressive and anticipatory discourses. The most important of them is the description of Ana's dance, inserted in chapters 5 and 29. In the first instance, we observe a ritual characteristic of the family, which refers to the legacy of Lebanese traditions. Then, in chapter 29, Ana adds several significant details that place the body at the center of all the subversions. That is, the narrative seems to want to show that it is not enough just to position oneself at the border. The step that each body may or may not take in this negotiation of space is significant. The dancer now appears with the small objects that her brother André secretly kept in a box. With them, and with calculated impetus, she reveals the differences at play: "confidently introducing her fiery decadence into the centre, shocking the surprised looks still further, dangling cries from each of the mouths, paralyzing all gestures for an instant, yet still dominating everyone with the violent impetus of her spirit" (103–104). The accumulated surplus is at the source of the passage from one code to another, from position to transposition, from formation to transformation, and from tradition to translation. For José Gil, in his studies on the language of the body, this type of performance is sent directly back to the corporeality of the audience. That is, the path of the dancer's "corpo-significante" [body-significant] is aimed at the spectator's "corpo-significado" [body-significance] (35).

In this context, Ana experiences the vertigo of displacement. The dancer's body is thus established as a "transdutor de signos" ["transducer of signals"] able to emit and receive signals, inscribe them on itself, and translate some of them into others (Gil, 32). As a demanding translator, Ana disturbs and fascinates the family, to whom now falls the task of forming – with the help of her body-grammar – the sentences she necessarily leaves incomplete (Gil 35). Favoring the passage from the closed regime of tradition to the regime of possibilities of translation, Ana expresses the limits of the exchanges between collectivity and individuals. This is possible because her body abandons its previous condition of muteness, chastity, and passivity and takes on the condition of the subject of memory, conveyor of meaning, and engine of knowledge and creation. Therefore, it can be said that, in the final stretch of the narrative, Ana's body is simultaneously the matrix and the place of reckoning of History (Weigel 88).

It is also important to highlight the change in verb tenses throughout the description of the scene: from the imperfect tense ("would make strident cymbals," "I would untie my shoes, take off my socks and, with my clean, white feet, scrape away the dry leaves") (used in chapter 5), we move to the past perfect tense ("made strident cymbals," "I untied my shoes, took off

248   *Nazir Ahmed Can*

my socks and, with clean, white feet, scraped away the dry leaves"). Used in chapter 29, this verb tense suggests that this was the last dance. In fact, the father, "possessed by divine wrath" (106) due to the provocation that exceeded the limits of family morality, murders his daughter with a cutlass. The tragedy, in fact, had already been anticipated at several moments in the narrative. Raduan Nassar summarizes in small segments the past of forbidden love, the future of death, and between them, a reflection on the transposition: "reason is generous, dear sister, it cuts through in any direction, will agree to any byway, as long as we handle the blade skillfully" (74). Ana's death ironically confirms both the grandfather's precept ("Maktub," "is it written") and the punishment foretold in the sacred book of Islam, cited between chapters 21 and 22: "Forbidden to you are your mothers, your daughters, and your sisters, (Koran, Chapter IV, 23)" (81).

In conclusion, *Ancient Tillage* is centered around two opposite interpretations of the border, which are also two rival conceptions about the representation of the world and to antagonistic forms of a relationship with a difference: the first is that of the father, summarized in the image of the fence that protects the house from the dangers of the world. The border, in this conception, is the manifestation of a defensive reaction of the world without translation. With the second interpretation, that of André, we know the incommensurability of the things that hide behind the rotted silence of the family. We travel, with the narrator, to the border where the characteristic passage of the world of translation is articulated. In the successive scale of interactions that he experiences, the young man deals with some of the most significant challenges (the secret, the unspeakable) and meets the most common fate of the entire endeavor of translation (betrayal). Aiming for a sense of balance distinct from that of his father, whose discourse is marked by stereotypes, André surrenders the exercise of transposition and, thence, establishes a new relationship with the land and with time. Therefore, two registers emerge in the narrative: the ancient tillage of the family patriarch, who assimilates and reduces the different into the identical in a process of deadly autophagy; and the labor of André, who, refusing the limiting and fallacious synthesis, keeps the tension and the mutual estrangement between the contexts of departure and arrival alive (Ribeiro, "A tradução" 84). This occurs when the narrative welcomes the word of the "foreigner." Reconfiguring the language from an exercise of tense comparison between opposing imaginaries, Raduan Nassar confirms the proximity between poetic invention and translation. At every moment, the work problematizes "the concept of original and the priority of original," presents the way "to negotiate differences and to make the difference manifest," and, finally to examine the estrangement "as a not only intercultural but also intracultural phenomenon," essential dimensions prescribed by the contemporary theory of translation (Ribeiro, "A tradução" 87). In the novel, moreover, we locate not only the "problem" of translation (untranslatability), but also the potential of this

The Idea of Translation in Ancient Tillage, by Raduan Nassar   249

practice for broadening the esthetic code of the literary field, for expanding the linguistic and cultural horizons of the frames of reference in play, and, finally, for recognizing the ethical responsibility that accompanies the task of mediating the difference.

If the practice of translation continues to be a risky operation always in search of a theory (Ricoeur 37), *Ancient Tillage* plays a decisive role in this undertaking – and has been doing so for nearly 50 years.

Notes

1. All translations from Portuguese, direct or paraphrased, except the quotes from *Ancient Tillage*, are my responsibility.
2. On Brazilian authors of Arab origin, see *A Literatura Brasileira e a Cultura Árabe*, by Moema de Castro e Silva Olival. In this work, the author analyzes the literary production of six Brazilian writers of Lebanese origin, including Raduan Nassar, and highlights their contribution to the field of cultural production in Brazil.
3. On the notion of transposition and its relationship with the concepts of migration, translation, and music, see Rice (*Transpositions: Migration, Translation, Music*).

Works Cited

Appadurai, Arjun. *Modernity At Large: Cultural Dimensions of Globalization*. U of Minnesota P, 1996.
Berman, Antoine. *L'épreuve de l'étranger*. Gallimard, 1995.
———. *La traduction et la lettre ou l'auberge du lointain*. Seuil, 1999.
Campos, Haroldo de. *Galáxias*. Editora Ex-libris, 1984.
Carvalho, Ruy Duarte de. *a câmara, a escrita e a coisa dita . . . fitas, textos e palestras*. Cotovia, 2008.
Coutinho, Priscilia. *Lavoura arcaica, un roman de la diaspora libanaise au Brésil*, Thèse de doctorat. Université Sorbonne, 2018.
Gil, José. *Metamorfoses do Corpo*. Relógio d'Água, 1997.
Large, Duncan et al. *Untranslatability: Interdisciplinary Perspectives*. Routledge, 2018.
Maalouf, Amin. *Les Identités meurtrières*. Grasset, 1998.
Mbembe, Achille. "As formas africanas de auto-inscrição." *Estudos afro-asiáticos*, vol. 23, n°. 1, 2001, pp. 171–209.
Nassar, Raduan. *Ancient Tillage*. Translated by Karen Sotelino, Penguin Books, 2016 [1975].
Olival, Moema de Castro e Silva. *Literatura Brasileira e a Cultura Árabe*. Editora Kelps, 2015.
Ribeiro, António Sousa. "A tradução como metáfora da contemporaneidade. Pós-colonialismo, fronteiras e identidades". *Colóquio de outono. Estudos de tradução. Estudos póscoloniais*, edited by Macedo, Ana Gabriela, and Maria Eduarda Keating, Universidade do Minho, 2005, pp. 77–87.
Ribeiro, António Sousa. "Traduzir e ser traduzido. Notas sobre discurso e migrações." *Revista Crítica de Ciências Sociais*. Número especial, 2018, pp. 55–70.

250 Nazir Ahmed Can

Rice, Alison. *Transpositions: Migration, Translation, Music*. Liverpool UP, 2021.

Ricoeur, Paul. *A metáfora viva*. Translated by Dion Davi Macedo, Loyola, 2005 [1975].

———. *Sobre a tradução*. Translated by Patrícia Lavelle, Editora da UFMG, 2011 [2004].

Venuti, Lawrence. *The Scandals of Translation: Towards an Ethics of Difference*. Routledge, 1998.

Weigel, Sigrid. *Cuerpo, Imagen y Espacio en Walter Benjamin. Una Relectura*. Translated by José Amícola, Paidós, 1999 [1996].

Index

Africa i, ix, x, 1, 2, 4, 9, 10, 12, 18, 19, 34, 36, 39, 40, 53, 71, 72, 79, 80, 82, 83, 84, 86, 90n2, 91n10, 92, 98, 101, 105, 106, 107, 112, 115, 116, 119, 132n2, 136, 137, 140, 145, 146, 148, 160n1, 163, 209, 222, 235
African Diaspora i, ii, iii, 1, 4, 5, 17, 63n2, 64n5, 66, 81, 105, 138, 142, 146, 148
African Migration 5, 18, 97, 101, 138
Afro-Hispanic i, ix, 1, 67, 80
Afropean 9, 12, 19, 140, 145, 149
Afro-Spanish 6, 9, 10, 83
Agboton, Agnès 9, 10, 81, 82, 83, 84, 85, 86, 87, 88, 89, 90, 90nn3, 4, 91n10, 92, 93
Al-Andalus 13, 16, 150, 151, 152, 153, 154, 155, 156, 160, 161n2, 162, 163, 171, 177, 220n6
Almeida, Djaimilia Pereira 139, 140, 141, 142, 148, 149
Alves, Adalberto 13, 116, 154, 161, 161n5
Amazigh 13, 28, 33n6, 35, 93
Angola 3, 10, 104, 105, 112, 135, 138, 140, 142, 143, 144, 148
Argentina xi, 2, 5, 14, 15, 16, 18, 193, 194, 195, 196, 198, 200, 201, 202, 203, 204, 205, 206, 208, 210, 217, 236
Asís, Jorge 195, 196, 197, 201, 205

Barcelona xii, 9, 81, 83, 84, 88, 90–91n7
Barros, Maria Filomena Lopes de 152, 155, 162, 167, 176
Bela-Lobedde, Desirée 89, 90, 92
Benin 5, 9, 81, 88

Blackness vi, 9, 11, 12, 89, 97, 98, 99, 105, 107, 109, 110, 112, 113, 138, 147
Bogotá 207, 214, 218, 219
Borges Coelho, António x, xii, 151, 152, 153, 163, 177
Brah, Avtar 68, 70, 77, 78, 80, 199, 202, 206
Brazil x, 2, 5, 14, 17, 18, 19, 115, 118, 120, 132n2, 137, 208, 237, 238, 239, 249n2
Buenos Aires 15, 196, 198, 202, 203

Camões, Luís Vaz de 14, 160, 165, 167, 177, 178, 237
Campoy-Cubillo, Adolfo 4, 7, 8, 19, 28, 33, 33n6, 53, 56, 65
Cape Verde 3, 5, 10, 72, 77, 121, 122, 138
Catalan/Catalonia i, viii, 2, 4, 24, 28, 29, 32n3, 33n6, 34, 81, 85, 88
Ceuta 5, 6, 8, 36, 37, 38, 39, 40, 41, 42, 43, 44, 47n1, 48, 48n3, 49, 82
Chihuahua vi, 17, 223, 226, 227, 229, 230, 234, 235
Chile 2, 5, 15, 16, 181, 182, 183, 184, 185, 186, 187, 188, 189, 190, 191, 192, 193
Chilestinian(s) vi, 15, 181, 183, 185, 191
Christian/Christianity 13, 15, 17, 24, 26, 35, 69, 137, 151, 152, 153, 154, 156, 157, 161n3, 162, 163, 164, 165, 168, 171, 173, 175, 178, 181, 182, 192, 212, 224, 238, 240
Civantos, Christina 16, 208, 210, 212, 221
Clariond, Jeannette 17, 223, 228, 229, 230, 231, 232, 233, 234, 235

252 *Index*

Colectivo Ioé 25, 26, 27, 30, 33
Colombia 2, 5, 16, 25, 208, 212, 214, 215, 216, 217, 218, 219, 220n1, 221, 222
coloniality 5, 12, 97, 100, 101, 103, 104, 108, 136, 139
Convivencia 170, 171, 220
counter-orientalism 2, 13, 150, 162
Crónica 39, 49, 181, 182, 185, 186, 187, 189, 192, 193, 209, 210, 211, 212, 215, 218, 221, 222, 235

decolonization 101, 104, 105, 114, 115
Diaspora i, v, vi, xi, 1, 3, 5, 9, 10, 12, 14, 16, 17, 19, 34, 63n2, 64n5, 66, 67, 68, 69, 70, 72, 73, 77, 78, 80, 81, 87, 92, 105, 110, 135, 136, 137, 138, 140, 142, 146, 148, 149, 160, 164, 176, 182, 184, 194, 195, 196, 198, 199, 200, 201, 202, 203, 204, 205, 206, 237, 249
Dib, Juana 201, 202, 205, 205n3, 206

El Hachmi, Najat 25, 28, 29, 30, 31, 32n4, 33, 33n6, 34, 35, 85, 92, 93
El Kadaoui Moussaoui, Saïd 85, 92, 93
Epalanga, Kalaf 139, 140, 144, 147, 148
Equatorial Guinea(n) i, viii, 4, 5, 8, 9, 68, 69, 72, 73, 77, 79, 80, 116, 122, 123
Europe i, viii, ix, xi, 2, 4, 5, 9, 10, 11, 12, 18, 19, 23, 24, 26, 32n1, 34, 35, 36, 39, 48, 63n2, 64n5, 65, 66, 71, 80, 82, 83, 84, 86, 92, 98, 100, 101, 102, 103, 110, 135, 139, 144, 145, 146, 147, 148, 149, 150, 154, 155, 164, 169, 175, 178, 188, 218, 238
Évora 108, 163, 165, 166, 167, 170, 176nn8, 9, 177

Fanon, Frantz 107, 112
Farahani, Fataneh 70, 71, 76, 77, 79n4, 80
Fayad, Luis 207, 208, 210, 211, 214, 215, 216, 217, 218, 219, 220n6, 221
feminism 61, 63n2, 66, 83
feminist 8, 50, 51, 54, 57, 58, 61, 62, 63, 63n2, 64n8, 64, 65, 66, 73, 80, 83, 87, 92, 109, 177
Fikes, Kesha 100, 112, 138, 139, 149
Foucault, Michel 68, 71, 72, 80

Freyre, Gilberto 97, 112, 132n2
Fuchs, Barbara 24, 34, 209, 221

Galia, Fátima 51, 56, 58, 59, 64n9, 65
García Márquez, Gabriel xi, 207, 208, 211, 212, 215, 217, 218, 220, 221
García-Sánchez, Inmaculada M. 25, 32, 34
gender viii, x, 5, 14, 50, 51, 61, 64n8, 70, 71, 74, 80, 86, 87, 91n8, 92, 118, 177, 181, 182, 195, 196
Geraldo e Samira: Uma ópera para Évora 163, 168, 169, 171, 172, 174, 177
Geraldo Sem Pavor 163, 165, 166, 167, 170, 171, 172, 173, 175, 176n11, 176, 177, 178
Gharb al-Andalus 13, 98, 150, 151, 152, 153, 154, 155, 160, 161n2, 162, 163, 170, 171
Global South 12, 98, 221
Guinea Bissau 5, 14, 105, 138, 164

Hasnaui, Zahra 50, 51, 54, 56, 59, 62, 64n7
Herculano, Alexandre 150, 166, 167, 175–176nn2, 10, 177
Hispanic-American Orientalism 5, 16, 207, 209, 219, 220n2
human rights 10, 36, 47n1, 48n3, 53, 54, 55, 56, 62, 119, 120

Iberia 35, 93, 152, 161nn2, 3, 209
Iberian Peninsula ii, 2, 4, 6, 13, 24, 81, 150, 160n1, 161n5, 163, 171, 175, 209
identity viii, ix, 2, 3, 4, 5, 6, 9, 10, 11, 12, 13, 14, 15, 16, 17, 18, 23, 28, 32, 32n2, 33n8, 47, 52, 67, 68, 69, 70, 71, 72, 73, 75, 77, 78, 79, 79n5, 85, 87, 88, 89, 90n3, 92, 93, 99, 104, 110, 111, 115, 122, 136, 142, 144, 145, 146, 147, 160, 165, 166, 167, 170, 175, 178, 183, 186, 188, 190, 194, 198, 205, 205n3, 206, 208, 209, 210, 214, 221, 222, 223, 224, 225, 226, 231, 232, 233, 234, 235, 239, 242
Islam 2, 5, 13, 14, 23, 32nn1, 2, 33, 34, 35, 59, 153, 155, 156, 157, 164, 165, 174, 175, 177, 178, 192, 221, 240, 248
Islamophobia 14, 23, 24, 32nn1, 2, 33, 34, 35, 174, 176, 177

Index 253

Jewish/Jew(s) viii, 5, 24, 26, 34, 171, 176n7, 220nn5, 6, 232, 235
journalism vi, 5, 15, 16, 181, 182, 183, 185, 186, 187, 188, 189, 191

Kushigian, Julia 2, 18, 222

Latin America(n) i, ii, iii, vi, viii, xi, xii, 1, 2, 3, 4, 5, 14, 15, 17, 62, 63n4, 80, 179, 181, 183, 185, 186, 188, 190, 192, 207, 208, 209, 210, 211, 218, 219, 220n2, 222, 224, 226, 235, 239
Lebanon/Lebanese 5, 15, 17, 19, 181, 190, 194, 195, 196, 201, 202, 205n4, 221n6, 223, 224, 225, 226, 227, 228, 229, 230, 231, 232, 233, 234, 234n1, 235, 236, 237, 238, 239, 247, 249n2
Levant/Levantine 15, 17, 208, 211, 213, 216, 222, 224, 225, 234
Lisbon vi, x, xi, 5, 11, 12, 18, 89, 100, 101, 103, 104, 105, 106, 109, 113, 114, 115, 116, 117, 118, 119, 120, 121, 122, 123, 125, 129, 132, 132n1, 133, 133n7, 139, 142, 144, 146, 147, 148
Lourenço, Eduardo 136, 137, 149
Luso-Arabic Literature vi, 5, 13, 150, 154, 155, 156, 159, 160, 161n5
Lusotropicalism/Lusotropicalist 11, 97, 113, 115, 126, 132n2, 137

Maghreb 2, 4, 33, 53, 65, 85, 222
Mahjar xi, 5, 14, 16, 18, 18n1, 19, 208, 211, 213, 214, 220, 222, 224, 226, 233, 235
Mallette, Karla 150, 151, 162
Maronite 17, 214, 218, 224
Martínez Assad, Carlos 223, 224, 225, 235
Martin-Márquez, Susan 4, 33n6, 34, 52, 53, 56, 62, 64n8, 65, 209, 222
Martín Muñoz, Gema 24, 34
Mashriq 5, 18, 195, 205
Mbomío Rubio, Lucía Asué 89, 92
medievalism 172, 174, 177
Mekuy, Guillermina 67, 68, 72, 73, 75, 77, 78, 79, 79n7, 80
Melibea Obono, Trifonia 67, 68, 70, 71, 72, 73, 74, 75, 76, 77, 78, 79, 80

Melilla 6, 36, 37, 38, 39, 40, 41, 42, 43, 44, 48, 48n3, 49, 82
Mértola 14, 153, 168, 169, 170, 173
Mestizaje v, 3, 9, 81, 87, 88
Mexico 2, 5, 16, 17, 62, 193, 208, 217, 222, 223, 224, 225, 226, 228, 229, 230, 234, 235, 236
Middle East i, 1, 3, 5, 14, 18, 49, 176, 177, 182, 183, 184, 189, 190, 191, 192, 205, 223, 224, 225, 230, 231, 234
Mil y un poemas saharauis v, 8, 50, 51, 52, 53, 54, 55, 56, 57, 59, 62, 63, 65, 66
Mohamed, Darak 51, 59, 61, 62, 66
Monteiro, Yara 139, 140, 143, 148, 149
Moor(s) vi, viii, 4, 13, 14, 24, 34, 132n2, 151, 152, 163, 164, 166, 167, 168, 169, 171, 172, 176nn7, 12, 13, 177, 209, 212, 222
Morocco/Moroccan i, v, viii, ix, 2, 3, 4, 5, 6, 7, 8, 19, 24, 25, 27, 29, 30, 31, 32, 33n6, 34, 35, 36, 37, 38, 39, 40, 41, 42, 43, 44, 45, 46, 47, 47n1, 48nn2, 4, 53, 58, 61, 64nn10, 11, 85, 93, 163, 176, 177
Mota Ripeu, O'sírima 67, 68, 72, 77, 78, 79, 79n6, 80, 128, 226, 235
Mozambique x, 3, 5, 10, 14, 105, 138, 156, 164
Musicamera Produções 168, 170, 171, 172, 173, 177
Muslim i, viii, 4, 5, 6, 13, 14, 19, 23, 24, 25, 26, 32nn1, 2, 56, 155, 156, 161n3, 162, 164, 168, 170, 174, 175, 178, 209, 214, 218, 220n6
Mutis, Álvaro 208, 210, 211, 213, 220, 222

Nassar, Raduan vii, 17, 237, 238, 239, 241, 248, 249, 249n2
North Africa(n) i, v, viii, ix, 4, 5, 6, 7, 13, 17, 18, 19, 23, 24, 25, 28, 34, 36, 39, 52, 53, 82, 163, 168, 204

One Thousand and One Arabian Nights/1001 *Arabian Nights* 52, 53, 62, 246
O'Reilly, Andrea 83, 86, 87, 91n8
orientalism x, xi, 2, 5, 13, 14, 16, 18, 19, 52, 53, 56, 64n6, 65, 66, 150, 162, 164, 165, 175, 177, 178, 207,

254 *Index*

209, 210, 211, 212, 214, 217, 218, 219, 220n2, 221, 222
Os Lusíadas 117, 165, 177
Osman, Elsa Serur 198, 201, 205
Ottoman Empire 15, 194, 195, 207, 208, 214, 216, 217, 218, 225, 226, 239

Palestine/Palestinian xi, 5, 15, 181, 183, 184, 190, 191, 192, 194, 204, 226, 228, 231
Pastor, Camila 16, 224, 226, 228, 235
Pitts, Johny 12, 19, 145, 146, 149
Polisario Front 7, 8, 58, 59, 64nn10, 11
Poppe, António 158, 159, 162
Porteadora/s 37, 38, 39, 40, 41, 42, 45, 46, 47
Portugal i, ii, iii, vi, ix, x, xi, 1, 2, 3, 4, 5, 10, 12, 13, 14, 17, 23, 39, 95, 97, 99, 100, 101, 102, 104, 105, 106, 107, 108, 109, 111, 112, 113, 114, 115, 116, 117, 119, 122, 126, 131, 132nn2, 4, 133, 134, 135, 136, 137, 138, 139, 140, 141, 142, 143, 144, 147, 148, 149, 150, 151, 152, 153, 154, 155, 160, 160n1, 161nn2, 3, 162, 163, 164, 165, 167, 168, 169, 170, 171, 173, 174, 175, 176, 176n4, 12, 177, 178
postcolonial 2, 9, 10, 11, 18, 28, 33n6, 35, 50, 54, 63n2, 65, 66, 69, 92, 93, 97, 100, 111, 113, 114, 122, 126, 139, 143

race ix, x, 5, 10, 11, 14, 33, 51, 63n2, 64n5, 65, 71, 85, 89, 92, 99, 111, 112, 113, 139, 140, 141, 146, 148, 181, 182, 188, 222, 226, 228, 232, 241
racial capitalism 97, 98, 99, 100, 112
racism xii, 2, 5, 9, 24, 32n5, 33, 83, 85, 88, 97, 101, 105, 107, 110, 122, 126, 132, 138, 139, 140, 141, 142, 143, 144, 145, 146, 148, 176, 234
Reconquista 6, 13, 24, 152, 163, 168, 170, 209, 212
Ribeiro, António Sousa 237, 239, 241, 243, 245, 248, 249
Ribeiro, Margarida Calafate xi, 122, 134, 136, 140, 149
Ricoeur, Paul 239, 241, 243, 249, 250

Rif /Rifian(s) 39, 40, 49
Robbins, Jill 7, 8, 19, 59, 66

Said, Edward 18, 19, 52, 56, 66, 150, 164, 172, 173, 175, 178, 222
Sala, Xavi 25, 34
São Paulo xii, 15, 17, 177, 238, 239
São Tomé and Príncipe 5, 10, 101, 105
Senegal 3, 115, 164
sexuality 50, 68, 69, 70, 71, 72, 73, 74, 75, 76, 77, 78, 79, 80, 177
Sousa Pereira, Armando de 166, 168, 171, 176, 178
South America(n) i, 56, 194, 195, 214, 207, 217
Spain i, ii, iii, v, viii, ix, 1, 2, 3, 4, 5, 6, 8, 9, 10, 13, 17, 21, 23, 24, 25, 27, 29, 31, 32nn1–4, 33n6, 33, 34, 35, 36, 37, 38, 39, 40, 41, 42, 43, 45, 46, 47, 50, 51, 52, 55, 57, 58, 59, 61, 62, 64nn5, 6, 65, 68, 69, 70, 71, 74, 77, 80, 81, 82, 83, 85, 87, 88, 89, 90, 91, 91n8, 93, 150, 152, 256, 160n1, 161n4, 162, 163, 168, 175, 176nn11–12, 209, 220n6
Spanish-Saharawi Fraternity 51, 53, 54, 58, 62
Sub-Sahara(n) 2, 4, 5, 9, 17, 53, 82, 160n1
Syria(n) 5, 15, 19, 181, 182, 190, 194, 195, 196, 201, 202, 203, 205n4, 207, 220n5, 226, 228, 231

Torres, Cláudio 14, 153, 162, 168
transborder 36, 40, 41, 42, 46, 48n3
Turco 15, 17, 199, 200, 201
Turk 15, 17, 151, 199, 226
Turkish 15, 231
Tvon, Telma 104, 109, 110, 112

Valete 101, 102, 110, 111, 112

Western Sahara 4, 5, 7, 8, 19, 51, 52, 56, 58, 59, 60, 61, 62, 63n4, 64n10, 65, 66, 69, 79

Yidi David, Odette 16, 19, 208, 222

Zerán, Faride 181, 182, 183, 185, 186, 187, 188, 189, 190, 191, 192, 193

Printed in the United States
by Baker & Taylor Publisher Services